AN EXCITING PAPERBACK COLLECTION
OF GREAT SCENES AND MONOLOGUES
FROM AMERICA'S AND BRITAIN'S
BEST CONTEMPORARY PLAYWRIGHTS.

Here is a wonderful, up-to-date material for scene study,
selected from the best plays from recent theatre seasons.
More than 20 monologues for both men and women, carefully chosen to display the widest range of dramatic ability,
are essential for auditioning actors. A large selection of
parts for women provide exciting opportunities to sharpen
acting skills in roles that brought accolades from New York's
toughest critics. More than 80 scenes in all, many previously
unpublished, allow every actor, professional, amateur or
student, to choose from either smart, sassy, often outrageous comedy or deeply moving drama—a unique, bal-
anced collection of the most successful contemporary plays.

THE ACTOR'S SCENEBOOK

THE ACTOR'S SCENEBOOK

*Scenes and Monologues
from Contemporary Plays*

Edited by
Michael Schulman and Eva Mekler

BANTAM BOOKS
TORONTO · NEW YORK · LONDON · SYDNEY · AUCKLAND

THE ACTOR'S SCENEBOOK
A Bantam Book / June 1984

ISBN 0-553-24348-9

ACKNOWLEDGMENTS

CAUTION: The use of the excerpts contained in this volume must
be confined to study and reference. They are fully protected under
the copyright laws of the United States of America, The British
Empire, the Dominion of Canada, and all other countries of the
Copyright Union. All rights, including professional, amateur,
motion pictures, recitation, lecturing, public reading, radio
broadcasting, television, video or sound taping, all other forms of
mechanical or electronic reproduction, such as information storage
and retrieval systems and photocopying, and the rights of transla-
tion into foreign languages are strictly reserved. For information,
contact the authors' representatives listed below or Bantam Books,
Inc., the Permissions Editor. For copyright notices, see the Ac-
knowledgments section on pages iv–viii, which constitutes an
extension of the copyright page.

Barefoot in the Park by Neil Simon. Copyright © 1964 by
Ellen Enterprises, Inc. Reprinted by permission of Random House,
Inc.

Talley's Folly by Lanford Wilson. Hill & Wang, Farrar Straus
& Giroux edition copyright © 1979 by Lanford Wilson. Reprinted
by permission of International Creative Management, 40 West
57th Street, New York, N.Y. 10019.

California Suite by Neil Simon. Copyright © 1977 by Neil
Simon. Reprinted by permission of Random House, Inc.

Key Exchange by Kevin Wade. Copyright © 1982 by Kevin
Wade. Copyright © 1981 by Kevin Wade as an unpublished
dramatic composition. Reprinted by permission of Writers and
Artists Agency, 162 West 56th Street, New York, N.Y. 10019.

Prisoner of Second Avenue by Neil Simon. Copyright © 1972
by Nancy Enterprises, Inc. Reprinted by permission of Random
House, Inc.

Romantic Comedy By Bernard Slade. Copyright © 1979,
1980 by Thornhill Productions, Inc. Reprinted by permission of
Hutto Management, Inc., 405 West 23rd Street, New York, N.Y.
10011.

The Dresser by Ronald Harwood. Copyright © 1980 by
Ronald Harwood Ltd. Reprinted by permission of Grove Press,
Inc.

Whose Life Is It Anyway? by Brian Clark. Copyright © 1978
by Brian Clark. Reprinted by permission of the Dramatic Publish-

CONTENTS

Scenes for One Man and One Woman

BAREFOOT IN THE PARK by Neil Simon   3

TALLEY'S FOLLEY by Lanford Wilson   12

CALIFORNIA SUITE by Neil Simon   18

KEY EXCHANGE by Kevin Wade   25

THE PRISONER OF SECOND AVENUE
  by Neil Simon   29

ROMANTIC COMEDY by Bernard Slade   36

THE DRESSER by Ronald Harwood   41

WHOSE LIFE IS IT ANYWAY? by Brian Clark   45

WHO'S AFRAID OF VIRGINIA WOOLF?
  by Edward Albee   48

THE WOOLGATHERER by William Mastrosimone   55

BETRAYAL by Harold Pinter   59

VIEUX CARRÉ by Tennessee Williams   63

BEDROOM FARCE by Alan Ayckbourn   68

TABLE SETTINGS by James Lapine   72

THE COLLECTOR by David Parker   75

DUET FOR ONE by Tom Kempinski   80

HOPSCOTCH by Israel Horovitz   89

THE AMERICAN CLOCK by Arthur Miller   95

MODIGLIANI by Dennis McIntyre   98

ANNE OF THE THOUSAND DAYS
  by Maxwell Anderson   104

AWAKE AND SING! by Clifford Odets   108

CALIGULA by Albert Camus   111

WAITING FOR LEFTY by Clifford Odets   114
JIMMY SHINE by Murray Schisgal   119
THE RUNNER STUMBLES by Milan Stitt   124
GIGI by Anita Loos   128
ONDINE by Jean Giraudoux   131
COME BACK, LITTLE SHEBA by William Inge   134
INNOCENT THOUGHTS, HARMLESS INTENTIONS
    by John Heuer   138

Scenes for Two Women

AGNES OF GOD by John Pielmeir   145
CRIMES OF THE HEART by Beth Henley   148
THE GINGERBREAD LADY by Neil Simon   152
UNCOMMON WOMEN AND OTHERS
    by Wendy Wasserstein   159
ON GOLDEN POND by Ernest Thompson   161
ALBUM by David Rimmer   166
A COUPLA WHITE CHICKS SITTING AROUND
    TALKING by John Ford Noonan   172
LUNCH HOUR by Jean Kerr   176
TABLE MANNERS (from THE NORMAN
    CONQUESTS) by Alan Ayckbourn   181
THE GREAT NEBULA IN ORION
    by Lanford Wilson   190
A DELICATE BALANCE by Edward Albee   193
LAUNDRY AND BOURBON by James McLure   196
ONCE A CATHOLIC by Mary O'Malley   202
MY SISTER EILEEN by Joseph A. Fields and
    Jerome Chodorov   206
EVERYTHING IN THE GARDEN by Edward Albee   210
EVERYBODY LOVES OPAL by John Patrick   215
MY CUP RANNETH OVER by Robert Patrick   220
THE FACULTY LOUNGE by Michael Schulman   226
TEACH ME HOW TO CRY by Patricia Joudry   230

Scenes for Two Men

CHAPTER TWO by Neil Simon   235
TRUE WEST by Sam Shepard   239
MASS APPEAL by Bill C. Davis   243
SAY GOODNIGHT, GRACIE by Ralph Pape   248
DA by Hugh Leonard   253
GEOGRAPHY OF A HORSE DREAMER
  by Sam Shepard   257
G. R. POINT by David Berry   261
LOOSE ENDS by Michael Weller   265
LONE STAR by James McLure   268
SCAPINO! by Frank Dunlop and Jim Dale   273
GALILEO by Bertolt Brecht   277
MR. ROBERTS by Thomas Heggen and Joshua Logan   281
LUTHER by John Osborne   285
TEAHOUSE OF THE AUGUST MOON
  by John Patrick   290
THE ANDERSONVILLE TRIAL by Saul Levitt   294

Scene for Three Characters
(and a Narrator)

THE LIFE AND ADVENTURES OF NICHOLAS
  NICKLEBY by David Edgar (from the novel by
  Charles Dickens)   299

Monologues for Women

A LOVELY SUNDAY FOR CREVE COEUR
  by Tennessee Williams   307
AGNES OF GOD by John Pielmeier   308
THE WEST SIDE WALTZ by Ernest Thompson   309
NUTS by Tom Topor   311
DEATH COMES TO US ALL, MARY AGNES
  by Christopher Durang   312

STOPS ALONG THE WAY by Jeffrey Sweet 313
A SEA OF WHITE HORSES by Peter Dee 315
THE FACULTY LOUNGE by Michael Schulman 316
IT'S BEEN WONDERFUL by John Patrick 318
LOVE IS A TIME OF DAY by John Patrick 320
WAITING FOR THE PARADE by John Murrell 321

Monologues for Men

SLY FOX by Larry Gelbart 325
KEY EXCHANGE by Kevin Wade 326
INDIANS by Arthur Kopit 327
LONE STAR by James McLure 328
STILL LIFE by Emily Mann 329
ROMANTIC COMEDY by Bernard Slade 331
THE FACULTY LOUNGE by Michael Schulman 332
FATHERS AND SONS by Thomas Babe 334
TEACH ME HOW TO CRY by Patricia Joudry 335
A PRAYER FOR MY DAUGHTER by Thomas Babe 337

OVERCOMING STAGE FRIGHT
by Michael Schulman

In the early 1970's I began teaching for the Lee Strasberg Theatre Institute. Because of my background in psychology and theatre, one of my goals was to apply the latest findings of clinical and research psychology to the craft of acting. Psychology and acting have a long history together, going back to the mutually enriching exchanges between Pavlov and Stanislavski during the early years of the Moscow Art Theatre.

The 1970's were an exciting time in psychology. A new understanding of the relationship between thought and action was emerging, and effective new procedures were being introduced in psychotherapy and educational settings across the country. A new term was coined to encompass these developments: Cognitive Behaviorism.

During the past dozen years as an acting teacher, starting back at the Strasberg Institute and continuing into my current work in New York and London with The British-American Acting Academy, I have been applying these new techniques to the various elements of the actor's craft, including concentration and confidence, emotional experience and expression, and physicalization and characterization. (At the same time, I brought the discoveries made in the acting class back to the psychotherapy office to be used by patients.) This chapter describes the concentration and confidence-training procedures we use for overcoming stage fright.

I. STAGE FRIGHT

In his recent autobiography, Laurence Olivier describes his experience with that bane of all actors: ''a merciless attack of stage fright with all its usual shattering symptoms.'' This ''attack'' hit Olivier at the height of his career in 1965, *after fifty years of experience as an actor.* In Olivier's own graphic words:

> My courage sank, and with each succeeding minute it became less possible to resist this horror. My cue came, and on I went to that stage where I knew with grim certainty I would not be capable of remaining more than a few minutes. I began to watch for the instant at which my knowledge of my next line would vanish. Only the next two now, no—one more . . . and then—NOW. I took one pace forward and stopped abruptly. My voice had started to fade, my throat closed up and the audience was beginning to go giddily round (why is it always anticlockwise?). . . . unhappily this malaise had a most obstinate reluctance to come to a conclusion. It persisted, and continued to torment me, for five whole years. . . .
>
> A shy performance of Othello is an absurdity. Early on in the course of it I had to beg my Iago, Frank Finlay, not to leave the stage when I had to be left alone for a soliloquy, but to stay in the wings downstage where I could see him, since I feared I might not be able to stay there in front of the audience by myself. Finally, everyone who had scenes with me had to know what was going on, in order to be able to cope in case of trouble.[1]

Virtually every actor, no matter how skilled or confident, has had to confront stage fright. It can show up at important auditions, when someone special is in the audience, when an acting partner intimidates you, or when a role calls for something you've never done before.

For the novice actor, overcoming stage fright is often the primary concern. Listen to Constantin Stanislavski's evocative description of an inexperienced actor's terrible fears at his first performance:

> This is the day of the exhibition performance . . . filled with a complete indifference until I reached my dressing room. But once inside, my heart began to pound and I felt nauseated.
>
> When I stepped away from the darkness of the wings to

---

[1] Laurence Olivier, *Confessions of An Actor: An Autobiography* (New York: Simon and Schuster, 1982), pp. 261-262.

the full illumination of the footlights, headlights and spotlights, I felt blinded. . . . but soon my eyes became accustomed to the light, I could see into the darkness, and the fear and attraction of the public seemed stronger than ever. I was ready to turn myself inside out, to give them everything I had; yet inside of me I had never felt so empty. The effort to squeeze out more emotion than I had, the powerlessness to do the impossible, filled me with a fear that turned my face and my hands to stone. All my forces were spent on unnatural and fruitless efforts. My throat became constricted, my sounds all seemed to go to a high note . . . . I was ashamed of every word, of every gesture.[2]

For some actors stage fright means butterflies in the stomach, sweaty palms, distracting and self-doubting thoughts. Some try to avoid these unpleasant experiences by trodding only well-beaten and comfortable paths. They play it safe, hoping to get by on their looks or charm.

Sometimes beginning acting students try to reduce their fears by letting everyone know not to take them too seriously. It's as if they are saying, "I know I'm going to be bad, so I won't really try." Or they use the equally self-defeating strategy of communicating to the audience, subtly but clearly, that they are not *really* like the character they are playing: *they,* of course, are not that vicious, cowardly, stupid, childish, or overtly sexual.

Often acting students fear that friends and family will think they are vain and self-centered; they dread someone asking them, "What makes you think you are worth paying money to watch?" Or conversely, "You think you're God's gift to the world, don't you?" An interviewer once asked Katherine Cornell whether she felt stage fright was caused by vanity. She replied, "Yes, of course it's vanity. It's egotism. You want to be so darned good—and that, I think, makes people shy and makes people self-conscious."[3]

On stage, different actors experience anxiety over different things. Some are embarrassed about expressing anger or sorrow; some are self-conscious about their laughs or smiles, or their faces when they cry. Others are afraid of being overwhelmed by

[2]Constantin Stanislavski, *An Actor Prepares,* trans. Elizabeth Reynolds Hapgood (New York: Theatre Arts Books, 1936), pp. 9-10.
[3]Lewis Funke and John E. Booth, eds., *Actors Talk About Acting* (New York: Avon Books, 1961), p. 124.

an emotion once it gets started. The one thing common to every actor's fear is that it undermines his or her concentration. When fear comes, concentration goes, and vice versa. Since fear and concentration are antagonists, the first step in learning to overcome stage fright is to learn *how to concentrate*.

II. CONCENTRATION

Every aspect of an actor's work depends on being able to concentrate. In class a student may stop a scene or an exercise and say, "I've lost my concentration." Or a teacher may inform a student, "You are not concentrating." But just what is this slippery substance that is so important and yet may vanish so easily? *What precisely is the behavior that we call "concentrating"? And what can an actor do to bring this behavior about more reliably?*

The Behavior of Concentrating. Once you choose something to focus your attention on you will say that you are "concentrating" when, during a moment of self-reflection, you find yourself on target, thinking about what you've chosen to think about. You say that you are "not concentrating" or that you've "lost your concentration" when you become aware that you are off-target, that your attention has been seized by something else.

A common "something else" is, of course, the actor's concern with what the audience thinks of him. Instead of attending to the stimuli and objectives of his character, the actor worries about whether his voice and body are attractive enough, or whether he is boring, or taking too long a pause, or whether he will time the up-coming laugh effectively. The actor is then, in the literal sense of the term, *self-conscious*—conscious of himself. His natural behavior becomes awkward, stilted; he no longer knows how to stand or walk or talk or even what to do with his hands—and he now has the added concern that his fear is obvious to everyone. The self-conscious actor has the experience of not living in the here-and-now of the character's life. Instead, he evaluates the moments just past and anticipates those coming up.

(This destructive self-consciousness is very different from the self-awareness that an actor uses to refine his or her work on a role. An actor must, of course, judge whether he has found a clear enough action to convey his character's objective, or whether his gestures are suitable for the period of the play, or whether his emotional intensity suits his character's temperament.)

Concentration may also be undermined by personal problems, fatigue, physical illness, an uncomfortable costume, or a hostile acting partner. The actor or actress must, in fact, *expect* to get distracted, because it is more than likely to happen; but he or she must also be prepared with *an effective technique for bringing his or her attention back on target*.

The concentration technique is deceptively simple: As soon as you become aware that you are off-target, that you are attending to the wrong thing, say to yourself, "Go back to my stimulus!" That simple phrase uttered to yourself is the key. Being off-target must become a *signal* to instruct yourself, insist to yourself, demand of yourself, "Go back to my stimulus." With practice this self-instruction will become second nature and you will catch yourself off-target sooner and sooner and learn to stay on target for longer and longer periods of time. Concentrating can become a well-learned skill, rather than something mysterious that you simply hope you will have and not lose.

The procedure is simple, but practice is important. Typically, when an actress first realizes that she has lost her concentration her immediate impulse is to scold herself (which only takes her further off-target) or to panic and quickly fake some result (like trying to sound angry by raising her voice). It takes practice to overcome these panic reactions and replace them with *self-instructions* that will bring your concentration back on target.

The Problem With Muscle Relaxation. A commonly recommended remedy for fear is muscle relaxation. But in practice, relaxation rarely works. If you are in an acting class that stresses relaxation training, look around and you will usually see that the best actors are not necessarily the best relaxers. One reason relaxation can't be relied on is that fear is controlled by the autonomic nervous system and muscle relaxation is controlled by the central nervous system. Your muscles can be relaxed and you can be afraid at the same time. Moreover, relaxing your muscles is a visible, often dulling, behavior that is not very useful in an actual performance. It often becomes merely another way to avoid carrying through whatever it is that you are afraid to do. The actor's goal should be a state of inner (autonomic) calm and physical ease; not a state of relaxed muscles.

When relaxation does work it is because the actor has *switched his focus* away from self-conscious thoughts to his muscles. But as we shall see in the confidence stimuli exercises, there are better things to switch your thoughts to than your muscles in order to overcome self-consciousness.

The following concentration exercises will give you practice in going back to a stimulus and instruct you on how to make your stimuli more compelling so they will hold your attention longer.

The Basic Concentration Exercise

Sit comfortably in a chair. You're going to concentrate on your thumbs. We choose a neutral stimulus like your thumbs so that you have to make an effort to stay focused on it; a compelling stimulus such as a person you love or hate is likely to hold your attention spontaneously, so you would not get the basic concentration practice that this exercise is designed to provide.

Make a commitment to keep your attention focused on your thumbs for the next four minutes. In trying to keep your thoughts on your thumbs—without looking at them or doing anything with them—you will notice periodically that your attention has shifted to other matters (to thoughts about whether you have understood the instructions, or whether you should have followed your parents' advice and gone to law school instead of acting school, or your daily affairs, unpaid bills, etc.). As soon as you become aware of any off-target thoughts, simply tell yourself, ''Go back to my thumbs.'' Shortly you will catch your thoughts wandering sooner and sooner and you will stay on target for increasingly longer periods of time. You are learning the basic concentration procedure.

When you are on target you will be thinking specific things about your thumbs. Your thoughts may be about how your thumbs look, or how they feel when responding to something (e.g., a pin prick), or how they feel internally (e.g., sensing your pulse), or what you have done or can do with them.

Asking Questions. Stimulate thoughts about your thumbs (or any other stimulus) by asking questions about them. For example, ask yourself if your thumbs are relaxed. Then try to relax them, carefully checking and rechecking the muscles around each joint. Because there is something immediately compelling about a question, this is a powerful technique that makes attending to a stimulus easier and more long-lasting. Ask yourself, ''What is the softest thing I touched today with my thumbs?'' Suddenly your thoughts will be filled with tactile and visual images.

The number of possible questions is endless: ''What is the

most painful thing that ever happened to my thumbs?" "What does my favorite fruit feel like to my thumbs?" "How does ice feel under my thumbs?" The point is that you can actually practice *the behavior of concentrating*. First, commit yourself to attending to a stimulus, then ask a question about that stimulus. Whenever you discover that your attention has shifted to a different stimulus, tell yourself to go back to the target stimulus and ask another (or the same) question.

Going Back to Stimuli. During an actual performance, the stimuli that you will go back to are derived from (1) the objectives and obstacles of your character, (2) your acting partners, (3) imagery based on your character's past experience, (4) imagery based on your own past experience, (5) your character's imagery projecting what *might* happen to him or her in the future, (6) the set, props, and costumes, and (7) your bodily sensations. These are the ingredients from which the actions and reactions—the very life—of your character will emerge. Therefore, the more thoroughly you have prepared, the more elements you will have to go back to if your concentration wanes.

Keep in mind that in life all our behavior is either an action or a reaction—an action in pursuit of an objective or a reaction in response to a stimulus. That's all there is. The life of your characters must be constructed out of precisely these same two classes of behavior, regardless of the period or style of the play.

There is one other kind of stimulus that an actor may usefully go back to: a "confidence stimulus." The *confidence stimulus procedure* is a highly effective tool for overcoming fears. It will be described in detail later in the chapter.

The Fourth Wall Exercise

All plays, including abstract ones, take place in some kind of physical environment. In order to maintain your concentration and experience the life of the character, you must fully create, immerse yourself in, and react to the physical environment. Sometimes the set designer will provide a quite literal replica of the setting of the play, but often—especially in a classroom situation—little or no physical setting is provided. But even the most complete and detailed sets leaves at least one side of the environment totally to the imagination of the actor: this is the "fourth wall," the area between the actor and the audience.

Actors never forget that they are on a stage playing for an

audience. They must, of course, make whatever vocal and bodily adjustments are necessary to be seen and heard. But at the same time—unless the scene requires them to play directly to the audience (as the Stage Manager does in *Our Town*)—they must "live" in an environment that surrounds them on all sides, that means either creating an imaginary fourth wall between themselves and the audience or creating an imaginary landscape that extends through and beyond the audience.

The key to successfully enclosing yourself in a physical environment is *specificity*. The more fully you visualize the details of your imaginary wall or landscape, the more fully those environments will exist for you. For example, if you want to imagine a huge bookcase as the fourth wall of your character's room, you should specify where different books are placed: the poetry on the third shelf to the right—and toward the center of the poetry section, a favorite collection of sonnets you received as a gift; plays are on the fourth row, to the left, arranged alphabetically by author, etc.

Now when you look in the direction of the audience you will have an array of specific stimuli that will keep your concentration connected to the character's life in that room. Now you can establish *for yourself,* and the audience as well, the sense that you are living in a real physical environment.

In the basic Fourth Wall exercise, your goal is to create an imaginary environment between yourself and the audience, one in which you can engage in some ongoing physical task. For example, you might visualize the wall of a kitchen with a stove, a sink, and cabinets. The task might be to make yourself breakfast. Or you might imagine a bookcase in a new apartment, with the task of removing your books from cartons and arranging them on the shelves.

These activities will bring you into direct face-to-face contact with the audience, but if your concentration remains on the task and the imaginary stimuli, the audience should hardly be seen. If you do find yourself focusing on the audience, *just go back to a specific detail* of your environment and activity. You might ask yourself, "Is there enough room on this shelf for all my theatre books?" Or, "Should I place the paperbacks on their sides or upright?" Or if you are creating a kitchen, you might ask, "Did I plug in the toaster?" Concentration will be helped by giving yourself obstacles. For example, you might discover burnt-on grease in the frying pan that must be scoured out before you can cook your breakfast.

Once you appear to have your concentration in this exercise under control, add another step. Imagine that someone, a friend perhaps, is in the next room, off to your right or left. Tell that person about a real incident you have experienced. Having to speak and tell a story often arouses self-conscious thoughts about the quality of your voice or how interesting your story is. Deal with this self-consciousness by continuously re-creating details of your fourth wall. Make sure you extend your imaginary environment to include the other room; and pick a specific friend so that your actual relationship to him or her will affect the way you tell your story.

When you do this exercise your focus will alternate between the different parts of your fourth wall, the details of the incident you are describing, some specific elements of the adjoining room, and visualizations of your friend's appearance and his or her reactions to your story. This alternation is to be expected. As long as you periodically re-create all the essential elements, your concentration will be maintained and you will feel *as if* you were functioning in a real physical environment. (The reality of imagined people, objects, and environments, though powerful and compelling, is, of course, not the same thing as the reality experienced with actual, tangible people and objects in real spaces. The actor does not experience hallucinations on stage, just as a person having a sexual fantasy in real life will have a powerful and compelling experience without failing to distinguish between the fantasy and the real thing.)

In performance, your concentration will not only depend on how specific you are with *imaginary* objects. Most of your attention will be directed toward your fellow actors and the real objects on stage. The more fully you personalize these and endow them with special meaning, the more fully and consistently you will experience the life and environment of the character. For example, the director may give you some business: pour some wine for a guest. It would be a mistake to treat this as an empty piece of stage business. Instead, you might add the circumstance that your character chose this particular wine especially for this occasion—perhaps to impress the guest. This circumstance will then affect the way you handle the bottle, how you taste the wine, and how you observe your guest as he drinks. Such added circumstances which must, of course, be fully consistent with the situation of the play, will both enrich your character's life in the scene and give you additional focal points for your concentration.

Morris Carnovsky provides us with a wonderful description of how to create a specific relationship to the objects on stage, and of the impact of this process on the actor's concentration and feeling of ease. He was playing the brother of Stockmann in *An Enemy of the People*. As he entered his brother's room Carnovsky went through a series of detailed thoughts about the room—all from his character's point of view:

> Here is the room. There is the lamp, that expensive lamp that my foolish brother bought. Here is a tablecloth. I don't have any such tablecloth in my house. This carpet is probably much finer than anything anybody in town has. What right has he to have a tablecloth and stuff like this around?[4]

Notice that each object in the room was endowed with meaning *for the character*. Only then could Carnovsky play the *life* of Stockmann's brother in that room.

The "Don't Go" Exercise

This is a more advanced concentration exercise and it includes strong emotional elements. We ask you to face the audience and visualize someone you care for, or have cared for in the past, leaving you. This may be a re-creation of a real incident in which you actually lost someone, or it may be done as a total fantasy by imagining what it would be like to lose some particular person currently in your life. Place the person you "see" in the middle of the audience area. When you do this exercise, create an imaginary environment between yourself and the departing person. You can move within this environment, but don't enter the audience or actually go to the imagined person.

As the person to stay, starting with the words, "Don't go." You can continue to use these same words, or any variation of these, such as, "Please stay!" "Don't leave me!" or any words of your own choosing. The person is leaving for a reason and you want him or her to stay. The goal is to play out an imaginary scene, but in a very structured way, limiting yourself to variations of "Don't go." In carrying this out, the imagined person should be active, moving or saying things to you, just as happens when we experience fantasies in our daily lives. Some students have imagined someone dying rather than someone leaving them. The exercise is carried out in the same way and no special problems occur.

Going Back in Time. If you create someone whom you have cared for in the past, but whom you no longer feel the same way toward, then you must begin by re-creating the *you* of that past time, with the needs, fears, and hopes that you had then. Don't try to behave and express feelings in a childlike or more youthful form; simply do your best to re-create your perceptions and self-perceptions of that time.

Respecting the Student's Privacy. It is important to note that in this and all other exercises that are based on a student's private life, the student is not asked to reveal who the imagined person actually is or anything about his or her relationship to that person.

Working Toward Self-Control. The classroom atmosphere for this and any other kind of emotional exercise must be one of disciplined self-control, where the actor learns to use his personal and emotional life fully, but systematically and respectfully— and always in the service of artistic ends; never for indulgent, therapeutic, or general unmasking purposes.

In addition, the student should always be in control of his own arousal process. That is, the emotion should always derive from the student's *own* stimuli. The teacher should prompt when necessary, but should never pressure or intimidate the student into an emotional reaction, nor provoke a reaction by manipulating his own relationship with the student. I have seen acting teachers, for the sake of evoking an emotion, antagonize, terrorize, humiliate, ridicule, and induce guilt feelings in students. Students often do become emotional through these means, but it is an unnecessarily painful process that places the control with the teacher rather than the student, and definitely does not teach the student how to generate and control emotional reactions on his own.

Concentration Difficulties. Concentration difficulties in this exercise come in various forms: (1) You are embarrassed about expressing such personal feelings publicly, though in real life you would, in fact, ask this person not to go if he or she were actually leaving you. (2) You would not even express this behavior privately. If the person were really leaving, you might *think* words like "Don't go" in your head, but would not speak them aloud. (3) You are afraid of feeling the emotions that might arise from this exercise or are afraid you will not be able to turn the emotions off. (4) You claim you've never cared for anyone strongly enough to want to ask him or her not to go.

Asking yourself the right questions will help keep you on target and away from self-conscious thoughts, and this will make it easier for you to overcome your fear and embarrassment about expressing strong personal feelings. Some useful questions are, "How will my life change if the person leaves me?" and "What about this person is special and irreplaceable?" It is also helpful to tell the person (in your mind, not out loud) what you've always wanted to say but never have. Your concentration will also be aided by reminding yourself to see the details of the person's face, particularly his or her eyes (looking at you or away from you, or crying, etc.), and to remember or imagine what it is like to touch or hold the person.

The way to gain confidence that you won't be overwhelmed by an emotion is to learn how to control and turn off an emotion at will. You can get out of an emotion by switching your concentration to pleasant stimuli, such as a relaxing bath or a lovely perfume or to someone who makes you feel good.

If you are one of those people who feels he has never cared for anyone very strongly, search your memory to find the person (or animal) that you have cared the most about, even going back into early childhood. Virtually all of us have had strong attachments to others at some point in our lives, but sometimes, to protect ourselves from the pain of rejection and loss of love, we convince ourselves that we don't really care for someone (or anyone) all that much. Such self-deception stands firmly in the way of an actor's development.

You can help yourself recall having loved or wanted someone by focusing your attention on the specific behavior, thoughts, and bodily sensations of loving or caring. Ask yourself, "Do I remember waiting and hoping to receive a telephone call from someone?" If the answer is yes, then try to remember your reaction when the person finally called (or didn't call). Two or three such questions are often sufficient to get you to think more concretely and more candidly about your emotional life.

The Privacy Exercise

Acting is a public event, and yet actors must maintain a strong sense of privacy on stage. They must never forget that an audience is watching, yet at the same time they must be fully concentrated on their characters' objectives and stimuli (or on personal stimuli from their own lives used as an aid in reaching certain strong emotional states).

Actors have trouble maintaining this privacy either because they are afraid of the audience or because they "play for" the audience, trying too hard to please them. The Privacy Exercise is useful for both groups.

You do the Privacy Exercise alone, in front of the class; although sometimes, as a first step, I will have all students work simultaneously. Start by imagining yourself in a familiar environment in which you ordinarily engage in some private, but not necessarily secretive behavior. (Asking someone who is having difficulty in concentrating to display truly secretive behavior in front of the class is akin to throwing someone who can't swim and is terrified of the water into the middle of a lake. In either setting it is bad teaching.) The private behavior should be physically active to some degree (unlike, for example, reading a book), and be something you do fairly regularly and that takes some time to complete. The activity may be virtually anything— cleaning something, shaving, putting on make-up, dancing to music, painting, etc.

To help establish the reality of your private environment you may use classroom props or items from your own home. Objects may also be created through the imagination as long as they are not too complex. For example, it would be too difficult to carry out typing a letter if one had to create all the sensory elements of an imaginary typewriter.

Do your best to engage in the selected activity as you do in life. The goal is to create a sufficient sense of privacy to engage in the activity unself-consciously. You will achieve this by: (1) focusing on the objectives of the activity (why you do it), (2) continuously re-creating the thoughts and images you usually have while engaging in the private activity, and (3) imagining the sensory details of the place where you do it and the objects you come in contact with there (for example, feeling the fabric of your living room chair or the carpet under your feet). If you find your thoughts filled with self-conscious concerns, instruct yourself to refocus your attention on the objectives or the objects.

Before doing the Privacy Exercise you should actually engage in the selected activity in your own environment. You will probably be surprised at many of the things you do. (If you get the chance, watch a classroom full of students in deep concentration during an exam: idiosyncratic behavior abounds.) Make periodic mental notes of your own behavior, but do not simply plan to copy these in the classroom. The idea is not to engage in a planned imitation of yourself, but to re-create your motivation and surroundings with enough specificity to bring about a true sense of privacy.

Give Yourself Obstacles. While doing the exercise make periodic observations of your own behavior. (For these brief instances, of course, you will not be concentrating on your objectives or environment.) If you find that your actions have become far more constrained and ''public'' than they were at home, or that you are adding extra touches in order to *look* more interesting, you can intensify your concentration *by providing yourself with an obstacle.* For example, if you are shaving, find a hair that is imbedded and won't come off easily, or a cut or blemish that must be approached with extra care.

When you are properly concentrated, *personal behavior* is likely to emerge. You may find yourself unself-consciously rubbing your lip or humming or sitting in a posture that you would not permit for yourself when your focus is on pleasing or impressing the viewers.

Actually, it is not that the actor becomes unconcerned with pleasing and impressing viewers—if this were so he might as well do all his acting alone in his living room. It is just that the criteria for pleasing and impressing are different from what he might have previously believed. He learns that the criteria are based on personal and passionate expression, rather than on arbitrarily attractive poses and postures.

Unnatural ''Naturalism.'' One pitfall is that the actor may misinterpret the terms ''personal'' and ''passionate'' and start inventing personal-*appearing* behavior that supposedly gives the impression of unself-consciousness. This may, in the extreme, lead to a lot of weird-looking behavior, done for its own sake; or to an excess of scratching, nose picking, and self-styled sloppiness, as if the goal in acting were to nurture these behaviors on stage because they are supposedly more ''natural.'' Such ''natural'' behavior doesn't make an actor either more personal or more expressive, but more mannered.

You may decide in advance that you would rather not make certain private behaviors public. That is your choice. The success of the exercise depends on learning how to maintain unself-conscious concentration while engaging in private activity in front of others. It does not depend on displaying everything you do when you are alone. If you exclude too much, though, you will be left with a highly censored "public" performance, and the whole purpose of the exercise will be undermined.

The Private Singing Exercise

This is a variation of the Privacy Exercise. Almost all of us sing when alone—at least sometimes. The goal of the exercise is to create the environment and circumstances in which we do our most uninhibited and expressive singing. Let yourself be playful or emotional or loud or whatever—just let it all out.

Addressing the Audience

Along with learning how to disregard the audience and feel private in their presence, students need to be taught how to deal with the audience directly. Many roles call for such direct contact and many actors find it very difficult to concentrate when looking right into the faces of the audience (even when they can't actually see the faces because of the stage lights). To overcome their nervousness they often try totally useless procedures (like trying to stare people down) that only serve to make both themselves and the audience uncomfortable.

In this exercise students do monologues or poems directly to the audience, making eye contact with individuals; sometimes they are asked to walk into the audience and take the hands of or touch individual audience members. The goal—and solution to concentration problems—is to really talk *to* the audience, and not merely *toward* them.

Some of the procedures that have been mentioned already are useful here too, such as reminding yourself to go back to the stimuli and objectives of the piece you are presenting. But something additional can also prove extremely helpful. Self-consciousness often disappears as soon as you begin to really communicate to the people you are speaking to—not as an impersonal "audience," but as a collection of individuals with the same kind of needs and feelings that you have. Ask yourself questions about those individuals and find the answers in their faces, bodies and postures. You might, for example, ask, "Have they experienced anything similar to what I am telling them?" "What kinds of joys and pains have they probably known?" "What are they probably afraid of?"

Authentic Interaction. In our everyday meetings with people, we think these kinds of questions quite spontaneously, and the way we interact with them is affected by the answers we give.

We meet someone and just on the basis of what we see in his or her face or stance, we make some judgments (or at least some guesses) about the kind of person they are. We make judgments about how friendly they will be if approached, or what their interests may be, or what feelings they have about themselves. And we continue to make and revise these kinds of judgments as we talk to them—particularly if we are pursuing some strong objective like trying to sell or convince them of something.

Asking yourself questions about the people you are speaking to, whether they are fellow actors on stage or audience members, is a reminder to really "see" that other person. (By "see" I definitely do not mean playing a scene staring into the other person's eyeballs. That kind of eyeballing is only seen in acting classes, never in life.) Asking questions *about others* will help overcome the self-consciousness and anxiety that stem from being overly concerned with how *you* are coming across to them.

The Rhythm Exercise

This exercise encourages students to engage in extreme physical and vocal behavior without inhibition or self-consciousness by building up a complex behavior pattern in a gradual, step by step fashion. In this exercise the whole class works together.

Start from a seated position. Hear a rhythm in your head. (The rhythm may change at any time during the course of the exercise.) Then move one part of your body in time to the rhythm. After a brief time, add a second part of your body, moving both parts simultaneously. Large movements are encouraged. Add a third part and a fourth. One of these parts should involve the torso.

Four parts of your body will be moving simultaneously and rhythmically. At any point you can change any of the movements or exchange one body part for any other. Stand up and continue the movements while moving around the room. Don't let the movements evolve into any kind of conventional or popular dance steps, as these lead only to stereotyped, practiced movements.

If you begin to feel silly or self-conscious, simply *go back to your stimulus*, the internal rhythm you have created. To re-engage your concentration, focus on a single movement from the entire pattern and express the rhythm fully with that one movement. (The other parts of the body ordinarily continue moving on their own, which is fine.) Next, add strong, rhythmic sounds to the total pattern. Pair up with a fellow student and make eye contact as you move together. Continue your sounds, communicating them to your partner—at times simultaneously and at times alternating vocalizing and listening.

In the last stage you will turn your rhythmic sounds into words. Tell your partner about a simple incident from the previous week (or even how the week was without incident). While continuing to move, you and your partner should alternate telling parts of your stories, trying to keep the same rhythm and pitch patterns that were used at the simple sound stage. The behavior during this final stage is generally very extreme and you're likely to be surprised by your lack of self-consciousness.

III. CONFIDENCE

We don't ordinarily choose to be afraid. The combination of thoughts, images, and bodily sensations which lead us to say to ourselves, "I am afraid," are unpleasant and embarrassing. They generally prevent us from doing our best work. Fear is a response to *specific* stimuli. For example, there are some people in whose presence we feel inadequate and insecure, with whom we are constantly watching ourselves. We behave awkwardly with them, perhaps stammering when speaking. But there are other people in whose presence we are more comfortable, more easily expressive, at our least self-conscious. Well, *the actor, through his imagination, can bring into auditions and performances those people or situations that make him feel strong and confident*. Whenever he's frightened he can imagine the people, places, objects, and animals that bolster his confidence and make him feel fearless and capable. These are called *confidence-stimuli*.

The goal is for *fear to become a signal* for immediately switching your concentration to your confidence-stimuli. The butterflies and trembles of fear will then give way to a feeling of strength across your chest and calmness in your body. The anticipation of failure will be replaced by a readiness for action. With confidence-stimuli, fear need no longer be indulged and time need no longer be wasted on worrying.

Among the many confidence-stimuli students have used are visualizing friends, family members, pets, various smells, the ocean, ballet slippers, the feel of a peach, sexual stimuli, music, sporting events, a basketball, a guitar, a special room, receiving an award. For some people, thinking of people or situations that make them angry leads to strong feelings of confidence.

When using a confidence-stimulus in performance, you only stay focused on it for a moment. Therefore, it doesn't matter if the feelings and thoughts aroused by the confidence-stimulus bear any resemblance to the feelings and thoughts of the character you are playing. The confidence-stimulus is for you, not the audience. The only requirement for a confidence-stimulus is that it makes you feel better about yourself and focuses you on your capabilities rather than your inadequacies.

The Confidence-Stimulus Exercise

The confidence-stimulus procedure must be practiced conscientiously since you will be countering the tangible stimuli of your fears (audiences, agents, casting directors) with the easily fleeting stimuli of your imagination. In class, students sit on chairs arranged in a semicircle. Then they are asked to choose a confidence-stimulus. If your confidence-stimulus is a person, imagine ("see") that person in front of you. The person should be alive: he or she should smile, talk, joke—whatever is necessary to make you feel the reality of his or her presence.

If the stimulus is some special place, imagine that you are there. If you are using an object, "see" it and "feel" it. Engage any and all senses that are appropriate to that stimulus.

For students not familiar with this kind of *sensory* creation, it isn't very difficult. Creating and responding to imaginary stimuli is something we all do spontaneously. Anyone who has had a sexual fantasy has gone through all the essential steps of a sensory exercise. To make your stimulus more vivid and enduring ask questions about it: What color are my grandmother's eyes? How does my best friend look when she smiles? Is the grain on the basketball new or worn? Look for the aspects of the stimulus that trigger your confidence and learn to switch away from the aspects that take you in other directions. (During any one exercise session, work with only one confidence-stimulus, but explore a number of such stimuli across a series of sessions.)

Once you have begun to imagine your stimulus, make a simple, voiced "ah" sound. The confidence-stimulus should affect the way the sound comes out. For many students the request that they make a sound leads to the immediate disappearance of the confidence-stimulus; it is replaced by self-conscious and self-evaluative thoughts about the quality of the sound about to be (or just) made. If this happens, *tell yourself* to go back to your stimulus and to take the risk of making a sound.

Sometimes if making a sound is particularly difficult for a student I will have her first make the sound "in her mind" only.

I then ask her to make a voiced sound, but remind her not to simply repeat the sound she heard in her mind. Before making the voiced sound she must re-create her confidence-stimulus so that the voiced sound, like the mental sound, comes out as *a reaction to something*.

You might begin to make a sound that *is* an organic reaction to your stimulus but, part way through, find that you are no longer focused on and reacting to your imagery; instead you are listening to and evaluating your sound. Rather than asking questions about your stimulus, you may find yourself asking such things as, "Do I sound like a fool?" Again, remind yourself to short-circuit these distracting thoughts and *go back to your stimulus*.

Proceed from a simple "ah" sound to more personal, expressive sounds, using any combination of vowels and consonants that express your feelings toward the stimulus. Then add expressive movements, starting with a simple arm movement and gradually adding other parts of the body until the whole body is involved in the expression of confidence. *Expressive* reactions, such as leaping, spinning and gliding are encouraged over *literal* reactions to the stimulus, such as hugging someone or bouncing a ball.

Although in actual performance situations reactions to a confidence-stimulus are not meant to be visible to the audience, in the classroom exercise public sounds and movements are useful. They provide you with obstacles to your concentration so that you may practice the process of *going back* to your confidence-stimulus when you feel self-conscious. In the exercise, place your confidence-stimulus in the space around you. In a performance, the stimulus should stay in your mind—behind your eyes, so to speak—otherwise the audience will become aware that you are stepping outside of the character for a moment.

Private Behavior. There is an extremely useful technique we use for increasing expressiveness in both exercises and scenes. Every actor has had the experience of knowing that he "felt more" than he actually expressed in his performance. How does the actor know this? He knows he felt more because in his mind *he saw himself* behaving in ways that he didn't let come through his body. And in his mind *he heard himself* speaking in ways or making sounds that he didn't let come through his voice. Our private selves are ordinarily far more expressive than our public selves. By tapping into his private self, the actor can become increasingly expressive and uninhibited.

For example, during the confidence-stimulus exercise (or any of the other stimulus exercises), stop moving and making sounds for a moment; then close your eyes and "see" (in your mind's eye) an image of yourself reacting to some details of the stimulus you have been using. Also "hear" the sounds your private self *wants* to make to that stimulus. It's as if you are watching a movie of yourself in your mind.

If your private self isn't very expressive, *tell it* to react to the stimulus with bolder, more expressive, more varied movements and sounds. The private you will comply. But don't consciously plan out the specific reactions of your private self because you will likely come up with only conventional actor-like forms of expression. Rather, simply give your private self a general command such as "Use your torso more" or "Get your arms involved," and then give it some specific aspect of the stimulus to react to. Then observe it passively.

After "observing" your private reactions, open your eyes (all sensory exercises are done with the eyes open) and re-create your stimulus for yourself. The goal now is to express through your body and voice the more expressive behavior that you observed your private self display.

It cannot be overemphasized that all reactions—both of the private self and the real self—must come *in response to a stimulus*. Otherwise your private self will only show you your own conventional ideas about how some action or emotion should be expressed, and your real self will only be able to engage in an awkward imitation of what you saw your private self do.

With practice, observation of the private self can be done without stopping the work and closing your eyes. When you feel you are not being expressive enough in an exercise or scene, you can instantly check your private self and let it lead you to more expressive reactions. In scene work, the private self can belong to your character, so that the style and form of expression you observe is appropriate to the role.

The Anti-Confidence to Confidence Exercise

The confidence-stimulus procedure can be practiced in real-life situations in which you feel anxious, inhibited, or embarrassed. You can also experience such situations through your imagination. You start by imagining what we call "an anti-confidence stimulus." Imagine yourself in a situation in which you feel shy, embarrassed, self-conscious, etc. When these feelings become strong, switch instantly to your confidence-stimulus. Once confident feelings are generated (with the aid of the question-asking procedure, if needed), continue to explore the confidence-stimulus for another minute. Then start the cycle over again by re-creating the anti-confidence stimulus. The cycle may be repeated a number of times in order to develop *the habit of switching* to your confidence-stimulus. Over a series of practice sessions, explore a number of different anti-confidence people and situations, including performance situations.

At times you might experience what seems like a tug of war for your consciousness between your confidence and anti-confidence stimuli. If this happens, simply remind yourself, "Go back to my confidence-stimulus," and ask yourself a question about it ("How does my grandmother sound when she sings to herself?"). By practicing with these imaginary unpleasant situations, you will be more likely to remember to use your confidence-stimulus when those first signs of fear arise in actual performance (or in any other situation). If you *choose* to be confident (not always an easy choice), the confidence-stimulus will provide a dependable tool for fulfilling that choice.

As you gain confidence in your acting craft you will need to rely on your confidence-stimulus much less often. You will understand the actor's process well enough so that if you lose your concentration, you will be able to focus directly on one of the basic acting elements, such as your character's objective or imagery. But it is still reassuring to know that if anxieties appear, you have a tool that can be relied upon—that you will not be helpless.

The Confidence-Substitution Exercise

Another procedure for increasing confidence is to bring your confidence-stimulus right into the performing situation. For example, to help overcome fear of the audience, imagine someone in the audience who makes you feel good about yourself, who you know is on your side. One way to practice this is to have each student speak a monologue or poem directly to the audience (their classmates) with the simple intention of making the meaning of what they are saying very clear to the listeners. In doing this, if you get nervous or self-conscious, immediately visualize your "confidence-person" sitting in the audience.

Do the next few lines *for* this person, feeling his or her

presence, as if he or she is really there. As you continue, place this person in different locations within the audience. See an expression on the face of your stimulus-person that will help you feel at ease and uninhibited—perhaps an encouraging smile from a loved one. (You can also use someone who makes you feel angry or indignant as your confidence-person; seeing a challenging gesture from that person might give you an ''I'll show you'' kind of confident feeling.) The principle here is that the actor's confidence-person is momentarily *substituted* for (actually, *added to*) the people in the audience.

Additions. In a variation of this procedure, an actress who loved cats visualized cat ears and whiskers on the faces of casting directors, agents, and other people who made her nervous. She had learned in class that the best way to do a ''substitution''—a technique employed in scene work to help generate authentic feelings and behavior—is to find something in the face or physique of your scene partner that reminds you of someone in your life who makes you feel the way your character has to feel. As this actress demonstrated, you can also, through imagery, *add* features to the person you are looking at.

The substitution and addition procedures will help you overcome feelings of helplessness in a scene as well as an interview. The procedures can also be used to create any other feelings that your character needs to experience in a scene. (When teaching actors how to bring personal stimuli from their own lives into a scene in order to intensify a reaction or make it more authentic, I prefer to use the term ''additions'' to the more traditional ''substitutions.'' Actors may *add* personal stimuli for brief moments, but should never actually drop out of the circumstances of the play and *replace* the character's stimuli with their own.)

The Confident-Character Exercise

Here is another valuable confidence technique, one that is based on our procedures for the creation of character. Essentially, what one does is create a *confident character.* For example, one student, whenever he felt anxious and too self-critical, would imagine that he was the famous dancer, Nureyev. He had seen an interview with Nureyev and had been very impressed by his poise and self-assurance. Most of us have done similar things at one time or another. Children are always turning themselves into their heroes when they play. This same device can be used for the serious business of overcoming fear.

When doing the confident character-work, don't try to imitate the personal mannerisms of your confident model. You would certainly want to be that detailed when you use a character model for developing a role, but in the confident-character exercise, the process is somewhat more subtle and the aspects of the model that one adopts are somewhat broader. The goal is to adopt the spirit and style of the confident model without becoming a facsimile: You remain yourself, but yourself possessed by a confident spirit.

Begin the exercise by first choosing a confident model. It can be someone you have known personally, or someone seen in a film or on television. The only requirements are that, to you, he or she appear confident and that you have a fairly clear image of his or her behavior. We have all known or seen people who have a confident style, a "comfortable-with-themselves" manner that we have admired or envied. Imagine yourself to be that person; imagine that they move in and take over your body.

Let them "possess" each part of your body—your neck, your shoulders, your arms and hands, your face, your eyes, your hips, thighs, and legs, your gait, your posture and the way you distribute your weight, the rhythm in your body, *all of you,* including your voice. If your model has a self-assured voice it is probably because of voice placement and resonance, or vocal rhythm, or the firmness and clarity of articulation, rather than his or her accent or some eccentricity of melody or pronunciation. Explore where your model's voice resonates from; it will probably not come from his or her throat.

One caution: If you choose a well-known actor as your model, don't pick one who "plays" at being confident—for example, someone who plays a macho character in films or television. Pick only people who in their real life seem to be confident; otherwise your confident character will be two steps removed from life and may wind up a caricature.

As the confident character "takes possession" of you, your sense of your body, your voice quality, your attitudes toward others, your expectations, your readiness for action will all feel different—more confident, more spontaneous. If done properly, you will not appear to others as if you are working on a character, in the sense of changing your entire behavioral style. What others will see is a confident version of you.

Sometimes this new feeling of strength is very disconcerting—it goes against old, safe habits. For some people, communicating to others, "I'm nobody," may have become a way to avoid the risk of rejection. *You've* said it—*they* don't have to. You can fight against the tendency to remain less than you know you can be by reminding yourself to take the risk and *go back to* your confident character: feel your neck, eyes, rhythm, etc. being taken over again.

As the exercise continues, take your character through a variety of tasks, such as carrying out everyday activities like polishing a car or washing dishes (with either actual or imaginary props). Never ask yourself how your character would do a particular task. You will have no idea. Just employ the steps to get "possessed" and do it.

In class the next step is to take your confident character into an improvisation or scene in order to practice using it when interacting with others. Never *pretend* to be confident in some external way. Let the form of the behavior derive solely from your model. Through your imagination, bring your confident character into contact with people and situations that intimidate you (that is, into contact with your anti-confidence stimuli). When you are possessed by your confident character, you will feel much more in control.

Sometimes as a last phase of any of the confidence exercises, I'll ask students to say the sentence, *"I can do anything"*—first to themselves, and then to each other. This is *not* meant to be a pep talk to oneself to pump up confidence. Feeling capable is the proper *outcome* of the confidence exercise, not something you can simply will. If the student feels truthful when he says "I can do anything," and there is no inner voice intruding with "No you can't" or "Who are you kidding?" the exercise has been effective. Then the student will feel he *can* take the risk of performing in front of others and he will accept as natural the fact that before he can act well he must act badly. He will give himself permission to fail in order to open up the possibility to learn. If the words, "I can do anything" feel hollow, as they will at times, the solution is: *Go back to your confidence stimulus or confident character.*

Creating Characters. One general note on character exercises: I know many teachers who are against using people as characters for theoretical reasons. They claim it leads to imitative acting, and that actors must find their characters only by exploring different sides of themselves. It is odd that when the actors these teachers admire the most (e.g., Marlon Brando, Laurence Olivier, Meryl Streep, Dustin Hoffman) talk about their acting process, they always refer to finding their characters through observing people.

Imitative acting occurs when you imitate the theatrical mannerisms of other actors, or when you fail to incorporate the physiological and psychological motivations that lie behind a model's behavioral style. I certainly agree that it is useful for an actor to find the sides of himself that are similar to his character. But, the process that I have called "getting possessed by a character" is the core of the technique great actors have always used for creating a unique and authentic life on stage.

In the Classroom. In the confidence exercises, as well as many other kinds of exercises, at the early stages of a student's work or as the student enters a new area of exploration, the teacher will need to prompt the student to go back to his stimuli. But eventually the student must become his own prompter, the voice providing the instruction must become his own. To help students make this transition it is useful for teachers to preface prompts with the words, "Tell yourself to..." Whether this instruction is completed by "... go back to your stimulus," or "... ask a question about your stimulus," or some other prompt, it is important to remind the student to take on the responsibility of prompting himself.

The classroom atmosphere and quality of interaction between teacher and student, of course, has a significant impact on the student's fear, concentration, and confidence. Some recommendations to teachers: Encourage any small gains on the part of a student. Let him know what the next steps for him to take are; but emphasizing only what students have done wrong, as opposed to what they have done better, will inevitably make them more self-conscious. If a teacher frightens or purposely intimidates a student (usually as a way to cover up his or her own inadequacies), he or she becomes part of the problem, rather than part of the solution.

There are some actors who enjoy the mild anxiety they feel before a performance. They feel it sharpens them and helps them prepare. These exercises are not designed to take away anything you find useful in your work, only the debilitating anxiety that undermines your craft.

SCENES FOR ONE MAN
AND
ONE WOMAN

BAREFOOT IN THE PARK
by Neil Simon

ACT II, SCENE 2

After 6 weeks of married bliss Corie and Paul Bratter are still adjusting to each other as well as to their tiny five floor walk-up (''6, if you count the stoop'') on Manhattan's east side. Corie's madcap zest for fun and adventure finds outlets in strange ways. She does fertility dances when she feels sexy and has a penchant for walking barefoot through Washington Square Park in 17° weather. Her fledgling lawyer husband likes to wear his gloves in the winter and won't eat any food whose name he can't pronounce. He is sensible and logical and, therefore, from Corie's point of view, he ''isn't any fun.''

Tonight Corie has arranged a blind date for her widowed mother with a flamboyant Hungarian neighbor, Mr. Velesco. He takes them all to an Albanian restaurant on Staten Island and plies them with dishes that are a bit too exotic for Paul's conservative palate and her mother's delicate stomach.

At 2 A.M. the four weary diners come traipsing home. Mr. Velesco gallantly offers to escort Corie's mother home—to New Jersey. While Corie is game for more fun, Paul is trying to contain his anger and cope with a spinning head and upset stomach. This clashing of temperaments quickly leads to their first spat.

CORIE: *(takes a beat, closes the door, smiles and turns to* PAUL*)* Well...how about *that*, Mr. ''This is going to be a fiasco tonight''?...He's taking her all the way out to New Jersey...at two o'clock in the morning...That's what I call ''The Complete Gentleman.'' (PAUL *looks at her with disdain, rises and staggers up the stairs into the bedroom.*) He hasn't

3

even given a thought about how he's going to get home... Maybe he'll sleep over... Hey, Paul, do you think...? No, not *my* mother... (*jumps up onto couch*) Then again anything can happen with the Sheik of Budapest.... Boy, what a night... Hey! I got a plan. Let's take the bottle of Scotch downstairs, ring all the bells and yell "Police"... Just to see who comes out of whose apartment... (*There is no answer from the bedroom.*) Paul?... What's the matter, darling...? Don't you feel well?

PAUL: (*Comes out of the bedroom, down the stairs, crossing to the closet. He is taking his coat off and is angry.*) What a rotten thing to do.... To your own mother.

CORIE: What?

PAUL: Do you have any idea how she felt just now? Do you know what kind of a night this was for her?

CORIE: (*impishly*) It's not over yet.

PAUL: You didn't see her sitting here two minutes ago. You were upstairs with that Hungarian Duncan Hines... Well, she was miserable. Her face was longer than that trip we took tonight. (*hangs up coat in closet*)

CORIE: She never said a thing to me.

PAUL: (*takes out hanger and puts jacket on it*) She's too good a sport. She went the whole cock-eyed way... Boy, oh boy... dragging a woman like that all the way out to the middle of the harbor for a bowl of sheep dip. (*hangs jacket up and crosses to dictionary on side table under radiator, takes tie off and folds it neatly*)

CORIE: (*follows him to table*) It was Greek bean soup. And at least *she* tasted it. She didn't jab at it with her knife throwing cute little epigrams like, "Ho, ho, ho... I think there's someone in there."

PAUL: (*puts tie between pages of dictionary*) That's right. That's right. At least I was honest about it. You ate two bowls because you were showing off for Al Capone at the next table. (PAUL *searches for wallet unsuccessfully.*)

CORIE: What are you so angry about, Paul?

PAUL: (*crossing to closet*) I just told you. I felt terrible for your mother. (*gets wallet out of jacket pocket*)

CORIE: (*following after him to the front of couch*) Why? Where is she at this very minute? Alone with probably the most attractive man she's ever met. Don't tell me *that* doesn't beat hell out of hair curlers and the Late Late Show.

PAUL: (*crossing up onto bedroom landing*) Oh, I can just hear it now. What sparkling conversation. He's probably telling her about a chicken cacciatore he once cooked for the High Lama of Tibet and she's sitting there shoving pink pills in her mouth.

CORIE: (*taking coat from couch and putting it on armchair R.*) You never can tell what people talk about when they're alone.

PAUL: I don't understand how you can be so unconcerned about this. (*goes into bedroom*)

CORIE: (*moving to stairs*) Unconcerned . . . I'm plenty concerned. Do you think I'm going to get one wink of sleep until that phone rings tomorrow? I'm scared to death for my mother. But I'm grateful there's finally the opportunity for something to be scared about . . . (*moves R., then turns back*) What I'm really concerned about is *you*!

PAUL: (*bursts out of bedroom, nearly slamming through door*) Me? Me?

CORIE: I'm beginning to wonder if you're capable of *having* a good time.

PAUL: Why? Because I like to wear my gloves in the winter?

CORIE: No. Because there isn't the least bit of adventure in you. Do you know what you are? You're a watcher. There are Watchers in this world and there are Do-ers. And the Watchers sit around watching the Do-ers do. Well, tonight you watched and I did.

PAUL: (*moves down stairs to* CORIE) Yeah . . . Well, it was harder to watch what you did than it was for you to *do* what I was watching. (*crosses back up stairs to landing*)

CORIE: You won't let your hair down for a minute. You couldn't even relax for one night. Boy, Paul, sometimes you act like a . . . a . . . (*gets shoes from under couch*)

PAUL: (*stopping on landing*) What . . . ? A stuffed shirt?

CORIE: (*drops shoes on couch*) I didn't say that.

PAUL: That's what you're implying.

CORIE: (*moves to R. armchair and begins to take off jewelry*) That's what you're anticipating. I didn't say you're a stuffed shirt. But you are extremely proper and dignified.

PAUL: I'm proper and dignified? (*moves to* CORIE) When . . . ? When was I proper and dignified?

CORIE: (*turns to* PAUL) All right. The other night. At Delfino's . . . You were drunk, right?

PAUL: Right. I was stoned.

CORIE: There you are. I didn't know it until you told me in the morning. (*unzips and takes off dress*) You're a funny kind of drunk. You just sat there looking unhappy and watching your coat.

PAUL: I was watching my coat because I saw someone else watching my coat . . . Look, if you want, I'll get drunk for you sometime. I'll show you a slob, make your hair stand on end. (*unbuttons shirt*)

CORIE: (*puts dress on chair*) It isn't necessary.

PAUL: (*starts to go, turns back*) Do you know . . . Do you know, in P.J. Clarke's last New Year's Eve, I punched an old woman? . . . Don't tell me about drunks. (*starts to go*)

CORIE: (*taking down hair*) All right, Paul.

PAUL: (*turns back and moves above couch*) When else? When else was I proper and dignified?

CORIE: Always. You're always dressed right, you always look right, you always say the right things. You're very close to being perfect.

PAUL: (*hurt to the quick*) That's . . . that's a *rotten* thing to say.

CORIE: (*moves up to* PAUL) I have never seen you without a jacket. I always feel like such a slob compared to you. Before we were married I was sure you slept with a tie.

PAUL: No, no. Just for very *formal* sleeps.

CORIE: You can't even walk into a candy store and ask the lady for a Tootsie Roll. (*playing the scene out, she moves D.R. of couch*) You've got to walk up to the counter and point at it and say, "I'll have that thing in the brown and white wrapper."

PAUL: (*moving to bedroom door*) That's ridiculous.

CORIE: And you're not. That's just the trouble. (*crosses to foot of stairs*) Like Thursday night. You wouldn't walk barefoot with me in Washington Square Park. Why not?

PAUL: (*to head of stairs*) Very simple answer. It was seventeen degrees.

CORIE: (*back to chair and continues taking down hair*) Exactly. That's very sensible and logical. Except it isn't any fun.

PAUL: (*down stairs to couch*) You know, maybe I *am* too proper and dignified for you. Maybe you would have been happier with someone a little more colorful and flamboyant . . . like the Geek! (*starts back to bedroom*)

CORIE: Well, he'd be a lot more laughs than a stuffed shirt.

PAUL: (*turns back on landing*) Oh, oh . . . I thought you said I wasn't.

CORIE: Well, you are now.

PAUL: (*reflectively*) I'm not going to listen to this. . . . I'm not going to listen . . . (*starts for bedroom*) I've got a case in court in the morning.

CORIE: (*Moves L.*) Where are you going?

PAUL: To sleep.

CORIE: *Now?* How can you sleep now?

PAUL: (*steps up on bed and turns back, leaning on door jamb*) I'm going to close my eyes and count knichis. Good night!

CORIE: You can't go to sleep now. We're having a fight.

PAUL: *You* have the fight. When you're through, turn off the lights. (*turns back into bedroom*)

CORIE: Ooh, that gets me insane. You can even control your emotions.

PAUL: (*storms out to head of stairs*) Look, I'm just as upset as you are . . . (*controls himself*) But when I get hungry I eat. And when I get tired I sleep. You eat and sleep too. Don't deny it, I've seen you. . . .

CORIE: (*moves R. with a grand gesture*) Not in the middle of a crisis.

PAUL: What crisis? We're just yelling a little.

CORIE: You don't consider this a crisis? Our whole marriage hangs in the balance.

PAUL: (*sits on steps*) It does? When did that happen?

CORIE: Just now. It's suddenly very clear that you and I have absolutely *nothing* in common.

PAUL: Why. Because I won't walk barefoot in the park in winter? You haven't got a case, Corie. Adultery, yes. Cold feet, no.

CORIE: (*seething*) Don't oversimplify this. I'm angry. Can't you see that?

PAUL: (*brings his hands to his eyes and peers at her through imaginary binoculars, then looks at his watch*) Corie, it's two-fifteen. If I can fall asleep in about half-an-hour, I can get about five hours' sleep. I'll call you from court tomorrow and we can fight over the phone. (*gets up and moves to bedroom*)

CORIE: You will *not* go to sleep. You will stay here and fight to save our marriage.

PAUL: (*in doorway*) If our marriage hinges on breathing fish balls and poofla-poo pie, it's not worth saving. . . . I am now going to crawl into our tiny, little, single bed. If you care to join me, we will be sleeping from left to right tonight. (*into bedroom and slams door*)

CORIE: You won't discuss it . . . You're *afraid* to discuss it . . . I married a coward . . . ! (*takes shoe from couch and throws it at bedroom door*)

PAUL: (*opens door*) Corie, would you bring in a pail? The closet's dripping.

CORIE: Ooh, I hate you! I hate you! I really, really hate you!

PAUL: (*storms to head of stairs*) Corie, there is one thing I learned in court. Be careful when you're tired and angry. You might say something you will soon regret. I-am-now-tired-and-angry.

CORIE: And a coward.

PAUL: (*comes down stairs to her at R. of couch*) And I will now say something I will soon regret . . . Okay, Corie, maybe you're right. Maybe we have nothing in common. Maybe we rushed into this marriage a little too fast. Maybe Love isn't enough. Maybe two people should have to take more than a blood test. Maybe they should be checked for common sense, understanding and emotional maturity.

CORIE: (That hurt.) All right . . . Why don't you get it passed in the Supreme Court? Only those couples bearing a letter from their psychiatrists proving they're well adjusted will be permitted to be married.

PAUL: You're impossible.

CORIE: You're unbearable.

PAUL: You belong in a nursery school.

CORIE: It's a lot more fun than the Home for the Fuddy Duddies.

PAUL: (*reaches out his hand to her*) All right, Corie, let's not get—

CORIE: Don't you touch me. . . . Don't you touch me. . . . (PAUL *very deliberately reaches out and touches her.* CORIE *screams hysterically and runs across the room away from him. Hysterically*) I don't want you near me. Ever again.

PAUL: (*moves toward her*) Now wait a minute, Corie—

CORIE: No. (*turns away from him*) I can't look at you. I can't even be in the same room with you now.

PAUL: Why?

CORIE: I just can't, that's all. Not when you feel this way.

PAUL: When I feel what way?

CORIE: The way you feel about me.

PAUL: Corie, you're hysterical.

CORIE: (*even more hysterically*) I am not hysterical. I know exactly what I'm saying. It's no good between us, Paul. It never will be again.

PAUL: (*throwing up his hands and sinking to the couch*) Holy cow.

CORIE: I'm sorry, I— (*She fights back tears.*) I don't want to cry.

PAUL: Oh, for pete's sake, cry. Go ahead and cry.

CORIE: (*height of fury*) Don't you tell me when to cry. I'll cry when I want to cry. And I'm not going to have my cry until you're out of this apartment.

PAUL: What do you mean, out of this apartment?

CORIE: Well, you certainly don't think we're going to live here together, do you? After tonight?

PAUL: Are you serious?

CORIE: Of course I'm serious. *I want a divorce!*

PAUL: (*Shocked, he jumps up.*) A *divorce*? What?

CORIE: (*pulls herself together, and with great calm, begins to go up stairs*) I'm sorry, Paul, I can't discuss it any more. Good night.

PAUL: Where are you going?

CORIE: To bed. (*turns back to* PAUL)

PAUL: You can't. Not now.

CORIE: You did before.

PAUL: That was in the middle of a fight. This is in the middle of a divorce.

CORIE: I can't talk to you when you're hysterical. Good night. (*goes into bedroom*)

PAUL: Will you come here . . . ? (CORIE *comes out on landing.*) I want to know why you want a divorce.

CORIE: I told you why. Because you and I have absolutely nothing in common.

PAUL: What about those six days at the Plaza?

CORIE: (*sagely*) Six days does not a week make.

PAUL: (*taken aback*) What does *that* mean?

CORIE: I don't know what it means. I just want a divorce.

PAUL: You know, I think you really mean it.

CORIE: I *do*!

PAUL: You mean, every time we have a little fight, you're going to want a divorce?

CORIE: (*reassuring*) There isn't going to be any more little fights. This is it, Paul! This is the end. Good night. (*goes into bedroom and closes door behind her*)

PAUL: Corie, do you mean to say—? (*He yells.*) Will you come down here!

CORIE: (*yells from bedroom*) Why?

PAUL: (*screams back*) Because I don't want to yell. (*The door opens and* CORIE *comes out. She stands at the top of the stairs. He points to his feet.*) All the way.

CORIE: (*seething, comes all the way down and stands where he pointed*) Afraid the crazy neighbors will hear us?

PAUL: You're serious.

CORIE: Dead serious.

PAUL: You mean the whole thing? With signing papers and going to court, shaking hands, goodbye, finished, forever, divorced?

CORIE: (*nodding in agreement*) That's what I mean...

PAUL: I see... Well... I guess there's nothing left to be said.

CORIE: I guess not.

PAUL: Right... Well, er... Good night, Corie. (*And he goes up stairs.*)

CORIE: Where are you going?

PAUL: (*turns back on landing*) To bed.

CORIE: Don't you want to talk about it?

PAUL: At two-thirty in the morning?

CORIE: I can't sleep until this thing is settled. (*moves to couch*)

PAUL: Well, it may take three months. Why don't you at least take a *nap*?

CORIE: You don't have to get snippy.

PAUL: Well, dammit, I'm sorry, but when I plan vacations, I'm happy and when I plan divorces I'm snippy. (*crosses to bookcase and grabs attaché case*) All right, you want to plan this thing, let's plan it. (*storms to coffee table and sweeps everything there onto floor with his hand*) You want a quick divorce or a slow painful one?

CORIE: (*horrified*) I'm going to bed. (*goes up stairs*)

PAUL: (*shouts*) You stay here or you get no divorce from me.

CORIE: (*stops on landing*) You can try acting civilized.

PAUL: (*putting down attaché case*) Okay, I'll be civilized. But charm you're not going to get. (*pushes chair towards her*) Now sit down!... Because there's a lot of legal and technical details to go through. (*opening attaché case*)

CORIE: Can't you do all that? I don't know anything about legal things.

PAUL: (*wheels on her and in a great gesture points an*

accusing finger at her) Ah, haa . . . Now *I'm* the Do-er and *you're* the Watcher! (*relentlessly*) Right, Corie? Heh? Right? Right? Isn't that right, Corie?

CORIE: (*with utmost disdain*) So this is what you're *really* like!

PAUL: (*grimacing like the monster he is*) Yes . . . Yes . . .

CORIE: (*Determined she's doing the right thing, she comes down stairs, and sits, first carefully moving the chair away from* PAUL.) All right, what do I have to do?

PAUL: First of all, what grounds? (*sitting on couch*)

CORIE: (*not looking at* PAUL) Grounds?

PAUL: (*taking legal pad and pencil out of case*) That's right. Grounds. What is your reason for divorcing me. And remember, my failure to appreciate knichis will only hold up in a Russian court.

CORIE: You're a scream, Paul. Why weren't you funny when we were happy?

PAUL: Okay . . . How about incompatible?

CORIE: Fine. Are you through with me?

PAUL: Not yet. What about the financial settlement?

CORIE: I don't want a thing.

PAUL: Oh, but you're entitled to it. Alimony, property? Supposing I just pay your rent. Seventy-five, sixty-three a month, isn't it?

CORIE: Ha ha—

PAUL: And you can have the furniture and the wedding gifts. I'd just like to keep my clothes.

CORIE: (*Shocked, she turns to* PAUL.) I hardly expected bitterness from you.

PAUL: I'm not bitter. That's a statement of fact. You're always wearing my pajamas and slippers.

CORIE: Only after you go to work.

PAUL: Why?

CORIE: Because I like the way they sm— never mind, it's stupid. (*She begins to sob, gets up and crosses up steps to bedroom.*) I'll sign over your pajamas and slippers.

PAUL: If you'd like, you can visit them once a month.

CORIE: (*turns back on landing*) *That's* bitter!

PAUL: You're damned right it is.

CORIE: (*beginning to really cry*) You have no right to be bitter.

PAUL: Don't tell me when to be bitter.

CORIE: Things just didn't work out.

PAUL: They sure as hell didn't.

CORIE: You can't say we didn't try.

PAUL: Almost two whole weeks.

CORIE: It's better than finding out in two *years*.

PAUL: Or twenty.

CORIE: Or fifty.

PAUL: Lucky, aren't we?

CORIE: We're the luckiest people in the whole world.

PAUL: I thought you weren't going to cry.

CORIE: Well, I am! I'm going to have the biggest cry I ever had in my life. And I'm going to enjoy it. (PAUL *drops pencil and pad into case, and buries his head in pillow from the couch.*) Because I'm going to cry so loud, I'm going to keep you awake all night long. Good night, Paul!...I mean, goodbye! (*She goes into bedroom and slams the door. We hear her crying in there.* PAUL *angrily slams his attaché case shut, gets up and moves towards stairs. At this moment, the bedroom door opens and* CORIE *throws out a blanket, sheet and pillow which land at* PAUL's *feet. Then she slams the door shut again. Again we hear crying from the bedroom.* PAUL *picks them up and glares at door.*)

PAUL: (*mimicking* CORIE) All night long. (*Seething,* PAUL *throws the bedding on the end table, and begins to try to make up the sofa with the sheet and blanket, all the while mumbling through the whole argument they have just had. As he puts the blanket over the sofa, he suddenly bursts out.*) Six days does not a week make.

TALLEY'S FOLLY
by Lanford Wilson

The time is 1944. The place is a deserted Victorian boathouse on the Talley place in Lebanon, Missouri. Matt Friedman has come to ask Sally Talley to marry him.

A foreigner and Jewish, Matt has struggled against his love for this vulnerable daughter of the wealthy Talley family. But after a year of doubts, he has decided to try his hand.

Sally is evasive, but she won't tell Matt why. Although she loves him, she has resigned herself to a life of spinsterhood.

The following scene takes place at the end of the play. Matt pressures Sally to tell him about her first beau. In the process she reveals the real reason why she has refused his proposal.

SALLY: I was engaged to Harley Campbell, his dad owned—

MATT: I don't believe it.

SALLY: You don't even know who he is.

MATT: I met him up at the house. He was the one that was saying, "You tell 'em, Buddy. You tell 'em, Buddy."

SALLY: Well, he used to be very good-looking.

MATT: I don't believe that either.

SALLY: (*not rhapsodic; detached, but this is an unpleasant memory*) He was a guard on the basketball team; I was a cheerleader. We grew up together. We were the two richest families in town. We were golden children. Dad owned a quarter of the garment factory; Harley's dad owned a third. These two great families were to be united in one happy factory. We used to walk through the plant holding hands, waving at all the girls; they loved us. When the workers asked for a showdown to discuss their demands, Dad brought us right into the meeting, onto the platform. Everybody applauded.

MATT: The youth, the beauty . . .

SALLY: The money. Here they are, folks. The future of the country. Do you love them or do you love them? Now back to work. They still don't have a union.

MATT: So how did it happen that Sally was disappointed in love?

SALLY: It all became academic. The Depression happened. Maybe we didn't look so golden. The factory almost closed.

MATT: I know the Depression came. So how did it happen that Sally was disappointed in love?

SALLY: (*with some difficulty*) I was sick for a long time. I got TB and missed school. I didn't graduate until a year after Harley did. It was a good excuse to drift apart. (*easier*) Then he went to Princeton, became engaged to a girl from New Jersey, his father killed himself.

MATT: Because he was engaged to a girl from New Jersey?

SALLY: Because by then it was 1931. He was in debt. He thought he would lose the factory. He didn't know how to live poor.

MATT: So?

SALLY: Harley quit school, Buddy and Harley and Dad worked at the factory, trying to save it. They're doing fine now.

MATT: I know. A government contract for army uniforms. So?

SALLY: Harley's wife left him eight years ago; he remarried a girl from Rogersville.

MATT: (*looks at her a moment*) So that's the truth, the whole truth, and nothing but the truth, so help you, Hannah.

SALLY: Yes.

MATT: You're real cute. (*pause*) Might as well get the gas, don't you think?

SALLY: You're not out of gas.

MATT: Yes, maybe I am. Maybe I lied.

SALLY: Well, if that's what it takes.

MATT: You know what I'm thinking? Over on track number nine? That Sally may not be who I thought she was, after all.

SALLY: Maybe not.

MATT: May not be. Maybe not. What kind of an answer to a mystery is that? What happened to change this Golden Girl into an embarrassment to the family? Into a radical old maid who is fired from teaching Sunday school? Why would this nice Harley leave you after all this time while you were sick with such a romantic disease? See, I'm a logical person. I have to have it all laid out like in a list, and that isn't logical.

SALLY: His family didn't want him to marry me, obviously.

MATT: They thought you weren't good enough for him?

SALLY: Come on. (*As she starts to move past him to the door, he reaches out and takes her wrist. The band, rather distant, plays a fanfare.*)

MATT: What?

SALLY: Yes. Don't do that.

MATT: Mr. Campbell was in debt and worried about being overextended, but the rich partner's daughter gets TB and the wedding is off?

SALLY: I don't know.

MATT: There's your music. Wasn't Harley the richest boy in town, you said?

SALLY: Yes.

MATT: And Sally was the richest girl in the countryside. This was the match of the decade. Bells were going to ring for such a match.

SALLY: Well, they didn't.

MATT: When the Depression comes, rich families must pool their resources.

SALLY: They didn't see it that way.

MATT: The Campbells are a large Missouri family, are they? Fifteen little Campbells?

SALLY: No.

MATT: Only Harley, two brothers and one sister?

SALLY: No.

MATT: Only Harley, and his brother.

SALLY: Harley and his sister.

MATT: Harley was the only son of a very prominent Laclede County family.

SALLY: Yes.

MATT: So why didn't they want their only son to marry the beautiful, popular cheerleader Talley girl whom he had been going steady with for three years?

SALLY: They didn't like me.

MATT: All those years he dated you over their protest?

SALLY: Not on your life.

MATT: No, because Harley did not do things against his parents' wishes.

SALLY: No.

MATT: But in fact you didn't graduate with Harley. You were delayed a full year.

SALLY: That's beginning to hurt, Matt.

MATT: You're pulling, I'm not pulling (*releases her, but stands in her path*) Why weren't you good enough for Harley?

SALLY: I got sick.

MATT: You got TB and went to Arizona, where you lived for the rest of your life.

SALLY: No.

MATT: You gave this contagious disease to their only son and he went away to Arizona and was never heard from again.

SALLY: The TB was not serious. There were complicating circumstances that caused me to be out of school.

MATT: There were complications. Sally was pockmarked and ugly and nobody wanted anything to do with her.

SALLY: You might say that.

MATT: This only son was repulsed by the sight of you.

SALLY: No, Matt. I was in the hospital for a month. I had a fever.

MATT: This Harley has a morbid fear of hospitals. I'm getting a fever is who's getting a fever.

SALLY: They didn't want it.

MATT: But your dad insisted.

SALLY: He didn't want it either.

MATT: You were pale and white and would not look good in a wedding dress.

SALLY: Matt.

MATT: You were a tramp and a vamp and would have ruined the reputation of this prominent family. Is what the story is?

SALLY: He was the heir. He had to carry on the family name!

MATT: And you were irresponsible; you had uncontrollable kleptomania and could not be trusted around the family money.

SALLY: I was sick! I had a fever.

MATT: You were delirious and drunken and no family would allow such a woman to marry their only son.

SALLY: (*She tries to run past him.*) I was sick for a year.

MATT: (*holds her again*) You were not sick. You went away. Why did you go away?

SALLY: I was at the house.

MATT: (*driving*) Why were you in the house for a year?

SALLY: I had a fever.

MATT: No. Because you had disgraced yourself.

SALLY: I had a pelvic infection.

MATT: Is that what you told people?

SALLY: They didn't know what was wrong with me.

MATT: Why were you hiding in the house?

SALLY: They couldn't get the fever down!

MATT: Why were you hiding?

SALLY: (*hitting him*) They couldn't break the fever! By the time they did, it didn't matter.

MATT: What were you hiding—

SALLY: Because it had eaten out my insides! I couldn't bear children. I can't have children. Let go of me. (*She breaks away, crying, falls against something, and sits.*)

MATT: What do you mean?

SALLY: I couldn't have children.

MATT: Sally, I'm here, you're okay. It's okay.

SALLY: Go away. Go away.

MATT: (*sitting beside her*) I didn't know. I thought you had had a child.

SALLY: I have had no child. There was no scandal. I was no longer of value to the merger.

MATT: It's okay. It's okay.

SALLY: Oh, stop. That's what I tell the boys. It's okay. Only they're dying of blood poisoning. Don't comfort me. I'm fine. Blast you. Let go.

MATT: I thought you had had a child by someone else. You're so crazy.

SALLY: I only wish I had.

MATT: This was a result of the TB?

SALLY: (*She looks at him for a long moment. Then finally, no longer crying*) The infection descended into the fallopian tubes; it's not uncommon with women at all. And so there couldn't be an heir to the garment empire. (*almost laughing*) It was all such a great dance. Everyone came to the hospital. Everyone said it made no difference. By the time Harley graduated, the Campbells weren't speaking to the Talleys. By then Dad was looking at me like I was a broken swing. It was a very interesting perspective.

MATT: Did you think that your aunt had told me you couldn't have children and I was making up the story of my life just to tease you?

SALLY: Possibly.

MATT: (*to the sky*) Eggs! Eggs! Eggs! Eggs! We're so terrified. But we still hope. You take a beautiful dress to work—Did you tell the nurses I was coming to see you?

SALLY: No!

MATT: And look at me. For five years I have been wearing the same tie to work. It is a matter of principle with me not to wear a different tie. I buy a new tie to come and see Sally. You see how corruption of principle begins.

SALLY: I had nothing to do with that.

MATT: Is that a new dress, by the way? I don't know that dress.

SALLY: Yes. It's no big deal.

MATT: It is an enormous deal! It is the new New Deal! It is a Big Deal!

SALLY: You didn't even say you liked it.

MATT: I like it, I love the dress. (*pause*) I was sitting up in St. Louis all this winter in a terrible quandary. It is not that I have been happy or not happy, but that I have not thought that I *could* be happy. (*beat*) But this winter I was terribly unhappy and I *knew* I was unhappy. I had fallen for a girl and could not give her the life she would surely expect, with a family, many children. (*Pause. Taking her hand*) You know what happened? Some mischievous angel has looked down and saw us living two hundred miles apart and said, You know what would be a kick in the head? Let's send Matt on a vacation to Lebanon.

SALLY: You believe in angels?

MATT: I do now, most definitely. Her name might be Lottie Talley, maybe. (*pause*) We missed your marching band.

SALLY: They'll play all evening.

MATT: (*pause*) So. We'll go up to the city tonight. Leave the car here—

SALLY: Oh, Matt, it's absurd to be talking like that; we're practically middle-aged.

MATT: So. We'll go up to the city tonight. Leave the car in town, take the midnight bus.

SALLY: (*pause*) I'll be up in a week or so.

MATT: (*pause*) I'll stay here at the hotel in Lebanon and wait.

SALLY: You have to work tomorrow.

MATT: So what?

SALLY: (*pause*) We'll go tonight. (*They kiss. The distant band strikes up a soft but lightly swinging rendition of "Lindy Lou." They laugh.*)

MATT: "Lindy Lou." (*Pause. They are sitting holding hands, perfectly relaxed.* MATT *looks around.*) You live in such a beautiful country. Such a beautiful countryside. Will you miss it?

SALLY: Yes.

MATT: Me too. Once a year we'll come back down, so we don't forget.

SALLY: All right.

MATT: (*looks at her for a long while, then his gaze drifts to the audience*) And so, all's well that ends... (*takes out his watch, shows time to* SALLY, *then to audience*)... right on the button. Good night. (*They embrace.*)

CALIFORNIA SUITE
by Neil Simon

ACT I, SCENE 1

Nine years ago Hannah and Billy got a divorce. She stayed in New York, continuing her cosmopolitan life and career as an

editor for *Newsweek*. Billy moved to Hollywood. He embraced
the California lifestyle wholeheartedly, and gave up political
writing for a successful career as a studio script writer. All they
now have in common is their seventeen-year-old daughter, Jenny.
Jenny has spent summers with her father, but now she wants to
live with him.

The scene takes place on a "hot" Thanksgiving Day in
Hannah's suite at the Beverly Hills Hotel. Jenny has flown to
California without permission, and Hannah has come after her,
to bring her home and rescue her from what she feels is the
vapid California lifestyle.

During the opening moments of the play, Hannah is on the
bedroom phone. First, she orders drinks. Then her New York
beau calls and she tells him she is determined to be strong with
Billy and Jenny. While she is on the phone, there is a knock on
the living room door. Hannah calls out that the door is open.
Billy enters, tanned and trim. He waits for her in the living
room.

(*She hangs up and sits there a moment. She takes a pencil and
jots down a note on the pad on the table next to the bed. She
is not in any great hurry to greet her visitor. She gets up, gives
herself another check in the mirror and goes to the doorway of
the living room. He turns and they look at each other.*)

HANNAH: Sorry. I was on the phone. It's snowing in New
York. We're going to have a white Thanksgiving. Don't you
love it? (*She sits. He is still standing. He smiles.*) Is that
wonderful, warm smile for me?

BILLY: You still have trouble saying a simple "Hello."

HANNAH: Oh, I *am* sorry. You always did get a big thrill out
of the "little" things in life . . . Hello, Bill.

BILLY: (*with generous warmth*) Hello, Hannah.

HANNAH: My God, look at you. You've turned into a young
boy again.

BILLY: Have I?

HANNAH: Haven't you noticed? You look like the sweetest
young fourteen-year-old boy. You're not spending your summers at camp, are you?

BILLY: Just three weeks in July. How are you?

HANNAH: Well, at this moment, nonplussed.

BILLY: Still the only one I know who can use "nonplussed"
in regular conversation.

HANNAH: Don't be ridiculous, darling, I talk that way at breakfast... Turn around, let me look at you.

BILLY: Shouldn't we kiss or shake hands or something?

HANNAH: Let's save it for when you leave... I love your California clothes.

BILLY: They're Bloomingdale's, in New York.

HANNAH: The best place for California clothes. You look so... I don't know—what's the word I'm looking for?

BILLY: Happy?

HANNAH: Casual. It's hard to tell out here—are you dressed up now, or is that sporty?

BILLY: I didn't think a tie was necessary for a reunion.

HANNAH: Is that what this is? When I walked in, I thought we were going to play tennis.

BILLY: Well, you look fit enough for it.

HANNAH: Fit? You think I look fit? What an awful shit you are. I look gorgeous.

BILLY: Yes, you do, Hannah. You look lovely.

HANNAH: No, no. *You* look lovely. *I* look gorgeous.

BILLY: Well, I lost about ten pounds.

HANNAH: Listen to what I'm telling you, you're *ravishing*. I love the way you're wearing your hair now. Where do you go, that boy who does Barbra Streisand?

BILLY: You like it, you can have my Thursday appointment with him... If you're interested, I'm feeling *very* well, thank you.

HANNAH: Well, of course you are. Look at that tan. Well, it's the life out here, isn't it? You have an office outdoors somewhere?

BILLY: No, just a desk near the window... Hey, Hannah, if we're going to banter like this, give me a little time. It's been nine years, I'm rusty.

HANNAH: You'll pick it right up again, it's like French. You see, that's what I would miss if I left New York. The bantering.

BILLY: San Francisco's only an hour away. We go up there and banter in emergencies.

HANNAH: Do you really?

BILLY: Would I lie to you?

HANNAH: I never liked San Francisco. I was always afraid I'd fall out of bed and roll down one of those hills.

BILLY: Not you, Hannah. You roll *up* hills.

HANNAH: Oh, good. You're bantering. The flight out wasn't a total loss... Aren't you going to sit down, Bill? Or do they call you Billy out here? Yes, they do. Jenny told me. Everybody calls you Billy.

BILLY: (*shrugs*) That's me. Billy.

HANNAH: It's adorable. A forty-five-year-old Billy. Standing there in his cute little sneakers and sweater. Please, sit down, Billy, I'm beginning to feel like your math teacher.

BILLY: I promised myself driving over here I would be pleasant. I am now being pleasant.

HANNAH: You drive everywhere, do you?

BILLY: Everywhere.

HANNAH: Even to your car?

BILLY: Would you mind if I called down for something to drink?

HANNAH: It's done.

BILLY: I don't drink double Scotches on the rocks any more. I gave up hard liquor.

HANNAH: Oh? What would you like?

BILLY: A cup of tea with lemon.

HANNAH: It's done . . . No hard liquor? At all?

BILLY: Not even wine. I'm big on apple juice.

HANNAH: Cigarettes?

BILLY: Gave them up.

HANNAH: Don't you miss the coughing and the hacking in the morning?

BILLY: It woke the dogs up. I have dogs now.

HANNAH: Isn't divorce wonderful? . . . What about candy? Please don't tell me you've given up Snickers?

BILLY: (*shrugs*) Sorry.

HANNAH: That *is* crushing news. You *have* changed, Billy. You've gone clean on me.

BILLY: Mind *and* body. That doesn't offend you, does it?

HANNAH: May they both live to be a thousand. I don't mean this to seem facetious, but how *do* you take care of yourself?

BILLY: I watch my diet, I've cut out meat, and you *do* mean to be facetious. You're dying to make a little fun of me. I don't mind. I have an hour to kill . . . Would you believe I run five miles every morning?

HANNAH: After what?

BILLY: The newspaper. I have lazy dogs . . . Shall I keep going? I swim twenty laps every night when I come home from the studio. Eight sets of tennis every weekend. I sleep well. I haven't had a pill in three and a half years. I take vitamins and I eat natural, unprocessed health foods.

HANNAH: Ah, aha! Health foods! At last, something in common.

BILLY: Don't tell me you've given up P.J. Clarke's chili burgers?

HANNAH: No, but I have them on whole wheat now . . . I'm enjoying this conversation. Tell me more about yourself. Jenny tells me you've taken up the banjo.

BILLY: The guitar. Classical *and* country.

HANNAH: Remarkable. And in New York you couldn't tune in Channel Five . . . More, more!

BILLY: I climb.

HANNAH: I beg your pardon?

BILLY: I climb. I climbed a ten-thousand-foot mountain in the Sierra Nevada last summer.

HANNAH: Well, that's no big deal. I climb that three times a week visiting my analyst.

BILLY: And no analyst.

HANNAH: Yes, I heard that. I'll accept the mountain climbing and, in a stretch, even the guitar. But no analyst? You ask too much, Billy. Why did you quit?

BILLY: I went sane.

HANNAH: Sane! How exciting. You mean you go out into the world every day all by yourself? (*He smiles, nods.*) Don't you ever get depressed?

BILLY: Yes.

HANNAH: When?

BILLY: Now.

HANNAH: I'm so glad the sun hasn't dried up your brain completely . . . Tell me more news.

BILLY: I moved.

HANNAH: Oh, yes. You're not in Hardy Canyon any more.

BILLY: Laurel. Laurel Canyon.

HANNAH: Laurel, Hardy, what the hell? And where are you now?

BILLY: Beverly Hills—a block north of Sunset Boulevard.

HANNAH: What style house?

BILLY: Very comfortable.

HANNAH: Well, I'm sure it is. But what style is it?

BILLY: Well, from the outside it looks like a small French farmhouse.

HANNAH: A small French farmhouse. Just one block north of Sunset Boulevard. Sounds rugged . . . I passed something coming in from the airport. I thought it was a Moroccan villa—turned out to be a Texaco station.

BILLY: We're a colorful community.

HANNAH: I love it from the air.

BILLY: And how is life over the subway?

HANNAH: Fine. I still live in our old apartment. But you would hate it now.

BILLY: What did you do to it?

HANNAH: Not a thing.

BILLY: And I heard you went in for an operation.

HANNAH: A hysterectomy. I was out the same day . . . And I believe you had prostate trouble.

BILLY: Small world, isn't it?

HANNAH: Well, our past sins have a way of catching up with us. . . . What else can I tell you about me?

BILLY: Jenny fills me in with everything.

HANNAH: Oh, I'm sure.

BILLY: I understand you have a new boyfriend.

HANNAH: A boyfriend? God forbid. I'm forty-two years old—I have a lover.

BILLY: Also a writer.

HANNAH: A newspaperman on the Washington *Post*.

BILLY: Really? Not one of those two who—

HANNAH: No.

BILLY: Right.

HANNAH: He's fifty-four. He has a heart condition, asthma and leans towards alcoholism. He also has the second-best mind I've met in this country since Adlai Stevenson. . . . And what's with you, mate-wise?

BILLY: Mate-wise? Mate-wise I am seeing a very nice girl.

HANNAH: Are you? And where are you seeing her to?

BILLY: (*annoyed*) Oh, come on, Hannah.

HANNAH: What did I say? Have I offended you?

BILLY: Can we cut the cute chitchat? I think we've got other things to talk about.

HANNAH: I'm sorry. I *have* offended you.

BILLY: My God, it's been a long time since I've been involved in smart-ass conversation.

HANNAH: I beg *your* pardon, but *you* were the one who said things like "I hear you have a boyfriend" and "I'm seeing a very nice girl." I am *not* the one with the Bobbsey Twin haircut and the Peter Pan phraseology.

BILLY: I can see you've really come to hunt bear, haven't you?

HANNAH: Hunt bear? Did I actually hear you say "hunt bear"? Is that the kind of nifty conversation you have around those Sierra Nevada campfires?

BILLY: Forget the tea. Maybe I *will* have a double Scotch.

HANNAH: It's ordered. You're safe either way.

BILLY: Can we talk about Jenny?

HANNAH: What's your rush? She's only seventeen. She's got her whole life ahead of her. If I'm going to turn my daughter over to you—which I am not—at least I'd like to know what you're like.

BILLY: Jenny is *our* daughter! *Ours!*

HANNAH: Maybe. We'll see. They've been very slow with the blood test. (*They glare at each other a moment. She suddenly smiles.*) So you live in a French farmhouse off Sunset Boulevard. Do you have a pool?

BILLY: Christ!

HANNAH: Come on, Billy, talk to me. I wrote down seventy-four questions to ask—don't make me look for the list. Do you have a pool? . . . Well, naturally you've got a pool. You've got a tan, so you've got a pool. . . . Is it kidney shaped? . . . Liver? . . . Possibly gall bladder?

BILLY: Pancreas, actually. The head surgeon at Cedars of Lebanon put it in. You're terrific. You haven't spent fifteen days of your life out here, but you know exactly how we all live, don't you? Too bad you're going back so soon. You're gonna miss the way we spend our holidays. Wouldn't it *thrill* you to see a pink-painted Christmas tree on my lawn . . . or a three-flavored Baskin-Robbins snowman wearing alligator shoes . . . with a loudspeaker on the roof playing Sonny and Cher singing "Silent Night"?

HANNAH: When you've seen it once, the thrill is gone.

KEY EXCHANGE
by Kevin Wade

Philip and Lisa are having a modern New York relationship. They bike in Central Park together, date a few times a week, sleep together, and even love each other. But no commitments please. They can date other people whenever they want. *Freedom,* that's the motto of this cosmopolitan couple.

But today Lisa has suggested they exchange keys to each other's apartments. She wants to "give it a go as a couple for a while, see what happens . . . Just you and me." Philip's reaction? Well, that's what the scene that follows is about. It takes place on a Sunday afternoon in summer in Central Park, on a small rise off Park Drive (which is closed to traffic and open to bicyclists on weekends). Their bikes are off to the side.

PHILIP: So great. So we get keys made for each other's apartments. So then you know what happens? I'll tell you what happens. Maybe one night I'm at a party, a bar, whatever, and I meet a girl, and right off we know it's the mutual attraction situation, and we have a little chat and a drink maybe, and next thing you know we're in a cab, and there's a physical thing that's happening, and we're chewing each other's faces and trying to decide where to go, you know, your place or mine, only hold the phone here, there is no decision to be made, because you've got a key to my place, and I don't know if you've dropped by or what, and I don't want to chance putting you or me in that awkward situation, so it's off to her place somewhere in the East Eighties where I've got to climb over her two roommates and three cats to do it on a foam mattress on the floor real, real quiet like because Sally my roommate has a commercial call-back at nine-thirty in the morning and this whole time I'm having some resentment

25

toward you because your having a key meant it had to be the cats and the floor and Sally the roommate asleep or nothing.

LISA: (*sharply*) Don't sweet talk me, Philip.

PHILIP: Don't get sarcastic.

LISA: Stop trying to let me down easy.

PHILIP: I'm just being honest with you. Okay, look, say it's the reverse situation, say you're out with some guy and it's getting personal and you want to invite him up, only you don't know if I've come by to watch a movie on the Home Box . . .

LISA: Okay, Philip, let's just drop it. Exchanging keys isn't really the issue anyway.

PHILIP: I'm sorry. Say what you were going to say.

LISA: Let's just drop it, okay.

PHILIP: You sure?

LISA: Yes. (*long pause*) Christ, you make me crazy sometimes.

PHILIP: So you're picking it up again.

LISA: Yes, I am. You give me this graphic harangue about the zipless fuck and then tell me you're just being honest. Well, you know what I think? I think you do that to try and keep safe distance, all that jazz like you're just some poor slob who's getting led around by his cock. Well, I'm not buying it, so stop trying to sell me on it.

PHILIP: Great. You're going to analyze me now. I love this. I eat this up. Maybe you've got some ink blots I could look at.

LISA: If you're trying to lose me, just say so. You don't need to make up long lurid stories. Do you want to not see each other anymore?

PHILIP: Gimme ten more minutes of amateur psychology and ask me again.

LISA: Oh, shit. This isn't going like I rehearsed it at all.

(*pause*)

PHILIP: You rehearsed it?

LISA: In my head. I knew you might resist the idea. I wanted to make it like exchanging gifts. I want to make this work.

PHILIP: (*going to her*) I do too.

LISA: You're a good man. And, usually a sane man, and that's rare. You're spunky. I like you a lot.

PHILIP: I like you a lot too.

LISA: We're good in bed. We like each other's cooking.

PHILIP: You laugh at my jokes.

LISA: I could be in love with you.

PHILIP: Me, too, I guess.

LISA: The thing about the keys, it's just sort of a pact. I thought maybe we could give it a go as a couple for a while, see what happens.

PHILIP: You mean exclusively?

LISA: Well, yes, exclusively. Just you and me. More than you and me, and it isn't a couple anymore.

PHILIP: I see what you mean.

LISA: We do casual real well. Hi, how are you? Saturday night? Okay, call me around five just to make sure. La di da.

PHILIP: I like it. I'm happy with you.

LISA: I like it too. But I feel stagnant. I want to go farther.

PHILIP: If we both like it where it is, which we both said we did, why do we have to go and change it?

LISA: I want to see if there's more to it. I want to see what happens if we make a commitment...

PHILIP: Oh, I knew that word would show up here...

LISA: Okay, strike commitment. How about an agreement? A trust? If there's a trust between us, will Papa Hemingway still ask you out for some drinks and a bullfight?

PHILIP: All right, Lisa...

LISA: I'm sorry. I'm jumping on you and I don't mean to. (*pause*) I can't do casual anymore.

PHILIP: You could just stop seeing other guys, just like that?

LISA: It wasn't me who insisted that it was important that we see other people.

PHILIP: You agreed.

LISA: You made a big thing about it, and I didn't care one way or the other at the time, so I agreed. I have a confession to make. I've been lying to you. Philip, I haven't been seeing other men.

PHILIP: You haven't? For how long?

LISA: Almost since the beginning.

PHILIP: That's over four months.

LISA: I know.

PHILIP: What about that doctor?

LISA: I made him up.

PHILIP: And your old boyfriend?

LISA: More lies. He's been in L.A. for a year.

PHILIP: That actor?

LISA: I photographed him. We had a drink. That was it.

PHILIP: Why'd you go to all the trouble?

LISA: It wasn't any trouble. It was kind of fun, actually. It's a rare relationship where you're cheating by being faithful. I didn't want you to feel pressured, so I invented a busy sex life for myself. I didn't meet anyone else I wanted to be with. Do you understand?

PHILIP: I guess so. Yes. (*pause*) Oh, Lisa, I hear you, I hear what you're saying. Half of me says sure, do it, she's a great dame and you're crazy about her and this could surely be IT, boyo, and the other half says sure, go ahead, but realize that somewhere down the line one of you will meet someone else, or it won't work out, and there will be tears and hurt and the whole shebang because you had to take a perfectly good thing and go off and hinge everything on it and weigh it down with keys and commitments and all, because we couldn't leave well enough alone.

LISA: I want to take the chance.

PHILIP: No going back, huh?

LISA: I'm not saying let's get married, sweetie, or even let's live together. I'm not that sure either. But I can't say oh, it was just a thought, no. I can't pretend not to want more.

PHILIP: Do I have to decide right now, about the keys?

LISA: No, of course not. I want you to think about it.

PHILIP: If we exchange keys, can I sneak into your bed in the middle of the night?

LISA: I wish you would.

PHILIP: Can I bring my pals?

LISA: No more than five at a time.

(*They kiss for a while. Philip crosses to his bicycle, putting on his gloves.*)

PHILIP: I'm going to ride for a while. You want to come?

LISA: No, I think I'll stay here for a while, wait for Michael to come back. I have a picture I want to show him. Come over for dinner tonight?

PHILIP: Ah, I can't.

LISA: Oh. Plans?

PHILIP: Sort of, yeah.

LISA: You have a date.

PHILIP: Well, yes, I do.

LISA: Oh.

PHILIP: I'll get out of it.

LISA: No, don't. Keep your date. And while you're trying to think of something to talk about with her between ordering drinks and getting in the sack, oh, shit, never mind. (*pause*)

Goddamnit, Philip, can't you lie once in a while? Yankees?
Box seat? First base line? Great, have a good time, call me
tomorrow.

PHILIP: I'll have a key for you tomorrow.

LISA: (*quickly*) I'm sorry. Just go. (*Philip is still.*) Please. Go.

THE PRISONER OF SECOND AVENUE
by Neil Simon

Act I, Scene 2

Mel Edison is at the end of his rope. A hard-core New Yorker
who lives in a modern Second Avenue highrise, Mel can no
longer cope with the daily inconveniences of city life: paper-thin
walls that transmit his neighbors' sex lives when he wants to
sleep; an air-conditioner that keeps the temperature of his bedroom at a constant 12°; and polluted air that kills everything
growing on the terrace. All this plus a growing anxiety about
losing his well-paid executive position have played havoc with
Mel's nerves and turned him into a prisoner of his own fears.
Mel's wife, Edna, tries to keep her equanimity while her husband's
world is coming apart, but when she comes home to find the
apartment burgled, she, too, has reached her limit.

Despite this tragic series of events, Neil Simon's comedy
gives us an hilarious portrait of a survivor, full of humor, pathos,
and a healthy dose of indignation.

In the following scene Mel has been out of work for four days
without Edna knowing about it. She has just come back from the
supermarket to find the apartment ransacked and proceeds to call
the police. Mel enters shortly afterwards in his now normal
dazed state.

---

*At the curtain's rise, the room is in a shambles. Chairs are
overturned; drawers are pulled open, their contents scattered
all over the floor; the bookcase has been cleared of half of its
shelves and articles of clothing are strewn about the room. It
is obvious what has happened.* EDNA *is on the phone. She is
shaking.*

EDNA: (*sobbing*) Edison, Mrs. Edna Edison... I've just been robbed... I just walked in, they took everything... Edison... I just walked in, I found the door open, they must have just left... 385 East 88th Street... Two minutes sooner, I could have been killed... Apartment 14A... I don't know yet. Television, the record player, books, clothing... They took lots of clothing. My dresses, my coats, all my husband's suits—there's not a thing left in his closet... I haven't checked the drawers yet... Would you, please? Send somebody right away... I'm all alone. My husband isn't home from work yet... *Mrs. Edna Edison.* I could have been killed. Thank you. (*She hangs up, then turns and looks at the room. She crosses the room, lifts a chair up and sets it right. Then she goes over to the bureau and starts to look through the drawers. As she discovers new things are missing, she sobs louder.*) All right... Calm down... A drink, I have to have a drink.

(*She rushes into the kitchen, gets a glass and a few cubes of ice from the refrigerator, then rushes back out into the living room. She rushes to the bar and looks. There are no bottles.*) The liquor's gone. They took the liquor. (*She puts the glass down, slumps into a chair, and sobs.*) Valium... I want a Valium. (*She gets up and rushes down the small corridor, disappearing into the bedroom. We hear noises as she must be looking through ransacked medicine chests. There are a few moments of silence.* EDNA *has probably fallen onto the bed, sobbing, for all we know. The front door is unlocked and* MEL *enters. He carries his suit jacket and the New York* Post. *His shirt sleeves are rolled up and he looks hot. He closes the door and hangs his jacket in the closet. Consumed with his own thoughts, he doesn't seem to even notice the room. He moves over to the chair, falls into it exhausted, puts his head back and sighs... His eyes open, then he looks at the room for almost the first time. He looks around the room, bewildered. From the bedroom we hear* EDNA's *voice.*) Mel?... Is that you, Mel? (MEL *is still looking at the room, puzzled.* EDNA *appears cautiously from the bedroom. She comes in, holding a vase by the thin end, and looks at* MEL.)

MEL: Didn't Mildred come in to clean today?
EDNA: (*puts the vase down*) Not today... Mondays and Thursdays.

MEL: What happened here?... Why is this place such a mess?

EDNA: We've been robbed.

(MEL *looks at her in a state of shock.... He slowly rises and then looks at the room in a new perspective.*)

MEL: What do you mean, robbed?

EDNA: (*starts to cry*) Robbed! Robbed! What does robbed mean? They come in, they take things out! *They robbed us!!!*

MEL: (*He keeps turning, looking at the room in disbelief—not knowing where to look first.*) I don't understand... What do you mean, someone just walked in and robbed us?

EDNA: What do you think?... They called up and made an appointment? *We've been robbed!*

MEL: All right, calm down. Take it easy, Edna. I'm just asking a simple question. What happened? What did they get?

EDNA: I don't know yet. I was out shopping. I was gone five minutes. I came back, I found it like this.

MEL: You couldn't have been gone five minutes. Look at this place.

EDNA: *Five minutes,* that's all I was gone.

MEL: Five minutes, heh? Then we'd better call the FBI, because every crook in New York must have been in here.

EDNA: Then that's who was here, because I was only gone five minutes.

MEL: When you came back into the building did you notice anyone suspicious-looking?

EDNA: *Everyone* in this building is suspicious-looking.

MEL: You didn't see anybody carrying any bundles or packages?

EDNA: I didn't notice.

MEL: What do you mean, you didn't notice?

EDNA: I didn't notice. You think I look for people leaving the building with my television set?

MEL: They took the television? (*He starts for the bedroom, then stops.*) A *brand new* color television?

EDNA: They're not looking for 1948 Philcos. It was here. They took it. I can't get a breath out.

MEL: All right, sit there. I'll get a drink.

EDNA: (*sitting down*) I don't want a drink.

MEL: A little Scotch. It'll calm you down.

EDNA: It won't calm me down, because there's no Scotch. They took the Scotch too.

MEL: *All* the Scotch?

EDNA: All the Scotch.

MEL: The Chivas Regal too?

EDNA: No, they're going to take the cheap Scotch and leave the Chivas Regal. They took it all, they cleaned us out.

MEL: (*gnashing his teeth*) Sons of bitches. (*He runs to the terrace door, opens it, steps out on the terrace and yells out.*) *Sons of bitches!* (*He closes the door and comes back in.*) All in five minutes, eh? They must have been gorillas to lift all that in five minutes.

EDNA: Leave me alone.

MEL: (*gnashing his teeth again*) Sons of bitches.

EDNA: Stop swearing, the police will be here any minute. I just called them.

MEL: You called the police?

EDNA: Didn't I just say that?

MEL: Did you tell them we were robbed?

EDNA: Why else would I call them? I'm not friendly with the police. What kind of questions are you asking me? What's wrong with you?

MEL: All right, calm down, because you're hysterical.

EDNA: I am not hysterical.

MEL: You're hysterical.

EDNA: You're *making* me hysterical. Don't you understand? My house has just been robbed.

MEL: What am I, a boarder? My house has been robbed too. My color television and my Chivas Regal is missing the same as yours.

EDNA: You didn't walk in and find it. *I* did.

MEL: What's the difference who found it? There's still nothing to drink and nothing to watch.

EDNA: Don't yell at me. I'm just as upset as you are.

MEL: I'm sorry. I'm excited too. I don't mean to yell at you. (*starts for the bedroom*) Let me get you a Valium, it'll calm you down.

EDNA: I don't want a Valium.

MEL: Take one. You'll feel better.

EDNA: I'm not taking a Valium.

MEL: Why are you so stubborn?

EDNA: I'm not stubborn. We don't have any. They took the Valiums.

MEL: (*stops*) They took the Valiums?

EDNA: The whole medicine chest. Valiums, Seconals, aspirin, shaving cream, toothpaste, razor blades. They left your toothbrush. You want to go in and brush your teeth, you can still do it.

MEL: (*smiles, disbelieving*) I don't believe you. *I don't believe you!*

(MEL *looks at her, then storms off and disappears into the bedroom.* EDNA *gets up and picks up a book from the floor. From the far recesses of the bathroom we hear* MEL *scream.*)

MEL: (*offstage*) *DIRTY BASTARDS!!!* (EDNA *is holding the book upside down and shaking it, hoping some concealed item will fall out. It doesn't.* MEL *storms back into the living room.*) I hope they die. I hope the car they stole to get away in hits a tree and turns over and burns up and they all die!

EDNA: You read about it every day. And when it happens to you, you can't believe it.

MEL: A television I can understand. Liquor I can understand. But shaving cream? Hair spray? How much are they going to get for a roll of dental floss?

EDNA: They must have been desperate. They took everything they could carry. (*shakes the book one last time*) They even found my kitchen money.

MEL: What kitchen money?

EDNA: I kept my kitchen money in here. Eighty-five dollars.

MEL: In cash? Why do you keep cash in a book?

EDNA: So no one will find it! Where else am I gonna keep it?

MEL: In a jar. In the sugar. Some place they're not going to look.

EDNA: They looked in the medicine chest, you think they're not going to look in the sugar?

MEL: *Nobody looks in sugar!*

EDNA: Nobody steals dental floss and mouthwash. Only sick people. Only that's who live in the world today. *Sick, sick, sick people!*

(*She sits, emotionally wrung out.* MEL *comes over to her and puts his arm on her shoulder, comforting her.*)

MEL: It's all right . . . It's all right, Edna . . . As long as you weren't hurt, that's the important thing.

(*He looks through the papers on the table.*)

EDNA: Can you imagine if I had walked in and found them here? What would I have done, Mel?

MEL: You were very lucky, Edna. Very lucky.

EDNA: But what would I have done?

MEL: What's the difference? You didn't walk in and find them.

EDNA: But supposing I did? What would I have done?

MEL: You'd say, "Excuse me," close the door and come back later. What would you do, sit and watch? Why do you ask me such questions? It didn't happen, did it?

EDNA: It *almost* happened. If I walked in here five minutes sooner.

MEL: (*walking away from her*) You couldn't have been gone only five minutes . . . It took the Seven Santini Brothers two days to move everything in, three junkies aren't gonna move it all out in five minutes.

EDNA: Seven minutes, eight minutes, what's the difference?

MEL: (*opens the door, looks at the lock*) The lock isn't broken, it's not jimmied. I don't even know how they got in here.

EDNA: Maybe they found my key in the street.

MEL: (*Closes the door. Looks at her*) What do you mean, "found your key?" Don't you have your key?

EDNA: No, I lost it. I thought it was somewhere in the house, but maybe I lost it in the street.

MEL: If you didn't have your key, how were you going to get back in the house when you went shopping?

EDNA: I left the door open.

MEL: You-left-the-door-open???

EDNA: I didn't have a key, how was I going to get back in the house?

MEL: *So you left the door open?* In a city with the highest crime rate in the history of the world, *you left the door open*?

EDNA: What was I going to do? Take the furniture with me? I was only gone five minutes. How did they know I was going to leave the door open?

MEL: They know! They know! A door opens, it doesn't lock, the whole junkie world lights up. "Door open, fourteenth floor, Eighty-eighth Street and Second Avenue." They know!

EDNA: They don't know anything. They have to go around trying doors.

MEL: And what did you think? They were going to try every door in this house except yours? "Let's leave 14A alone, fellas, it looks like a nice door."

EDNA: If they're going to go around trying doors, they have twenty-three hours and fifty-five minutes a day to try them. I didn't think they would try ours the five minutes I was out of the house. I gambled! I lost!

MEL: What kind of gamble is that to take? If you lose, they get everything. If you win, they rob someone else.

EDNA: I *had* to shop. There was nothing in the house to eat tonight.

MEL: All right, now you have something to eat and nothing to eat it with . . . Why didn't you call up and have them send it?

EDNA: Because I shop in a cheap store that doesn't deliver. I am trying to save us money because you got me so worried the other night. I was just trying to save us money . . . Look how much money I saved us.

(EDNA *starts to pick up things.*)

MEL: What are you doing?

EDNA: We can't leave everything like this. I want to clean up.

MEL: Now?

EDNA: The place is a mess. We have people coming over in a few minutes.

MEL: The *police*? You want the place to look nice for the police? . . . You're worried they're going to put it down in their books, "bad housekeeper"? . . . Leave it alone. Maybe they'll find some clues.

EDNA: I can't find out what's missing until I put everything back in its place.

MEL: What do you mean? You know what's missing. The television, the liquor, the kitchen money, the medicine chest and the hi-fi . . . That's it, isn't it? (*pause*) Isn't it? (EDNA *looks away.*) Okay, what else did they get?

EDNA: Am I a detective? Look, you'll find out.

(*He glares at her and looks around the room, not knowing where to begin. He decides to check the bedroom. He storms down the hall and disappears.* EDNA, *knowing what to expect, sits on a chair in the dining area and stares out the window. She takes out a hanky and wipes some dirt from the window sill.* MEL *returns calmly—at least outwardly calm. He takes a deep breath.*)

MEL: Where are my suits?

EDNA: They were there this morning. They're not there now. They must have taken your suits.

MEL: (*still trying to be calm*) Seven suits? Three sports jackets? Eight pairs of slacks?

EDNA: If that's what you had, that's what they got.

MEL: I'm lucky my tuxedo is in the cleaners.

EDNA: (*still staring out the window*) They sent it back this morning.

MEL: Well, they did a good job of it...Cleaned me out...Left a pair of khaki pants and my golf hat... Anybody asks us out to dinner this week, ask them if it's all right if I wear khaki pants and a golf hat. DIRTY BASTARDS!!!!

ROMANTIC COMEDY
by Bernard Slade

ACT II, SCENE 2

Jason and Phoebe have been collaborating on Broadway romantic comedies for ten years. When they met, Phoebe was a Vermont school teacher and Jason was a well-known playwright about to marry the sophisticated daughter of a diplomat. Jason and Phoebe launched a successful partnership: Phoebe kept the egotistical, sharp-tongued Jason in line, and he helped her achieve success and fame.

Sometime during their ten-year partnership Phoebe fell in love with Jason. But she has kept her feelings a secret. After all, Jason is faithful to his wife, Allison, and Phoebe adores their two children.

When Phoebe discovers that Jason is having an affair with Kate Mallory, the leading lady of their new play, she breaks up the partnership, marries her journalist beau, Leo, and moves to Paris.

The scene below takes place two years later. Phoebe has just turned up unexpectedly at Jason's house. After an awkward exchange of greetings, Jason's manager, Blanche, exits and they are left alone.

JASON: How's Leo?

PHOEBE: Fine. He's out apartment hunting right now. (JASON *nods.*) Oh, Timmy and little Phoebe send their love.

JASON: You saw them?

PHOEBE: We drove up to Tarrytown for the weekend.

JASON: How's Allison?

PHOEBE: Very well. I suppose you know she's running for Congress. (*He nods. A small pause*) You live alone?

JASON: All alone. (*a small pause*)

PHOEBE: I'm sorry I walked out on you, Jason. I mean at that time—in the middle of a production.

JASON: It wouldn't have made any difference if you'd stayed. Nothing could have helped that play. (*He frowns.*) And, since we're on that subject, I said a lot of things in the heat of anger before you left that—

PHOEBE: You don't have to apologize for—

JASON: No, no—there's something I said that's really been bothering me and I'd like to retract it. It was stupid and childish and I should never have said it.

PHOEBE: What?

JASON: I never had my nose fixed.

PHOEBE: I know.

JASON: How?

PHOEBE: It was out of character.

JASON: For me to have it done?

PHOEBE: No, for you to admit it.

JASON: (*gives her a wintry smile*) I'd forgotten what an excellent judge of character you were.

PHOEBE: Why are you nursing such a grudge?

JASON: (*turns to face her*) You're asking that seriously?

PHOEBE: It's rather important we clear the air.

JASON: Why?

PHOEBE: You'll understand later. All right, I admit I left you at an inopportune time—but is that any reason to go into a childish sulk?

JASON: Childish? You turned my life upside down, you ruined my marriage!

PHOEBE: (*puzzled*) How did I ruin your marriage?

JASON: (*evasively*) Look, I really don't see any point in re-hashing all this.

PHOEBE: In what way did I ruin your marriage?

JASON: All right! Do you know why Allison left me?

PHOEBE: She found out about you and Kate Mallory.

JASON: And how do you think she found out? Why do you think she kept her nose to the scent like a Tennessee bloodhound?

PHOEBE: I have no idea.

JASON: Allison kept asking me why you'd walked out and wouldn't accept any of the reasons I gave her. It was maddening. She said for you to leave me I must have done something absolutely horrendous.

PHOEBE: Why did she think that?

JASON: Look, she was quite demented at the time—totally irrational—it made no sense at all.

PHOEBE: What didn't?

JASON: She said that all the years you and I were together you'd been in love with me.

PHOEBE: I was in love with you.

JASON: Well—now you can see why I bear you a certain— animosity.

PHOEBE: No, I don't.

JASON: For God's sake, you might have had the decency to tell me!

PHOEBE: You were married. You know what a stickler for form you were.

JASON: (*uncomfortably*) Well, you certainly kept it hidden very well.

PHOEBE: (*calmly*) Allison knew.

JASON: Yes—well, I don't know how she sensed that.

PHOEBE: Maybe it was the way I hung on every word you said and started to perspire when you came within two feet of me.

JASON: I have that effect on a lot of people. Anyway, I resent being the last to know.

PHOEBE: You were the first, Jason. You always knew and you enjoyed it. Oh, I can't say I blame you. You had the best of everything. Two women who adored you and had devoted their lives to satisfying your every whim. (*She turns to look at him.*) And you revelled in it.

JASON: Did you come up with that idea all by yourself?

PHOEBE: No, I went into analysis.

JASON: Why?

PHOEBE: You're an arrogant, often unfeeling, difficult man and yet for some ten years I was totally infatuated by you. I am now married to a nice, sensitive man and if my marriage was going to work, I believed it was important to come up with the reasons for my relationship with you.

JASON: (*quietly*) Why do you think I'm unfeeling?

PHOEBE: Jason, do you know that the only time I ever saw you cry was when a pit orchestra struck up? Never in real life.

JASON: Tears are simply the appearance of emotion. Not emotion itself.

PHOEBE: You mean you could be feeling something but it's for you to know and everyone else to find out?

JASON: What other blinding revelations did you experience?

PHOEBE: That when I found out about you and Kate Mallory I was angry with you because I really wanted you to make love with me.

JASON: You know, I liked you better before you came out of your shell.

PHOEBE: It's not easy for me to stand here and say these things, Jason.

JASON: It's not a lot of fun where I'm standing either. Look, is this encounter part of your therapy?

PHOEBE: Partly. Naturally, I wanted to find out how I would feel when I saw you.

JASON: How's it going so far?

PHOEBE: Are you just being flip or do you really want an answer?

JASON: You used to be able to tell.

PHOEBE: I also wanted to see you for professional reasons. Have you read "Romantic Comedy"?

JASON: What's that?

PHOEBE: It's the title of my book.

JASON: I'm sorry, I've been rather pressed for time lately. (*She looks at him.*) Well, don't look at me as if I haven't completed a homework assignment. I simply haven't got around to it yet.

PHOEBE: I thought you might be curious. No matter. I want to adapt it into a play and I want you to collaborate with me on it.

JASON: Why?

PHOEBE: There are two reasons. First, I'd like to tell you how I got the idea.

JASON: Is that absolutely necessary?

PHOEBE: It was a funny quote by Hemingway.

JASON: Yes, he's always cracked me up.

PHOEBE: He said that he and a woman had been in love for forty years but whenever she was single he was married and when he was single she was married. He said "we were the victims of an unsynchronized passion." That started me thinking about us. I really started the book as therapy. Of course, in the writing I fantasized the relationship to make it interesting. I suppose what I'm saying is that you should write it with me because I stole your character.

JASON: Isn't this where you came in fourteen years ago?

PHOEBE: Well, that didn't turn out too badly, did it?

JASON: You said there were two reasons.

PHOEBE: The second one should be obvious. You're the best dramatist of this sort of material I know.

JASON: There's a third reason.

PHOEBE: Oh?

JASON: You think I need the money and my life is a shambles.

PHOEBE: Yes—well, I'd be less than honest if I said I wasn't aware of that. But that has nothing—well, very little—to do with my offer. It's not your lack of money that worries me, Jason. It's your lack of spirit. You need to work.

JASON: (*Slowly rises. Icily angry*) I am not a charity case!!

PHOEBE: I never said you were.

JASON: (*tightly controlled*) No, you said a lot more. Well, now let *me* say a few things. You come waltzing in here, clutching your tawdry little best seller and expect me to kiss the hem of your Givenchy dress! Well, you've made a few assumptions that need correcting. First, I may have been going through a somewhat fallow period but my career did not freeze into a "still life" the moment you left. I was writing plays when you were a teenage ticket taker and I suspect I'll be writing them long after you're a plump matron making funny speeches about your septic tank to the P.T.A. Next, your infantile psychological insights about my character and your infatuation with an unfeeling, insensitive older man. Well, I'm exactly ten years older than you, which doesn't exactly make me an aging Caesar to your pubescent Cleopatra! (*She moves to get her things.*) Wait a minute, I'm not through!

PHOEBE: I know. You haven't come up with a good exit line yet.

JASON: (*growing ever more angry*) Next, your concern over my alleged lack of emotion. How the hell can you presume to know what I feel or don't feel? How do you know that when you left I wasn't quite—bruised. (*She doesn't say anything.*

He picks up her baseball cap, waves it in front of her.) Well, I kept your damned hat, for God's sake!! Of course, I was remembering a warm, vulnerable, compassionate, unique girl who used to blush, not the woman you've become! You know what you've become? You've become—*CRISP*! One of those confident, crisp fashion-plate bitches who think they know the secret of the world and I wouldn't work with you if you were a combination of Moliere and Mary Tyler Moore!! (*Stung, her tears are now partly from anger.*) And, since this is obviously the last time we'll ever see each other, *I was not inadequate in Chicago!!* I happened to be drunk and when a man is drunk, he—uh—he— (*He suddenly doubles over, his face contorted with pain, gasping for breath.*)

PHOEBE: What is it?

JASON: You'd better—stick around. I—think—I'm having—a heart attack. (*He collapses rather theatrically onto the floor.*)

PHOEBE: Oh, come on, Jason. We did that in "Innocent Deception" and it didn't work well there either.

JASON: (*groaning*) Stay with me, Phoebe.

PHOEBE: Jason? (*He doesn't answer. Uncertainly*) Jason, don't play the fool. This is not funny. (*He turns his head towards her, breathing with difficulty. The realization hits her that he is not faking.*) Oh, my God!! (*She rushes to his side, frantically tries to find his pulse, races for a bottle of brandy, uncorks it, rushes back, kneels beside him, raises his head.*) Here—drink this brandy!

JASON: (*feebly*) What—what year—is it?

THE DRESSER
by Ronald Harwood

Act II

England, January, 1942. German bombs are dropping from over-head. But tonight, in a theatre in the English provinces, Sir, the last of the great British actor-managers, will perform King Lear—if he can just hold his weary spirit and ailing body together long enough to remember all his lines and entrance cues. Tonight, like every other night during the past sixteen years of touring the provinces, Norman, his dresser, will do his best to say just what Sir needs to hear so he can go on.

The play takes place backstage in the theatre. It is intermission. The performance is going well. Irene, the pretty ingenue/assistant stage manager has been working hard to get Sir to notice her, and finally he has. When they are alone in his dressing room he touches her body, almost kisses her—but doesn't. He lifts her off the ground into his arms, and then waves her away for no apparent reason. As she runs out she is stopped by Norman, who has been trying vainly to hear the goings-on through the locked door. In the scene below, Norman demands that Irene tell him what went on in the dressing room. He must know everything about Sir if he is to keep him going.

At the end of the scene, Her Ladyship, Sir's wife and leading lady, enters. She is no longer young and no longer light enough to lift easily, but she is still playing Cordelia to his Lear. She wants Sir to retire, wants them to relinquish the "fantasy" titles of "Sir" and "Her Ladyship," and wants him to finally accept that he will never be the esteemed actor he hoped he would be.

NORMAN: Well now, my dainty duck, my dear-o.
IRENE: Let go of me.
NORMAN: What was all that about?

(*pause*)

IRENE: He seems better.
NORMAN: Better than what or whom as the case may be?
IRENE: I didn't think he'd get through the performance tonight.
NORMAN: He's not through it yet. (*pause*) I'm waiting.
IRENE: For what?
NORMAN: A graphic description of events. Out with it. Or I shall slap your face. Hard. You had better know that my parentage is questionable, and that I can be vicious when aroused.
IRENE: I thought we were friends.
NORMAN: I thought so, too, Irene. I shall long remember welcoming you into the company in the prop room of the Palace Theatre, Newark-on-Trent, the smell of size and carpenter's glue, the creaking of skips and you locked in the arms of the Prince of Morocco, a married man, ever such a comic sight with his tights round his ankles and you smeared black. I said

"Don't worry, mum's the word, but don't let it happen again." We talked, brewed tea on a paint-stained gas-ring. You expressed gratitude and I said, "Now you're one of the family." And this is how you repay me.

IRENE: What am I supposed to have done?

NORMAN: You tell me.

IRENE: About what?

NORMAN: About Sir. The Guv'nor, the Chief, Father, Him from whom all favours flow. You know who Sir is, Irene.

IRENE: I'm late. I have to help Her Ladyship with her armour.

NORMAN: Her Ladyship's armour will keep. Perhaps you didn't hear my question. What did Sir do?

IRENE: I'm not telling you—

(*He grabs her closer and threatens to strike her.*)

NORMAN: I'll mark you for life, ducky.

IRENE: You strike me and I'll tell him, I'll tell Sir, I'll tell Sir, I will, I'll tell Sir—

(*He lets go of her.*)

NORMAN: Tell Sir? On me? I quake in my boots. I shan't be able to eat my tea. Tell Sir? Gadzooks, madam, the thought of it, you telling Sir on me. Ducky, in his present state, which totters between confusion and chaos, to tell Sir anything at all would take a louder voice and clearer diction than that possessed by the most junior member of this Shakespearean troupe, the assistant stage manager, dog's body, general understudy, map-carrier and company mattress, namely you. You won't be able to tell Sir you'd let him touch your tits on a Thursday matinee in Aberystwyth. Tell Sir. You think I don't know the game? You think I've dressed the rotten bugger for sixteen bloody years, nursed him, spoiled him, washed his sweat-sodden doublet and hose and his foul underpants night after night without knowing every twist and turn of what is laughingly known as his mind? Never mind tell Sir. I'll tell you. He did something, something unseen and furtive, something that gave him pleasure. "That's more like it!" More like what, Irene? I have to know all that occurs. I have to know all he does.

(*pause*)

IRENE: He lifted me up in his arms.

NORMAN: Lifted you up?

IRENE: And I understood, I understood what he meant. "So young, so young," he said, and lifted me up. "That's more like it," he cried and I knew, cradled in his arms, that it was youth and newness he was after—(NORMAN *laughs*.)—why do you laugh? I was there, it happened, it's true, I felt it. He was trembling and so was I. Up in his arms, part of him, "that's more like it," and he lowered me, waved me away and I ran off. Youth. And with my eyes closed I imagined what it would be like to be carried on by him, Cordelia, dead in his arms, young.

NORMAN: Never mind a young Cordelia, ducky, he wants a light Cordelia. Light, ducky, light. Look at yourself. Look at Her Ladyship.

IRENE: You don't understand. He needs youth—

NORMAN: "That's more like it." You're lighter than she is, ducky. (*He laughs. Pause*) You're not the first to be placed on the scales. How do you think Her Ladyship got the job? Her Ladyship, when a slip of a girl, went from map-carrier to youngest daughter overnight. I remember it well. That was the tour the Doge of Venice gave Launcelot Gobbo clap.

(IRENE *begins to cry softly.*)

NORMAN: It's not youth or talent or star quality he's after, ducky, but a moderate eater. (*pause*) We could cope with anything in those days. Turmoil was his middle name. (NORMAN *sways a little, then controls himself. He becomes tearful but holds back.*) So. Ducky. Keep well away. The old days are gone, the days of vim and vigour, what's to come is still unsure. Trip no further, pretty sweeting. We can't have any distractions. Not anymore. Not if things are to be lovely. And painless. (*pause*) Don't disobey me, will you? The fateful words, "You finish on Saturday" have a decidedly sinister ring. . . .

WHOSE LIFE IS IT ANYWAY?
by Brian Clark

Act I

Ken Harrison has decided he wants to die. Paralyzed from the neck down as a result of an automobile accident, there is no hope of recovery. A former sculptor and art teacher, this once energetic and vital young man is now condemned to hospital care for the rest of his life.

Ken assesses his situation rationally and prefers to end his life rather than live only through the grace of doctors and machines. But this is easier said than done. Everyone around him—doctors, social workers, nurses—refuse to take him seriously until he hires a lawyer to plead his case.

When Ken first shares his views with Dr. Scott, she prescribes Valium to calm him down. He refuses, arguing that he does not want his mind dulled by sedatives. She reconsiders and informs her superior, Dr. Emerson, that she now feels Ken is in control of himself and does not need the tranquilizer. Dr. Emerson disagrees and, against Ken's wishes, administers the drug.

In the following scene Ken is upset after a meeting with a social worker who ignored his arguments against living by telling him he was just "depressed" and would get over it. The social worker leaves and Dr. Scott enters. She is apologetic about the incident with Dr. Emerson.

DR. SCOTT: And what was all the fuss about?
KEN: I'm sorry about that. The last thing I want is to bring down Emerson again with his pharmaceutical truncheon.

45

DR. SCOTT: I'm . . . sorry about that.

KEN: I don't suppose it was your fault.

DR. SCOTT: Can I give you some advice?

KEN: Please do; I may even take it.

DR. SCOTT: Take the tablets; the dose is very small—the minimum—and it won't really blunt your consciousness, not like the injection.

KEN: . . . You're on.

DR. SCOTT: Good . . . I was glad to hear about your decision to try and get your compensation settled.

KEN: How did you? . . . Oh, I suppose Sister checked with you.

DR. SCOTT: She did mention it . . .

KEN: You have lovely breasts.

DR. SCOTT: I beg your pardon?

KEN: I said you have lovely breasts.

DR. SCOTT: What an odd thing to say.

KEN: Why? You're not only a doctor, are you? You can't tell me that you regard them only as mammary glands.

DR. SCOTT: No.

KEN: You're quite safe.

DR. SCOTT: Of course.

KEN: I'm not about to jump out of bed and rape you or anything.

DR. SCOTT: I know.

KEN: Did it embarrass you?

DR. SCOTT: Surprised me.

KEN: And embarrassed you.

DR. SCOTT: I suppose so.

KEN: But why exactly? You are an attractive woman. I admit that it's unusual for a man to compliment a woman on her breasts when only one of them is in bed, only one of the people that is, not one of the breasts, but that wasn't the reason, was it?

DR. SCOTT: I don't think it helps you to talk like this.

KEN: Because I can't do anything about it, you mean.

DR. SCOTT: I didn't mean that exactly.

KEN: I watch you walking in the room, bending over me, tucking in your sweater. It's surprising how relaxed a woman can become when she is not in the presence of a man.

DR. SCOTT: I am sorry if I provoked you . . . I can assure you . . .

KEN: You haven't "provoked" me, as you put it, but you are a woman and even though I've only a piece of knotted string between my legs, I still have a man's mind. One change that I have noticed is that I now engage in sexual banter with your nurses, searching for the double entendre in the most innocent remark. Like a sexually desperate middle-aged man. Then they leave the room and I go cold with embarrassment. It's fascinating, isn't it? Laughable. I still have tremendous sexual desire. Do you find that disgusting?

DR. SCOTT: No.

KEN: Pathetic?

DR. SCOTT: Sad.

KEN: I am serious you know . . . about deciding to die.

DR. SCOTT: You will get over the feeling.

KEN: How do you know?

DR. SCOTT: From experience.

KEN: That doesn't alter the validity of my decision now.

DR. SCOTT: But if we acted on your decision now, there wouldn't be an opportunity for you to accept it.

KEN: I grant you, I may become lethargic and quiescent. Happy when a nurse comes to put in a new catheter, or give me an enema, or to turn me over. These could become the high spots of my day. I might even learn to do wonderful things, like turn the pages of a book with some miracle of modern science, or to type letters with flicking my eyelids. And you would look at me and say: "Wasn't it worth waiting?" and I would say: "Yes" and be proud of my achievements. Really proud. I grant you all that, but it doesn't alter the validity of my present position.

DR. SCOTT: But if you became happy?

KEN: But I don't want to become happy by becoming the computer section of a complex machine. And morally, you must accept my decision.

DR. SCOTT: Not according to my morals.

KEN: And why are yours better than mine? They're better because you're more powerful. I am in your power. To hell with a morality that is based on the proposition that might is right.

DR. SCOTT: I must go now. I was halfway through Mr. Patel.

(*She walks to the door.*)

KEN: I thought you were just passing. Oh, Doctor . . . one more thing . . .

DR. SCOTT: Yes?
KEN: You still have lovely breasts.

WHO'S AFRAID OF VIRGINIA WOOLF?
by Edward Albee

ACT I

George and Martha are an unlikely couple. She is loud and brash and enjoys degrading George in public. He is a mild-mannered history professor, soft-spoken and seemingly obliging to his domineering wife. But George is equal to the sadistic banter Martha constantly throws at him. He can hold his own. His style is more subtle, but equally cutting.

Beneath the anguish and bitterness that characterize their married life, they share a special understanding. They respect each other's ability to withstand the pain they inflict on each other and they hold fast to the limits they have set in the game of mutual torment that constitutes their marriage. Until this evening.

Tonight Martha will violate one of their sacred rules and George will kill the son they have created and nurtured in their imaginations for years. And he will do it in front of the handsome young biology professor and his wife that Martha has invited home for a late night drink.

As the scene opens George and Martha have just returned from a Saturday night faculty party hosted by Martha's father, who is president of the university where George teaches.

(*Set in darkness. Crash against front door,* MARTHA'S *laughter is heard. Front door opens, lights are switched on.* MARTHA *enters, followed by* GEORGE.)

MARTHA: *Jesus...*
GEORGE: *...SHHHHHHH...*
MARTHA: *...H. Christ...*
GEORGE: For God's sake, Martha, it's two o'clock in the...
MARTHA: Oh, George!
GEORGE: Well, I'm sorry, but...

MARTHA: What a cluck! What a cluck you are.

GEORGE: It's late, you know? Late.

MARTHA: (*Looks about the room. Imitates Bette Davis*) What a dump. Hey, what's that from? "What a dump!"

GEORGE: How would I know what...

MARTHA: Aw, come on! What's it from? *You* know...

GEORGE: ...Martha...

MARTHA: WHAT'S IT FROM, FOR CHRIST'S SAKE?

GEORGE: (*wearily*) What's what from?

MARTHA: I just told you; I just did it. "What a dump!" Hunh? What's that from?

GEORGE: I haven't the faintest idea what...

MARTHA: Dumbbell! It's from some goddamn Bette Davis picture...some goddamn Warner Brothers epic...

GEORGE: I can't remember all the pictures that...

MARTHA: Nobody's asking you to remember every single goddamn Warner Brothers epic...just one! One single little epic! Bette Davis gets peritonitis in the end...she's got this big black fright wig she wears all through the picture and she gets peritonitis, and she's married to Joseph Cotten or something...

GEORGE: ...Some*body*...

MARTHA: ...some*body*...and she wants to go to Chicago all the time, 'cause she's in love with that actor with the scar...But she gets sick, and she sits down in front of her dressing table....

GEORGE: What actor? What scar?

MARTHA: *I* can't remember his name, for God's sake. What's the name of the *picture*? I want to know what the name of the *picture* is. She sits down in front of her dressing table...and she's got this peritonitis...and she tries to put her lipstick on, but she can't...and she gets it all over her face...but she decides to go to Chicago anyway, and...

GEORGE: *Chicago!* It's called *Chicago*.

MARTHA: Hunh? What...what is?

GEORGE: The picture...it's called *Chicago*....

MARTHA: Good grief! Don't you know *anything*? *Chicago* was a 'thirties musical, starring little Miss Alice *Faye*. Don't you know *anything*?

GEORGE: Well, that was probably before my *time*, but...

MARTHA: Can it! Just cut that out! This picture...Bette Davis comes home from a hard day at the grocery store...

GEORGE: She works in a grocery store?

MARTHA: She's a housewife; she buys things . . . and she comes home with the groceries, and she walks into the modest living room of the modest cottage modest Joseph Cotten has set her up in. . . .

GEORGE: Are they married?

MARTHA: (*impatiently*) Yes. They're married. To each other. Cluck! And she comes in, and she looks around, and she puts her groceries down, and she says, "What a dump!"

GEORGE: (*pause*) Oh.

MARTHA: (*pause*) She's discontent.

GEORGE: (*pause*) Oh.

MARTHA: (*pause*) Well, what's the name of the picture?

GEORGE: I really don't know, Martha. . . .

MARTHA: Well, think!

GEORGE: I'm tired, dear . . . it's late . . . and besides . . .

MARTHA: I don't know what you're so tired about . . . you haven't *done* anything all day; you didn't have any classes, or anything. . . .

GEORGE: Well, I'm tired . . . If your father didn't set up these goddamn Saturday night orgies all the time . . .

MARTHA: Well, that's too bad about you, George. . . .

GEORGE: (*grumbling*) Well, that's how it is, anyway.

MARTHA: You didn't *do* anything; you never *do* anything; you never *mix*. You just sit around and *talk*.

GEORGE: What do you want me to do? Do you want me to act like you? Do you want me to go around all night *braying* at everybody, the way you do?

MARTHA: (*braying*) I DON'T BRAY!

GEORGE: (*softly*) All right . . . you don't bray.

MARTHA: (*hurt*) I do not *bray*.

GEORGE: All right. I said you didn't bray.

MARTHA: (*pouting*) Make me a drink.

GEORGE: What?

MARTHA: (*still softly*) I said, make me a drink.

GEORGE: (*moving to the portable bar*) Well, I don't suppose a nightcap'd kill either one of us. . . .

MARTHA: A nightcap! Are you kidding? We've got guests.

GEORGE: (*disbelieving*) We've got what?

MARTHA: Guests. GUESTS.

GEORGE: GUESTS!

MARTHA: Yes . . . guests . . . people . . . We've got guests coming over.

GEORGE: When?

MARTHA: Now!

GEORGE: Good Lord, Martha . . . do you know what time it . . . *Who's* coming over?

MARTHA: What's-their-name.

GEORGE: Who?

MARTHA: WHAT'S-THEIR-NAME!

GEORGE: Who is what's-their-name?

MARTHA: I don't know what their name is, George. . . . You met them tonight . . . they're new . . . he's in the math department, or something. . . .

GEORGE: Who . . . who are these people?

MARTHA: You met them tonight, George.

GEORGE: I don't remember meeting anyone tonight. . . .

MARTHA: Well you did. . . . Will you give me my drink, please. . . . He's in the math department . . . about thirty, blond, and . . .

GEORGE: . . . and good-looking. . . .

MARTHA: Yes . . . and good-looking. . . .

GEORGE: It figures.

MARTHA: . . . and his wife's a mousey little type, without any hips, or anything.

GEORGE: (*vaguely*) Oh.

MARTHA: You remember them now?

GEORGE: Yes, I guess so, Martha. . . . But why in God's name are they coming over here now?

MARTHA: (*in a so-there voice*) Because Daddy said we should be nice to them, that's why.

GEORGE: (*defeated*) Oh, Lord.

MARTHA: May I have my drink, please? Daddy said we should be nice to them. Thank you.

GEORGE: But why now? It's after two o'clock in the morning, and . . .

MARTHA: Because Daddy said we should be nice to them!

GEORGE: Yes. But I'm sure your father didn't mean we were supposed to stay up all *night* with these people. I mean, we could have them over some Sunday or something. . . .

MARTHA: Well, never mind. . . . Besides, it *is* Sunday. Very early Sunday.

GEORGE: I mean . . . it's ridiculous . . .

MARTHA: Well, it's *done*!

GEORGE: (*resigned and exasperated*) All right. Well . . . where are they? If we've got guests, where are they?

MARTHA: They'll be here soon.

GEORGE: What did they do . . . go home and get some sleep first, or something?

MARTHA: They'll *be* here!

GEORGE: I wish you'd *tell* me about something sometime. . . . I wish you'd stop *springing* things on me all the time.

MARTHA: I don't *spring* things on you all the time.

GEORGE: Yes, you do . . . you really do . . . you're always *springing* things on me.

MARTHA: (*friendly-patronizing*) Oh, George!

GEORGE: Always.

MARTHA: Poor Georgie-Porgie, put-upon pie! (*as he sulks*) Awwwww . . . what are you doing? Are you sulking? Hunh? Let me see . . . are you sulking? Is that what you're doing?

GEORGE: (*very quietly*) Never mind, Martha . . .

MARTHA: AWWWWWWWWWWW!

GEORGE: Just don't bother yourself. . . .

MARTHA: AWWWWWWWWWW! (*no reaction*) Hey! (*no reaction*) HEY! (GEORGE *looks at her, put-upon.*) Hey. (*She sings.*)

> Who's afraid of Virginia Woolf,
> > Virginia Woolf,
> > Virginia Woolf. . . .

Ha, ha, ha, HA! (*no reaction*) What's the matter . . . didn't you think that was funny? Hunh? (*defiantly*) I thought it was a scream . . . a real scream. You didn't like it, hunh?

GEORGE: It was all right, Martha. . . .

MARTHA: You laughed your head off when you heard it at the party.

GEORGE: I smiled. I didn't laugh my head off. . . . I smiled, you know? . . . it was all right.

MARTHA: (*gazing into her drink*) You laughed your goddamn head off.

GEORGE: It was all right. . . .

MARTHA: (*ugly*) It was a scream!

GEORGE: (*patiently*) It was very funny, yes.

MARTHA: (*after a moment's consideration*) You make me puke!

GEORGE: What?

MARTHA: Uh . . . you make me puke!

GEORGE: (*thinks about it . . . then . . .*) That wasn't a very nice thing to say, Martha.

MARTHA: That wasn't *what*?

GEORGE: . . . a very nice thing to say.

MARTHA: I like your anger. I think that's what I like about you most . . . your anger. You're such a . . . such a simp! You don't even have the . . . the what? . . .

GEORGE: . . . guts? . . .

MARTHA: PHRASEMAKER! (*pause . . . then they both laugh*) Hey, put some more ice in my drink, will you? You never put any ice in my drink. Why is that, hunh?

GEORGE: (*takes her drink*) I always put ice in your drink. You eat it, that's all. It's that habit you have . . . chewing your ice cubes . . . like a cocker spaniel. You'll crack your big teeth.

MARTHA: THEY'RE MY BIG TEETH!

GEORGE: Some of them . . . some of them.

MARTHA: I've got more teeth than you've got.

GEORGE: Two more.

MARTHA: Well, two more's a lot more.

GEORGE: I suppose it is. I suppose it's pretty remarkable . . . considering how old you are.

MARTHA: YOU CUT THAT OUT. (*pause*) You're not so young yourself.

GEORGE: (*with boyish pleasure . . . a chant*) I'm six years younger than you are. . . . I always have been and I always will be.

MARTHA: (*glumly*) Well . . . you're going bald.

GEORGE: So are you. (*pause . . . they both laugh*) Hello, honey.

MARTHA: Hello. C'mon over here and give your Mommy a big sloppy kiss.

GEORGE: . . . . oh, now . . .

MARTHA: I WANT A BIG SLOPPY KISS!

GEORGE: (*preoccupied*) I don't *want* to kiss you, Martha. Where *are* these people? Where are these *people* you invited over?

MARTHA: They stayed on to talk to Daddy. . . . They'll be here. . . . *Why* don't you want to kiss me?

GEORGE: (*too matter-of-fact*) Well, dear, if I kissed you I'd get all excited . . . I'd get beside myself, and I'd take you, by force, right here on the living room rug, and then our little guests would walk in, and . . . well, just think what your father would say about *that*.

MARTHA: You pig!

GEORGE: (*haughtily*) Oink! Oink!

MARTHA: Ha, ha, ha, HA! Make me another drink . . . lover.

GEORGE: (*taking her glass*) My God, you can swill it down, can't you?

MARTHA: (*imitating a tiny child*) I'm firsty.

GEORGE: Jesus!

MARTHA: (*swinging around*) Look, sweetheart, I can drink you under any goddamn table you want...so don't worry about me!

GEORGE: Martha, I gave you the prize years ago....There isn't an abomination award going that you...

MARTHA: I swear...if you existed I'd divorce you....

GEORGE: Well, just stay on your feet, that's all....These people are your guests, you know, and...

MARTHA: I can't even see you...I haven't been able to see you for years....

GEORGE: ...if you pass out, or throw up, or something....

MARTHA: ...I mean, you're a blank, a cipher....

GEORGE: ...and try to keep your clothes on, too. There aren't many more sickening sights than you with a couple of drinks in you and your skirt up over your head, you know....

MARTHA: ...a zero....

GEORGE: ...your *heads*. I should say...(*the front door bell chimes.*)

MARTHA: Party! Party!

GEORGE: (*murderously*) I'm really looking forward to this, Martha...

MARTHA: (*same*) Go answer the door.

GEORGE: (*not moving*) You answer it.

MARTHA: Get to that door, you. (*He does not move.*) I'll fix you, you...

GEORGE: (*fake-spits*)...to you...(*door chime again*)

MARTHA: (*shouting...to the door*) C'MON IN! (*to George, between her teeth*) I said, get over there!

GEORGE: (*moves a little toward the door, smiling slightly*) All right, love...whatever love wants. (*stops*) Just don't start on the bit, that's all.

MARTHA: The bit? The bit? What kind of language is that? What are you talking about?

GEORGE: The bit. Just don't start in on the bit.

MARTHA: You imitating one of your students, for God's sake? What are you trying to do? WHAT BIT?

GEORGE: Just don't start in on the bit about the kid, that's all.

MARTHA: What do you take me for?

GEORGE: Much too much.

MARTHA: (*really angered*) Yeah? Well, I'll start in on the kid if I want to.

GEORGE: Just leave the kid out of this.

MARTHA: (*threatening*) He's mine as much as he is yours. I'll talk about him if I want to.

GEORGE: I'd advise against it, Martha.

MARTHA: Well, good for you. (*knock*) C'mon in. Get over there and open the door!

GEORGE: You've been advised.

MARTHA: Yeah . . . sure. Get over there!

GEORGE: (*moving toward the door*) All right, love . . . whatever love wants. Isn't it nice the way some people have manners, though, even in this day and age? Isn't it nice that some people won't just come breaking into other people's houses even if they do hear some sub-human monster yowling at 'em from inside . . . ?

MARTHA: SCREW YOU!

THE WOOLGATHERER
by William Mastrosimone

Act I

Rose is a strange, fragile five-and-dime store salesgirl who lives in a seedy apartment in South Philadelphia. When she meets Cliff, a witty truck driver, she invites him back to her apartment. He entertains her with jokes and pranks while she tells him bizarre stories: her friend Brenda had a nervous breakdown when a boyfriend left her; Mrs. Majusko is a nosy neighbor who listens to her with a glass to the wall; Rose saw a group of kids at the zoo stone to death a rare breed of cranes (''derricks'').

In fact, everything about Rose is strange. She never curses, eats very little, and doesn't care if her only window is boarded up. But Cliff is attracted to her delicate innocence and makes a move to kiss her. She recoils. She is afraid of human contact and keeps Cliff at arm's distance by talking about ''true love.'' Angry at being rebuffed, Cliff tells her what he believes really "counts" in a relationship.

CLIFF: Hey, one thing counts out there, Rosie-schmosie. Scratch! And you gotta leap in the fuckin dogfight and grab all you can grab. And while you're out grabbin it, true love's screwin the guy next door. And if you lose it, you get true love's consolation prize—alimony payments! So don't hit me with this stale bag of wholesale pigshit about true love because I been there and I know better. (*pause*) Alls I said was I want to hold you and you gotta make a big deal.

ROSE: It's not my fault I'm this way!

CLIFF: Look, I don't want to hear about no bad childhood.

ROSE: I have to be very careful because of my hemophilia.

CLIFF: Your what?

ROSE: I happen to have a very very rare blood disease. If I get cut I could bleed to death.

CLIFF: This ain't happening.

ROSE: Just a little scratch bleeds for days! And if I get a deep cut, that's it!

CLIFF: I said I want to hold you, not bite you!

ROSE: So I have to be very careful!

CLIFF: So how's a flesh and blood man supposed to get near you? I talk, I draw blood. I touch, you go icy. I mean, hey, maybe we should carry this thing on over the telephone. Germless. And when it starts to hurt, you could hang up.

ROSE: I don't have a phone.

CLIFF: I'm not talking about phones! I'm talking about me and you! I'm here, you're there, and there's no wall between us except the one you keep building up in that head of yours!

ROSE: I don't know what wall you're talking about.

CLIFF: Hey, Rosie, I didn't order a pound of nonpareils because I got a sweet tooth. I didn't come up here to discuss Brenda or seaweed soup or homophillioes or dinosaurs or flamingoes. I came up here to be with you. You. And hold you. Make love to you.

ROSE: (*pause*) I don't want to cheat.

CLIFF: So you do have a man, eh?

ROSE: Yes.

CLIFF: So why the fuck did you invite me up here.

ROSE: And he doesn't curse or smoke or pretend he wants to talk when he wants to touch and doesn't make fun!

CLIFF: What's he, a priest? Sister Rose and Father Clean!

ROSE: Shut up!

CLIFF: What do you guys do for thrills? Whip each other with rosaries?

ROSE: Be quiet.

CLIFF: Hallelujah! Father Clean and the Boneless Sardine!

ROSE: Shut up! You're jealous!

CLIFF: O, I think I'll go home and punch a cotton ball!

ROSE: I hate you!

CLIFF: O gosh! I think I'll go hang myself!

ROSE: You're just like them!

CLIFF: I think I'll go to the zoo and stone a long-legged derrick!

ROSE: Stop it!

CLIFF: Or jump out the window! But how can I? Some whacko boarded it up and another whacko won't take it down!

ROSE: Go to hell!

CLIFF: You cursed! O, what a trashmouth! Mrs. Majusko! Call the Sanitation Department!

ROSE: FUCK YOU! (*Her hands snap to her mouth, she turns to the wall. Long pause*)

CLIFF: Rose, you don't watch your mouth, I'm leavin.

ROSE: Now for the rest of my life, I could never say I never cursed!

CLIFF: O big fuckin deal! That your only problem in life? You been cooped up too long, Rosie-dozie!

ROSE: If I never met you, this would've never happened!

CLIFF: If! If! If! If my aunt had balls, she'd be my uncle! (*pause*) Well, look, champ, I was lookin for a little wham-bam-thank-you-ma'am, but I guess I turned over the wrong rock. So, catch ya later.

ROSE: Can I have your sweater?

CLIFF: Come again?

ROSE: Never mind.

CLIFF: No no no no no. What did you ask me?

ROSE: Nothing . . . I was just . . . Nothing.

CLIFF: Could you have my sweater?

ROSE: If you don't want it.

CLIFF: Well, yeah, I was just about to toss it in the garbage on the way out.

ROSE: You must think I'm crazy.

CLIFF: Noooooooooooooooooooooo.

ROSE: Never mind.

CLIFF: Can I ask what for?

ROSE: I don't know. To remember you by.

CLIFF: Remember me by.

ROSE: But never mind.

CLIFF: It's my work sweater.

ROSE: I should've never asked.

CLIFF: It's dirty and I slept in it. Blew my nose in it.

ROSE: Never mind.

CLIFF: You don't want me to stay but you want to remember me by. That's one that goes way over my head, champ. So let's just leave it at that. Take good care of it. It's used to travelling across country at 65 m.p.h.

ROSE: Thank you.

CLIFF: And be careful. It goes through amber lights.

ROSE: Thank you.

CLIFF: It's 100% virgin wool. Meant to be. For you.

ROSE: Thank you.

CLIFF: The label fell out. But see this hole?

ROSE: Yes?

CLIFF: I burned it there so I know which's the front. But I don't want to assume anything, Rosie. Maybe you like the front on the back. Me myself, I like the front on the front.

ROSE: Thank you.

CLIFF: Rose?

ROSE: Yeah?

CLIFF: Can I have your shoe?

ROSE: I thought you was different.

CLIFF: It was all in your head. Catch ya later.

ROSE: Bye.

CLIFF: Yeah.

ROSE: Hope you get the new job.

CLIFF: Yeah.

ROSE: Think your truck's fixed?

CLIFF: What's it matter?

ROSE: Will you ever drive through Philadelphia again?

CLIFF: Who knows?

ROSE: Bye.

CLIFF: Yeah.

ROSE: Thank you.

CLIFF: Yeah.

ROSE: Bye. Cliff?

CLIFF: Yeah?

ROSE: Will you be cold without your sweater?

CLIFF: Me? Cold? Hey, Rosie, you're lookin at the only survivor of the Great Ice Age. (*Exit* CLIFF. *His footfalls fade down the stairwell.* ROSE *rushes to the door.*)

ROSE: Cliff? (*Lights fade quickly.*)

BETRAYAL
by Harold Pinter

ACT II, SCENE 5

The play starts in the spring of 1977 and moves backward in time to the winter of 1968, to the day when Emma and Jerry became secret lovers. In Scene One, Emma and Jerry meet in a pub. It's been two years since their last meeting when they ended their seven-year affair—ended it largely because their declining passion for each other no longer made up for the inconvenience of their afternoon rendezvous.

This morning Emma called Jerry because last night she and Robert, her husband and Jerry's oldest friend, spent the night talking. Robert told her about other women in his life and they decided to separate. Today Emma called Jerry because she needed to talk to someone.

As the scenes progress we learn that Robert actually discovered Emma's affair with Jerry four years earlier, but neither he nor she ever told Jerry that he knew. Robert managed to accept the "betrayal," keeping his wife, his best friend, and his own liaisons secret without anyone becoming too uncomfortable.

Scene Five is the discovery scene. Emma and Robert are vacationing in Venice in the summer of 1973. They are in a hotel room. Emma is on the bed reading a new best seller by one of Jerry's authors (Jerry is a literary agent), a book that Robert, who is a publisher, turned down.

(*Hotel room. Venice. 1973. Summer.* EMMA *on bed reading.* ROBERT *at window looking out. She looks up at him, then back at the book.*)

EMMA: It's Torcello tomorrow, isn't it?

ROBERT: What?

EMMA: We're going to Torcello tomorrow, aren't we?

ROBERT: Yes. That's right.

EMMA: That'll be lovely.

ROBERT: Mmn.

EMMA: I can't wait. (*pause*)

ROBERT: Book good?

EMMA: Mmn. Yes.

ROBERT: What is it?

EMMA: This new book. This man Spinks.

ROBERT: Oh that. Jerry was telling me about it.

EMMA: Jerry? Was he?

ROBERT: He was telling me about it at lunch last week.

EMMA: Really? Does he like it?

ROBERT: Spinks is his boy. He discovered him.

EMMA: Oh. I didn't know that.

ROBERT: Unsolicited manuscript. (*pause*) You think it's good, do you?

EMMA: Yes, I do. I'm enjoying it.

ROBERT: Jerry thinks it's good too. You should have lunch with us one day and chat about it.

EMMA: Is that absolutely necessary? (*pause*) It's not as good as all that.

ROBERT: You mean it's not good enough for you to have lunch with Jerry and me and chat about it?

EMMA: What the hell are you talking about?

ROBERT: I must read it it again myself, now it's in hard covers.

EMMA: Again?

ROBERT: Jerry wanted us to publish it.

EMMA: Oh, really?

ROBERT: Well, naturally. Anyway, I turned it down.

EMMA: Why?

ROBERT: Oh . . . not much more to say on that subject, really, is there?

EMMA: What do you consider the subject to be?

ROBERT: Betrayal.

EMMA: No, it isn't.

ROBERT: Isn't it? What is it then?

EMMA: I haven't finished it yet. I'll let you know.

ROBERT: Well, do let me know. (*pause*) Of course, I could be thinking of the wrong book. (*silence*) By the way, I went into American Express yesterday. (*She looks up.*)

EMMA: Oh?

ROBERT: Yes. I went to cash some travellers cheques. You get a much better rate there, you see, than you do in a hotel.

EMMA: Oh, do you?

ROBERT: Oh yes. Anyway, there was a letter there for you. They asked me if you were any relation and I said yes. So they asked me if I wanted to take it. I mean, they gave it to me. But I said no, I would leave it. Did you get it?

EMMA: Yes.

ROBERT: I suppose you popped in when you were out shopping yesterday evening?

EMMA: That's right.

ROBERT: Oh well, I'm glad you got it. (*pause*) To be honest, I was amazed that they suggested I take it. It could never happen in England. But these Italians . . . so free and easy. I mean, just because my name is Downs and your name is Downs doesn't mean that we're the Mr. and Mrs. Downs that they, in their laughing Mediterranean way, assume we are. We could be, and in fact are vastly more likely to be, total strangers. So let's say I, whom they laughingly assume to be your husband, had taken the letter, having declared myself to be your husband but in truth being a total stranger, and opened it, and read it, out of nothing more than idle curiosity, and then thrown it in a canal, you would never have received it and would have been deprived of your legal right to open your own mail, and all this because of Venetian *je m'en foutisme*. I've a good mind to write to the Doge of Venice about it. (*pause*) That's what stopped me taking it, by the way, and bringing it to you, the thought that I could very easily be a total stranger. (*pause*) What they of course did not know, and had no way of knowing, was that I am your husband.

EMMA: Pretty inefficient bunch.

ROBERT: Only in a laughing Mediterranean way. (*pause*)

EMMA: It was from Jerry.

ROBERT: Yes, I recognized the handwriting. (*pause*) How is he?

EMMA: Okay.

ROBERT: Good. And Judith?

EMMA: Fine. (*pause*)

ROBERT: What about the kids?

EMMA: I don't think he mentioned them.

ROBERT: They're probably all right, then. If they were ill or something he'd have probably mentioned it. (*pause*) Any other news?

EMMA: No. (*silence*)

ROBERT: Are you looking forward to Torcello? (*pause*) How many times have we been to Torcello? Twice. I remember how you loved it, the first time I took you there. You fell in love with it. That was about ten years ago, wasn't it? About . . . six months after we were married. Yes. Do you remember? I wonder if you'll like it as much tomorrow. (*pause*) What do you think of Jerry as a letter writer? (*She laughs shortly.*) You're trembling. Are you cold?

EMMA: No.

ROBERT: He used to write me at one time. Long letters about Ford Madox Ford. I used to write to him, too, come to think of it. Long letters about . . . oh, W.B. Yeats, I suppose. That was the time when we were both editors of poetry magazines. Him at Cambridge, me at Oxford. Did you know that? We were bright young men. And close friends. Well, we still are close friends. All that was long before I met you. Long before he met you. I've been trying to remember when I introduced him to you. I simply can't remember. I take it I *did* introduce him to you? Yes. But when? Can you remember?

EMMA: No.

ROBERT: You can't?

EMMA: No.

ROBERT: How odd. (*pause*) He wasn't best man at our wedding, was he?

EMMA: You know he was.

ROBERT: Ah yes. Well, that's probably when I introduced him to you. (*pause*) Was there any message for me, in his letter? (*pause*) I mean in the line of business, to do with the world of publishing. Has he discovered any new and original talent? He's quite talented at uncovering talent, old Jerry.

EMMA: No message.

ROBERT: No message. Not even his love? (*silence*)

EMMA: We're lovers.

ROBERT: Ah. Yes. I thought it might be something like that, something along those lines.

EMMA: When?

ROBERT: What?

EMMA: When did you think?

ROBERT: Yesterday. Only yesterday. When I saw his handwriting on the letter. Before yesterday I was quite ignorant.

EMMA: Ah. (*pause*) I'm sorry.

ROBERT: *Sorry?* (*silence*) Where does it . . . take place? Must be a bit awkward. I mean we've got two kids, he's got two kids, not to mention a wife. . . .

EMMA: We have a flat.

ROBERT: Ah. I see. (*pause*) Nice? (*pause*) A flat. It's quite well established then, your . . . uh . . . affair?

EMMA: Yes.

ROBERT: How long?

EMMA: Some time.

ROBERT: Yes, but how long exactly?

EMMA: Five years.

ROBERT: *Five years?* (*pause*) Ned is one year old. (*pause*) Did you hear what I said?

EMMA: Yes. He's your son. Jerry was in America. For two months. (*silence*)

ROBERT: Did he write to you from America?

EMMA: Of course. And I wrote to him.

ROBERT: Did you tell him that Ned had been conceived?

EMMA: Not by letter.

ROBERT: But when you did tell him, was he happy to know I was to be a father? (*pause*) I've always liked Jerry. To be honest, I've always liked him rather more than I've liked you. Maybe I should have had an affair with him myself. (*silence*) Tell me, are you looking forward to our trip to Torcello?

VIEUX CARRÉ
by Tennessee Williams

SCENE NINE

In a studio apartment of a rundown rooming house in New Orleans a lovely and elegant young woman is trying to rouse her handsome and brutish lover from a deep narcotic sleep. After living with this sexual wonder for several weeks, Jane decides she must curb her uncommon passion for this "addicted delinquent . . . barker at a strip show joint."

She has just learned that her leukemia is no longer in remission. Very soon she will deteriorate into an invalid and she cannot rely on Tye to be responsible for her. He is a child, a dope addict, and unable to support her basic financial needs. In a desperate emotional state she decides to prostitute herself to a Brazilian gentleman she met in a bar.

(*The lights come up on* JANE'S *studio area. The shuttered doors to the windows overlooking the courtyard below are ajar.* JANE *is trying to rouse* TYE *from an unnaturally deep sleep. It is evident that she has been engaged in packing her effects and his.*)

JANE: Tye, Tye, oh—Christ . . .

(*He drops a bare arm off the disordered bed and moans slightly. She bends over to examine a needle mark on his arm.*)

TYE: —Wh—?

(JANE *crosses to the sink and wets a towel, then returns to slap* TYE'S *face with it. He begins to wake slowly.*)

Some men would beat a chick up for less'n that, y'know.

JANE: All right, get out of bed and beat me up, but get *up*.

TYE: (*stroking a promontory beneath the bed sheet*)—Can't you see I *am* up?

JANE: I don't mean that kind of up, and don't bring strip show lewdness in here this—Sunday afternoon.

TYE: Babe, don't mention the show to me t'day.

JANE: I'd like to remind you that when we first stumbled into this—crazy—co-habitation, you promised me you'd quit the show in a week.

TYE: For what? Tight as work is for a dude with five grades of school and no skill training from the Mississippi sticks?

JANE: You could find something less—publicly embarrassing, like a—filling station attendant.

TYE: Ha!

JANE: But of course your choice of employment is no concern of mine now.

TYE: Why not, Babe?

JANE: I'm not "Babe" and not "Chick"!

TYE: You say you're not my chick?

JANE: I say I'm nobody's chick.

TYE: Any chick who shacks with me's my chick.

JANE: This is my place. You just—moved in and stayed.

TYE: I paid the rent this month.

JANE: Half of it, for the first time, my savings being as close to exhaustion as me.

(*There is the sound of a funky piano and a voice on the Bourbon Street corner; "I've stayed around and played around this old town too long."* JANE'S *mood softens under its influence.*)

Lord, I don't know how I managed to haul you to bed.

TYE: Hey, you put me to bed last night?

JANE: It was much too much exertion for someone in my—condition.

TYE: (*focusing on her more closely*)—Honey, are you pregnant?

JANE: No, Lord, now who'd be fool enough to get pregnant by a Bourbon Street strip show barker?

TYE: When a chick talks about her condition, don't it mean she's pregnant?

JANE: All female conditions are not pregnancy, Tye. (*She staggers, then finishes her coffee.*) Mine is that of a desperate young woman living with a young bum employed by gangsters and using her place as a depository for hot merchandise. Well, they're all packed. You're packed too.

TYE: —Come to bed.

JANE: No, thank you. Your face is smeared with lipstick; also other parts of you. I didn't know lip rouge ever covered so much—territory.

TYE: I honestly don't remember a fuckin' thing after midnight.

JANE: That I do believe. Now have some coffee, I've warmed it. It isn't instant, it's percolated.

TYE: Who's birthday is it?

JANE: It's percolated in honor of our day of parting.

TYE: Aw, be sweet, Babe, please come back to bed. I need comfort, not coffee.

JANE: You broke a promise to me.

TYE: Which?

JANE: Among the many? You used a needle last night. I saw the mark of it on you.

TYE: No shit. Where?

JANE: (*returning to the bedside*) There, right there on your— (*He circles her with his arm and pulls her onto the bed.*) I've been betrayed by a—sensual streak in my nature. Susceptibility to touch. And you have skin like a child. I'd gladly support you if I believed you'd—if I had the means to and the time to. Time. Means. Luck. Things that expire, run out. And all at once you're stranded.

TYE: Jane, you—lie down with me and hold me.

JANE: I'm afraid, Tye, we'll just have to hold each other in our memories from now on.

TYE: (*childishly*) Don't talk that way. I never had a rougher night in my life. Do I have to think and remember?

JANE: Tye, we've had a long spell of dreaming, but now we suddenly have to.

TYE: Got any aspirin, Babe?

JANE: You're past aspirin, Tye. I think you've gone past all legal—analgesics.

TYE: You say words to me I've never heard before.

JANE: Tye, I've been forced to make an urgent phone call to someone I never wanted to call.

TYE: Call?

JANE: And then I packed your personal belongings and all that lot you've been holding here. Exertion of packing nearly blacked me out. Trembling, sweating—had to bathe and change.

TYE: Babe?

JANE: You're vacating the premises, "Babe." It's *afternoon*.

TYE: Look, if you're knocked up, have the kid. I'm against abortion.

JANE: On moral principles?

TYE: Have the kid, Babe. I'd pull myself together for a kid.

JANE: You didn't for me.

TYE: A baby would be a livin' thing between us, with both our blood.

JANE: Never mind.

(*Voices in the courtyard are heard.*)

NURSIE: Any donations t'keep the cou'tyard up, just drop it in my apron as you go out, ladies!...

JANE: Those tourists down there in the courtyard! If I'd known when I took this room it was over a tourist attraction—

TYE: It's the Festival, Babe. It ain't always Festival.... Gimme my cigarettes, ought to be some left in a pocket.

JANE: (*throwing his pants and a fancy sport shirt on the bed*) Here, your clothes, get in them.

TYE: (*putting on his shorts*) Not yet. It's Sunday, Babe ...Where's Beret? I like Beret to be here when I wake up.

JANE: Not even a cat will wait ten, twelve hours for you to sleep off whatever you shot last night. How did a girl well educated and reasonably well brought up get involved in this...Oh, I'm talking to myself.

TYE: I hear you, Babe, and I see you.

JANE: Then...get up and dressed.

TYE: It's not dark yet, Babe. Y'know I never get dressed till after dark on Sundays.

JANE: Today has to be an exception. I'm...expecting a caller, very important to me.

TYE: Fashion designer?

JANE: No. Buyer...to look at my illustrations. They're no good, I'm no good. I just had a flair, not a talent, and the flair flared out, I'm...finished. These sketches are evidence of it! (*She starts tearing fashion sketches off the wall.*) Look at me! Bangles, jangles! All taste gone! (*She tears off her costume jewelry.*)

TYE: Babe, you're in no shape to meet a buyer.

JANE: (*slowly and bitterly*) He's no buyer of anything but me.

TYE: —Buyer of *you*? Look. You said that you were expecting a buyer to look at your drawin's here.

JANE: I know what I said, I said a buyer to look at my illustrations, but what I said was a lie. Among other things, many other undreamed of before, you've taught me to practice deception.

VOICES OFFSTAGE: Edwina, Edwina, come see this dream of a little courtyard. Oh, my, yaiss, like a dream.

JANE: I know what I said, but let's say, Tye, that I experienced last week a somewhat less than triumphant encounter with a buyer of fashion illustrations at *Vogue Moderne*. In fact, it left me too shattered to carry my portfolio home without a shot of Metaxas brandy at the Blue Lantern, which was on the street level of the building. It was there that I met a gentleman from Brazil. He had observed my entrance, the Brazilian, and apparently took me for a hooker, sprang up with surprising agility for a gentleman of his corpulence, hauled me to his table, and introduced me to his *camaradas*,

"Señorita, this is Señor and Señor and Señor," declared me, "*Bonita, muy, muy, bonita*"—tried to press a hundred-dollar bill in my hand. Well, some atavistic bit of propriety surfaced and I, like a fool, rejected it—but did accept his business card, just in case—This morning, Tye, I called him. "Señorita Bonita of the Blue Lantern awaits you, top floor of seven-two-two Toulouse," that was the invitation that I phoned in to the message desk—He must have received it by now at the Hotel Royal Orleans, where the Presidential Suite somehow contains him.

TYE: Who're you talkin' about?

JANE: My expected caller, a responsible businessman from Brazil. Sincerely interested in my bankrupt state...

TYE: Forget it, come back to bed and I'll undress you, Babe, you need rest.

JANE: The bed bit is finished between us. You're moving out today.

(*He slowly stumbles up, crosses to the table, and gulps coffee, then grasps her arm and draws her to bed.*)

No, no, no, no, no, no!

TYE: Yes, yes, yes, yes, yes!

BEDROOM FARCE
by Alan Ayckbourn

Act I

Kate and Malcolm are a young married couple who are getting ready to receive guests for a housewarming party. However, some of their friends have rather complicated and unnerving relationships. Trevor and Suzanne are a battling couple whose marriage is on the rocks. Jan, who dated Trevor before he married Suzanne, is coming to the party without her husband who is bedridden with a bad back. These troublesome and potentially embarrassing relationships have Malcolm worried that the party will not be the fun-loving shindig he planned.

While they get dressed and review their party preparations, Kate and Malcolm enjoy teasing each other in their accustomed fashion—by hiding shoes and hair brushes in unexpected places.

(*Cross-fade to* MALCOLM *and* KATE'S. MALCOLM *comes in with one of* KATE'S *shoes. He looks for somewhere to hide it. He tucks it down the bottom of the unmade bed.* MALCOLM *sits in the chair innocently.* KATE *calls off, then enters, holding the other shoe.*)

KATE: Malcolm! Malcolm... I know you're up here, Malcolm. Come on, Malcolm, what have you done with it?

MALCOLM: What?

KATE: My other shoe. What have you done with it?

MALCOLM: I don't know.

KATE: Oh really... (*seeing the cardboard package*) What's all this?

MALCOLM: Ah-ha.

KATE: Where did it come from?

MALCOLM: I got it today.

KATE: I didn't see you.

MALCOLM: You don't see everything.

KATE: What is it?

MALCOLM: A little surprise. Nothing much. A little house-warming present from me to you.

KATE: Whatever is it?

MALCOLM: Later, later. When they've all gone.

KATE: Whatever is it? It's an ironing board.

MALCOLM: An ironing board...

KATE: What have you done with my shoe?

MALCOLM: Shoe? Shoe?

KATE: (*giving up*) Oh...

MALCOLM: (*taking off his shoes*) It's going to be a really good party tonight, I can feel it.

KATE: I hope so. Oooh. Something to confess.

MALCOLM: What?

KATE: You know that shelf you put up in the kitchen.

MALCOLM: Yes.

KATE: It's fallen down again.

MALCOLM: Again...

KATE: I was ever so careful.

MALCOLM: I told you it wasn't designed for great heavy weights.

KATE: I only stood the cruet on it. I deliberately didn't go near it in case it fell down. Oh, I'm terribly hot. Have I got time for a bath?

MALCOLM: Just about.

KATE: Now, the food's all going on the big table. Then I've cleared the sideboard for the drinks. And they can put their coats here on the bed—oh look, I haven't made the bed. Where is it then? (*She starts to make the bed.*)

MALCOLM: What?

KATE: You know what. My blooming shoe.

(MALCOLM *whistles to himself and starts to take off his sweater.*)

You going to wear your nice shirt?

MALCOLM: Which one?

KATE: Your nice one.

MALCOLM: All right.

KATE: You look nice in that.

MALCOLM: Yes, it's going to be a really good party. Who've we got coming then?

KATE: Oh—everyone—I asked everyone. Except Nick, he can't come.

MALCOLM: Nick?

KATE: Yes, he hurt his back, poor thing.

MALCOLM: Ah.

KATE: Jan phoned me. He hurt it this morning. She's coming though.

MALCOLM: Good. Good.

KATE: And who else is there. Ken and Margaret, of course. And John and Dorothy and Wilfrid and Gareth and Gwen and Mike and Dave and Carole and Dick and Lottie. Gordon and Marge, of course and—er—Susannah and Trevor . . .

MALCOM: Trevor?

KATE: Yes.

MALCOLM: And Susannah?

KATE: Yes.

MALCOLM: Oh dear, oh dear.

KATE: Well, I had to. They've had us round twice.

MALCOLM: I see. Well, that's that isn't it?

KATE: Well.

MALCOLM: That's that. Where is it then?

KATE: What?

MALCOLM: The shirt.
KATE: Oh, it's in the airing cupboard. I washed it.
MALCOLM: Right.

(MALCOLM *goes.*)

KATE: Could you turn my bath on?
MALCOLM: *(off)* Right.

(KATE *finds her shoe in the bed.*)

KATE: Oh really. (*She eyes the present. She sees* MALCOLM's *shoes. She snatches them up and stuffs them into one of the pillowcases.* MALCOLM *returns with the shirt.*) Very funny.
MALCOLM: Eh?
KATE: My shoe. Very funny.
MALCOLM: Ah.
KATE: And I don't want any more foreign bodies in my side of the bed tonight, thank you very much.
MALCOLM: Foreign bodies?
KATE: You know, hair brushes and all my bottles and jars— you know.
MALCOLM: Wasn't me.
KATE: You and your jokes. Is my bath running?
MALCOLM: Yes. Now look, you say Jan's coming and Susannah's coming and Trevor's coming?
KATE: Yes.
MALCOLM: (*putting on his shirt*) That's marvellous. If Trevor and Susannah don't have a fight, then it's ten to one Jan and Susannah will have a fight. . . .
KATE: I hope not.
MALCOLM: Well, the first sign of any trouble they're all out, I'm telling you. This is going to be a good party. I'm not having any of that. (*He has put on his shirt.*)
KATE: Has that shrunk?
MALCOLM: I don't know, has it?
KATE: It looks as if it's shrunk. Or else you're getting fat.

(KATE *goes off.*)

MALCOLM: Fat? You cheeky thing. (*calling*) Hey, Blodge. Blodge. (*He takes off the shirt.*)
KATE: *(off)* What?
MALCOLM: What have you done with my shoes?
KATE: *(off)* Ah-ha.
MALCOLM: What have you done with them? What's she

done with them? (*He sees her shoes. He hides them in the bed.*)

KATE: (*off*) Ooooh!

MALCOLM: What?

(KATE *returns, partially undressed.*)

KATE: Did you put that brush in my bath?

MALCOLM: Brush? What brush?

KATE: Well, you shouldn't do that. It's very unhygienic. Honestly.

(KATE *goes.* MALCOLM, *laughing, follows her.*)

TABLE SETTINGS
by James Lapine

At the center of James Lapine's comedy is Mother who is sixty, from Minsk, and has a passion for food. All the characters in this fast-paced play are known only by the titles they hold within the family: Younger Son, Girl Friend, Older Son, Granddaughter, etc. They comprise the archetypical Jewish family with all its infighting and tugs of love. Younger Son, by virtue of his title, spends most of his time getting stoned and "looking for himself," while Mother wants him to look for a job. His Girl Friend is a social worker for whom "communication is very important." In the following scene she feels obligated to indulge in the modern compulsion to express herself.

(YOUNGER SON *rushes into the space with* GIRL FRIEND *yakking behind.*)

GIRL FRIEND: (*exasperated*) Look, I'm just trying to get things out in the open. I'm a little bit older than you. I've been married—things are different for me—I'm working on opening up—talking things out.

YOUNGER SON: So talk things out—

GIRL FRIEND: I don't love you.

YOUNGER SON: Fine.

GIRL FRIEND: I mean I do love you, but I'm not in love with you . . .

YOUNGER SON: Fine.

GIRL FRIEND: Which makes it difficult for me to see you.

YOUNGER SON: Why does that make it difficult?

GIRL FRIEND: Difficult because I am a person who really needs to be in love.

YOUNGER SON: Yeah, so?

GIRL FRIEND: So, you're not really the kind of person I want to be in love with . . .

YOUNGER SON: Oh?

GIRL FRIEND: . . . besides which, you really don't want me falling in love with you.

YOUNGER SON: I don't?

GIRL FRIEND: Take it from me, you hardly know me. The minute I declare my love for someone, I feel compelled to be unfaithful.

YOUNGER SON: Me, too.

GIRL FRIEND: There, you see, I could never have a relationship with someone who was unfaithful to me.

YOUNGER SON: That makes no sense, but I think I understand perfectly. *(lovingly)* Look, if you want to cheat on me, you can.

GIRL FRIEND: That's just what I mean—you're so goddamned wishy-washy. Can't you take a stand? I hate being able to walk all over you. It's just not going to work.

YOUNGER SON: Okay, okay. Relax.

GIRL FRIEND: Besides which, I have a confession to make that's very embarrassing and is really going to turn you off.

YOUNGER SON: Try me.

GIRL FRIEND: I have crabs.

(YOUNGER SON *stops dead.*)

I picked them up at the clinic somehow.

YOUNGER SON: *(at a loss for words)* . . . that's too bad.

GIRL FRIEND: That's too bad? That's all you can say? Don't you ever express anger?

YOUNGER SON: What is it with you anyway?

GIRL FRIEND: I think it's important that we be able to tell each other everything—without being uptight.

YOUNGER SON: Tell me anything. I'm not uptight.

GIRL FRIEND: What if I tell you I've slept with women?

YOUNGER SON: Women?

GIRL FRIEND: That's what I said.

YOUNGER SON: That doesn't threaten me.

GIRL FRIEND: Any psychiatrist will tell you that it's a natural urge to be attracted to your own sex. But if the idea of that bothers you, you certainly can tell me.

YOUNGER SON: I used to have this thing for little girls.

GIRL FRIEND: What kind of thing?

YOUNGER SON: You know . . .

GIRL FRIEND: Little women you mean?

YOUNGER SON: Girls.

GIRL FRIEND: Girls?

YOUNGER SON: Girls.

GIRL FRIEND: *(disgusted)* Girls. *(big breath)* Well, anything goes, right? We live in the unshockable age. Words have no meaning. Everybody's done everything.

YOUNGER SON: Right. We're free! And we're oh so contemporary. Liberation is the name of the day.

GIRL FRIEND: Do you have any idea what Freud says about doing ''things'' with little girls?

YOUNGER SON: Fuck Freud.

GIRL FRIEND: *(angry again)* Shut up.

YOUNGER SON: You suck your thumb. What do your psychiatrists say about that?

GIRL FRIEND: *(hurt)* I do not!

YOUNGER SON: You do too. At night when you go to bed.

(He makes a thumb-sucking motion.)

GIRL FRIEND: That's an unforgivable accusation!

YOUNGER SON: *(pulling back)* I think it's kind of cute.

GIRL FRIEND: It's retentive, that's what it is—but no more so than you, hiding under that hideous hat of yours with a joint stuck in your mouth like some maternal nipple substitute!

YOUNGER SON: *(flies off the handle)* All right. You won. Look, I'm angry.

(He slams his hand against the wall or the table.)

Let's call the whole thing off.

GIRL FRIEND: *(a moment of silence)* Well, I feel sort of better now that everything's out in the open. Communication is very important.

YOUNGER SON: So's mental health. I shudder to think what you do to your patients.

GIRL FRIEND: If they can survive me, you *know* they're ready for the real world.

(*silence*)

Let's just be friends, huh? Let's not succumb to the predisposed notions of conventional relationships. What do you say?

(*He shrugs.*)

You're awfully cute, you know that?

(*He shrugs again. She goes over to him and gives him a kiss.*)

YOUNGER SON: (*He walks away.*) Under this new unconventional disposition, do friends get to make ... whoopee?
GIRL FRIEND: I don't see why not.

THE COLLECTOR
by David Parker from the novel by John Fowles

ACT III, SCENE 2

Ferdinand Clegg is a passionate collector of butterflies. When he sees Miranda Grey at a café near the Slade Art School, he is struck by her beauty and becomes passionately obsessed with her. She is everything he is not: upperclass, good-looking, confident and popular. This prim, "well-mannered" but "self-deprecating" young man begins to fantasize about meeting and marrying her. He dreams of capturing her and keeping her imprisoned so she can grow to love him.

Knowing that he "wouldn't stand a chance in London" with a girl like Miranda, Clegg decides to "collect" her and make his dreams come true. He kidnaps this beautiful human specimen and locks her in a lonely country house where he has stocked a cellar with everything to her liking: art books, so she can continue her studies, clothing just her size, food, and music.

Miranda, of course, tries to escape. But her attempts are useless. Clegg has constructed his cellar prison carefully.

The following scene takes place after weeks of captivity. Miranda has just tried to escape by hitting Clegg with a table leg she managed to dislodge. Desperate and willing to try anything, she offers him her body. Clegg resists because he "can't make love properly."

(MIRANDA, *wearing a housecoat, comes from the dressing room with her blood-stained dress, which she puts to soak in a bowl of cold water. She goes to the dressing table and studies her forehead in the mirror. She opens one of the drawers in the dressing table and notices the underwear supplied by* CLEGG, *holding up a black bra and stockings. Thoughtfully, she selects the most provocative underwear and returns to the dressing room.*

The door swings silently open and CLEGG *enters cautiously. He listens.* MIRANDA *coughs.* CLEGG *creeps slowly towards the dressing room, peers through a gap in the plastic door, then silently returns to the main door. Carefully he slides the bolts forward then slams them open. He knocks on the door, smiling as he does so.*)

MIRANDA: (*off*) Don't tell me who it is—let me guess.

(CLEGG *locks the door and straightens the rug.*)

CLEGG: You've come round then?
MIRANDA: (*off*) How's your head?
CLEGG: I'm lucky not to be dead. (*He sits on the bed.*)
MIRANDA: (*coming from the dressing room*) I apologize. Sincerely. I'm very sorry. I was wrong. Violence begets violence. Serves me right.
CLEGG: Fine pacifist you are.
MIRANDA: I know, I'm sorry. (*She looks at his forehead solicitously.*) Let me see. It's all right, I'm not going to hurt you.
CLEGG: Ow—ouch...
MIRANDA: Did you wash it?
CLEGG: Ow—yes.
MIRANDA: Not with antiseptic?
CLEGG: Oh, come on—it's all right. What's the game now?
MIRANDA: I'm very sorry I did what I did and I should like to thank you for not retaliating—you had every right to.
CLEGG: I accept your apologies. How's *your* head?

MIRANDA: Just bruised. (*She turns his hand, looking at his watch.*) How long was I out for?

CLEGG: I've been gone about an hour.

MIRANDA: Couldn't have been long, then. (*still holding his hand*) What have you been doing?

CLEGG: Having a bath.

MIRANDA: Mmmm. I thought so. You smell all talcum powdery. (*She coughs, suddenly and violently.*)

(CLEGG *rises and breaks away to the kitchen.*)

CLEGG: Can I get you anything?

MIRANDA: A very large drink.

(CLEGG *pours two drinks. She takes a drawing block and pencil from the bookcase.*)

Will you pose for me?

CLEGG: You don't want to draw me.

MIRANDA: I do.

CLEGG: What for?

MIRANDA: It'll give me something to remember you by.

(*He hands her a drink then sits on the bed. She draws.*)

Ferdinand . . .

CLEGG: Yes?

MIRANDA: I want you to help me.

CLEGG: Carry on.

MIRANDA: I've got a friend—a girl—who's got a man in love with her.

CLEGG: Oh yes.

MIRANDA: He's so much in love he's kidnapped her.

CLEGG: What a coincidence.

MIRANDA: Isn't it? Well—she wants to be free again. (*She lies full-length on the floor in front of him, still drawing.*) This girl doesn't know what to do. What would you advise?

CLEGG: Patience.

MIRANDA: What must happen before he'll release her?

CLEGG: Anything might happen.

MIRANDA: All right. Don't let's play games. (*She turns, lying on her back, looking up at him.*) Tell me what I must do to be set free? Marriage is no good, you can't trust me.

CLEGG: Yet.

MIRANDA: If I went to bed with you? Well—would you like to have me?

CLEGG: I didn't think you were that sort.

MIRANDA: I'm just trying to find your price.

CLEGG: Like a washing machine?

MIRANDA: Oh, God! Just answer yes or no. Do you want me to go to bed with you?

CLEGG: Not like we are now.

MIRANDA: What are we like now?

CLEGG: I thought you were supposed to be the clever one.

MIRANDA: You feel I'm just looking for a way to escape. Whatever I did would be for that?

CLEGG: Yes.

MIRANDA: If you felt I was doing it for some other reason— just for fun?

CLEGG: I can buy what you're talking about in London any time I like.

MIRANDA: Then you haven't got me here because you find me sexually attractive?

CLEGG: I find you very attractive—the most.

MIRANDA: Kiss me, then. (*He kisses her forehead.*) Not like that.

CLEGG: I don't want to.

MIRANDA: Why not?

CLEGG: I might—go too far.

MIRANDA: So might I. (*She unfastens her housecoat.*)

CLEGG: You know what I am.

MIRANDA: What are you?

CLEGG: Not the sort you like.

MIRANDA: Just relax. Don't be nervous. Don't be ashamed. Put the lights out. Let's just have the firelight.

(*He goes to the door, unlocks it, reaches round it and switches off the light. She stands. He locks the door.*)

What's wrong—Ferdinand?

CLEGG: Nothing's wrong.

MIRANDA: There's nothing to be frightened of.

CLEGG: I'm not frightened.

MIRANDA: Come back here, then. Come on.

(*He goes hesitantly towards her.*)

CLEGG: It's not right. You're only pretending.

(*She drops off her housecoat. She wears a black bra, panties, suspender belt and stockings.*)

MIRANDA: Am I?

CLEGG: You know you are.

MIRANDA: (*gently*) Come here.

(*She kisses him, taking off his jacket as she does so. She unbuttons his shirt, slips it off his shoulders and pulls him on to the bed. She kisses him, puts his hands round her waist, and begins to unbutton his trousers.*)

CLEGG: No—please—I can't—I can't . . .

MIRANDA: You can't make love properly?

CLEGG: Mmmmm.

MIRANDA: It doesn't matter. It happens to lots of men. Doesn't it please you when I touch you? You seemed to like it when I kissed you.

CLEGG: It's when it gets past the kissing. It's not your fault. I'm not like other people. I dream about it but—it can't ever be real.

MIRANDA: Who told you that?

CLEGG: Doctor. A psychiatrist.

MIRANDA: What sort of dreams did you have about me?

CLEGG: All sorts.

MIRANDA: Sexy ones?

CLEGG: I'd be holding you. You'd be asleep. With the wind and the rain outside or something like that.

MIRANDA: Would you like to try that now?

CLEGG: It wouldn't do any good. I wish you'd never started this.

MIRANDA: Why do you think I did it? Just to escape?

CLEGG: Not—love.

MIRANDA: You must realize that I've sacrificed all my principles tonight because I want to help you. To show you that sex—sex is just an ordinary activity. People jeer and titter and make it dirty, but it's not. Anything two people do in love isn't dirty. I did something for you out of a *kind* of love. I think you owe me something. (*She pulls her housecoat on.*)

CLEGG: (*dressing*) What?

MIRANDA: At least try to understand.

CLEGG: Yes.

MIRANDA: Is that all?

CLEGG: I don't feel like talking.

MIRANDA: You could have told me. You could have stopped me at the very beginning.

CLEGG: I did. I tried.

MIRANDA: You must understand. It was a *kind* of love. It's fantastic. We're further apart than ever.

CLEGG: You hated me before. Now I suppose you despise me as well?

MIRANDA: I pity you. I pity you for what you are and for not understanding.

(CLEGG *exits*.)

DUET FOR ONE
by Tom Kempinski

SESSION 3

Stephanie Abrahams came to Dr. Feldmann, a German psychiatrist practicing in London, for a consultation. She came, she said, because "my husband thought I was fairly upset with things and might benefit from some kind of I don't know, support or guidance, and I agreed with him."

As the playwright describes her, "she is a striking-looking woman, middle-class, well educated...outspoken, often aggressive, witty...sarcastic sometimes, and seemingly confident." Stephanie has worked hard her entire life to become a respected concert violinist. She is now thirty-four years old, and she has succeeded in her dream. She seemed to be achieving everything she ever wanted: a career as an esteemed artist, a loving husband, wealth, an exciting life. And then she was struck with multiple sclerosis. The deteriorating muscular control has already begun. She will no longer be able to play the violin.

Stephanie enters the office in an electrically powered wheelchair. She immediately asserts her independence and communicates her disrespect for Feldmann. She has overcome adversities in the past, and she will do the same now. She is a realist. She has new goals and new plans: teaching, and assisting her husband, David, in his career as a world-famous composer.

But she has also thought about suicide, and sometimes, when she is feeling quite all right, "really," tears just "suddenly start coming, flooding down."

Dr. Feldmann, who "gives off the real feeling that one's problems are understood and sympathized with," tries to help Stephanie face her despair, her fear about the future of her marriage, her deep sense of defeat, and her underlying hopelessness about what life has in store for her. She fights him every step of the way. Her defenses include aloofness, insults, intellectual challenges, seduction—and silences that are excruciating for both of them.

This scene is their third session. Stephanie left the previous session enraged by Feldmann's suggestion that she might be worried that her husband will leave her. The lights come up as Stephanie is talking.

(STEPHANIE *and* FELDMANN *are both in their seats, he comfortably leaning back slightly, she tense, and sitting with her back to him.*)

STEPHANIE: . . . In fact, if David *hadn't* asked me to come back again, I do assure you, you wouldn't have seen me for dust again, ever. However, he *did* ask me to come back again, so to please him, I have, and he asked me to apologize, so to please him and only to please him, I'll do that too. I'm sorry.

(FELDMANN *smiles.*)

FELDMANN: I don't get the feeling from your tone that you mean that.

STEPHANIE: In which case my tone is an accurate reflection of my thinking, Dr. Feldmann.

FELDMANN: I understand. So you came back purely because your husband has asked you to do so?

STEPHANIE: You've understood my English perfectly. For the first time, I might add.

FELDMANN: But you did come for your own reasons too, of course.

STEPHANIE: Ah. Sorry. You obviously *didn't* understand my English perfectly. *Mea culpa* entirely, I'm sure. Very well, then, I'll try again. (*She now articulates each word very precisely with gaps between syllables.*) I own-ly—came—be-cause—my—huz-band—askt—me—toooo. Iz—th-at—cle-ar—nowww?

FELDMANN: Excuse me. I understood you to say that you never agreed with your husband on principle. If you agreed to what he asked on this occasion, presumably you therefore had your own reason for doing so, independent of merely his request.

STEPHANIE: Oh brilliant. Quite superb, in fact. Speaking as an ex-violinist, I must say, I always found logical people to be so tremendously, incredibly, *boring, if* you don't mind me saying so.

(*silence*)

I'm not sleeping well. I suppose it's those bloody other tablets you changed me on to. I either want to come off them entirely... No, come to think of it, I don't. I want some sleeping tablets.

FELDMANN: The irritability has disappeared, I take it.

STEPHANIE: Yes. As a matter of fact, it has. Though not with regard to your good self, I might add. There it has increased considerably.

FELDMANN: Are you waking up in the night, or do you have difficulty in getting to sleep at all? Or both?

(STEPHANIE *is still completely frozen towards him.*)

STEPHANIE: I have difficulty getting to sleep. Once asleep, I sleep perfectly well.

FELDMANN: I don't think sleeping tablets will be necessary. What time...?

STEPHANIE: Still terrified I'll kill myself, are we? Very bad for the great doctor's image, I imagine. But since I imagine most of your patients have committed suicide, perhaps one more will hardly register in the statistics. As long as they keep coming, and the money keeps flowing in, hmm? How can I kill myself anyway, on the pills? I thought they were precisely designed to lift your mood, so that you *didn't* kill yourself.

FELDMANN: It's true. They do lift your mood. If you were still, however, distressed in your thoughts, you might stop taking them, and then...

STEPHANIE: And then it's cutting-wrist time, is it?

FELDMANN: Is that how you imagine doing this to yourself?

(STEPHANIE *imitates* FELDMANN's *gesture of shrugging his shoulders and turning her hands face-up, back to him.*)

What time in the evening do you take the Imipramine?

STEPHANIE: Despite the fact that, of course you're quite right, and I'm a *desperate* case and can't cope at *all* at the moment, despite this *tragic* fact, I'm actually so busy all day and in the evening too, that I always forget to take them six hours after the others, and I take them when I go to the bathroom before going to bed, actually.

FELDMANN: Ah yes. I thought so. It is the Imipramine that is stopping you getting to sleep. Taken late, it affects some persons in this way. I think if you were to take them earlier by the amount of hours you find it takes you to get to sleep, you would find you had no further trouble.

STEPHANIE: (*sarcastically*) Wonderful!

(*silence*)

FELDMANN: Is there anything else you would like to discuss?

STEPHANIE: No.

FELDMANN: You do not wish to say anything about the matters we touched last time?

STEPHANIE: No.

(*pause*)

FELDMANN: Would you prefer to end this session early and leave now?

STEPHANIE: Frightfully big of you. I have paid my money, and shall stay.

FELDMANN: But you do not wish to talk about anything at all.

STEPHANIE: No.

FELDMANN: I see. (*pause*) I wanted us to discuss your father, as a matter of fact.

STEPHANIE: Really.

FELDMANN: Yes. I feel that you have mentioned him a number of times, but have not really said fully what you felt about him, what really went on between you, and so on, and yet you must have much to say about him, as he brought you up and so on. This is an important area we have to look at more closely.

(*silence*)

Did you love your father?

STEPHANIE: Of course.

FELDMANN: Did you get on well with him?

STEPHANIE: Very.

FELDMANN: But I received the impression that he was not very interested in your musical side.

STEPHANIE: You're quite mistaken.

FELDMANN: Oh really. Are you saying he approved of you becoming a concert violinist?
STEPHANIE: Exactly.

(FELDMANN *has written no notes. He knows this is all pointless.*)

FELDMANN: Miss Abrahams. We are really wasting our time with this type of defensive behaviour, you know.
STEPHANIE: Good.

(*pause*)

FELDMANN: I recall another patient I once tried to treat who also would not speak. The poor man wasted an enormous amount of money for nothing. He made me feel extremely guilty, I remember.
STEPHANIE: I suppose you're going to tell me that because he didn't talk to you, he went off and lead a miserable life, are you? Is that the moral for me of this little fairy tale?

(FELDMANN *smiles.*)

FELDMANN: Quite the contrary, as a matter of fact. He married an extremely rich woman, and all his symptoms disappeared. It was a very chastening experience for a young doctor, I assure you.
STEPHANIE: Don't think you're going to soften me up with these boring little tales of a failed doctor's life story. I'm fully aware of your little game, believe me.
FELDMANN: Sometimes the silence is as painful for me as it is for my patient, I assure you, Miss Abrahams.
STEPHANIE: How simply *awful* for you, Doctor.
FELDMANN: (*sighing*) It's true, I assure you.
STEPHANIE: Oh give it a rest, will you! You're lying. You're just telling lies to try and win me round. What do you take me for? You're lying; it's as plain as plain chocolate, mate....

(STEPHANIE *stops in mid-sentence, and stares into herself.* FELDMANN *waits a moment for something else. When nothing comes, he probes.*)

FELDMANN: (*quietly*) What is it, Miss Abrahams?
STEPHANIE: (*quietly, half to herself*) That's what I used to say to my father, when he invented some nonsense to try and get back into favour with me. That's what I used to say....

(*Slight pause.* STEPHANIE's *sarcastic defense is breached.*)

FELDMANN: Do you feel your father was often false with you?

STEPHANIE: (*quietly*) Yes. Pretty often. Yes. About my playing mostly, yes.

FELDMANN: In which way, precisely?

STEPHANIE: He'd upset me saying something unpleasant about my playing, and then, when I cried, he'd pretend he hadn't meant it. I wasn't convinced.

FELDMANN: When your mother was alive, she supported you in your endeavours of course, you said.

STEPHANIE: Totally, yes.

FELDMANN: Then how did you manage when she died?

STEPHANIE: I coped, I was upset. We've been through this before.

FELDMANN: Excuse me, what I meant was, how did you manage with regard to your playing?

STEPHANIE: Well—I suppose, at first, I suppose it was all right, because Daddy just went on regarding it as my little girl's hobby. (*slight pause*) Then—well, then I started to say I wanted to take it up seriously, for life, sort of thing. Well at first he just sort of pooh-poohed it, you know, "Yes, yes, tut, tut," and so on. And I started to dig my heels in and then the rows started. "I'll stop paying for your lessons; a wandering minstrel's no life for my daughter; scraping cat-gut for a living", and so on. So then I said I wouldn't do any school-work if he stopped me. (*During this speech, we more and more see a new side of her; it is the side that underpins her sarcasm and determination; a great strength, which grew out of her determined struggle against her father to pursue what she had to pursue—her music. She fought and triumphed. As the speech progresses, she reflects more and more this iron in her soul.*) I remember that row; it was one tea-time, after school. I had shepherd's pie. He was so furious when I said I wouldn't do my schoolwork. He couldn't believe I'd stand up to him, I mean cross him like that. He hit me. Here. And then he said that settled it, he *was* going to stop paying for my lessons—and he did. Actually did stop paying for my music lessons. And I didn't write an essay, do a sum, paint a picture, read a book; nothing. That went on for five weeks and three-and-a-half days. Then he paid again. (*pause*) Then he tried snidey things. He said he was tired after working all day for me; didn't I have any consideration practising when he was trying to get a bit of rest? I went and practised at a friend's, so he stopped that too. I think he wanted me back in the house to have me on hand to continue the battle. Then he tried saying my playing was absolutely wonderful, and I didn't need to practise so much; I was up to standard already. Incredible isn't it, really; so blatant, so transparent. I didn't budge an inch; three hours a day; every day, rain or shine. *And* did my homework too. Round three, he developed mysterious illnesses. Always very vague, but very painful; migraines, heart murmurs, back pains, so I had to do everything around the house; cramps, I don't know. One day I told him to hurry up and die, 'cos it would save a lot of doctors' bills, and I could use the money for my lessons. I remember that was during a cramp period. The cramps vanished miraculously and he knocked me over the blue armchair. . . . (*She stops again, hard-faced. Then she softens a little.*) He was just a little businessman, really, you know. He couldn't really grasp it. He couldn't really grasp what I was about at all; it wasn't . . . He just didn't, I don't know; there just wasn't anywhere in his head that could grasp it, you see. But he was determined. And he was bitter. And was lonely too, I suppose. And guilty. Everything jumbled. But very determined. "I want my child to be something better than me; better than a small-time shopkeeper; is a scraper something better, is it? Is that something better? It's for people's spare time. Something to discuss over dinner for the top people. But it's not serious. Be a doctor, a surgeon, they have women on boards of directors now. Be *something* useful. This is for fun, for amusement." Oh it was unending. (*She toughens.*) And I fought him every inch of the way. Every word, every comment, every innuendo, every insult. I read up about women artists, asked my teachers for examples. I went out every day and brought back some weapon to fight him with. (*Pause. not regretfully*) And gradually he weakened. He'd sulk. Long silences. Days he wouldn't speak. But I spoke. When he had nothing to say except sit there feeling sorry for himself, I'd come in with some story of a famous musician playing to some king or some famous person, or winning a prize. I piled on the attack the more he retreated, because he'd suddenly find new energy and come out with some violent, bitter bit of rubbish he'd heard somewhere from some idiot in the shop; a pianist committing suicide; that woman who played in the nude; artists were no better than scum, they were the most promiscuous people on the planet, it said so in the *Daily Mirror*, or some rag, *Tit-Bits* I think one bit of rubbish he found in. And then round four was crying and begging and pleading and what would become of him in his old age. I told him once he could come to my concerts on a stretcher. He was so respectable. So narrow. So petty in his horizons. Ugh! I hated him for it. . . .

(*long pause*)

FELDMANN: (*quietly*) And yet, wouldn't you have liked to please him, if it had been possible, if you could have, perhaps.

STEPHANIE: (*her voice hard*) I know you're the expert on the subconscious goings-on here, Dr. Feldmann, and maybe I did want to please him, but if I did, I didn't let myself know it. I didn't let it get into my thoughts. I knew what I had to do. It was meant, see. Meant. It was meant. And no handmade chocolate maker was going to stop me playing, see. Not my father, not the Pope, not the Chief Rabbi, not even God, if he'd joined in the objections. I knew where *I* was going. (*slight pause*) You won't be surprised to hear that I can't eat chocolate. Not since a long time ago.

(*long pause*)

FELDMANN: So you won?
STEPHANIE: Yes! I won. Bach or Plain Assorted. Which do you think's for people's spare time. Oh yes. Definitely. I definitely won.
FELDMANN: You showed great determination in the face of severe pressure, wouldn't you say so?
STEPHANIE: Yes.

(*slight pause*)

FELDMANN: (*quietly*) As you are showing it now, perhaps. You believe it can overcome all opposition, perhaps. From inside, from outside. Is that so?
STEPHANIE: Let's just say that it helps, wouldn't you say?

(*slight pause*)

FELDMANN: Tell me, please. What would you say you had gained as a prize from your victory?

(STEPHANIE *smiles a radiant smile from deep inside.*)

STEPHANIE: Oh Dr. Feldmann. Look around you. Look at

your tapes and your records. You know them; you listen to them. You don't really need me to answer that, do you?

FELDMANN: Nevertheless, I should like to hear what you have to say.

STEPHANIE: But why? Why? We know. We both know. Millions of people know, and we know. I can't tell you better than you know yourself.

FELDMANN: (*after a slight pause*) Miss Abrahams. You have just told me of a great struggle you engaged in to achieve a certain goal. I would like to hear your feelings about the results of that struggle.

STEPHANIE: Well, I don't feel sorry for Dad, or guilty, if that's what you mean.

FELDMANN: No, no. I meant music, Miss Abrahams.

(*Pause.* STEPHANIE *fills like a balloon with joy.*)

STEPHANIE: (*slowly at first*) Well—music. (*pause*) Music. Music, Dr. Feldmann, is the purest expression of humanity that there is. Because, you see, it's magic; but real magic, true mystery, not trickery. You can say it is sound, as speech is sound, as bird song is sound, but it isn't. It's itself. A piece of music which expresses pain or sorrow, or loneliness, it sounds nothing like what a lonely man says or does, but it expresses it, and even better than the person does. Magic. You see, there's no God, you know, Dr. Feldmann, but I know where they got the idea; they got it from music. It is a kind of heaven. It's unearthly. It lifts you out of life to another place. That was my prize, that's what I won.

(STEPHANIE *is utterly radiant.* FELDMANN *has built to this moment. Now he picks the fruit of his skillful husbandry.*)

FELDMANN: (*quietly*) And now?

(STEPHANIE *carries her radiance over into her next speech. But quite soon tears begin to flow, and she cries, but not from the depth of her high-flown feelings, but from their opposite, as from deep, deep down, her feelings answer* FELDMANN'S *question because she is admitting for the first time that she can no longer make music, and the pain of that. So as she persists, by determination, in her sublime feelings on the surface, the depth of her anguish shows through, forces its way to the top, try as she may to keep it down. She talks through her sobs, over them, coughs them down, wipes them away, cries and talks at the same time; but gradually the truth asserts itself, and destroys her great pretence.*)

STEPHANIE: Now I shall pour my magic into others; who will make my sounds for me. They'll come to me because they know I climbed the peaks, made peaks of my own that weren't even there before, and then climbed those too. (*She begins to cry.*) At first they will only be able to scale the lower slopes. And then, in struggle and great joy, in pain and ecstasy, they'll climb too. And they'll do it because I shall pour my magic through their souls; my hand will be near to steady them when they threaten to fall or turn aside and my strength will give them strength. (*She is suppressing and releasing gulps of anguish by now.*) I have a special room in my house where I practise. It's blue. . . . (*shuddering gulps of weeping shake her entire body*) I—can never—never—play—the —the—the—violin again! Never—never—never—never—never again. What do hulks do, Dr. Feldmann? (*She is in despair.*) You see, Dr. Feldmann, you can't change this condition with determination.

HOPSCOTCH
by Israel Horovitz

In a playground overlooking Lake Quannapowitt in Wakefield, Massachusetts, a young woman is playing hopscotch. Suddenly she speaks to a man who has been watching her from a distance. At first it may seem as if these two people are strangers. But as their conversation continues, a shared past is revealed. Elsa was sixteen when she became pregnant with Will's child. He didn't wait around to settle into the dull routine of small-town living. He had the world to see and he left Wakefield. Now, almost fifteen years later, he's back for a visit.

As the play progresses, the bitter truth of Elsa and Will's relationship emerges through subtle hints and innuendos. She strings him along until the passionate hatred for the man she once loved can no longer be contained.

(ELSA *is discovered, drawing hopscotch grid on asphalt with yellow chalk. She throws a pebble into the first square and hops to it, picks it up, continues hopping to end of grid, turns, returns to starting position: her game has begun. Music plays to completion. As* ELSA *plays, we sense she is bothered by something or someone offstage, beyond auditorium. As music fades out,* ELSA *calls out into and above auditorium.*)

ELSA: You like what you're seein'?

(*No response. She returns to her game. When she reaches the end of the grid, she turns, stops, calls out again.*)

Hey, c'mon now, will ya! If you're gonna gawk, gawk from where I can gawk back! Fair's fair!

(*No response. She throws pebble; plays.*)

I'll turn my back, I won't watch. You can either come out and show yourself . . . or go away. . . . (*Pause. Calls louder*) Either way's okay with me! You gotta do one or the other, okay?

(*She turns her back to auditorium. A moment of silence passes.*)

(*A young man,* WILL, *appears in auditorium. He will stop a moment and then walk swiftly and directly onto stage, directly to* ELSA. *He will never alter his course, once he begins to move to her. She turns; sees him. She is obviously frightened.*)

I'm not frightened, you know . . .

(WILL *continues his move to her.*)

This place is crawling with people, you know that?

(ELSA *is frozen in fear.* WILL *continues to move to her.*)

You better just back down, huh? This place is crawling with people . . . I mean, there's no danger here, right? . . .

(WILL *reaches* ELSA. *He takes her in his arms and kisses her on the lips. She is overwhelmed by his size and acquiesces, at first, to his embrace and kiss. She then responds with noticeable strength and emotion. They hold their kiss awhile. They break apart, holding a fixed stare between them.*)

That was a good one . . . (*She smiles. She throws pebble.*) Strong silent type, huh? (*hops*)

WILL: (*looking in baby carriage*) Where's the baby?

ELSA: Playing. Why?

WILL: Yours?

ELSA: Sure. (*She throws the pebble and begins her hopscotch game again.*)

WILL: Where's your husband? Working?

ELSA: It's daytime, isn't it? (*points to sky*) That big round bright thing up there's the sun. When you can see it, you can pretty much figure it's daytime. And when it's daytime, people are working.... (*smiles*) Most people.

WILL: This what you do for a living?

ELSA: (*smiles*) Naw. Not yet. I'm not turning pro till after the next Olympics....

(*She throws pebble again and plays.* WILL *sits and watches a moment.*)

ELSA: You married?

WILL: Me? Naw.

ELSA: Ever close?

WILL: To being married? (*pauses*) Naw. Not even close.

ELSA: How come?

WILL: I looked around me. All my married friends were spending their weekends playin' softball. Their wives were home spending their weekends complaining about bein' left alone...while their husbands were playin' softball.

ELSA: That's why?

WILL: Sure. I hate softball. All's I needed was to get married and haveta start bullshit like *that*! You know what I mean? (*He smiles.*)

ELSA: You've got a lotta charm and a wonderful sense of humor.

WILL: You noticed?

ELSA: MMMmmm. I never miss a trick. (*She begins to play again.*)

WILL: I see you waited....

ELSA: For what?

WILL: Babies.

(*She stops. She looks at him, suddenly. He nods to carriage.*)

WILL: I could tell from the age. Still in a carriage and all.

ELSA: (*She plays.*) Oh, yuh. I waited. (*She smiles.*)

WILL: Boy or girl?

ELSA: Well, now. It's gotta be one or the other, right?

WILL: Nine chances outta ten, yuh.

ELSA: Girl.

WILL: Name?

ELSA: Lorali.

WILL: How's that again?

(*She throws.*)

ELSA: Lorali. (*She plays.*)

WILL: That's pretty. Yours?

ELSA: (*Stops, looks at him*) My name?

(*He smiles.*)

ELSA: The same: Lorali. (*She resumes play.*) I'm Lorali the Second, she's Lorali the Third. My grandmother was Lorali and my mother was Lorali, Junior... (*smiles*) Very common name around these parts. (*She throws.*)

WILL: No kidding. I never heard it in my life before, now I hear of four of them... And in a jerk town, like Wakefield, too....

ELSA: Very well known and very well respected name, too.... (*She plays.*)

WILL: Around these parts, huh? (*stands*) Wakefield, Massachusetts, United States of America, North America, Western Hemisphere, Earth, Universe, Infinity... New England. (*smiles*) I'm very deep.

ELSA: Oh, yuh. So's the lake.

WILL: What d'ya call it?

ELSA: The lake?

WILL: Yuh. The lake.

ELSA: Janet. I call it Janet. (*She turns to him.*) See these shoes? (*points to her shoes*) These are the twins. (*nods to bench*) The bench is Nanny Mary Poppins and you are what we see of Silver as he rides off into the sunset: a horse's ass! (*stops, controls her anger by turning away from him*) Unbelievable! (*faces him again*) Lake Quannapowitt. Named for the local Indians... a tribe that vanished.

WILL: Oh, right... I forgot.

(*Silence. Ten count*)

ELSA: (*She plays.*) You wanna know about my husband? (*stops at 10*)

WILL: Sure. What does he do for a living? Break backs?

ELSA: Naw. Not for a living; he just breaks backs as a weekend hobby kind of thing...

WILL: He sounds nice...

ELSA: He's a minister.

WILL: No kidding?

ELSA: No kidding.

WILL: What kind of minister?

ELSA: Protestant.

WILL: A Protestant minister. You don't say? What denomination?

ELSA: (*She will hop backward one square as she speaks each word or phrase.*) Baptist. (*pauses*) Blond. (*pauses*) Blue eyes. Both of them....(*pauses*) Six-five-and-a-half...(*pauses*) Square jaw, thick neck . . . (*pauses*) He's a hunk. (*She crosses to* WILL.)

WILL: He is?

ELSA: Mmmm...

WILL: A hunk?

ELSA: Mmmmm...

WILL: Of what?

ELSA: Huh?

WILL: A hunk of what?

(ELSA *returns to grid, resumes game.*)

ELSA: You just passing through . . . or are you planning to start a business here? Hey! Maybe pizza. (*smiles*) Santoro hit it big with subs—maybe you could be pizza. Wakefieldians eat a hell of a lot of pizza. A pizza palace with a real gimmick could be a real hot-shit success!

WILL: Anybody ever tell you you've got a mouth like a toilet?

ELSA: (*stops*) Oh, yuh. Coupla guys. They didn't get too far with me, though . . . not with an obvious line like that. (*smiles*) You know . . . maybe a quick feel, but nowhere solid. (*pauses*) I've never been a sucker for an obvious come-on line. I like something more subtle. . . .

WILL: (*stands*) A gun, a knife? That sort of thing?

ELSA: No. Uh uh. (*smiles*) Money's more what I had in mind.

WILL: (*after pretending to fish in his pockets*) Jeez . . . what a shame! (*He crosses to the grid, smiles.*) I used all my spare change on the train from North Station. . . .

ELSA: (*She plays to 10 and back, stops.*) Hey, well, listen! You can't win 'em all! I had a guy here just the other aftanoon . . . a real blowah . . . real bullshit ahtist type, ya know. . . . He tried to pay me with magic beans. . . .

WILL: No kidding?

ELSA: No kidding.

WILL: Was he youngish?

ELSA: Yuh, youngish . . .

WILL: Sho't?

ELSA: Yuh. Wicked sho't. Nearly teensy. . . .

WILL: Was he leading a cow on a rope?

ELSA: That's him!

WILL: (*sits on bench*) Never heard of 'im. (*pauses, changes attitude suddenly*)

ELSA: (*plays again*) You do night work, huh?

WILL: Huh?

ELSA: You work anywhere?

WILL: Yuh. I work.

ELSA: What kind?

WILL: I work for a big company. . . . Construction.

ELSA: Oh, really? You construct things?

WILL: Me, personally? Nope. Opposite. I tear things down. I'm in the destruction end. . . . Wrecking.

ELSA: (*She moves to* WILL *at bench.*) Gee, it, well, sounds like you've done really well with yourself . . . very successful. (*pauses*) Wrecking, huh? (*pauses*) They pay you a lot of money to do that? (*She sits beside* WILL *on bench.*)

WILL: Money? Sure, well . . .

ELSA: Sounds like it took a lot of schooling. . . .

WILL: Schooling? Well, I . . .

ELSA: You have a big desk? . . .

WILL: C'mon . . .

ELSA: . . . a big *position!*

WILL: You s'posed ta be *cute* now or somethin'?

ELSA: Me? Cute? Uh-uh.

WILL: (*forces a calm pitch to his voice*) I have a middle-sized position. . . . Middle management, they call us. (*smiles*) It's a middle-sized position.

ELSA: Do you like it?

WILL: (*yells*) My position? Do I like my middle-sized position?

(*There is an embarrassed pause.*)

I'm still awful tired from traveling. My nerves are all edgy. . . .

ELSA: Don't sweat it. (*hops*) I can understand that. . . .

THE AMERICAN CLOCK
by Arthur Miller

Act II

The American Clock is about the effect of the Great Depression on people who believed "with all their hearts" in the American dream. As one character puts it, "By the year 1929 you had a general belief that every American was inevitably going to get richer every year."

No one held that belief more strongly than the Baum family. One day Moe Baum had a successful business and a fortune in stocks. The next day the market crashed and Moe and his wife, Rose, and their son, Lee, and Grandpa, who had emmigrated from Europe, were struggling to survive. We see the collapse of their lives and the collapse of the American spirit through the eyes of Lee Baum, as he matures from a carefree boy into a young radical and then into a weary middle-aged sportswriter who still can't quite understand how it all happened.

At the time of the scene below, Lee is living on his own, on relief. As the scene begins, he tells the audience about Edie. "Any girl with an apartment of her own was beautiful. She made thirty-six dollars a week. She was one of the dialogue writers for the *Superman* comic strip."

LEE: Edie, can I sleep here?

EDIE: Oh, hi, Lee—yeah, sure. Let me finish and I'll put a sheet on the couch. If you have any laundry throw it in the sink. I'm going to wash later. (*He stands behind her as she works.*) This is going to be a terrific sequence.

LEE: It's amazing to me how you can keep your mind on it.

EDIE: Why! Superman is one of the greatest teachers of class consciousness.

LEE: Really?

EDIE: Of course. He stands for justice. You can't have justice under capitalism, so the implications are terrific.

LEE: You're beautiful when you talk about politics, you know that? Your face gets an emanation—

EDIE: (*smiling*) Don't be such a bourgeois horse's ass.

LEE: Edie, can I sleep in your bed tonight?

EDIE: Where'd you get an idea like that?

LEE: I'm lonely.

EDIE: Why don't you join the Party, for God's sake?

LEE: Aren't you lonely?

EDIE: (*flushing*) I don't have to go to bed with people to be connected to mankind.

LEE: Forget I said that, will you? I'm ashamed of myself.

EDIE: I don't understand how a person who knows Marxism can hold aloof from the struggle. You're lonely because you refuse to be part of history. Why don't you join the Party?

LEE: . . . I guess I don't want to ruin my chances; I want to be a sportswriter.

EDIE: Well maybe you could write for the *Worker* sports page.

LEE: The *Daily Worker* sports page? It's a joke.

EDIE: Then help improve it.

LEE: Tell me the truth. You really think this country can go socialist?

EDIE: Where have you been? We're living in the middle of the greatest leap in class consciousness that's ever happened. Hundreds of people are joining the Party every week! Why are you so goddamn defeatist?

LEE: I was in Flint, Michigan, when the sit-down strikes started. I thought I'd write a feature story, try to sell it. It was a very confusing experience. The solidarity was enough to bring tears to your eyes. But I interviewed about thirty of them afterwards. You ought to talk to them.

EDIE: Well they're still backward. I know that.

LEE: They're not backward, they're normal. Normally anti-Semitic, anti-Negro, and anti-Soviet. They're building unions and that's good, but inside their heads it's full of fascism.

EDIE: How can you say a thing like that?

LEE: I talked to thirty men, Edie, and I found one who even knew what socialism was. There's an openly fascist organization in Detroit—the Knights of the White Camellia—

EDIE: I know that—

LEE: It's full of auto workers. All I mean is—I'm afraid there isn't going to be time to save this country. I mean—you're afraid too, aren't you? Or are you?

EDIE: You really want my answer?

LEE: I do, yes.

EDIE: Tomorrow we're picketing the Italian consulate; Mussolini's sending Italian troops into the Spanish civil war. Come. Do something. You love Hemingway so much, read what he just said. "One man alone is no fucking good." As decadent as he is, even he's learning. If you want to be any good you've got to believe. It really is the final conflict, like the song says. They're fighting it out in Spain and they're going to win; the German workers are going to rise up any day now and destroy Nazism. . . .

LEE: Your face gets so beautiful when you—

EDIE: Anyone can be beautiful if what they believe is beautiful. I believe in my comrades. I believe in the Soviet Union. I believe in the victory of the working class here and everywhere, and I believe in the peace that will come to the world when the people take power.

LEE: . . . But what about now, Edie?

EDIE: Now doesn't matter. The future matters! (*She removes her hand from his and limps to her writing table.*) I've got to finish this strip. I'll make up the couch in a minute.

LEE: You're a marvelous girl, Edie. Now that I'm on relief I'll take you out to dinner—I'll pay, I mean.

EDIE: (*smiles*) You are something. Why must you pay for me just because I'm a woman?

LEE: Right. I forgot about that. (*He stands. She works. He saunters up behind her and looks at her work.*) Why don't you have Superman get laid? Or married even?

EDIE: He's too busy. (*She laughs softly as she works, and he suddenly leans down to kiss her, turning her face. She starts to respond, then pushes his hand away.*) What are you doing! (*He looks down at her, nonplussed. She seems about to weep, angry and flying apart.*) I thought you were a serious person! (*She stands.*)

LEE: You suddenly looked so beautiful. . . .

EDIE: But you don't want me! Why do you make everything trivial? You have no real faith in anything, do you?

LEE: Must I agree with everything you believe before I can—

EDIE: Yes! It is all one thing. Everything is connected. The same cynicism you look at the auto workers with lets you pretend to have a serious conversation when all you want is to jump into my bed.

LEE: I can't see the connection between the auto workers and—

EDIE: I have to ask you not to sleep here.

LEE: Edie, because I don't go along with all your ideas, is that—

EDIE: I'm asking you to leave. You are not a good person! (*She bursts into tears, gets up, and goes into the dark.*)

MODIGLIANI
by Dennis McIntyre

Act 1, Scene 4

For ten years Modigliani has been living and painting in Paris. For ten years he has worn shabby clothes, slept on cots in cold, damp studios, and borrowed money to eat. The struggle has taken its toll. He is a tormented and frightened man, torn between wanting to stop painting and being unable to do so. He gets drunk whenever he gets close to alcohol and is given to violent outbursts to release his frustration. Tonight, after sneaking into an elegant restaurant just "to stare at a few of Lautrec's ladies," he was chased by indignant waiters and broke a window and cut his hand before he fled.

With the police after him, Modigliani runs to the apartment of Zbo, a down and out art dealer who believes in the artist's talent. Good news awaits. Zbo has managed to interest Guillaume Chéron, a famous art dealer, in one of Modigliani's sketches. Instead of cheering him, the news frightens Modigliani even more. Chéron won't buy anything. His struggle is useless. He has no talent.

Still terrified of the police and dreading his meeting with Chéron, Modigliani returns to the studio he shares with his mistress, Beatrice, a poet.

(*He picks up the hammer. He begins to sculpt again.* BEATRICE *enters while he is sculpting. She watches him sculpt—pleased.*

She carries a basket. He begins coughing again—but he continues to work. The coughing becomes more and more violent—and he stops sculpting.)

BEATRICE: *(lighting the lamp)* How can you work in the dark?

MODIGLIANI: I was waiting for you.

BEATRICE: What?

MODIGLIANI: I was waiting for you—that's all. I was keeping busy.

BEATRICE: What'd you do to your hand?

MODIGLIANI: I cut it. *(the sculpture)* I was wiping off some dust.

BEATRICE: *(takes his hand)* Did you wash it?

MODIGLIANI: *(withdrawing his hand)* Yes.

BEATRICE: I know you didn't wash it—and you can't work with an open cut. *(She starts to move toward a basin. He takes her hand.)*

MODIGLIANI: Bea—I washed it. I put alcohol on it. It's not bleeding. I can make a fist. *(shows)* See? *(pulls her toward him)* I've got some good news.

BEATRICE: *(feeling it)* Take off your shirt first. You're soaked.

MODIGLIANI: I've only got one shirt. It's not that wet.

BEATRICE: *(moves—gets the blanket—drapes it over his shoulders)* Here. *(massaging his neck)* Max and I stayed up all night working on my poem. You're in it—you know. Two verses. I'm going to make you famous. What's your good news?

MODIGLIANI: Remember that night I drew you about twenty times?

BEATRICE: What night?

MODIGLIANI: ''Rosalie's.'' Max was treating. He'd just sold a poem. No—wait—we've got to celebrate. Is there anything to drink?

BEATRICE: *(points—the basket)* Whiskey. Half now— *(the sculpture)* half when you finish her.

MODIGLIANI: What'd you do? Steal it?

BEATRICE: Of course I stole it. Somebody's got to steal around here—you fucking aristocrat.

MODIGLIANI: *(takes out the bottle—raises the bottle to her—quotes)* ''Age cannot wither her—nor custom stale.''

BEATRICE: *(the whiskey)* Wait. *(He drinks. He coughs. She takes the bottle. She drinks.)*

MODIGLIANI: (*coughing*) Beatrice—if you're going to steal it—at least pick a better brand.

BEATRICE: (*coughing*) It sure tightens up your ass—doesn't it?

MODIGLIANI: (*runs his hands up and down her hips*) Yes—it does.

BEATRICE: (*moves away*) No—it's too cold. (*the sculpture*) And it's not finished.

MODIGLIANI: (*runs a hand over her shoulder*) Don't you want to hear my good news?

BEATRICE: What is it?

MODIGLIANI: I'll tell you in bed.

BEATRICE: But you've got the blanket—

MODIGLIANI: I'll share it.

BEATRICE: I'm not sleepy.

MODIGLIANI: I'll make you sleepy.

BEATRICE: All right—I'll go to bed. You sculpt.

MODIGLIANI: Later.

BEATRICE: No—now. Sculpt me asleep. (*He grabs at her. She jumps out of the way. They circle the room.*)

MODIGLIANI: Beatrice—

BEATRICE: What's that—Modigliani?

MODIGLIANI: If I catch you—

BEATRICE: Yes—Modigliani? (*He charges at her. She avoids him.*)

MODIGLIANI: Why'd you leave Capetown? It's near the sea—isn't it?

BEATRICE: Maybe I met a painter and had a child.

MODIGLIANI: (*charges—misses her*) Did you?

BEATRICE: Maybe my father caught me dancing in a saloon without my clothes and whipped me over the bar with a walking stick.

MODIGLIANI: (*charges—misses her*) Did he?

BEATRICE: Who knows? I've lived a very exciting life.

MODIGLIANI: (*charges*) Then how would you like a little more excitement?

(*He catches her. They fall on the bed. The bed collapses. They laugh—hug each other. A fierce love play. He begins unbuttoning her dress.*)

BEATRICE: I love you—Modigliani! Yes!

MODIGLIANI: Then how would you like to go to Martinique with me?

BEATRICE: Swim?

MODIGLIANI: I can't swim.

BEATRICE: So much for Martinique.

MODIGLIANI: Zbo's got me a dealer. That's my good news. He's coming on Friday.

BEATRICE: Zbo's always got you a dealer.

MODIGLIANI: (*seducing*) But this time it's true. Guillaume Chéron.

BEATRICE: Chéron? (*laughs*) Oh—Modi—

MODIGLIANI: (*seducing*) No—Zbo wrote him. He sent him a sketch of you. He loved it. I read the letter. Zbo's meeting him at the Rotonde terrace.

BEATRICE: Chéron?

MODIGLIANI: Yes.

BEATRICE: Guillaume Chéron?

MODIGLIANI: Yes. I hope the sun's out Friday. Chéron's used to the sun. He lives in Nice.

BEATRICE: (*coldly*) I know where he lives.

MODIGLIANI: What's the capital of Martinique?

BEATRICE: (*moves away*) Forget Martinique. He won't buy.

MODIGLIANI: What do you mean he won't buy? Hey—Bea— don't say that.

BEATRICE: Why not? Zbo couldn't sell Chéron a Da Vinci.

MODIGLIANI: Zbo can sell.

BEATRICE: What's he sold? Modi—Chéron's an important man. See him yourself.

MODIGLIANI: No.

BEATRICE: All he has to do is buy one painting.

MODIGLIANI: No—Bea—

BEATRICE: But you've got a better chance without Zbo.

MODIGLIANI: No!

BEATRICE: Don't you want to get sold? My God—Modi— Zbo limps into galleries with your paintings stuffed under his arms!

MODIGLIANI: Who cares how they arrive?! They get there— don't they?!

BEATRICE: And that's about all! Dealers care! They love to unwrap them. There has to be a string. Their fingers are trained. It's a ritual—and Zbo completely ignores it.

MODIGLIANI: They've got eyes—don't they?!

BEATRICE: Modi—it's the voice. It's the smile.

MODIGLIANI: They're both in my paintings!

BEATRICE: Dealers need a guide!

MODIGLIANI: And Zbo happens to know!

BEATRICE: Zbo knows who posed! Modi—he smells—

MODIGLIANI: I smell!

BEATRICE: But you know it. Modi—that beard—His clothes—He doesn't wear socks most of the time—His coat's ripped in the back—

MODIGLIANI: (*shows*) Zbo's money!

BEATRICE: (*points*) My whiskey! Does that make me an agent?!

MODIGLIANI: He's selling Hanka's dresses this afternoon so he can eat!

BEATRICE: Then he'll probably go hungry! Paintings—dresses—what's the difference?!

MODIGLIANI: (*rummaging*) What happened to the cigarettes?

BEATRICE: Who worships the Louvre?!

MODIGLIANI: Why didn't you steal some cigarettes?!

BEATRICE: Who painted them?!

MODIGLIANI: There's a reason!

BEATRICE: What? Your clothes? I'll wash them.

MODIGLIANI: No—there's a window—

BEATRICE: What window?

MODIGLIANI: Dealer's don't know—that's all!

BEATRICE: They know about Picasso!

MODIGLIANI: The bastard's a factory—that's why!

BEATRICE: So what?! He's got galleries on their knees!

MODIGLIANI: Zbo's worked for me—He trusts me—

BEATRICE: He envies you! He tried painting—and he can't paint. Did you ever see his sketch of Hanka? Ridiculous! He tried writing—and he can't write. Let go of him—Modi! Do it yourself. Do you think Picasso'd hang onto Zbo? No! Picasso's interested in museums! Picasso's interested in galleries! Picasso's interested in seeing his paintings hung on a wall—(*gestures—the studio*) not rolled up and shoved in drawers—or under the bed! What are you interested in?! (*He turns away.*) Damn you! Damn you—Modigliani! (*runs a hand over the sculpture*) You won't sell your work—and you won't work!

MODIGLIANI: I tried. I'll cough.

BEATRICE: Then paint! Remember painting?!

MODIGLIANI: Do you know what time it is?!

BEATRICE: What time is it?!

MODIGLIANI: (*flustered*) It's too cold to paint!

BEATRICE: (*Slaps it.*) It's my ass! (*begins to undress*) Another nude! Why not?! Let's enlarge Zbo's collection!

MODIGLIANI: There isn't enough paint.

BEATRICE: There's enough to start!

MODIGLIANI: Sure! If I scraped a painting and heated the chips!

BEATRICE: (*pointing*) There's a tube in the drawer—and one in that can!

MODIGLIANI: Two colors!

BEATRICE: Three! You'll probably cough on the canvas!

MODIGLIANI: What canvas?

BEATRICE: There's one left. Right over there. Against the wall. I'm meeting Max this afternoon—so we'll have to hurry.

MODIGLIANI: My line'd be off. There isn't enough light.

BEATRICE: Light has nothing to do with it! Stand by the window!

MODIGLIANI: The window's dirty!

BEATRICE: Then I'll open it for you.

MODIGLIANI: (*quickly*) There aren't any brushes—Good brushes—

BEATRICE: (*moves to the desk*) I saved one. (*opens a drawer*) I stuck it behind my poems. (*rummaging*) I stole it from Picasso. (*finds it*) Here.

MODIGLIANI: Bea—I'm not going to use Picasso's brush!

BEATRICE: It's a brush! It makes lines! Take it!

MODIGLIANI: One brush! What can I paint with one brush?!

BEATRICE: Me! All set—Modigliani? Should I lie on my stomach this time?

MODIGLIANI: My hand—I cut it—

BEATRICE: No—I've got it. Why don't I just sit down? Drape Zbo's money over my crotch. (*pushes him*) Let's go—Modigliani! You're supposed to be a painter—aren't you?! Then paint!

MODIGLIANI: I can't paint—I—

BEATRICE: Sure you can! Paint! (*pushes him*) Paint for Zbo!

MODIGLIANI: How?! My hand's bleeding!

BEATRICE: Go on! (*grabs his right hand*) Paint! (*He rips his hand away and slaps her across the face.*)

MODIGLIANI: (*as he slaps her*) No! (*Silence. She dresses.* MODIGLIANI *wandering.*) Bea—Bea—I'm hungry—

BEATRICE: Draw a restaurant.

ANNE OF THE THOUSAND DAYS
by Maxwell Anderson

ACT II, SCENE 7

Against the dictates of the Pope, Henry VIII divorces Katherine of Aragon and makes Anne Boleyn his second wife and Queen. Henry wants a male heir and he is willing to risk a complete break with the Catholic Church by exchanging his older wife (with whom he has a daughter) for the youthful and lovely Anne. In order to accomplish this monumental break he must be appointed and recognized head of the Church of England by his ministers. Most of Henry's lords are willing to do his bidding, but Sir Thomas More, his Lord Chancellor, is not. Encouraged by his new bride to "Let them die," Henry executes his opposition and becomes supreme head of the Church.

After a thousand days as Queen, Anne has given Henry only a daughter and several miscarriages. His love for her has begun to fade along with his hopes for a son when he meets Jane Seymour. Perhaps yet another wife will give him the heir he so desperately wants. Since Anne will not consent to a divorce, Henry accuses her of adultery and tacitly encourages his ministers to find her guilty of treason.

In the following scene Henry has come to ask Anne, for the last time, to consent to a divorce and avoid forcing him to have her executed.

HENRY: And yet it could be true. (*to* ANNE) You were no virgin when I met you.first. You told me as much. You knew what it was to have men.

ANNE: Have you stepped into your own trap, my lord? Any evidence you have against me you yourself bought and paid for. Do you now begin to believe it?

HENRY: (*looks at her steadily for a moment, then turns*) I was a fool to come here!

ANNE: Why did you come?

HENRY: Because I wanted to know!
Because I wanted to know! And still I
don't know!
And no man ever knows!

ANNE: Whether I was unfaithful to you?

HENRY: Yes! Just that! Whether you were unfaithful to me
while I loved you! But I'll never know! Whether you say aye
or no. I won't be sure either way! Fool that I am! That all men
are!

ANNE: There are fools and fools, King Henry.
You've shut me up here
to be tried for adultery and treason toward you.
You've done this because you love elsewhere—
and I know it—
But now you come here
to make sure whether there were truly adultery,
because that would touch your manhood—
or your pride!
And you wait and listen, a cat in a corner,
watching the pet mouse before it dies.
And then you come out—to make sure!
And, oh fool of fools,
even so, my heart and my eyes
are glad of you.
Fool of all women that I am,
I'm glad of you here!
Go then. Keep your pride of manhood.
You know about me now.

HENRY: Nan—

ANNE: Mind, I ask no pity of you—

HENRY: Nan! I have no wish to harm you.
I am much moved by what you said. I'd rather
a year cut out of my life than do you wrong.
After those words of yours.
Did you say—did you
say truly, you were glad of me here?

ANNE: I won't say it again.
But I did say it.
And it was true.

HENRY: Then,
let's do all this gently, Nan,

for old times' sake.
I have to prove that I can father a king
to follow me.
You and I,
we'll not have a son now.
God has spoken there.
Go quietly. Sign the nullification.

ANNE: No. We were king and queen, man and wife together. I keep that.
Take it from me as best you can.

HENRY: You do leave no choice.

ANNE: Would you let this grind on the way it's going?

HENRY: You would, if it served your purpose.

ANNE: I?

HENRY: I remember
Your saying, "Let them die," upon a time.
You've forgotten it, no doubt.

ANNE: No, I did say it.
These things look different from the other end.
If I'd known then what I feel now—
I couldn't have done it.

HENRY: No.

ANNE: I've been your wife.
Could you do it to me?

HENRY: Yes. If you stood in my way.
Defiantly. As you do.

ANNE: You're not old. You've been long a king.
But you're still young and could change.
You said—on that one day when we loved each other—
you remember—that one day when I loved you
and you loved me—that you would change—would seek justice—
would be such a king as men had hoped you'd be
when you came to the throne? It's not too late for that.
Only if you harden in your mind toward me,
and say, it's nothing, like the other rats and rabbits
let her be cut and torn and buried—
then I think it will be indeed too late.
The king—the great king
you might have been, will have died in you.

HENRY: Now I'll tell you truly.
I do want to begin again.
And I can't with you.
You brought me into blood—that bloody business

of the death of More and all the pitiful folk
who were like him and wouldn't sign.
Your hand was to that. It's blood-stained.

ANNE: And yours? Not yours?
Will you give back what you stole from the monasteries,
and the men executed?
Will you resume with Rome?
When you do that I'll take your word again,
But you won't do it. And what you truly want—
you may not know it—
Is a fresh, frail, innocent maid who'll make you feel
fresh and innocent again, and young again;
Jane Seymour is the name. It could be anyone.
Only virginal and sweet. And when you've had her
you'll want someone else.

HENRY: It's not true.

ANNE: Meanwhile, to get her,
you'll murder if you must.

HENRY: (*angry*) Why, then you've decided.—And so have I.

(*He starts away.*)

ANNE: (*flashing out*) Before you go, perhaps
You should hear one thing—
I lied to you.
I loved you, but I lied to you! I was untrue!
Untrue with many!

HENRY: This is a lie.

ANNE: Is it? Take it to your grave! Believe it!
I was untrue!

HENRY: Why, then, it's settled.
You asked for it. You shall have it.

ANNE: Quite correct.
Only what I take to my grave you take to yours!
With many! Not with one! Many!

HENRY: (*to* NORFOLK) She's guilty!
Proceed with this mummery.

AWAKE AND SING!
by Clifford Odets

Act II

Hennie Berger grew up in the poverty-caked streets of the Bronx during the Great Depression. She wanted more, but didn't know how to get it. Hennie thought she could escape the trap of her bickering, nagging family by finding a rich man to give her a new life. But it didn't work out that way. At 26, she found herself pregnant by a salesman who ran out on her when she told him of her predicament. Bitter and disillusioned, she married Sam Feinschreiber, a European, "a lonely man, a foreigner in a strange land" and gave her child a name and a home. A year later Hennie is at her wit's end, tired of the pampering husband she never loved and the endless days of washing diapers and trying to make ends meet on the meager salary that Sam brings home.

Moe Axelrod is in love with Hennie—or "Paradise," as he calls her. A friend of the Berger family and a product of the same struggling Bronx neighborhood, Moe went off to World War I and lost a leg. "Life has taught him a disbelief in everything, but he will fight his way through." Moe was Hennie's first lover and he believes he will always be "part of her insides." He's willing to fight for her, even if she did marry someone else.

Hennie's brother, Ralph, has just left the living room of the Berger apartment after telling Hennie and Moe that he won't settle for a shabby life of skimping and sacrifice, that he intends to carve out a future for himself through determination and hard work. Moe is now alone with Hennie and ready to make his pitch to her for a better life together.

MOE: The kid's a fighter! (*to* HENNIE) Why are you crying?
HENNIE: I never cried in my life. (*She is now.*)

MOE: (*Starts for door. Stops*) You told Sam you love him. . . .

HENNIE: If I'm sore on life, why take it out on him?

MOE: You won't forget me to your dyin' day—I was the first guy. Part of your insides. You won't forget. I wrote my name on you—indelible ink!

HENNIE: One thing I won't forget—how you left me crying on the bed like I was two for a cent!

MOE: Listen, do you think—

HENNIE: Sure. Waits till the family goes to the open air movie. He brings me perfume. . . . He grabs my arms—

MOE: You won't forget me!

HENNIE: How you left the next week?

MOE: So I made a mistake. For Chris' sake, don't act like the Queen of Roumania!

HENNIE: Don't make me laugh!

MOE: What the hell do you want, my head on a plate! Was my life so happy? Chris', my old man was a bum. I supported the whole damn family—five kids and Mom. When they grew up they beat it the hell away like rabbits. Mom died. I went to war; got clapped down like a bedbug; woke up in a room without a leg. What the hell do you think, anyone's got it better than you? I never had a home either. I'm lookin' too!

HENNIE: So what?!

MOE: So you're it—you're home for me, a place to live! That's the whole parade, sickness, eating out your heart! Sometimes you meet a girl—she stops it—that's love. . . . So take a chance! Be with me, Paradise. What's to lose?

HENNIE: My pride!

MOE: (*grabbing her*) What do you want? Say the word—I'll tango on a dime. Don't gimme ice when your heart's on fire!

HENNIE: Let me go! (*He stops her.*)

MOE: WHERE?

HENNIE: What do you want, Moe, what do you want?

MOE: You!

HENNIE: You'll be sorry you ever started—

MOE: You!

HENNIE: Moe, lemme go—(*trying to leave*) I'm getting up early—lemme go.

MOE: No! . . . I got enough fever to blow the whole damn town to hell. (*He suddenly releases her and half stumbles backwards. Forces himself to quiet down*) You wanna go back to him? Say the word. I'll know what to do. . . .

HENNIE: (*helplessly*) Moe, I don't know what to say.

MOE: Listen to me.

HENNIE: What?

MOE: Come away. A certain place where it's moonlight and roses. We'll lay down, count stars. Hear the big ocean making noise. You lay under the trees. Champagne flows like—(*Phone rings.* MOE *finally answers the telephone.*) Hello?...Just a minute. (*looks at* HENNIE)

HENNIE: Who is it?

MOE: Sam.

HENNIE: (*starts for phone, but changes her mind*) I'm sleeping....

MOE: (*in phone*) She's sleeping....(*Hangs up. Watches* HENNIE *who slowly sits*) He wants you to know he got home O.K....What's on your mind?

HENNIE: Nothing.

MOE: Sam?

HENNIE: They say it's a palace on those Havana boats.

MOE: What's on your mind?

HENNIE: (*trying to escape*) Moe, I don't care for Sam—I never loved him—

MOE: But your kid—?

HENNIE: All my life I waited for this minute.

MOE: (*holding her*) Me too. Made believe I was talkin' just bedroom golf, but you and me forever was what I meant! Christ, baby, there's one life to live! Live it!

HENNIE: Leave the baby?

MOE: Yeah!

HENNIE: I can't...

MOE: You can!

HENNIE: No...

MOE: But you're not sure!

HENNIE: I don't know.

MOE: Make a break or spend the rest of your life in a coffin.

HENNIE: Oh God, I don't know where I stand.

MOE: Don't look up there. Paradise, you're on a big boat headed south. No more pins and needles in your heart, no snake juice squirted in your arm. The whole world's green grass and when you cry it's because you're happy.

HENNIE: Moe, I don't know...

MOE: Nobody knows, but you do it and find out. When you're scared the answer's zero.

HENNIE: You're hurting my arm.

MOE: The doctor said it—cut off your leg to save your life! And they done it—one thing to get another.

CALIGULA
by Albert Camus (trans. by Stuart Gilbert)

Act I

When his sister Drusilla dies, Caligula is thrown into a crisis. The world is not what he thought it was, and for all his power as Emperor of Rome, he cannot change the fact that "men die and they are not happy." He roams the countryside by himself for three days trying to come to grips with the repugnant knowledge of his own powerlessness. When he returns to the place, he is a changed man. He now believes that the only way to experience true freedom is to attain the impossible: "to drown the sky in the sea, to infuse ugliness with beauty, to wring a laugh from pain." He does not care that in trying to grasp this impossible freedom he will have to sacrifice friendship, honor, justice, and love. Caligula the boy-emperor has become Caligula the monster.

In the scene below Caligula has just informed his senators that from now on his rule will be arbitrary and absolute—without regard to justice or the law. His mistress, Cæsonia, is stunned by his transformation. When they are alone she notices that he is distressed.

CÆSONIA: Crying?

CALIGULA: Yes, Cæsonia.

CÆSONIA: But, after all, what's changed in your life? You may have loved Drusilla, but you loved many others—myself included—at the same time. Surely that wasn't enough to set you roaming the countryside for three days and nights and bring you back with this . . . this cruel look on your face?

CALIGULA: (*swinging round on her*) What nonsense is this? Why drag in Drusilla? Do you imagine love's the only thing that can make a man shed tears?

CÆSONIA: I'm sorry, Caius. Only I was trying to understand.

CALIGULA: Men weep because . . . the world's all wrong. (*She comes toward him.*) No, Cæsonia. (*She draws back.*) But stay beside me.

CÆSONIA: I'll do whatever you wish. (*sits down*) At my age one knows that life's a sad business. But why deliberately set out to make it worse?

CALIGULA: No, it's no good; you can't understand. But what matter? Perhaps I'll find a way out. Only, I feel a curious stirring within me, as if undreamed-of things were forcing their way up into the light—and I'm helpless against them. (*He moves closer to her.*) Oh, Cæsonia, I know that men felt anguish, but I didn't know what that word anguish meant. Like everyone else I fancied it was a sickness of the mind—no more. But no, it's my body that's in pain. Pain everywhere, in my chest, in my legs and arms. Even my skin is raw, my head is buzzing, I feel like vomiting. But worst of all is this queer taste in my mouth. Not blood, or death, or fever, but a mixture of all three. I've only to stir my tongue, and the world goes black, and everyone looks . . . horrible. How hard, how cruel it is, this process of becoming a man!

CÆSONIA: What you need, my dear, is a good, long sleep. Let yourself relax and, above all, stop thinking. I'll stay by you while you sleep. And when you wake, you'll find the world's got back its savor. Then you must use your power to good effect—for loving better what you still find lovable. For the possible, too, deserves to be given a chance.

CALIGULA: Ah, but for that I'd need to sleep, to let myself go—and that's impossible.

CÆSONIA: So one always thinks when one is over-tired. A time comes when one's hand is firm again.

CALIGULA: But one must know where to place it. And what's the use is the amazing power that's mine, if I can't have the sun set in the east, if I can't reduce the sum of suffering and make an end of death? No, Caesonia, it's all one whether I sleep or keep awake, if I've no power to tamper with the scheme of things.

CÆSONIA: But that's madness, sheer madness. It's wanting to be a god on earth.

CALIGULA: So you, too, think I'm mad. And yet—what is a god that I should wish to be his equal? No, it's something higher, far above the gods, that I'm aiming at, longing for with all my heart and soul. I am taking over a kingdom where the impossible is king.

CÆSONIA: You can't prevent the sky from being the sky, or a fresh young face from aging, or a man's heart from growing cold.

CALIGULA: (*with rising excitement*) I want...I want to drown the sky in the sea, to infuse ugliness with beauty, to wring a laugh from pain.

CÆSONIA: (*facing him with an imploring gesture*) There's good and bad, high and low, justice and injustice. And I swear to you these will never change.

CALIGULA: (*in the same tone*) And I'm resolved to change them.... I shall make this age of ours a kingly gift—the gift of equality. And when all is leveled out, when the impossible has come to earth and the moon is in my hands—then, perhaps, I shall be transfigured and the world renewed; then men will die no more and at last be happy.

CÆSONIA: (*with a little cry*) And love? Surely you won't go back on love!

CALIGULA: (*in a wild burst of anger*) Love, Caesonia! (*He grips her shoulders and shakes her.*) I've learned the truth about love; it's nothing, nothing! That fellow was quite right—you heard what he said, didn't you—it's only the Treasury that counts. The fountainhead of all. Ah, now at last I'm going to live, really *live*. And living, my dear, is the opposite of loving. I know what I'm talking about—and I invite you to the most gorgeous of shows, a sight for gods to gloat on, a whole world called to judgment. But for that I must have a crowd—spectators, victims, criminals, hundreds and thousands of them. (*He rushes to the gong and begins hammering on it, faster and faster.*) Let the accused come forward. I want my criminals, and they all are criminals. (*still striking the gong*) Bring in the condemned men. I must have my public. Judges, witnesses, accused—all sentenced to death without a hearing. Yes, Caesonia, I'll show them something they have never seen before, the one free man in the Roman Empire. (*To the clangor of the gong the palace has been gradually filling with noises; the clash of arms, voices, footsteps slow or hurried, coming nearer, growing louder. Some soldiers enter, and leave hastily.*) And you, Caesonia, shall obey me. You must stand by me to the end. It will be marvelous, you'll see. Swear to stand by me, Caesonia.

CÆSONIA: (*wildly, between two gong strokes*) I needn't swear. You know I love you.

CALIGULA: (*in the same tone*) You'll do all I tell you.

CÆSONIA: All, all, Caligula—but do, please, stop. . . .
CALIGULA: (*still striking the gong*) You will be cruel.
CÆSONIA: (*sobbing*) Cruel.
CALIGULA: (*still beating the gong*) Cold and ruthless.
CÆSONIA: Ruthless.
CALIGULA: And you will suffer, too.
CÆSONIA: Yes, yes—oh, no, please . . . I'm—I'm going mad,
I think!

WAITING FOR LEFTY
by Clifford Odets

1. JOE AND EDNA

It is the middle of the Great Depression and Edna Mitchell is
fed up with poverty. Her husband, Joe, can barely eke out a
living as a taxi cab driver, bringing six to seven dollars a week.
Today their furniture was repossessed, the kids went to bed
without supper, and Edna doesn't even have enough money to
resole her little girl's shoes. After years of struggle and hardship
she's tired of seeing her husband exploited by the cab owners
and union racketeers, and tired of listening to Joe's vague
promises that things have to get better. Edna wants him to stand
up and fight for his right to earn a decent living. She wants him
to fight back and win some dignity as well as a livable wage.
She wants him to strike!

Joe protests. He's afraid to confront the bosses, afraid he'll get
hurt if he speaks up, and afraid of losing the little he has because
there are no other jobs. He's willing to wait out the hard times
without rocking the boat. Sick with disgust at his cowardice,
Edna threatens to leave if he doesn't start fighting for his family.

(*A tired but attractive woman of thirty comes into the room,
drying her hands on an apron. She stands there sullenly as* JOE
*comes in from the other side, home from work. For a moment
they stand and look at each other in silence.*)

JOE: Where's all the furniture, honey?

EDNA: They took it away. No installments paid.

JOE: When?

EDNA: Three o'clock.

JOE: They can't do that.

EDNA: Can't? They did it.

JOE: Why, the palookas, we paid three-quarters.

EDNA: The man said read the contract.

JOE: We must have signed a phoney. . . .

EDNA: It's a regular contract and you signed it.

JOE: Don't be so sour, Edna. . . . (*tries to embrace her*)

EDNA: Do it in the movies, Joe—they pay Clark Gable big money for it.

JOE: This is a helluva house to come home to. Take my word!

EDNA: Take MY word! Whose fault is it?

JOE: Must you start that stuff again?

EDNA: Maybe you'd like to talk about books?

JOE: I'd like to slap you in the mouth!

EDNA: No you won't.

JOE: (*sheepishly*) Jeez, Edna, you get me sore some time. . . .

EDNA: But just look at me—I'm laughing all over!

JOE: Don't insult me. Can I help it if times are bad? What the hell do you want me to do, jump off a bridge or something?

EDNA: Don't yell. I just put the kids to bed so they won't know they missed a meal. If I don't have Emmy's shoes soled tomorrow, she can't go to school. In the meantime let her sleep.

JOE: Honey, I rode the wheels off the chariot today. I cruised around five hours without a call. It's conditions.

EDNA: Tell it to the A & P!

JOE: I booked two-twenty on the clock. A lady with a dog was lit . . . she gave me a quarter tip by mistake. If you'd only listen to me—we're rolling in wealth.

EDNA: Yeah? How much?

JOE: I had "coffee and—" in a beanery. (*hands her silver coins*) A buck four.

EDNA: The second month's rent is due tomorrow.

JOE: Don't look at me that way, Edna.

EDNA: I'm looking through you, not at you. . . . Everything was gonna be so ducky! A cottage by the waterfall, roses in Picardy. You're a four-star-bust! If you think I'm standing for it much longer, you're crazy as a bedbug.

JOE: I'd get another job if I could. There's no work—you know it.

EDNA: I only know we're at the bottom of the ocean.

JOE: What can I do?

EDNA: Who's the man in the family, you or me?

JOE: That's no answer. Get down to brass tacks. Christ, gimme a break, too! A coffee and java all day. I'm hungry, too, Babe. I'd work my fingers to the bone if—

EDNA: I'll open a can of salmon.

JOE: Not now. Tell me what to do!

EDNA: I'm not God!

JOE: Jeez, I wish I was a kid again and didn't have to think about the next minute.

EDNA: But you're not a kid and you do have to think about the next minute. You got two blondie kids sleeping in the next room. They need food and clothes. I'm not mentioning anything else—But we're stalled like a flivver in the snow. For five years I laid awake at night listening to my heart pound. For God's sake, do something, Joe, get wise. Maybe get your buddies together, maybe go on strike for better money. Poppa did it during the war and they won out. I'm turning into a sour old nag.

JOE: (*defending himself*) Strikes don't work!

EDNA: Who told you?

JOE: Besides that means not a nickel a week while we're out. Then when it's over they don't take you back.

EDNA: Suppose they don't! What's to lose?

JOE: Well, we're averaging six–seven dollars a week now.

EDNA: That just pays for the rent.

JOE: That is something, Edna.

EDNA: It isn't. They'll push you down to three and four a week before you know it. Then you'll say, "That's somethin'," too!

JOE: There's too many cabs on the street, that's the whole damn trouble.

EDNA: Let the company worry about that, you big fool! If their cabs didn't make a profit, they'd take them off the streets. Or maybe you think they're in business just to pay Joe Mitchell's rent!

JOE: You don't know a-b-c, Edna.

EDNA: I know this—your boss is making suckers outa you boys every minute. Yes, and suckers out of all the wives and the poor innocent kids who'll grow up with crooked spines and sick bones. Sure, I see it in the papers, how good orange juice is for kids. But damnit our kids gets colds one on top of the other. They look like little ghosts. Betty never saw a grapefruit. I took her to the store last week and she pointed to stack of grapefruits. "What's that!" she said. My God, Joe—the world is supposed to be for all of us.

JOE: You'll wake them up.

EDNA: I don't care, as long as I can maybe wake you up.

JOE: Don't insult me. One man can't make a strike.

EDNA: Who says one? You got hundreds in your rotten union!

JOE: The union ain't rotten.

EDNA: No? Then what are they doing? Collecting dues and patting your back?

JOE: They're making plans.

EDNA: What kind?

JOE: They don't tell us.

EDNA: It's too damn bad about you. They don't tell little Joey what's happening in his bitsie witsie union. What do you think it is—a Ping-Pong game?

JOE: You know they're racketeers. The guys at the top would shoot you for a nickel.

EDNA: Why do you stand for that stuff?

JOE: Don't you wanna see me alive?

EDNA: (*after a deep pause*) No . . . I don't think I do, Joe. Not if you can lift a finger to do something about it, and don't. No, I don't care.

JOE: Honey, you don't understand what—

EDNA: And any other hackie that won't fight . . . let them all be ground to hamburger!

JOE: It's one thing to—

EDNA: Take your hand away! Only they don't grind me to little pieces! I got different plans. (*starts to take off her apron*)

JOE: Where are you going?

EDNA: None of your business.

JOE: What's up your sleeve?

EDNA: My arm'd be up my sleeve, darling, if I had a sleeve to wear. (*puts neatly folded apron on back of chair*)

JOE: Tell me!

EDNA: Tell you what?

JOE: Where are you going?

EDNA: Don't you remember my old boyfriend?

JOE: Who?

EDNA: Bud Haas. He still has my picture in his watch. He earns a living.

JOE: What the hell are you talking about?

EDNA: I heard worse than I'm talking about.

JOE: Have you seen Bud since we got married?

EDNA: Maybe.

JOE: If I thought . . . (*He stands looking at her.*)

EDNA: See much? Listen, boyfriend, if you think I won't do this it just means you can't see straight.

JOE: Stop talking bull!

EDNA: This isn't five years ago, Joe.

JOE: You mean you'd leave me and the kids?

EDNA: I'd leave *you* like a shot!

JOE: No . . .

EDNA: Yes! (JOE *turns away, sitting in a chair with his back to her. Outside the lighted circle of the playing stage we hear the other seated members of the strike committee. "She will . . . she will . . . it happens that way," etc. This group should be used throughout for various comments, political, emotional and as general chorus. Whispering . . . The fat boss now blows a heavy cloud of smoke into the scene.*)

JOE: (*finally*) Well, I guess I ain't got a leg to stand on.

EDNA: No?

JOE: (*suddenly mad*) No, you lousy tart, no! Get the hell out of here. Go pick up that bull-thrower on the corner and stop at some cushy hotel downtown. He's probably been coming here every morning and laying you while I hacked my guts out!

EDNA: You're crawling like a worm!

JOE: You'll be crawling in a minute.

EDNA: You don't scare me that much! (*indicates a half inch on her finger*)

JOE: This is what I slaved for!

EDNA: Tell it to your boss!

JOE: He don't give a damn for you or me!

EDNA: That's what I say.

JOE: Don't change the subject!

EDNA: This is the subject, the *exact subject*! Your boss makes this subject. I never saw him in my life, but he's putting ideas in my head a mile a minute. He's giving your kids that fancy disease called the rickets. He's making a jellyfish outta you and putting wrinkles in my face. This is the subject every inch of the way! He's throwing me into Bud Haas' lap. When in hell will you get wise—

JOE: I'm not so dumb as you think! But you are talking like a red.

EDNA: I don't know what that means. But when a man knocks you down you get up and kiss his fist! You gutless piece of baloney.

JOE: One man can't—

EDNA: (*with great joy*) I don't say one man! I say a hundred, a thousand, a whole million, I say. But start in your own union. Get those hack boys together! Sweep out those racketeers like a pile of dirt! Stand up like men and fight for the crying kids and wives. Goddamnit! I'm tired of slavery and sleepless nights.

JOE: (*with her*) Sure, sure! . . .

EDNA: Yes. Get brass toes on your shoes and know where to kick!

JOE: (*suddenly jumping up and kissing his wife full on the mouth*) Listen, Edna, I'm goin' down to 174th Street to look up Lefty Costello. Lefty was saying the other day . . . (*He suddenly stops.*) How about this Haas guy?

EDNA: Get out of here!

JOE: I'll be back! (*Runs out. For a moment* EDNA *stands triumphant.*)

JIMMY SHINE
by Murray Schisgal

ACT I, SCENE 1

Jimmy Shine is an oddball painter living in a Greenwich Village loft. After an unsuccessful week of trying to paint, he enlists the services of Rosie, a local prostitute, to alleviate his frustration and give him some human comfort. But today Rosie wants Jimmy to pay for his pleasures, especially since he forgot to the last time. They begin to quibble about the money when the phone rings. It is Elizabeth Evans, a girl that Jimmy loved in his youth who married his best friend.

(JIMMY SHINE *is seated against headboard in bed, a hairy piece stuck to his bare chest. He smokes a cigar, drinks from a can of beer, tosses it into paper basket, listlessly picks up a newspaper and tries to read it, gives up, calls to* ROSIE *who is in bathroom.*)

JIMMY: (*throws newspaper to floor, shouts*) Hey! (*no answer*) Hey!

ROSIE: Wha'?

JIMMY: You still in there?

ROSIE: No!

JIMMY: Come on out, huh?

ROSIE: Hold your horses. (*He gets up, wraps bedsheet around him.*)

JIMMY: How long you gonna be in there? (*He goes to bathroom door.*)

ROSIE: Will you leave me alone a minute? (JIMMY *opens door,* ROSIE *slams it shut, screaming "Jimmy!" She locks door.*)

JIMMY: (*sulking*) You're mad at me, aren't you?

ROSIE: I'm not mad at you.

JIMMY: You're mad at me. I can tell by your voice.

ROSIE: I'm not mad at you.

JIMMY: I'm rarely wrong about such things. Sooner or later everybody gets mad at me. It's been that way all my life. Hey!

ROSIE: (*shouts back from bathroom*) What?

JIMMY: You coming out?

ROSIE: I'll be out! I'll be out!

JIMMY: When? Next year? What am I supposed to do here, all by myself? That wasn't the deal, Rosie. The deal was that you were coming up here to stay with me, in bed, all morning, that was the deal. But you didn't keep the deal. You're like all the others. You're a non-deal keeper. (*knocks on bathroom door*) Rosie!

ROSIE: What?

JIMMY: Talk to me!

ROSIE: What's there to talk about?

JIMMY: Anything. About anything. I'm going out of my mind here. I've been locked up in this room for a week and I'm not painting, I'm not working...(*plays Beethoven 5th theme on piano*) Hanging around here I'm getting so sick and depressed. . . . Rosie!

ROSIE: What?

JIMMY: Talk to me.

ROSIE: Shh! Don't bother me now.

JIMMY: (*bends down and looks through keyhole*) You're mad at me, aren't you?

ROSIE: I'm not mad at you.

JIMMY: Why are you shaving the hair under your arm?

ROSIE: (*shouts*) Get away from that door, Jimmy!

JIMMY: That's the only blade I have so you'd better put it back where you . . . (*He pulls away from keyhole, his eye covered with shaving cream which Rosie has "shot" through the keyhole from a pressurized can.*) That's not funny, Rosie. I don't see anything funny about it. (*He scoops shaving cream off eye and chest-piece.*) Aw . . . you ruined my fur. (*takes chest-piece off and puts it under pillow on bed*)

ROSIE: (*entering from bathroom*) OK. Wha' d'you wanna talk about? Pull up the zipper.

JIMMY: (*doing so*) You didn't hear anything I said before, did you?

ROSIE: Wha'?

JIMMY: Forget it.

ROSIE: Wha' did you say?

JIMMY: Forget it, Rosie. Just forget it!

ROSIE: What's the matter? You've been picking on me all morning, I swear.

JIMMY: Picking on you! I'm trying to get some consideration, some sympathy out of you! Is that too much of one human being to ask from another human being?

ROSIE: (*takes mirror from wall, leans it against ice in sink, puts on jewelry*) Look, Jimmy, what I came up here to give you I gave you already so how about payin' me so I can get outta here?

JIMMY: You'd leave me alone, wouldn't you? In my present state of mind, you'd actually leave me alone.

ROSIE: You can go out, who's stoppin' you? You're 30 years old, you don't have to stay up here all by yourself.

JIMMY: That's easy for you to say. You have places to go, business to take care of.

ROSIE: So find another job. What's the big deal?

JIMMY: You really have a heart of gold, don't you. You like seeing me loading furniture, running errands, chopping off fish-heads. That appeals to you, doesn't it?

ROSIE: Why don't you go back an' paint? You got all your stuff up here. Painters make good money. . . .

JIMMY: Because I'm not painting any more. Because I haven't painted for a whole year. Because I got sick and tired of painting bones. Bones, bones, bones. (*sings*) "Dem bones, dem bones, dem dry bones, dem bones, dem bones, dem wet bones . . ."

ROSIE: (*takes blond wig out of large carry-all bag*) You could make somebody crazy, I swear. I'm goin'. (*Puts on wig in front of mirror. Jimmy goes into bathroom.*) Jimmy . . . (*He re-enters, with can of shaving cream, which he "threatens" Rosie with, she jumps onto bed.*) Cut it out, Jimmy.

JIMMY: Aha! I finally have you where I want you, Rosie Pitkin.

ROSIE: Never mind you finally have me where you want me. There's the matter of the ten bucks you owe me from last time and the ten bucks you owe me this time. . . .

JIMMY: I owe you ten bucks from last time?

ROSIE: Yeah, you owe me ten bucks from last time!

JIMMY: For what?

ROSIE: For what? For whatta you think!

JIMMY: Oh.

ROSIE: That's right.

JIMMY: I thought it was on the house last time.

ROSIE: (*starts to put on shoe*) On the house? I never did anything in my life on the house!

JIMMY: (*pulling her towards bed on one foot*) You wanna try?

ROSIE: No fooling around now, Jimmy. I ain't got all day. I got another appointment. Now will you just give me the money?

JIMMY: (*lying on bed*) All right, Rosie, you can take any painting you want.

ROSIE: What do I want with a painting? If you don't have the money, why don't you sell that piano-thing there? You could get a couple of hundred for it.

JIMMY: You really want the money.

ROSIE: Yes.

JIMMY: You went to bed with me for the money, is that it?

ROSIE: That's it.

JIMMY: No other reason.

ROSIE: No other reason. (JIMMY *sticks his thumb into mouth, turns away from* ROSIE, *snuggling into the sheets.* ROSIE, *shaking his shoulder*) Jimmy.

JIMMY: Leave me alone.

ROSIE: I want my money, Jimmy.

JIMMY: (*sits up in bed, shouts*) What's wrong with you? I'm dying! How can you keep nagging me about monetary remuneration?

ROSIE: I'm warning you, Jimmy...

JIMMY: All right, Rosie. If that's what you came for...(*pointing to pants on floor near bed*) There. The money's in the left-hand pocket. Take it and please go. (*starts to read newspaper*) We have nothing further of any consequence to talk about.

ROSIE: (*turning pants pocket inside out, one after another, all empty*) Why are you mad at me for? I'm the one who should be mad I have to fight with you....

JIMMY: (*as she searches*) Take whatever you find in there. I don't care. It's not even worth discussing. (*The telephone rings.* JIMMY *picks up receiver.*) When you hear the dial tone, you will be disconnected. (*He hangs up.*)

ROSIE: Jimmy, if you don't give me the money...

JIMMY: What are you talking about? I told you to take it from my pants pocket.

ROSIE: Your pants pocket? There's no money in your pants pocket! Look for yourself! (*She throws the pants at him.*)

JIMMY: (*wagging his head with feigned fury*) Don't you pull that gambit on me, Rosie Pitkin! I've been around too long to be taken in by that swindle! (*The phone rings again.* JIMMY *picks up receiver.*) Forty-third precinct, pickpocket division... Who? Elizabeth? No, no, everything's fine. It's...(*He gets up and takes the phone across the room as he talks.*) It's just such a surprise hearing from you, Elizabeth...Sure, sure you can come up...as soon as you can...(ROSIE *starts taking off her shoes.*) That's right, top floor...I'll be waiting...Right. (*He hangs up. To* ROSIE) It was Elizabeth.

ROSIE: (*starting to undress*) I'm delighted.

JIMMY: She's coming here!

ROSIE: Oh, that's nice.

JIMMY: Rosie, you have to go. She's coming up. She'll be here.

ROSIE: Let's make love, Jimmy. You've aroused my appetite.

JIMMY: Rosie, please. You can't stay. Not now!

ROSIE: First you give me my twenty bucks, Jimmy.

JIMMY: (*takes money from can on sink*) Look, here's ten dollars. Come back in a couple of hours and I'll give you the rest, I promise. (*He is putting her shoes in her handbag.*)

ROSIE: (*trying to get her clothes back on*) You're lucky I have another appointment or else I'd stay here all day!

JIMMY: (*throwing her out the door, half-undressed*) Go! Go!

Keep your appointment! Rosie, you can get dressed in the
street. Have a good time! (*He slams door shut.*) Elizabeth is
coming. . . .

THE RUNNER STUMBLES
by Milan Stitt

ACT III

In a remote parish of northern Michigan Father Rivard ostensi-
bly tries to finish a theological treatise he has been instructed to
write. But he is distracted by Sister Rita, a nun who arrives to
help in the parish school. Father Rivard finds his sexual and
emotional passions suddenly ignited. He is drawn to Sister Rita
with an intensity so strong that he is filled with guilt and
self-loathing. When he discovers that she returns his love, he is
beside himself. He cannot forsake his vows and the parishioners
who need him. He must fight his need for her as well as his
growing doubts about God.

During a fire in town, a ditch is dug through Sister Rita's
garden. Exhausted after working with the townspeople to put out
the blaze, she returns to her room. Father Rivard enters.

NUN: (*at window*) Where is my garden? The fire ditch. They
dug the fire ditch right through my garden. All the bulbs are
dug up. The roses. They burned. (*During* NUN'S *speech,*
PRIEST *abruptly enters, crosses to* NUN. PRIEST *holds* NUN
until sobbing subsides. NUN *falls to knees in front of* PRIEST
who sits on stool.)

PRIEST: At night I wonder how you are feeling, what you
think, if you're happy, if you can sleep. Even when I pray, I
wonder what you're doing. I look up through a window if it's
recess or listen for your steps in the hall. I can only concentrate if I pray about you. Almost to you. (*He is about to kiss
her.*)

NUN: Please. Tell me what it is.

PRIEST: I have. (*silence*) I love you. (*They kiss, stand and embrace.*)

NUN: (*sitting on stool as* PRIEST *sits on bench*) I never dared think—I thought who else would have me but the Church? But with you I'm not nothing, am I?

PRIEST: No. You're not.

NUN: (*standing to put diary away*) I'm just like everyone else.

PRIEST: What's that?

NUN: (*starting to pass* PRIEST) Just my diary. I always keep it in the drawer. But it's all right now, isn't it? (*handing it to* PRIEST) Do you want to read it?

PRIEST: It's drawings.

NUN: Not all of it. (*She sits on bench with* PRIEST *to look at diary.*)

PRIEST: No. Of course not. This can't be Sister Immaculata, can it?

NUN: I think she must have been in a grump that day.

PRIEST: Every day. Did you show her this?

NUN: No one's ever seen it. I offered to show it to Mother Vincent, but she said the only sin it could possibly be is boring.

PRIEST: She was wrong. This is so easy. Why was I so stupid? I don't understand why it seemed so worthy to—

NUN: Why do we have to understand? Has trying to understand been so wonderful?

PRIEST: No.

NUN: Who's that?

PRIEST: Me? Well, you sure got the eyelashes. How could you know how I'd look without a beard?

NUN: I guessed.

PRIEST: Well, you'd be disappointed.

NUN: I don't think so.

PRIEST: You make me so happy. And you made me so miserable.

NUN: I never meant to. (*leading* PRIEST *to window, still holding diary*) Look. Where I stood all those nights. See. We can be with all the other people now. We aren't so different after all, are we? Don't look at the Church. Look down there with the other families. We'll be like that too.

PRIEST: We can't move down there.

NUN: We'll have our own children.

PRIEST: Children.

NUN: Oh yes. I should have known. Oh, all those nights. Known that if the Church wasn't everything, that you would give me something in its place. I think I always knew I was not a true Bride of Christ.

PRIEST: You thought of this before.

NUN: No. Just the confusion. In there you'll see. I just didn't know.

PRIEST: What did you write?

NUN: It doesn't matter, does it?

PRIEST: Read it to me.

NUN: Someday, whenever, you can read it all—

PRIEST: Read it to me. Now. Read it.

NUN: (*looking as she sits on stool*) Well, any page these last few weeks. "I think Father Rivard must be right. Maybe the Church is only for rules, but God is for people. According to the rules everything I feel is wrong, yet nothing feels wrong. Do I have a conscience? Yes, I do. Do I belong in the Church? I don't know. He makes me so confused."

PRIEST: We can never lose our faith.

NUN: We won't.

PRIEST: You can't even think of it.

NUN: (*standing*) Now look. The lights are going on in their homes. We can think of that. We'll be down there and then— (PRIEST *suddenly pulls her from window R.*) What is it?

PRIEST: Mrs. Shandig is coming up the hill.

NUN: But we can tell her. Everyone.

PRIEST: No.

NUN: Why?

PRIEST: (*moving to exit*) Because I, I—I'm their priest. She depends on me. They all do. I'm the only way they have of understanding.

NUN: People understand. (*She crosses to stop his exit. He grabs her by the arms.*)

PRIEST: It's not how you think it is. Their homes have photographs of babies in coffins. Adolescents pour kerosene on kittens, and their fathers laugh when they set the fire. Sometimes wives cannot cook breakfast. Their fingers are broken from their husbands' beatings. It's only because they think I'm different; it's only because they think I'm worthy that I can help them. I must be worthy.

NUN: (*putting arms around his neck*) I think you're worthy. Please. You said you loved me. I know you're too good, too precious to escape, desert me when—

PRIEST: I'm not, not what you think. I, I, I've destroyed all that. For the Church. (*pushing her onto stool*) There's nothing left for you. I can't be a husband. I can't be (*kneeling in front of her*) be a father. There's nothing left but cruelty. That's all I know. That's all I worship. All I need. Not the resurrection, life. It's the nails. My salvation. Only the agony. There's no chance for—

NUN: You're not cruel. It'll be different now.

PRIEST: Damn you. Trying to break me down, make me forget. (*taking her head in his hands, forcing her to look out window*) Planting those flowers out there as if you, you could make the world beautiful. What makes you think you could change anything? Promising me things will be better. You make them worse. It's not my fault you lost your faith. It's not. You never had any if it dies so easily. (*He starts to rip up diary. She wrestles it from him.*)

NUN: No. That was before. You can stop. That's gone. It's gone.

PRIEST: (*grabbing* NUN *by shoulders, shaking her with violence, causing her to drop diary*) With them, with them, I can make it look all right. They only want me to say those words. They don't want to know me. You can't know me. I'll destroy you. You can't know me. You'd hate me. I hate myself.

NUN: I don't hate you. God doesn't hate you.

PRIEST: (*trying to exit*) Don't talk about God.

NUN: (*holding him from exit*) We still have God.

PRIEST: I don't want God. I don't want you. (*starting to choke* NUN) I hate God. I hate God. I want to kill God. I always wanted to kill— (NUN *falls on floor. For a moment of silence, she appears dead.* PRIEST *slaps her on back. She coughs. He drags her to bench. He gets wet cloth, sits next to her, wiping her brow.* MRS. SHANDIG *begins to enter up ramp. She is looking back down in the valley to see if fire is out.*)

NUN: (*as she stops choking*) I'm sorry. I'm sorry. What you said. Hating God. It's my fault too. You couldn't—

PRIEST: No. No. It's me. (MRS. SHANDIG *enters.*)

NUN: We have to help each other. It's all we have now. We only have each other.

GIGI
dramatized by Anita Loos
(from the novel by Colette)

ACT II, SCENE 3

Gigi is a charming, effervescent girl who is being groomed by her grandmother and Aunt Alicia to be a fashionable mistress to some rich and debonair Parisian. When she turns sixteen, they decide that Gaston Lachaille (nicknamed Tonton), a friend of the family, is the perfect choice for her. They set about ensnaring the handsome Gaston and finally propose their "arrangement" to him. He is caught, now thoroughly in love with Gigi, and he eagerly agrees with the women's plans.

But the independent-minded Gigi has her own ideas about how people in love should live together. She has left a message for Gaston at his club to come to her home because she has personal matters to discuss with him.

GIGI: Won't you come in?
GASTON: Thanks.

(GIGI *walks down right of table*—GASTON *left of it. They pause.*)

GIGI: So you got my message at the Club, did you?
GASTON: Why no—I haven't been there.
GIGI: Then why did you come here?
GASTON: I wanted to make sure you got home safely from your Aunt's, that's all.
GIGI: Oh! (*glances at* GASTON, *trying to make conversation*) Well, Tonton,—you look very elegant in your swallowtail.
GASTON: It's a cutaway, stupid.
GIGI: Of course it is. Where are my brains? Will you sit down?

(GASTON *takes chair from left of dining table, places it left center as* GIGI *takes chair from right of table, and places it right center.*)

GASTON: Yes. (*Sits, but rises quickly, until* GIGI *has seated herself. He sits again.*) Sorry! (*slight pause*) Gigi—(*gives a slight tug at his chair towards her*)—there's something I'd like to ask you. Tell me something. Did you know what I went to see your Aunt Alicia about today?

GIGI: (*half-turned towards him*) I understand you told Aunt Alicia that you would be willing to—

GASTON: (*interrupting her*) Please! I know what I said to your Aunt. It isn't necessary for you to repeat it. (*again moves his chair a few inches towards hers*) Just tell me what it is you don't want. And then tell me what it is you *do* want. I'll give it to you if I can.

GIGI: Really?

GASTON: I'll try.

GIGI: Well, you told Aunty that you wished to give me a future.

GASTON: A very good one, Gigi.

GIGI: It would be a good one, if I wanted it, Tonton. But the way you want things—well—it seems I'm to leave here, and go away with you and sleep in your bed.

GASTON: (*avoiding her gaze*) Don't, Gigi—please.

GIGI: But why should I be ashamed to say things to you, that you weren't ashamed to say to Aunt Alicia? I know very well that if you gave me a future, Tonton, I'll have my picture in the papers—I'll go to the Flower Festival at Nice, and to the races at Trouville. But every time we have a quarrel, *Gil Blas* will tell all about it, and when you leave me for good, as you did when you had enough of Gaby Fougere—

GASTON: How did you know about that? (*again moving his chair towards her*) Have they told you these things?

GIGI: Nobody had to tell me. I just know what everybody else in the world knows. I know that you're a very fashionable man. I know that Maryse Chuquet stole some letters from you, and that you had to bring suit against her. I know that the Countess Pariewsky was upset because you wouldn't marry a divorced woman, and that she shot at you with a revolver.

GASTON: (*Moves his chair. He is now very close to her.*) But all those things had nothing to do with *you*, Gigi. That's all finished. It's in the past. (*takes her hands*)

GIGI: That's true, Tonton—up to the point when it begins again. It isn't your fault that you're fashionable. But you see, I just haven't any desire to be fashionable myself. (*draws her hands away from his*) So things like that don't tempt me. (*rises*) You see, that's the way it is. (*steps down right, turns away from him*) That's just how it happens to be.

GASTON: (*rises*) Gigi—I'd like to be sure you're not simply trying to hide the fact that I'm not pleasing to you. If I'm not, it's better that I know about it right away.

GIGI: (*looks at him*) Why no, Tonton, I'm very happy when I see you. (*going to him*) The proof is, that I'm going to propose something myself. You may come here as usual, only more often. No one will see anything wrong with it, because you're a friend of the family. You can bring me licorice and champagne for my birthday, and on Sunday, we'll play a simply monstrous game of piquet. Well—isn't that a much better way to do things, than to have the newspapers print that I'm sleeping with you, so that everyone in Paris knows about it?

GASTON: But—there's one thing, Gigi, you seem to have overlooked. And that is that—that I'm in love with you.

GIGI: (*utterly dazed*) You're in love with me? But you never told me that before!

GASTON: I'm telling you now.

GIGI: (*horror-stricken, pushes her chair upstage, and moves closer to* GASTON) What kind of a horrible man are you, anyway?

GASTON: Gigi!

GIGI: You're in love with me! And you want to drag me into a life that can only bring me suffering? Where everybody talks viciously about everybody else—where the newspapers write nasty stories—? You're in love with me! But it doesn't stop you for a moment from wanting to drag me into something that's bound to end up with a separation—with quarrels—with revolvers—with laudanum? With another woman for you and another man for me? And then another, and another, and another! (*breaks into a sob, and covers her face with her hands*)

GASTON: But Gigi—listen to me—

GIGI: (*bursting in*) Go away! I never want to see you again. I'd never have believed it of you—you couldn't be in love with anyone—Get out of here!! (*shrieks*) Get out—Get out!!!

ONDINE
by Jean Giraudoux
(English version by Maurice Valency)

Act II

A handsome young knight, Hans, rides out into an enchanted forest. If he comes back alive after one month, he can marry the beautiful, dark-haired Princess Bertha. His bravery in the forest will prove his love for her and bring him glory at court as well as marriage to Bertha. But things don't always turn out as expected, even in a fairy tale.

Hans happens upon a peasant hut deep in the forest. There he meets Ondine, a golden-haired sea nymph, and he loses his heart to her perfect beauty and grace. They return to court and are married. But the cunning Bertha is not ready to accept rejection and she plots to win him back.

In the scene below, Bertha and Hans have been chasing an escaped bird when they suddenly collide.

(*The bird flies in and settles on the fountain.* BERTHA *runs in from the right and catches it.*)

BERTHA: Again! What a bad bird you are!

HANS: Again! What an obstinate beast! (*He enters the room with the glove in his hand, just as* BERTHA *runs up with the bird. They collide.* HANS *takes her hands to keep her from falling. They recognize each other.*) Oh! I beg your pardon, Bertha.

BERTHA: Oh! I'm sorry, Hans.

HANS: Did I hurt you?

BERTHA: Not a bit.

HANS: I'm a clumsy brute, Bertha.

BERTHA: Yes. You are. (*There is a moment of embarrassed silence. Then each turns and walks off slowly.* BERTHA *stops.*) Pleasant honeymoon?

HANS: Marvelous.

BERTHA: A blonde, I believe?

HANS: Blonde, like the sun.

BERTHA: Sunlit nights! I prefer the darkness.

HANS: Each to his taste.

BERTHA: It was dark that night under the oak tree. My poor Hans! You must have suffered!

HANS: Bertha!

BERTHA: I didn't suffer. I loved it.

HANS: Bertha, my wife is coming in at any moment.

BERTHA: I was happy that night in your arms. I thought it was for always.

HANS: And so it could have been, had you not insisted on sending me into the forest on a wild-goose chase. Why didn't you keep me with you, if you wanted me?

BERTHA: One takes off a ring sometimes to show to one's friends. Even an engagement ring.

HANS: I'm sorry. The ring didn't understand.

BERTHA: No. And so it rolled, as rings do, under the nearest bed.

HANS: I beg your pardon!

BERTHA: Forgive me. I shouldn't have mentioned a bed. Among peasants, you sleep in the straw, I believe? You pick it out of your hair the morning after. Is it fun?

HANS: One day you will see.

BERTHA: No, I don't think so. Black hair and straw don't go well together. That's for blondes.

HANS: You may be right. Although in love, these details don't seem to matter. But, of course, you've never had that experience.

BERTHA: You think?

HANS: When you're in love, you don't think of yourself so much. You think of the other. You will see one day. But when it happens to you, don't let your lover go.

BERTHA: No?

HANS: Don't send him into senseless danger and loneliness and boredom.

BERTHA: One would say you had a bad time in the black forest.

HANS: You are haughty. But when you meet the man you love, take my advice—pocket your pride, throw your arms around his neck and tell him, before all the world, that you love him.

BERTHA: (*She throws her arms around his neck.*) I love you.

(*She kisses him, then tries to run off. But he holds her by the hands.*)

HANS: Bertha!

BERTHA: Let me go, Hans.

HANS: What game are you playing with me now, Bertha?

BERTHA: Be careful, Hans. I have a bird in my hand.

HANS: I love another woman, Bertha.

BERTHA: The bird!

HANS: You should have done that before, Bertha.

BERTHA: Hans, don't squeeze my hand so. You're going to kill it.

HANS: Let the bird go, Bertha.

BERTHA: No. Its little heart is beating with fear. And just now I need this little heart next to mine.

HANS: What is it you want of me, Bertha?

BERTHA: Hans—Oh! (*opening her hand and showing the bird*) There. You've killed it.

HANS: Oh, Bertha! (*taking the bird*) Forgive me, Bertha. Forgive me. (BERTHA *looks at him a long moment. He is completely contrite.*)

BERTHA: Give it to me. I'll take the poor little thing away. (*She takes it from him.*)

HANS: Forgive me.

BERTHA: I want nothing of you now, Hans. But once, I wanted something for you, and that was my mistake. I wanted glory—for the man I loved. The man I had chosen when I was a little girl, and whom I led one night under the oak tree on which long ago I had carved his name. I thought it was a woman's glory to lead her lover not only to his table and his bed, but to whatever in the world is hardest to find and most difficult to conquer. I was wrong.

HANS: No, Bertha. No, Bertha.

BERTHA: I am dark. I thought that in the darkness of the forest this man would see my face in every shadow. I am dark, I trusted my love to the darkness. How could I have known that in these shadows, he would come one night upon a head of gold?

HANS: How could anyone have known it?

BERTHA: That was my error. I have confessed it. And that's the end of it. I shall carve no more initials in the bark of trees. A man alone in a dream of glory—that's already foolish. But a woman alone in a dream of glory is completely ridiculous. So much the worse for me.

HANS: Forgive me, Bertha?
BERTHA: Farewell, Hans.

COME BACK, LITTLE SHEBA
by William Inge

ACT II, SCENE 3

Doc and Lola Delaney have been married for twenty years. When they met, Doc was a student planning to go to medical school. But the pretty, childlike Lola captured his heart and they had an indiscreet affair. She became pregnant, he married her and became a chiropractor instead of a doctor. They settled down to a dull life in a "run-down neighborhood in a Midwestern city." Doc became an alcoholic and Lola's good looks faded into slovenliness.

When the play opens, Doc has been on the wagon for a year. He has reconciled himself to his shabby existence and his kind-hearted but stupid wife. Lola spends her time meddling in other people's lives to fill the emptiness of her own days. (She miscarried and has remained childless.) Her latest preoccupation is Marie, their 18-year-old boarder, who is engaged to Bruce, but enjoys flirting with Turk, a fellow student. In her innocence, Lola encourages Marie to "have a good time" and enjoy her youth. Doc is disgusted with Lola's meddling. When he discovers she has gone as far as reading Marie's telegrams, he is furious.

It is 5:30 in the morning. The night before, Lola prepared a special meal for Marie and Bruce. But Doc didn't come home for dinner. In fact, he didn't come home at all. Lola is distraught, fearing he has started to drink again. She calls Doc's friend, Mr. Anderson.

LOLA: (*At telephone. She sounds frantic.*) Mr. Anderson? Mr. Anderson, this is Mrs. Delaney again. I'm sorry to call you so early, but I just *had* to . . . Did you find Doc? . . . No, he's not home yet. I don't suppose he'll come home till he's drunk all he can hold and wants to sleep.... I don't know what else to think, Mr. Anderson. I'm scared, Mr. Anderson. I'm awful scared. Will you come right over?... Thanks, Mr. Anderson. (*She hangs up and goes to kitchen to make coffee. She finds some left from the night before, so turns on the fire to warm it up. She wanders around vaguely, trying to get her thoughts in order, jumping at every sound. Pours herself a cup of coffee, then takes it to living room, sits and sips it. Very quietly* DOC *enters through the back way into the kitchen. He carries a big bottle of whiskey which he carefully places back in the pantry, not making a sound, hangs up overcoat, then puts suitcoat on back of chair. Starts to go upstairs. But* LOLA *speaks.*) Doc? That you, Doc?

(*Then* DOC *quietly walks in from kitchen. He is staggering drunk, but he is managing for a few minutes to appear as though he were perfectly sober and nothing had happened. His steps, however, are not too sure and his eyes are like blurred ink pots.* LOLA *is too frightened to talk. Her mouth is gaping and she is breathless with fear.*)

DOC: Good morning, honey.

LOLA: Doc! You all right?

DOC: The morning paper here? I wanta see the morning paper.

LOLA: Doc, we don't get a morning paper. *You* know that.

DOC: Oh, then I suppose I'm drunk or something. That what you're trying to say?

LOLA: No, Doc . . .

DOC: Then give me the morning paper.

LOLA: (*scampering to get last night's paper from console table*) Sure, Doc. Here it is. Now you just sit there and be quiet.

DOC: (*resistance rising*) Why shouldn't I be quiet?

LOLA: Nothin', Doc . . .

DOC: (*Has trouble unfolding paper. He places it before his face in order not to be seen. But he is too blind even to see; he speaks mockingly.*) Nothing, Doc.

LOLA: (*cautiously, after a few minutes' silence*) Doc, are you all right?

DOC: Of course, I'm all right. Why shouldn't I be all right?

LOLA: Where you been?

DOC: What's it your business where I been? I been to London to see the Queen. What do you think of that? (*Apparently she doesn't know what to think of it.*) Just let me alone. That's all I ask. I'm all right.

LOLA: (*whimpering*) Doc, what made you do it? You said you'd be home last night . . . 'cause we were having company. Bruce was here and I had a big dinner fixed . . . and you never came. What was the matter, Doc?

DOC: (*mockingly*) We had a big dinner for *Bruce*.

LOLA: Doc, it was for you, too.

DOC: Well . . . I don't want it.

LOLA: Don't get mad, Doc.

DOC: (*threateningly*) Where's Marie?

LOLA: I don't know, Doc. She didn't come in last night. She was out with Bruce.

DOC: (*back to audience*) I suppose you tucked them in bed together and peeked through the keyhole and applauded.

LOLA: (*sickened*) Doc, don't talk that way. Bruce is a nice boy. They're gonna get married.

DOC: He probably *has* to marry her, the poor bastard. Just 'cause she's pretty and he got amorous one day . . . Just like I had to marry *you*.

LOLA: Oh, Doc!

DOC: You and Marie are both a couple of sluts.

LOLA: Doc, please don't talk like that.

DOC: What are you good for? You can't even get up in the morning and cook my breakfast.

LOLA: (*mumbling*) I will, Doc. I will after this.

DOC: You won't even sweep the floors, till some bozo comes along to make love to Marie, and then you fix things up like Buckingham Palace or a Chinese whorehouse with perfume on the lampbulbs, and flowers, and the gold-trimmed china *my mother* gave us. We're not going to use these any more. My mother didn't buy those dishes for whores to eat off of.

(*He jerks the cloth off the table, sending the dishes rattling to the floor.*)

LOLA: Doc! Look what you done.

DOC: Look what I *did,* not *done.* I'm going to get me a drink. (*goes to kitchen*)

LOLA: (*follows to platform*) Oh, no, Doc! You know what it does to you!

DOC: You're damn right I know what it does to me. It makes me willing to come home here and look at you, you two-ton old heifer. (*takes a long swallow*) There! And pretty soon I'm going to have another, then another.

LOLA: (*with dread*) Oh, Doc! (LOLA *takes phone.* DOC *sees this, rushes for the butcher knife from kitchen-cabinet drawer. Not finding it, he gets a hatchet from the back porch.*) Mr. Anderson? Come quick, Mr. Anderson. He's back. He's *back*! He's got a hatchet!

DOC: God damn you! Get away from that telephone. (*He chases her into living room where she gets the couch between them.*) That's right, phone! Tell the world I'm drunk. Tell the whole damn world. Scream your head off, you fat slut. Holler 'til all the neighbors think I'm beatin' hell outuv you. Where's Bruce now—under Marie's bed? You got all fresh and pretty for him, didn't you? Combed your hair for once—you even washed the back of your neck and put on a girdle. You were willing to harness all that fat into one bundle.

LOLA: (*about to faint under the weight of the crushing accusations*) Doc, don't say any more. . . . I'd rather you hit me with an ax, Doc. . . . Honest I would. But I can't stand to hear you talk like that.

DOC: I oughta hack off all that fat, and then wait for Marie and chop off those pretty ankles she's always dancing around on . . . then start lookin' for Turk and fix him too.

LOLA: Daddy, you're talking crazy!

DOC: I'm making sense for the first time in my life. You didn't know I knew about it, did you? But I saw him coming outta there, I saw him. You knew about it all the time and thought you were hidin' something. . . .

LOLA: Daddy, I didn't know anything about it at all. Honest, Daddy.

DOC: Then *you're* the one that's crazy, if you think I didn't know. You were running a regular house, weren't you? It's probably been going on for years, ever since we were married.

(*He lunges for her. She breaks for kitchen. They struggle in front of sink.*)

LOLA: Doc, it's not so; it's not so. You gotta believe me, Doc.

DOC: You're lyin'. But none a that's gonna happen any more. I'm gonna fix you now, once and for all. . . .

LOLA: Doc . . . don't do that to me. (LOLA, *in a frenzy of fear, clutches him around the neck holding arm with ax by his side.*)

Remember, Doc. It's *me*, Lola! You said I was the prettiest
girl you ever saw. Remember, Doc! It's me! Lola!

DOC: (*The memory has overpowered him. He collapses, slowly
mumbling.*) Lola . . . my pretty Lola. (*He passes out on the
floor,* LOLA *stands now, as though in a trance.*)

INNOCENT THOUGHTS, HARMLESS INTENTIONS
by John Heuer

ACT II

Ernie Blagg is an ugly American. A squad leader in a remote
Alaskan outpost during the Korean War, he is a crude example of
an insensitive, uneducated American threatened by unfamiliar
surroundings. Unsure of his masculinity, he sadistically needles
his soldiers in order to inflate his own ego. He uses his authority
to abuse everyone around him and swindle extra privileges for
himself. When he meets Inga, a young Eskimo woman, he
quickly moves to seduce her and then brags about it in the
barracks.

The scene below takes place the morning after their first sexual
encounter.

(INGA *secrets herself under the covers of the daybed and* ERNIE
*enters from U.L. laying a robe, his shirt and undershirt on the
L. table. He then steps down to the end of the bed proceeding
to do push-ups. The U. barracks light fades as a D.L. light
rises on* INGA's *apartment. While* ERNIE *does push-ups, she
stirs, pulls herself out from under the covers to stretch and get
comfortable. She is completely naked.*)

ERNIE: (*without looking*) Sounds like someone has finally
decided to join the living.

INGA: Excuse me?

ERNIE: I was beginning to think you were going to skip today
altogether.

INGA: Sleep is good. I like sleeping.

ERNIE: That's your big hobby, eh? (*Rising from his push-ups,* *he sees her sitting naked.)* What do you think you're doing?

INGA: Resting. When the Trading Post is not open, I do not get out of bed quickly.

ERNIE: Will you put something on!

INGA: Why must I have something on?

ERNIE: A civilized person does not sit around with no clothes on.

INGA: I had no clothes on all night. You were here in bed with me and you had no clothes on, too.

ERNIE: *(crossing U. to the table)* That's different. It's at night when the lights are out. I don't want to see you sitting around with all the lights on, naked.

INGA: Should you then close your eyes so I can get my robe?

ERNIE: Never mind. *(He grabs the robe from the table and, without looking, hands it over the counter, but is not close enough for her to reach.)*

INGA: You can look. I am holding the blanket under my chin. *(He holds out the robe so she can slip her arms into the sleeves.)* Should I put it on under the blanket? *(Dismissing her, he turns away. She pulls the covers over her head.)* It is difficult to put clothes on under a blanket. *(With the robe on she pulls the blanket off her head and, seeing that he is shirtless, immediately sits with her back turned.)*

ERNIE: Now what in hell's the matter with you?

INGA: You are not wearing clothes.

ERNIE: *(proceeding to put on his clothes)* I got my pants on, that's all that's important. Well, . . . ? How do you feel? *(She looks puzzled.)* You virgins are all alike. The first time you get it, you got no idea what to do with it. A guy I met once told me that after he was drafted, just before leaving, his old man told him that if he laid any girls who weren't regular white girls his, you know, private, would turn black.

INGA: *(as he crosses down to sit by her on the bed)* Have you turned black?

ERNIE: Don't be silly.

INGA: *(grabbing at the front of his pants)* Let me see!

ERNIE: Hey, come on, stop it! Jesus! So, tell me, what do you think? How does it feel? *(dropping his tone a register)* You're a big girl now.

INGA: I think you were too fast.

ERNIE: Oh, do you? Like I suppose you know all about it!

INGA: You wanted strongly to know.

ERNIE: Yeah, sure, but don't go trying to make out you know

what it's all about. I know better. For Chrissake you laid
there all the while and never moved a muscle.

INGA: I did not have time.

ERNIE: How much time do you think a person needs?

INGA: (*as she begins fixing the daybed*) I am sorry you are not
happy. I will try harder. Before this I always had more time.

ERNIE: Oh, Jesus, what king of bullshit are you trying to
spread around? I'm not your local muck-luck from down the
street, you know. You can't con me; you've never had it.

INGA: I have two children.

ERNIE: Aw, come on. I mean, come on. What'd you do, get
married at ten?

INGA: Excuse me?

ERNIE: You're not old enough. Two kids? Come on. What do
you think, I'm blind? You're no more'n sixteen; seventeen,
maybe.

INGA: (*crossing U. to the table*) By your counting I am
twenty-three years.

ERNIE: Twenty-three?! Bullshit! (*From behind the counter
she takes a plate and tangerine which she proceeds to peel
and set out for him.*)

INGA: I was born in the year of nineteen twenty-nine. In
school they said that was a year of great importance in the
United States.

ERNIE: (*crossing U. to her*) Christalmighty! When I was a
freshman you were already a senior! It's embarrassing as hell!
Jesus, at that rate . . . you really aren't a virgin, are you?

INGA: I do not think so.

ERNIE: (*sitting at the table to eat the tangerine*) Where these
kids at?

INGA: They stay with my father and mother in the mountains.
That is why I work here for money to send them supplies.

ERNIE: You ever have a husband or don't you people know
about that yet?

INGA: (*crossing D., facing away from him*) He died in a
fishing accident.

ERNIE: (*as* INGA *continues converting the daybed*) Oh, fisherman,
was he? Shucks, I thought you wouldn't go for anything less
than an honest-to-god Kodiak bear killer. But, anyhow, I guess
the main thing I should understand is, he could fuck better
than me.

INGA: Excuse me?

ERNIE: Never mind. Probably doesn't translate anyway.

Well, . . . I sure been taken this time. The least you could've done was given me some idea. It's rotten your just hiding it all. Guess I better just pack up and leave.

INGA: (*rushing back U. to him*) I am not telling you you have to go away. I had wished we might become better . . . related.

ERNIE: (*as he finishes dressing*) Forget it. When my time is up in this snowpile, it's back to the States in double quick time. I got a wife and kid to look out for.

INGA: You have a wife and child?

ERNIE: Yeah. Baby boy. Why?

INGA: I do not understand last night. You are not faithful?

ERNIE: Just a damn minute. I happen to be very faithful! You'd never catch me messing around with another girl back home.

INGA: I am a girl.

ERNIE: I mean a regular American girl. But don't get me wrong; I'm not saying you ain't pretty. Two kids and all, you're still pretty.

INGA: What is different?

ERNIE: Nothing. It's just that you're not regular. That's all.

INGA: Would you have been with me if we were in the United States?

ERNIE: But we're not! Will you stop being a cramp!

INGA: I will tell you a great truth. If Kokolikatuk were still here, you would not know me!

ERNIE: Oh, come on. I may not speak the language, but, I know all the stories about how you people wife swap and woman share. I'm not stupid!

INGA: If you were passing a night so cold the sled dogs dig holes in the drifts, he would not give me to keep you warm. (*In a fury she crosses back D. to finish converting the daybed.*)

ERNIE: So what?! As far as I can see he doesn't even figure into it. If he was still hanging around I wouldn't even be talking to you. I'm not the type to go sticking my nose in, you know. Besides which, you can complain about my action if you want to, but, I'll bet dollars to doughnuts since him you don't get made a whole lot. Now considering I get into Fairbanks a good twice a month, taking every pass that icebox can cough up, I may stop around again. (*Having finished the daybed,* INGA *pauses at the head, extreme D.L., and surreptitiously reaches under the mattress, then buries her hands in the folds of her robe, remaining with her back turned. Ernie crosses D. to her.*) You shouldn't knock it. I mean, you ain't exactly got guys wearing out your front stoop. So what d'you say? (*Grabbing her shoulder, he turns her into him for a hug only to suddenly gasp and stiffen.* INGA *takes a step back to show that she is holding a large hunting knife tucked, blade up, tight into his crotch.*) I . . . don't like . . . being held . . . this way.

INGA: I do not like the way you hold me.

ERNIE: You just . . . carefully . . . put the blade down.

INGA: You can step away.

ERNIE: What you're doing . . . is dangerous.

INGA: What you do is dangerous. I have tried to understand you, I have tried to be friendly to you; strange white man from the United States. (*She yanks the blade from between his legs.*)

ERNIE: (*feeling his crotch*) Hey, careful! You realize what you could've done? You crazy or something? (*Advancing, she backs him all the way up above the table area into the corner formed by the L. wall and the attic partition.*)

INGA: You ask to hear my language: Kha-y-no, wha-nga-tik! It is the same as we call a sled dog so sick in its mind it will bite everything, even itself!

ERNIE: Look, will you stand still a minute?

INGA: I have been six seasons without my man of the nets and umiaks. This is my second long night without him. He had no brothers and I am lonely. I despise myself for that weakness. But, when next I meet a white soldier from the United States, I will know what I have learned!

ERNIE: You're pointing that blade at a member of the United States Army, now you better just hand it over. I don't want to hurt you. But, I warn you, I'm very highly trained.

INGA: Come take it. I beg for you to take it! I have killed a reindeer with this. It was much larger than you. (*Feeling a rush of adrenalin,* ERNIE *boldly advances on her.*)

ERNIE: You stand still for just a second and I will; I'm not scared of you! I'm from Fort Dix, New Jersey. In hand-to-hand combat I'm very highly trained. I'm lethal!

INGA: (*faking a retreat down the steps to the end of the daybed*) Then take the knife from me. Show me your strength, white man of the United States Army! (*He reaches towards her recklessly; she strikes out, narrowly missing his hand.*)

ERNIE: You stupid, ignorant savage. That's all you are! A stupid savage! Fucking you was no more than fucking an animal!

SCENES FOR TWO WOMEN

AGNES OF GOD
by John Pielmeier

ACT I, SCENE 10

A young nun is found unconscious in her room suffering from excessive loss of blood. In a wastepaper basket, a dead infant is discovered with an umbilical cord knotted around its neck. The nun, Agnes, has no recollection of the event and claims she is innocent. She is indicted for manslaughter and brought to trial. But first the court must determine whether she is legally sane. Dr. Martha Livingstone, a psychiatrist, is assigned to the case.

First Dr. Livingstone interviews Mother Miriam Ruth, head of the convent. Although she cannot explain the events, Mother Miriam believes Agnes is "an unconscious innocent," and fears her fragile purity will be destroyed by psychiatry.

Dr. Livingstone is intrigued by her patient and discovers some extraordinary facts about her early life: Agnes came to the convent at 17, after her mother died. She had been locked in her house most of her life. She had very little schooling and never saw a movie or read a book. In fact, she had almost no communication with anyone except her disturbed, alcoholic mother who saw angels every time she had a headache. At 10, Agnes saw her own angel and found God. One night during her first year at the convent, she bled from the palms.

Dr. Livingstone believes all these events can be explained. Mother Miriam maintains "a miracle is an event without explanation," and she is afraid to have Agnes' "mind cut open" by psychiatry. While the two women battle over what is real and what is miraculous, Agnes reluctantly submits to sessions with the doctor.

In the following scene Dr. Livingstone probes Agnes' love/hate relationship with her mother. At first Agnes refuses to cooperate and answer personal questions. But after a while her defenses weaken and she pours out the painful events of her early life.

DOCTOR: But you're troubled, aren't you?

AGNES: That's because you keep reminding me. If you go away then I'll forget.

DOCTOR: And you're unhappy.

AGNES: Everybody's unhappy! You're unhappy, aren't you?

DOCTOR: Agnes.

AGNES: Aren't you?!

DOCTOR: Sometimes, yes.

AGNES: Only you think you're lucky because you didn't have a mother who said things to you and did things that maybe weren't always nice, but that's what you think, because you don't know that my mother was a wonderful person, and even if you did know that you wouldn't believe it because you think she was bad, don't you.

DOCTOR: Agnes.

AGNES: Answer me! You never answer me!

DOCTOR: Yes, I do think your mother was wrong, sometimes.

AGNES: But that was because of me! Because *I* was bad, not her!

DOCTOR: What did you do?

AGNES: I'm always bad.

DOCTOR: What do you do?

AGNES: (*in tears*) No!

DOCTOR: What do you do?

AGNES: I breathe!

DOCTOR: What did your mother do to you? (AGNES *shakes her head.*) If you can't tell me, shake your head, yes or no. Did she hit you? (*"No."*) Did she make you do something you didn't want to do? (*"Yes."*) Did it make you uncomfortable to do this? (*"Yes."*) Did it embarrass you? (*"Yes."*) Did it hurt you? (*"Yes."*) What did she make you do?

AGNES: No.

DOCTOR: You can tell me.

AGNES: I can't.

DOCTOR: She's dead, isn't she?

AGNES: Yes.

DOCTOR: She can't hurt you anymore.

AGNES: She can.

DOCTOR: How?

AGNES: She watches, she listens.

DOCTOR: Agnes, I don't believe that. Tell me. I'll protect you from her.

AGNES: She...

DOCTOR: Yes?

AGNES: She...makes me...take off my clothes and then...

DOCTOR: Yes?

AGNES: ...she makes...fun of me.

DOCTOR: She tells you you're ugly?

AGNES: Yes.

DOCTOR: And that you're stupid.

AGNES: Yes.

DOCTOR: And you're a mistake.

AGNES: She says...my whole body...is a mistake.

DOCTOR: Why?

AGNES: Because she says...if I don't watch out...I'll have a baby.

DOCTOR: How does she know that?

AGNES: Her headaches.

DOCTOR: Oh yes.

AGNES: And then...she touches me.

DOCTOR: Where?

AGNES: Down there. (*silence*) With her cigarette. (*silence*) Please, Mummy. Don't touch me like that. I'll be good. I won't be your bad baby any more. (*Silence. The* DOCTOR *puts out her cigarette.*)

DOCTOR: Agnes, dear, I want you to do something. I want you to pretend that I'm your mother. I know that your mother's dead, and you're grown now, but I want you to pretend for a moment that your mother has come back and that I'm your mother. Only this time, I want you to tell me what you're feeling. All right?

AGNES: I'm afraid.

DOCTOR: (*She takes* AGNES' *face in her hands.*) Please. I want to help you. Let me help you. (*silence*)

AGNES: All right.

DOCTOR: Agnes, you're ugly. What do you say to that?

AGNES: I don't know.

DOCTOR: Of course you do. Agnes, you're ugly. (*silence*) What do you say?

AGNES: No, I'm not.

DOCTOR: Are you pretty?

AGNES: Yes.

DOCTOR: Agnes, you're stupid.

AGNES: No, I'm not.

DOCTOR: Are you intelligent?

AGNES: Yes, I am.

DOCTOR: Agnes, you're a mistake.

AGNES: I'm not a mistake! I'm here, aren't I? How can I be a mistake if I'm really here? God doesn't make mistakes. *You're* a mistake! I wish you were dead! (AGNES *bursts into tears. The* DOCTOR *takes her in her arms.*)

DOCTOR: It's all right. Just pretend, right? (AGNES *nods.*) Thank you. (*The* DOCTOR *dries* AGNES' *eyes.*) Agnes, I'd like to ask a favor of you. You can say no, if you don't like what I'm asking.

AGNES: What?

DOCTOR: I'd like permission to hypnotize you.

AGNES: Why?

DOCTOR: Because there are some things that you might be able to tell me under hypnosis that you aren't able to tell me now.

AGNES: Does Mother Miriam know about this?

DOCTOR: Mother Miriam loves you very much just as I love you very much. I'm certain that she wouldn't object...to anything that would help you.

AGNES: Do you really love me? Or are you just saying that?

DOCTOR: I really love you.

AGNES: As much as Mother Miriam loves me? (*silence*)

DOCTOR: As much as God loves you. (*silence*)

AGNES: All right.

DOCTOR: Thank you.

CRIMES OF THE HEART
by Beth Henley

ACT III

The three McGrath sisters of Hazlehurst, Mississippi are having their problems. Lenny is thirty today and sure she's going to be an old maid. Meg, the middle sister, left Hazlehurst to seek adventure as a pop singer, but things didn't work out. She wound up losing her voice and spending some time in the Los Angeles County Hospital psychiatric ward. And Babe, the youngest, is out on bail after having shot her nasty husband, Zackery, who was suspicious that she was having an affair with a local black boy named Willie Jay—which she was.

Meg returned home yesterday, after receiving a telegram about Babe's situation, and, with much effort, she finally convinces Babe to tell her entire story to a lawyer, Mr. Barnette Lloyd— who it turns out has a "personal vendetta" against Zackery and who quickly develops a crush on Babe.

But Babe finally decides to follow in her mother's footsteps and hang herself. She finds some red rope and goes upstairs. As the scene begins the kitchen is empty. Lenny has gone out to pick "pawpaws" (a kind of fruit), elated after a phone conversation with a man she loved, but who she mistakenly thought had lost interest in her. Meg has gone off to pick up the cake for Lenny's surprise birthday party.

(*There is a moment of silence, then a loud, horrible thud is heard coming from upstairs. The telephone begins ringing immediately. It rings five times before* BABE *comes hurrying down the stairs with a broken piece of rope hanging around her neck. The phone continues to ring.*)

BABE: (*to the phone*) Will you shut up! (*She is jerking the rope from around her neck. She grabs a knife to cut it off.*) Cheap! Miserable! I hate you! I hate you! (*She throws the rope violently around the room. The phone stops ringing.*) Thank God. (*She looks at the stove, goes over to it, and turns the gas on. The sound of gas escaping is heard.* BABE *sniffs at it.*) Come on. Come on . . . Hurry up . . . I beg you—hurry up! (*Finally,* BABE *feels the oven is ready; she takes a deep breath and opens the oven door to stick her head into it. She spots the rack and furiously jerks it out. Taking another breath, she sticks her head into the oven. She stands for several moments tapping her fingers furiously on top of the stove. She speaks from inside the oven. . . .*) Oh, please. Please. (*After a few moments, she reaches for the box of matches with her head still in the oven. She tries to strike a match. It doesn't catch.*) Oh, Mama, please! (*She throws the match away and is getting a second one.*) Mama . . . Mama . . . So that's why you done it! (*In her excitement she starts to get up, bangs her head and* *falls back in the stove.* MEG *enters from the back door, carrying a birthday cake in a pink box.*)

MEG: Babe! (MEG *throws the box down and runs to pull* BABE'S *head out of the oven.*) Oh, my God! What are you doing? What the hell are you doing?

BABE: (*dizzily*) Nothing. I don't know. Nothing. (MEG *turns off the gas and moves* BABE *to a chair near the open door.*)

MEG: Sit down. Sit down! Will you sit down!

BABE: I'm okay. I'm okay.

MEG: Put your head between your knees and breathe deep!

BABE: Meg—

MEG: Just do it! I'll get you some water. (MEG *gets some water for* BABE.) Here.

BABE: Thanks.

MEG: Are you okay?

BABE: Uh-huh.

MEG: Are you sure?

BABE: Yeah, I'm sure. I'm okay.

MEG: (*getting a damp rag and putting it over her own face*) Well good. That's good.

BABE: Meg—

MEG: Yes?

BABE: I know why she did it.

MEG: What? Why who did what?

BABE: (*with joy*) Mama. I know why she hung that cat along with her.

MEG: You do?

BABE: (*with enlightenment*) It's 'cause she was afraid of dying all alone.

MEG: Was she?

BABE: She felt so unsure, you know, as to what was coming. It seems the best thing coming up would be a lot of angels and all of them singing. But I imagine they have high, scary voices and little gold pointed fingers that are as sharp as blades and you don't want to meet 'em all alone. You'd be afraid to meet 'em all alone. So it wasn't like what people were saying about her hating that cat. Fact is, she loved that cat. She needed him with her 'cause she felt so all alone.

MEG: Oh, Babe . . . Babe. Why, Babe? Why?

BABE: Why what?

MEG: Why did you stick your head into the oven?!

BABE: I don't know, Meg. I'm having a bad day. It's been a real bad day; those pictures; and Barnette giving up his vendetta; then Willie Jay, heading north; and—Zackery called me up. (*trembling with terror*) He says he's gonna have me classified insane and send me on out to the Whitfield asylum.

MEG: What! Why, he could never do that!

BABE: Why not?

MEG: 'Cause you're not insane.

BABE: I'm not?

MEG: No! He's trying to bluff you. Don't you see it? Barnette's got him running scared.

BABE: Really?

MEG: Sure. He's scared to death—calling you insane. Ha! Why, you're just as perfectly sane as anyone walking the streets of Hazlehurst, Mississippi.

BABE: I am?

MEG: More so! A lot more so!

BABE: Good!

MEG: But, Babe, we've just got to learn how to get through these real bad days here. I mean, it's getting to be a thing in our family. (*slight pause as she looks at* BABE) Come on now. Look, we've got Lenny's cake right here. I mean don't you wanna be around to give her her cake; watch her blow out the candles?

BABE: (*realizing how much she wants to be here*) Yeah, I do, I do. 'Cause she always loves to make her birthday wishes on those candles.

MEG: Well, then we'll give her her cake and maybe you won't be so miserable.

BABE: Okay.

MEG: Good. Go on and take it out of the box.

BABE: Okay. (*She takes the cake out of the box. It is a magical moment.*) Gosh, it's a pretty cake.

MEG: (*handing her some matches*) Here now. You can go on and light the candles.

BABE: All right. (*She starts to light the candles.*) I love to light up candles. And there are so many here. Thirty pink ones in all plus one green one to grow on.

MEG: (*watching her light the candles*) They're pretty.

BABE: They are. (*She stops lighting the candles.*) And I'm not like Mama. I'm not so all alone.

MEG: You're not.

BABE: (*as she goes back to lighting candles*) Well, you'd better keep an eye out for Lenny. She's supposed to be surprised.

MEG: All right. Do you know where she's gone?

BABE: Well, she's not here inside—so she must have gone on outside.

MEG: Oh, well, then I'd better run and find her.

BABE: Okay 'cause these candles are gonna melt down. (MEG *starts out the door.*)

MEG: Wait—there she is coming. Lenny! Oh, Lenny! Come on! Hurry up!

BABE: (*overlapping and improving as she finishes lighting candles*) Oh, no! No! Well, yes—yes! No, wait! Wait! Okay!

THE GINGERBREAD LADY
by Neil Simon

ACT II

Polly is seventeen—she's sober, mature and responsible. Evy is forty-three—she's erratic, self-destructive, very witty—and an alcoholic just barely on the wagon. She is also Polly's mother, although their roles have somehow gotten reversed with Polly doing all the nagging and scolding and setting up of house rules.

During her growing-up years, Polly lived with her father and stepmother while Evy attained some degree of popularity as a nightclub singer. During that time Evy acquired a penchant for too much liquor and food, and nasty men.

The play opens with Evy returning home from Happy Valley, "a sanitarium for drunks." She is dry and forty-two pounds thinner. Enter Polly with suitcase in hand, determined to finally live with, get to know—and take care of—her mother.

This scene begins after they have been together for three weeks. Polly is worried because Evy is late for dinner. (The movie version of *The Gingerbread Lady* is called *Only When I Laugh*.)

(*It is three weeks later, about nine o'clock at night.* POLLY *is thumbing through a private phone book. She finds a number and dials. She looks at her watch, concerned.*)

POLLY: (*into the phone*)...Hello?...Is this Joe Allen's Bar?...Could you tell me if Evelyn Meara is there, please?...*Evy* Meara, that's right...I see...Was she there at all today?...

(*The front door opens, unseen by* POLLY. EVY *enters carrying a Saks Fifth Avenue shopping bag.*)

EVY: I'm here, I'm here. Just what I need, a trusting daughter. (*She closes the door.*)

POLLY: (*into the phone*) Never mind. Thank you.

(*She hangs up and turns to* EVY. EVY *puts down the packages.*)

EVY: If you knew what a terrific day I had you wouldn't be worrying about me....I've got sensational news....I was picked up today....He was eighty-six years old with a cane and a limp, but he really dug me. I don't think he could see me or hear me too good but we really hit it off....If I don't get any better offers this week, I'm going to contact him at the Home. Hello, pussycat, give your mother a kiss. (*She kisses* POLLY *on the cheek;* POLLY *receives it coldly.*) What's wrong?

POLLY: It's almost nine o'clock.

EVY: You're kidding?

POLLY: (*points to the clock on the mantel*) I'm not kidding. It's almost nine o'clock.

EVY: All right, don't get excited. What did I miss, the eclipse, what happened?

POLLY: You don't call, you don't leave a note, you don't tell me where you're going to be. I'm expecting you home for dinner at six-thirty and you don't show and I'm scared to death. What happened? Where were you?

EVY: Hanging around the men's room in the subway...I had a good day. You want to hear the details or you want to yell at me?

POLLY: I want to yell at you.

EVY: You can't yell at me, I'm your mother. I missed your dinner. Oh, God, Polly, I'm sorry. What did you make?

POLLY: I don't know. Something out of the cookbook. It was brown and it was hot....If you want some, it's in the kitchen now. It's yellow and it's cold.

EVY: (*hugging her*) Don't be mad at me. All I've got in the world is you and that eighty-six-year-old gimp—don't be mad at me. Let me tell you what happened today.

POLLY: Did you eat?

EVY: Yes, I think so. . . . Listen to what happened. I ran into this old girl friend of mine who used to work in the clubs—

POLLY: What do you mean, you think so? Don't you know if you ate or not?

EVY: I ate, I ate! I had a sandwich for lunch. I'll run up to Lenox Hill and take an x-ray for you. . . . Will you listen to my story?

POLLY: You mean you haven't had anything to eat except lunch?

EVY: It didn't say "lunch" on the sandwich. Maybe it was a "dinner" sandwich, I don't know. What are you taking in school this week, nagging? Let me tell you my story.

POLLY: You don't sleep well and I never see you eat, so I'm worried about you.

EVY: Who says I don't sleep well?

POLLY: I watch you at night.

EVY: Then *you're* the one who doesn't sleep well.

POLLY: You're in the living room until five, six in the morning, pacing and smoking and coughing. I hear you in there.

EVY: It's the television. I listen to cancer commercials.

POLLY: Making phone calls in the middle of the night . . . Who were you calling at four o'clock in the morning?

EVY: The weather bureau.

POLLY: At four o'clock in the morning?

EVY: I like to know what it's going to be like at five o'clock. . . . Jesus! Two more years of this, you're going to be a professional pain in the ass.

POLLY: Okay, fine with me. If you don't give a crap, I don't give a crap.

EVY: And watch your goddamned language.

POLLY: If you don't watch yours, why should I watch mine?

EVY: I talk this way. It's an impediment. You want me to wear braces on my mouth?

POLLY: You might as well. You never *eat* anything except a cup of coffee for breakfast.

EVY: What the hell difference does it make?

POLLY: Because if you don't take care of your body, it's not going to take care of you.

EVY: I don't want to take care of my body. I want somebody else to take care of it. Why do you think I'm talking to eighty-year-old men?

POLLY: You're infuriating. It's like talking to a child.

EVY: (*turns away*) I don't get any respect. How the hell am I going to be a mother if I don't get any respect?

POLLY: How am I going to respect you when you don't respect yourself?

EVY: (*looks up in despair*) Oh, Christ, I'm a flop mother. Three weeks and I blew it. Don't be angry, Polly. Don't be mad at me.

POLLY: And stop apologizing. You're my mother. Make *me* apologize to you for talking the way I did.

EVY: It won't happen again, sweetheart, I promise.

POLLY: (*vehemently*) Don't promise *me*, promise yourself! I can't live my life *and* yours. *You've* got to take over, *you've* got to be the one in charge around here.

EVY: Listen, you're really getting me crazy now. Why don't you write all the rules and regulations nice and neat on a piece of paper and I'll do whatever it says. Put on one page where I yell at you, and one page where you yell at me. . . . Now you want to hear what happened to me this afternoon or not?

POLLY: (*It's hard not to like* EVY; POLLY *smiles at her.*) What happened this afternoon?

EVY: I think I have a job.

POLLY: You're kidding. Where?

EVY: Well . . . (*pacing*) I was in Gucci's looking for a birthday present for Toby . . . when suddenly I meet this old girl friend of mine who used to be a vocalist in this singing group. . . . Four Macks and a Truck or some goddamned thing . . . Anyway, she can't get over my gorgeous new figure and asks what I'm doing lately and I tell her. . . . I'm looking for good honest work, preferably around a lot of single men, like an aircraft carrier, Okinawa, something like that . . . You're looking at me funny. If you're thinking of heating up the cold yellow stuff, forget it.

POLLY: I'm just listening.

EVY: All right . . . Well, she starts to tell me how she's out of the business now and is married to an Italian with four restaurants on Long Island and right away I dig he's in with the mob. I mean, one restaurant, you're in business; four restaurants, it's the Mafia. . . . Anyway, he's got a place in Garden City and he's looking for an attractive hostess who says, "Good evening, right this way please," and wiggles her behind and gets a hundred and ninety bucks a week. . . . So I played it very cool, and nonchalantly got down on my knees, kissed her shoes, licked her ankles and carried her packages out the store.

POLLY: A hostess in a restaurant? Is that what you want to do?

EVY: No, what I *want* to do is be a masseur at the New York Athletic Club but there are no openings. . . . Can I finish my story?

POLLY: Why don't you finish your story?

EVY: Thank you, I'll finish my story. . . . So we go around the corner to Schrafft's and she buys me a sherry and we sit there chatting like a couple of Scarsdale debutantes—me, the former lush, and her, a chippie married to Joe Bananas. . . . And she writes down the address and I have to be—(*consults a scrap of paper from her pocket*)—at the Blue Cockatoo Restaurant in Garden City at ten o'clock tomorrow morning, where Lucky Luciano's nephew will interview me. All this in one day, *plus* getting my knees rubbed by an eight-six-year-old degenerate on the crosstown bus . . . And you're going to sit there and tell me there's no God. . . . (*She looks at* POLLY *expectantly, hoping* POLLY *will be as exuberant and enthusiastic about her prospects as she is. But* POLLY *just glares at her.*) . . . What's the matter?

POLLY: You had a glass of sherry?

EVY: (*turns away*) Oh, Christ.

POLLY: Why did you have a glass of sherry?

EVY: Because the waitress put it down in front of me.

POLLY: They don't put it down in front of you unless you order it. I don't understand you.

EVY: I don't understand *you*! I rush home happy, excited, bubbling with good news and who do I find when I get here—a seventeen-year-old cop! I am not loaded, I am not smashed, I am thrilled to death because I spent a whole day out of this house and I came home alive and noticed and even wanted.

POLLY: Do you need a drink to feel that?

EVY: I was tense, I was afraid of blowing the job. So I had one stinking little drink. Did you ever have a cocktail in Schrafft's? Half of it is painted on the glass.

POLLY: That isn't the point. You could have had coffee or tea or milk.

EVY: Thank you, Miss, when do we land in Chicago? . . . I don't want to talk about it any more. Go inside and study.

When you pass French, we'll discuss it in a foreign language. Until then, shape up or ship out or whatever the hell that expression is.

POLLY: (*a pause*) No, listen... (*looks at her quietly a moment*) I think it's terrific.

EVY: You think what's terrific?

POLLY: About today, about getting the job. I really do. When will you start?

EVY: Well, in the first place, I didn't get it yet. And in the second place, I'm not so sure I'm going to take it.

POLLY: (*puzzled*) Then what's all the excitement about?

EVY: About being asked... About being wanted.

POLLY: I'm sorry—I don't think I understand.

EVY: (*goes over to* POLLY *and holds her head in her arms*) Please God, I hope you never do... (*smiles at her, trying to be more cheerful*) Listen, how about one more chance at being a mother? If I screw up, you can buy out my contract for a hundred dollars and I'll move out.

POLLY: (*takes* EVY'S *hand*) Who's going to bring me up?

EVY: (*shrugs*) I'll set you on automatic... (*crosses back to her shopping bag*) Hey, come on, get dressed. We have a party that started fifteen minutes ago.

POLLY: What party?

EVY: Toby's birthday. (*She takes a present from the shopping bag.*) She's forty years old today. She's promised to take off her make-up and reveal her true identity.

POLLY: I've got to study. I have a science test on Monday.

EVY: Flunk it! Men don't like you if you're too smart. (*She takes out a bottle of champagne. She looks at* POLLY, *who stares at her meaningfully.*) I'm pouring! That's all I'm doing is pouring.

POLLY: Who's coming?

EVY: Jimmy, Marty and Toby.

(EVY *starts to cross to the kitchen with the champagne bottle, and* POLLY *starts for the bedroom.*)

POLLY: What should I wear? How about the blue chiffon?

EVY: You can wear black crepe as long as your boobs don't bounce around.

(*She moves toward the kitchen.*)

POLLY: (*at the bedroom door*) Mother?

EVY: Yes?

POLLY: Don't take that job. You're too good for it. Hold out for something better.

EVY: I'm so glad you said that. Who the Christ even knows where Garden City is? . . . Hey, let's have a good time tonight. I'm beginning to feel like my old self again.

POLLY: Hey, listen, I forgot to tell you. We have a lunch date tomorrow.

EVY: (*in kitchen, busy with bottles*) Who has a lunch date?

POLLY: We do. You, me and Daddy.

(EVY *stops what she's doing and comes out to the kitchen doorway.*)

EVY: (dismayed) *What* Daddy?

POLLY: *My* Daddy. You remember, Felicia's husband? . . . Twelve o'clock at Rumpelmayer's.

EVY: Why didn't you tell me?

POLLY: Because I never see you. *Now* I see you. He just wants to have lunch with us, talk, see how we're getting along.

EVY: We're getting along fine.

POLLY: He knows. He just wants to see.

EVY: You mean he's checking to see what shape I'm in? Christ, he's going to look in my ears, under my fingernails— I'll never pass.

POLLY: He just wants to talk.

EVY: Is he gonna ask questions, like what's the capital of Bulgaria?

POLLY: Stop worrying. It'll be all right. I've got to get dressed. Oh, and if he does, the capital is Sofia. (*She goes into the bedroom.*)

EVY: (*standing there a moment*) Just what I needed. A physical examination in Rumpelmayer's. (*starts into the kitchen.*) I should have had *two* sherries today.

UNCOMMON WOMEN AND OTHERS
by Wendy Wasserstein

Act II, Scene 5

Rita and Samantha are seniors at Mt. Holyoke College, a prestigious Eastern women's school. Samantha is attractive, tasteful, "like a Shetland...sweater, a classic." Rita is her counterpart: outrageous and flamboyant; she has been known to wear "cowbells on her dress." Both women are part of a group that share the joys, confusions and fears of college days. Through it all they emerge as distant and different individuals, each struggling in her own fashion to come to grips with the future.

RITA: Hey, man, wanna go out and cruise for pussy?

SAMANTHA: Beg your pardon?

RITA: Come on, man.

SAMANTHA: (*putting hair brush in her mouth as if it were a pipe*) Can't we talk about soccer? Did you see Dartmouth take us? They had us in the hole.

RITA: I'd sure like to get into a hole.

SAMANTHA: Man, be polite.

RITA: (*gives* SAMANTHA *a light punch on the arm*) Fuck, man.

SAMANTHA: (*softly at first*) Shit man. (*She laughs hysterically.*)

RITA: Fucking "A" man.

SAMANTHA: Excuse me.

RITA: Samantha, you're losing the gist.

SAMANTHA: I just feel more comfortable being the corporate type. Won't you sit down? Can I get you a drink? Want to go out and buy Lacoste shirts and the State of Maine?

RITA: (*picking up* SAMANTHA'S *bag of nuts*) Nice nuts you got there.

SAMANTHA: Thank you. You can only get them west of the Mississippi.

RITA: (*chewing on the nuts*) I'll give you a vasectomy if you give me one. (*pause*)

SAMANTHA: (*She breaks her male character.*) Rita, I liked the game when we said who we would marry much better. All right. (*She goes back into character.*) Anyway, I don't want a vasectomy. I like homes and babies.

RITA: (RITA *picks up Piglet.*) Hey, man, what's this? You got a fucking doll, man, with two button eyes, a pink little ass, and a striped T-shirt. I could really get into this. This dollie got a name, man? Piglet?

SAMANTHA: (*disliking game*) I don't know.

RITA: What's the matter, man? You afraid I think you're a pansy or something?

SAMANTHA: (*drops character*) Rita, cut it out.

RITA: Samantha, I'm only playing.

SAMANTHA: We're twenty-one years old and I don't want to play.

RITA: Then why do you have the fucking doll?

SAMANTHA: (*Taking doll, she begins to exit.*) I like my doll. I've had it ever since my Dad won it when I was in sixth grade at the Naperville Fair.

RITA: (*dropping doll and character*) Samantha, you don't like me.

SAMANTHA: I like you, Rita. We're just very different. And I don't want to play anymore.

RITA: Do you know what, Samantha? If I could be any one of us, first I would be me. That's me without any embarrassment or neurosis—and since that's practically impossible, my second choice is, I'd like to be you.

SAMANTHA: But, Rita, when you're thirty you'll be incredible.

RITA: Samantha, at least you made a choice. You decided to marry Robert. None of the rest of us has made any decisions.

SAMANTHA: (*pause*) Thanks, Rita.

RITA: Well, I don't want to spend oodles of time with you. You're not a fascinating person. But I do want to be you. Very much. (*pause*) You're the ideal woman.

SAMANTHA: Robert says that I never grew up into a woman. That I'm sort of a child-woman. I've been reading a lot of books recently about women who are wives of artists and actors and how they believe their husbands are geniuses, and they are just a little talented. Well, that's what I am. Just a little talented at a lot of things. That's why I want to be with Robert and all of you. I want to be with someone who makes a public statement. And, anyway, if I'm going to devote my uncommon talents to relationships, then I might as well nurture those that are a bit difficult. It makes me feel a little special.

RITA: (*taking* SAMANTHA's *hand*) You are special, Samantha. We're all special.

SAMANTHA: It's a quiet intelligence. But I like it. (*pause*) Hey, Rita, when's your birthday? Because when we get out of here, we probably won't see each other very much. But I want to be sure to send you a birthday card. I like you, Rita.

RITA: It's March 28. I'm an Aries. Aries women are impulsive and daring, but have terrible domineering blocks.

SAMANTHA:
March 28 is the day of Rita's birthday, hipooray.
She talks of cocks and Aries blocks
But what's so neeta, about my Rita
Is I know secretly, she's very sweeta.
(*starts to giggle*) Pretty fucking gross, man, huh! (*She gives Rita a light punch and they begin to exit together.*)

RITA: (*gives her a light punch and starts to giggle*) Yeah, pretty fucking gross, man. (*Scene ends as they continue to giggle and exit with their arms around each other.*)

ON GOLDEN POND
by Ernest Thompson

ACT II, SCENE 1

Ethel and Norman Thayer have spent every summer of their fifty years together vacationing on Golden Pond. Norman is nearly eighty years old, a retired professor with a heart problem and a failing memory. But he is still sharp-tongued, crusty and lovable—despite his caustic wit. Their forty-year-old divorced daughter, Chelsea, has gone off to Europe with her dentist boyfriend, leaving his teenage son to spend the summer with her parents. To everyone's surprise, Billy brings new life to Golden Pond and especially to Norman.

The following scene takes place at the end of the summer. Chelsea has returned from Europe and has come to bring Billy back to California with her. As she approaches the house she hears her mother singing old camp songs to herself. Perhaps because this reminds Chelsea of her own early years on Golden Pond, she tells her mother about her childhood grudges toward Norman and why she never felt loved by him.

ETHEL: How'd you get here?

CHELSEA: I rented a car. A Volare. It's made by Plymouth. I got it from Avis. (*She walks to* ETHEL. *They embrace.*) They *do* try hard.

ETHEL: You're not supposed to come till the fifteenth.

CHELSEA: Today's the fifteenth.

ETHEL: No!

CHELSEA: 'Fraid so.

ETHEL: Well. No wonder you're here.

CHELSEA: Still have the kid or did you drown him?

ETHEL: Still have him.

CHELSEA: Are he and Norman asleep?

ETHEL: You must be joking. They're out on the lake already, antagonizing the fish. Still have Bill or did you drown him?

CHELSEA: Still got him. But he's not with me. He went back to the coast. He had a mouth that needed looking into.

ETHEL: Oh. You must have left Boston at the crack of dawn.

CHELSEA: I left Boston in the middle of the night. I felt like driving. I didn't feel like getting lost, but it worked out that way.

ETHEL: If you'd come more often, you wouldn't get lost.

CHELSEA: You're right. If I promise to come more often will you give me a cup of coffee?

ETHEL: All right. I could do that. Yes. You must have had a lovely time in Europe. You look wonderful.

(*She exits into the kitchen.*)

CHELSEA: I do? I did. I had a lovely time. (*peers out at the lake*)

ETHEL: (*offstage*) I always thought Norman and I should travel, but we never got to it somehow. I'm not sure Norman would like Europe.

CHELSEA: He wouldn't like Italy.

ETHEL: (*offstage*) No?

CHELSEA: Too many Italians.

ETHEL: (*enters*) I've got the perker going. See the boys?

CHELSEA: Yes. What are they doing out there? It's starting to rain.

ETHEL: Ah, well. I told Norman not to go. The loons have been calling for it. I'm afraid Norman doesn't give them much credence.

CHELSEA: They're going to get drenched.

ETHEL: I think between the two of them they have sense enough to come in out of the rain. At least I hope they do.

(*A moment passes as they look out at the lake.*)

Isn't it beautiful?

CHELSEA: (*She nods and looks at* ETHEL.) Look at you. You've had that robe for as long as I can remember.

ETHEL: (*She tries to arrange it.*) It looks like it, doesn't it?

CHELSEA: It looks great.

(*She stares at* ETHEL, *She steps to her and hugs her emphatically.*)

ETHEL: You're in a huggy mood today. What's the matter?

CHELSEA: You seem different.

ETHEL: You mean old.

CHELSEA: I don't know.

ETHEL: Well, that's what happens if you live long enough. You end up being old. It's one of the disadvantages of a long life. I still prefer it to the alternative.

CHELSEA: How does it really make you feel?

ETHEL: Not much different. A little more aware of the sunrises, I guess. And the sunsets.

CHELSEA: It makes *me* mad.

ETHEL: Ah, well, it doesn't exactly make me want to jump up and down.

(CHELSEA *hugs* ETHEL *again.*)

Oh, dear. They're not digging the grave yet. Come sit down. You must be exhausted.

(ETHEL *sits.* CHELSEA *wanders.*)

CHELSEA: Have Billy and Norman gotten along all right?

ETHEL: Billy is the happiest thing that's happened to Norman since Roosevelt. I should have rented him a thirteen-year-old boy years ago.

CHELSEA: You could have traded me in. (ETHEL *laughs.*) Billy reminds me of myself out there, way back when. Except I think he makes a better son than I did.

ETHEL: Well, you made a very nice daughter.

CHELSEA: Does Billy put the worm on the hook by himself?

ETHEL: I'm really not sure.

CHELSEA: I hope so. You lose points if you throw up, I remember that. I always apologized to those nice worms before I impaled them. Well, they'll get even with me someday, won't they?

ETHEL: You're beginning to sound an awful lot like your father.

CHELSEA: Uh oh. (*changing direction*) Thank you for taking care of Billy.

ETHEL: Thank *you*. I'm glad it gives us another chance to see you. Plus, it's been a tremendous education. Norman's vocabulary will never be the same but that's all right.

CHELSEA: (*turning to the mantel and picking up a picture*) Look at this. Chelsea on the swim team. That was a great exercise in humiliation.

ETHEL: Oh, stop it. You were a good diver.

CHELSEA: I wasn't a good diver. I was a good sport. I could never do a damn back flip.

ETHEL: Well, we were proud of you for trying.

CHELSEA: Right. Everyone got a big splash out of me trying. Why do you think I subjected myself to all that? I wasn't aiming for the 1956 Olympics, you know. I was just trying to please Norman. Because he'd been a diver, in the eighteen hundreds.

ETHEL: Can't you be home for five minutes without getting started on the past?

CHELSEA: This house seems to set me off.

ETHEL: Well, it shouldn't. It's a nice house.

CHELSEA: I act like a big person everywhere else. I do. I'm in charge in Los Angeles. I guess I've never grown up on Golden Pond. Do you understand?

ETHEL: I don't think so.

CHELSEA: It doesn't matter. There's just something about coming back here that makes me feel like a little fat girl.

ETHEL: Sit down and tell me about your trip.

CHELSEA: (*an outburst*) I don't want to sit down. Where were you all that time? You never bailed me out.

ETHEL: I didn't know you needed bailing out.

CHELSEA: Well, I did.

ETHEL: Here we go again. You had a miserable childhood. Your father was overbearing, your mother ignored you. What else is new? Don't you think everyone looks back on their childhood with some bitterness or regret about something? You are a big girl now, aren't you tired of it all. You have this unpleasant chip on your shoulder which is very unattractive. You only come home when I beg you to, and when you get here all you can do is be disagreeable about the past. Life marches by, Chelsea, I suggest you get on with it.

(ETHEL *stands and glares at* CHELSEA.)

You're such a nice person. Can't you think of something nice to say?

CHELSEA: I married Bill in Brussels.

ETHEL: You did what in Brussels?

CHELSEA: I married Bill.

ETHEL: Does it count in this country?

CHELSEA: 'Fraid so.

ETHEL: (*stepping to* CHELSEA *and kissing her*) Well, bless you. Congratulations.

CHELSEA: Thank you.

ETHEL: You have an odd way of building up to good news.

CHELSEA: I know.

ETHEL: Bill seems very nice.

CHELSEA: He's better than nice. He's an adult, too. I decided to go for an adult marriage this time. It's a standard five-year contract with renewable options. If it doesn't work out I still get to keep my gold caps.

ETHEL: What about Billy?

CHELSEA: Bill gets to keep Billy.

ETHEL: Will Billy live with you?

CHELSEA: Yes. That's part of the reason Bill had to get back to L.A. He's murdering his ex-wife. She doesn't want the kid anyway.

ETHEL: Do you?

CHELSEA: Yes.

ETHEL: Well, I'm so pleased.

CHELSEA: Nothing to it. I'm twice as old as you were when you married Norman. Think that means anything?

ETHEL: I hope it means that Bill will be only half as much trouble. Norman will be so surprised.

CHELSEA: I'll bet.

ETHEL: All he wants is for you to be happy.

CHELSEA: Could have fooled me. He always makes me feel like I've got my shoes on the wrong feet.

ETHEL: That's just his manner. He enjoys keeping people on their toes.

CHELSEA: I'm glad *he* gets pleasure out of it.

ETHEL: Dear God, how long do you plan to keep this up? Hmm?

CHELSEA: I don't know. I . . . can't talk to him. I've never been able to.

ETHEL: Have you ever *tried*?

CHELSEA: Yes, we've discussed the relative stupidity of Puerto Rican baseball players. I don't even know him.

ETHEL: Well, he'll be along any minute. I'll be happy to introduce you. You don't get to know a person by staying away for years at a time.

CHELSEA: I know. Maybe someday we can try to be friends.

ETHEL: Chelsea, Norman is eighty years old. He has heart palpitations and a problem remembering things. When exactly do you expect this friendship to begin?

CHELSEA: I don't know . . . I'm afraid of him.

ETHEL: Well, he's afraid of you. You should get along fine.

ALBUM
by David Rimmer

Act I, 3: Ticket to Ride

It's August, 1965. Trish is sixteen years old and, of course, she's mad about the Beatles. She plays their music all day long. All night long she dreams of romantic dates with John Lennon. She writes down the words to the Beatles' songs in the photo album her mother gave her, scribbling across old pictures of herself and her family. This beloved album has become Trish's security against all her adolescent fears about sex, boys, and her own budding needs.

When her best friend, Peggy, returns from summer camp, Trish immediately wants to know about Peggy's sexual adventures and if she is still a virgin.

The scene below takes place in Trish's room. Her parents are about to leave, but first they want her to turn down her blaring transistor radio.

(TRISH, *16, is sprawled on the floor downstage, one hand holding up a picture of John Lennon, as she gazes at it, a transistor radio next to her, blaring. She's wearing summer clothes, shorts and a sleeveless blouse; her body is beginning to fill out, she's looking more like a girl, her hair a little longer, more in control, her face less hidden. She listens to an offstage voice and reluctantly responds to it.*)

TRISH: *Okay! Okay! (She grudgingly turns down the radio, and the volume of "Ticket to Ride" goes down. She gets up, muttering and grumbling as she walks around the room in frustration.)* Haven't you gone yet? . . . God . . . *(She looks out the window and hears the sound of a car starting up and pulling away. She yells.)* I'll listen as loud as I want! *(Afraid she said it too loud, she takes a quick look outside, then, relieved, goes to her radio, and turns it back up. She sings along with the second verse of the song, changing the lyrics to show her anger toward her parents: from "She" and "me" to "I" and "you." As she sings, she takes out her mother's picture album and a pen, and a pack of cigarettes with matches and ashtray—all hidden under the bed. She sits on the floor and defiantly lights a cigarette. After a second or two of pleasure, the smoke gets in her eyes, and she reacts in pain. Then she turns her attention to the album, leafing through it, writing in it, turning down the radio a bit.)* Writin' in your sacred old picture album again, Mom. "A Thousand Stars," "Surfer Girl." Ecch. Ancient history. *(smiles)* "Eight Days A Week," "Help!" "Ticket To Ride." Here's what happens, Mom: I meet John Lennon at a party and he needs help just like a regular person, he's having problems with Cynthia and he's just waiting for the right bird to fly away with and I'm it and we run away together and leave you and your old album behind. And he's my Ticket to Ride. . . . *(She kisses the picture of John on the lips; then gets up.)* Sick. Gotta stop fallin' in love with pictures. *(looks out the window)* C'mon, get dark. *(The sound of a car pulling into the driveway scares her. She fans the air for smoke, hides the cigarettes, runs to the window.)* Shit! Back already? Can't you give me any peace—? (*yelps in delight*) Peggy! (*looks closer*) Barb? And a guy—? (*She runs out the door as the radio plays, and after a second or two, she and* PEGGY, *16 too, rush back into the room.* PEGGY *is wearing summer clothes, looks great in them. She seems the same, maybe a little more cynical and bored; no cracks in her front yet. They're playfully arguing, giggling like crazy, words overlapping, as they run to the window, music slowly fading down and out.*)

PEGGY: I had the worst summer of all time—

TRISH: No, I had the worst summer of all time—

PEGGY: No, I did—*Wait!* What's Barb doin'?

TRISH: Who's that guy, he looks so hoody—Move!

PEGGY: I can't see! God, I can't believe she's gonna do it with him—

TRISH: Do what?

PEGGY: It.

TRISH: *It?* You mean—How do you know? How can you tell?

PEGGY: She told me.

TRISH: Oh.

PEGGY: Wait! He's bending down! Look!

TRISH: Oh my God, he's goin' for it already! (*sound of car engine gunning*)

PEGGY: Nah, he's just revvin' it up. What a grub. Rory. (*They both giggle.*) She could've picked a guy with a better name.

TRISH: And one that didn't look like he just got out of state prison. (*Sounds of the car pulling away; they watch it drive out of sight.*)

PEGGY: She said to stay here and wait for her 'til she gets back. Then she'll tell us all about it.

TRISH: God, you go away for a summer and look what happens. You didn't do it too, didya?

PEGGY: Wanna hear somethin' sad? Midnight died—

TRISH: Your cat?

PEGGY: He got hit by a car. Splat. (PEGGY *starts checking out the room.*) Oh my God, you got your own phone now? (*picks up the receiver, speaks into it*) Princess. (*sits on the bed, looks into the album*) And still gettin' hot over pictures . . . ?

TRISH: Shut up! What about Barb?

PEGGY: What about her?

TRISH: The first time you do it, it hurts, doesn't it? And it bleeds?

PEGGY: I guess.

TRISH: (*wondrous*) But only for a second. Then every time afterwards it doesn't . . . Hey—

PEGGY: *What?*

TRISH: Do you think—no—

PEGGY: *What?*

TRISH: You think you'd—Think you'd ever do it with one of the Beatles?

PEGGY: *Dugan!*—God!—

TRISH: If you had the chance—

PEGGY: I don't know—

TRISH: Would you?—

PEGGY: Cut it out—

TRISH: *Come on,* would you?—

PEGGY: All right, yeah, I guess so—

TRISH: Which one?

PEGGY: Dugan, gimme a break. Haven't you gotten over the Beatles yet?

TRISH: I'll never get over them—

PEGGY: (*leafing through album*) I remember when it was Brian Wilson and the Beach Boys.

TRISH: Bullshit.

PEGGY: You kiss your mother with that mouth?

TRISH: (*sighs*) I've never even seen a boy's, you know.

PEGGY: I saw my brother's in the bathtub once. (*They both giggle.*)

TRISH: Really? What'd it look like?

PEGGY: Like a mushroom. With a little eye at the end of it. Then when it gets big, it's like a mushroom on top of a rocket.

TRISH: It gets big? I thought it just, you know, stood up. Like an erection. (*hesitant pause*) Do you know, um, do the balls go in with it or do they stay outside?

PEGGY: (*embarrassed*) Gross!—

TRISH: My mother never told me anything she was supposed to. She said stuff like, "A kiss should end the evening, not begin it." And "Why buy a cow when you can already taste the milk?"

PEGGY: What does that mean?

TRISH: Don't do it before you're married.

PEGGY: Vomitous.

TRISH: I wonder if Barb'll have to get married.

PEGGY: *Will you shut up about Barb?*

TRISH: What's the matter? You did it too, didn't you?

PEGGY: No, I—Never mind.

TRISH: Some friend. You and Barb go off and do it and leave me— (*stops and stares at* PEGGY)

PEGGY: What're you doin'?

TRISH: Tryin' to see if you look different.

PEGGY: What?

TRISH: You look different after you do it. That's what happens.

PEGGY: How can you look different?

TRISH: I don't know! You turn into a woman and you look different. Don't ask me. (*beat*) You look the same to me. Didya feel different after you did it?

PEGGY: *Will· you leave me alone?*

TRISH: What's the matter?

PEGGY: No—I—did—not—feel—different.

TRISH: Why not?

PEGGY: *Dugan!*

TRISH: Peggy . . . What—? Aren't you gonna tell me about it?

PEGGY: Why?

TRISH: 'Cause you're my friend, that's why.

PEGGY: Why don't you just wait for Barb to get back. She's your friend too.

TRISH: 'Cause—She's not my friend the way you are. Okay? *'Cause I want you to tell me!* (PEGGY *smiles, drifts off for a second, glances at some of* TRISH's *old toys.*)

PEGGY: Remember that time when we were little kids and we became blood sisters?

TRISH: Yeah, and the knife slipped and I got an infection. I still got the scar.

PEGGY: Lemme see. (TRISH *holds out her hand.* PEGGY *takes it in hers, holds it, then bites it.* TRISH *cries "Ow!", backs away, her hand at her mouth, sucking at the sore.*)

TRISH: You're weird. God, if it changes you this much, I don't know if I wanna do it.

PEGGY: (*coming over to her*) I'm sorry! I'm sorry, I just wanted to be blood sisters again. (*She takes* TRISH's *hand and gently kisses it on the sore spot and then walks away. Amazed,* TRISH *just stares at her.*) I met this guy from another town. I didn't even know his name.

TRISH: God . . .

PEGGY: Shh—Don't talk. (*beat*) I drove down to the Quarry with him, and we parked the car. (TRISH *sits down, listening, all rapt attention.*) There wasn't anybody else there. There was a full moon, I could see it through the windshield. We got in the back seat . . . 1st Base, 2nd Base, 3rd Base . . . He kept touching me down there. You remember the first time you felt . . . you got wet?

TRISH: Tell me about now.

PEGGY: First time it happened to me was way back with Billy. That was nice. (*looks at* TRISH, *who's still anxiously waiting*) Okay, we're in the back seat, and practically all our clothes are off. Then he goes and gets a rubber. Eeuu. And he gets on top of me and starts moanin' and groanin' like he was dyin' or something. Then I feel something touching me down there and I think, "Okay, okay, it's only gonna hurt a second." But it keeps hurting, and it isn't going in. I said, "What's the matter?" And he said, "No, it's okay, it's okay." He wanted me to put my hand on it. It was all slimy. And he keeps trying and trying and it still won't go in. He was sweating on me. I felt so squished. I pushed him off me, and he was just sitting there with this stupid look on his face, and I thought, "This is it?" So I said to him, "There's something wrong with one of us." He didn't say anything.

TRISH: (*her face fallen*) That isn't true.

PEGGY: I'm never doin' it again. First and last.

TRISH: (*can't believe it*) That happened to *you*?

PEGGY: No, it happened to Shelley Fabres. (TRISH *just stares at* PEGGY, *who keeps her face turned away. Pause. The phone rings.* TRISH, *never taking her eyes off* PEGGY, *answers it.*)

TRISH: Hello? . . . Barb? . . . What—? (*listens*) . . . God . . . Yeah, where are ya? . . . Okay, we'll be right there. . . . I promise. . . . Just keep listenin' to your radio, okay? . . . What—? They played "Satisfaction" and now they're playin' "Wooly Bully"? Great. Okay, we're comin'. Bye. (*Hangs up. Stands there stunned.*) She started doin' it with the guy, and he asked if she was a virgin or not. She said yeah, he said forget it, and he kicked her out of the car and left her on the beach.

PEGGY: Figures.

TRISH: How're you supposed to get to *not* be a virgin? (TRISH *stands still, not sure what to do.* PEGGY *lies down on the bed and looks at* TRISH's *pictures.* TRISH *puts her sandals on, then turns back to* PEGGY.) Come on . . . We better go. . . .

PEGGY: Maybe it's better with pictures. (TRISH *yanks* PEGGY *up and they both go out the door, arms around each other.*)

A COUPLA WHITE CHICKS SITTING AROUND TALKING
by John Ford Noonan

Act II, Scene 1

Having just moved up from Texas to the upwardly mobile county of Westchester, N.Y., Hannah Mae Bindler needs a friend. She is brash, big-hearted—an ex-cheerleader with irrepressible charm. Her cowgirl style is a sharp contrast to the Yanky formality of her neighbor, Maude Mix. But Hannah has taken a liking to this Westchester housewife, and pursues a friendship with a single-mindedness that borders on war. Everything about Maude fascinates Hannah: the *Better Homes and Gardens* decor of her house, her pin-neat kitchen, her compulsive cooking style—even her blend of coffee. Hannah is intrigued. She wants to be friends.

Unfortunately, Maude is not feeling particularly friendly this weekend. Her husband, Tyler, is off on a weekend spree with his secretary, and she is trying to keep her composure while she decides what to do about her failing marriage. When Hannah bursts on the scene, Maude tries her best to keep her out of her kitchen and out of her life. But Hannah persists.

Hannah's husband, Carl Joe, is displeased with her new friendship. She spends too much time watching Maude through binoculars when she should be paying attention to him. He tries to break up the friendship by seducing Maude on her kitchen table. Emotionally weakened by her marital problems, Maude yields and immediately regrets it. When Hannah drops by for a morning cup of coffee, Maude tells her what happened. But Hannah is nonplussed. Carl Joe was just testing their friendship, trying to break it up. She tells Maude, "If I had to share Carl Joe with anyone, I'm real glad that anyone was you." Maude is fed up with the whole situation and throws her out.

The next morning Hannah turns up with a broken wrist, a black eye and a mug for some of Maude's special coffee.

HANNAH MAE: (*speaks from outside door*) Hello? Anyone home? (*tries to open screen door, discovers it locked*) Screen door's locked! Flip the latch. (*no response*) Maude, how long you planning to keep your shades pulled down?

MAUDE: Till you stop.

HANNAH MAE: About yesterday—

MAUDE: What happened with your husband yesterday is something I am very sorry about and will always live to regret. One of those unexplainable events. Like snow in July. However, yesterday was Wednesday and today is Thursday. I am back with my cookies. Order has been restored. I have regained my hold on things. I am back in clothes I feel comfortable in. I am wearing an apron. Today I am doing seven sheets of vanilla ice box wafers for next Tuesday's League of Women Voters tag sale and six more for the Westchester County Fresh Air Fund. Hear what I'm saying? I want you to go back home, now.

HANNAH MAE: Before I go back home, don't you want to autograph my cast?

MAUDE: What cast?

HANNAH MAE: Come over here and see for yourself.

MAUDE: (*crosses to oven, puts cookie sheet in, turns and faces door*) I can see fine from here. (*runs to door, opens it*) Did that bastard beat you up?

HANNAH MAE: (*Walks in, leans against door frame. She is wearing large white cast on left arm. Right eye is bruised and half closed. She is wearing sunglasses.*) No, I walked into a door, I need to sit down. (MAUDE *helps* HANNAH MAE *to kitchen table and into chair.*) Got any coffee on? (*suddenly producing two coffee cups*) I bought a new cup for myself, and here's one for the one you threw at me yesterday. (MAUDE *takes two cups to coffee pot, fills one, returns to table.* HANNAH MAE *tastes coffee.*) There's something you do with the cinnamon I still gotta figure out. (HANNAH MAE *puts cup down on table.*)

MAUDE: All I do actually is—

HANNAH MAE: Could you move your chair over here and sit beside me? (MAUDE *moves chair next to* HANNAH MAE.) Could you put your arm around me?

MAUDE: (*putting arm around* HANNAH MAE) How's that?

HANNAH MAE: Could you sway me back and forth real gentle? (MAUDE *sways her back and forth.*) A little more . . .

(MAUDE *does so,* HANNAH MAE *takes off her sunglasses and shows* MAUDE *her bandaged right eye.*)

MAUDE: That bastard really did a job on you.

HANNAH MAE: Goddang if I didn't do the whole mess to myself.

MAUDE: What?

HANNAH MAE: Self-inflicted wounds, Honey, self-inflicted.

MAUDE: I don't believe you.

HANNAH MAE: Carl Joe arrives on the five-forty-seven. I'm dressed perfect. Dinner's a killer. He stuffs his face. I wipe his mouth. My plan's going perfect, I'm leading the sucker to slaughter! Next I take off his shoes—I'm on the verge of doing a job on his insteps—only I can't hold my anger back another second. I smash his shoes to the floor and I scream, "Lug, the wandering hands is one thing but this next-door hustling's gotta stop!" He screams back, "What next-door hustling?" I smile and say real quiet and slow, "I know about you and Miss Maude." He smiles and says real quiet back, "Nothing happened between us. She's got no proof!"

MAUDE: No proof? There's me.

HANNAH MAE: I grab his shoe and whack him hard on the side of his head. "Goddang liar!" He bolts out of the chair. For twenty years every day I've been afraid of pushing him too far. . . . I mean, to live all that time threatened by something that never comes but at any minute could . . . only now it's here! Before he can even make a fist, WHAP! I get him with the shoe again. It's him that's afraid of me. Twice more I hit him. WHAP, WHAP. He rolls over and the chase begins. Ain't never felt so good in my life. Only trouble is I wrecked my eye falling against the coffee table in the living room and my wrist, well, that got broke falling down the back stairs trying to tackle the lug. Self-inflicted, but sure feels good. So!

MAUDE: So?

HANNAH MAE: Yes or no?

MAUDE: Yes or no what?

HANNAH MAE: I need to hear it from you. Did it happen?

MAUDE: Yes.

HANNAH MAE: (*taking* MAUDE's *face in her hands*) Right into my eyes.

MAUDE: Yes, we did it! Yes, yes, yes!! (HANNAH MAE *bursts out of room.* MAUDE *runs to door, holds it open.*) Hannah Mae, WHAT ARE YOU DOING?!

HANNAH MAE: (*returns, suitcase in each hand and crosses* *left past* MAUDE, *puts suitcases down*) What's your situation "guest-room-wise"?

MAUDE: Listen, I—

HANNAH MAE: Don't stand there with your mouth open, do you or don't you?

MAUDE: Do I or *don't* I WHAT?

HANNAH MAE: Have any extra bedrooms on the side of your house facing my house? (*crosses to "her window," lifts shade*) Gotta be able to see every move that bastard makes.

MAUDE: (*picks up suitcases*) Our extra bedrooms all face the other way.

HANNAH MAE: Then it'll have to be your bedroom.

MAUDE: What?!!

HANNAH MAE: (HANNAH MAE *crosses to* MAUDE.) You and Tyler sleep together or in separate beds?

MAUDE: Separate but—

HANNAH MAE: It's perfect. I'll use his bed, and you can keep yours! That way I'll be close enough to protect you.

MAUDE: From what?

HANNAH MAE: (HANNAH MAE *pulls* MAUDE *downstage near dishwasher.*) Carl Joe Bindler will stop at nothing to get back at you for what you've done to me.

MAUDE: What I've done to you!!!

HANNAH MAE: Not only that but he says you led on.

MAUDE: Wait a minute. I thought he said nothing happened.

HANNAH MAE: (*crosses to table*) He said you served him a cup of your wonderful coffee, threw your skirt over your head, and hopped up on the table. He says if you hadn't closed your eyes and started begging for it, he couldn't have snuck out the door and run to safety like he did!

MAUDE: That's it! That bastard's not getting away with this.

HANNAH MAE: That's what I say too! (*crosses to her suitcases, picks them up*) So where do you want my bags?

MAUDE: Up the stairs, hook a left.

(HANNAH MAE *exits up left with suitcases, leaves them offstage.* MAUDE *lifts shades, returns chairs to table.* HANNAH MAE *re-enters kitchen, crosses downstage.*)

HANNAH MAE: Maude, I need someone to stand behind me all the way, are you that kind of friend?!

MAUDE: (*crosses to* HANNAH MAE) Absolutely! Your bed's on the far side of the room—the red bedspread with the big initial "T" on it—now get going!

HANNAH MAE: Usually I'm afraid to be happy but here comes my cowgirl yell. (*yelling out*) YIP-PEE-I-OW, YIP-I-OW, YIP-PEE-I-OW—YIP-OH YIPEE!

LUNCH HOUR
by Jean Kerr

ACT 1

Oliver DeVreck is spending his summer in Amagansett trying to finish his new book when he is interrupted by a young woman who is looking for his wife. Carrie Sachs has never met either Oliver or his wife, Nora, but she knows Nora is having an affair with her husband, Peter. Not knowing quite how to handle this situation, Carrie has decided to confront it head on.

But Nora is not home. Nervous and a bit befuddled, the lovable Carrie spills the beans about the affair to Oliver and insists that the only thing to do is wait for Nora to return. Oliver is stunned. He wants her to leave. While he answers a phone call in the next room, Nora returns.

In the meantime Carrie has decided that the best way to save her marriage is to convince Nora that she is having an affair of her own—with Oliver.

(NORA *does appear with both arms overloaded with wobbly shopping bags.*)

CARRIE: Oh, hello, Mrs. DeVreck. Come right in. Here, let me take one of those.

NORA: (*as* CARRIE *quickly snatches one of the bags from her*) Well, you are the soul of hospitality! And who are you? And where is my husband?

CARRIE: He's in the bedroom. (*turns her attention to taking one bag to table near settee R.*)

NORA: (*There's something she doesn't like about this.*) In the bedroom? (*heading for it*) Oliver! Oliver!

CARRIE: (*grabbing her arm as she puts down bag*) Wait,

wait—please. He's on the phone. But he knows I'm going to talk to you. We agreed to that.

NORA: And does any part of this agreement include telling me who you are? Oh, of course. How slow-witted I am! You are Mrs. Amagansett.

CARRIE: But you didn't believe that for a minute. I could tell by the way you underlined the word "who." You said— (*imitating her on phone*) "Who?" (*extending her hand suddenly*) I'm Carrie Sachs. How do you do?

NORA: (*startled, ignoring the hand*) You're Peter's wife?

CARRIE: And you're Peter's girl friend. This bag feels cold. I'm going to put it in the kitchen for you. (*taking it from the table toward where refrigerator might be, off*) This stuff could melt. They say you can refreeze things, but I wouldn't. (*She keeps popping back and forth.*) Let me get that other bag. I notice you have skim milk in here. I notice things like that because of all my diets.

NORA: Mrs. Sachs, won't you sit down? And let me explain about that foolish phone call Peter made.

CARRIE: (*keeping at work on the grocery bags to overcome her nervousness, all of which is making* NORA *nervous*) No, thank you, I've been sitting all day—

NORA: I don't know exactly what to say— (*And it's difficult for her to think with* CARRIE *so busy.*) Please put the groceries down. Please sit down.

CARRIE: (*deposits grocery bag on small table, R., turns toward* NORA) I'd rather stand.

NORA: (*rising, and speaking more firmly*) Please sit down.

CARRIE: (*about to take off again*) I think I'd better—

NORA: (*swiftly intercepting her, speaking to her as though training a dog*) Sit!

(CARRIE *does sit, reluctantly, stiffly.*)

Look, you must believe me. The whole thing between Peter and me was nothing. One day my car broke down in front of the fish market, so I walked over to the cab stand. Naturally, there were no cabs— (*She too has seated herself, on the sofa, trying to be easy.*)

CARRIE: They're *never*! It's really a disgrace, the cab situation.

NORA: (*going on, with an effort*) So a car pulled up and this man said, "I'm not a taxi, I'm Peter Sachs, but if you're going anywhere down the Montauk I'd be happy to drop you." So I got in the car.

CARRIE: That messy car! Peter's so ambivalent about being rich. Because it's a Mercedes, he won't ever get it washed. And then that front seat—all littered with sneakers and old road maps! I'd rather have a clean Chevy.

(*She takes out a cigarette. Without a word,* NORA—*whose nerves have just snapped—shifts closer to* CARRIE, *snatches* CARRIE'S *pack of cigarettes and, her hand noticeably trembling, lights up. She takes a deep drag and is finally able to continue.*)

NORA: In any case, he said he was suddenly starving, and so was I, and so we had lunch. We've had lunch several times since— (*Suddenly she breaks off, gets to her feet, changes her tone entirely.*) Look. This is too important to lie about. One day we were walking back to the car. And I guess he wanted to know what time it was. Anyway, he reached down and picked up my wrist to look at my watch—he wasn't wearing one. It was as simple as that. He was holding my wrist and we didn't say anything. But I knew what was going to happen and I was so happy—and so sorry.

CARRIE: (*affected, covering it by jumping up and snatching a magazine out of a floor rack*) That bag is beginning to make a puddle.

NORA: What are you doing?

CARRIE: (*slipping magazine under the bag on the table*) I'm just putting a magazine under here. You'll get a white ring. Of course, you can get it out with lemon oil. But sometimes it takes two applications. (*sits down again abruptly, facing* NORA *as though nothing had been interrupted*)

NORA: (*deep breath, making a last-ditch effort*) Look, what I'm trying to tell you is—I think I'm in love with Peter. (*forcing herself*) I *am* in love with Peter.

(CARRIE *is on her feet again.*)

Now what are you doing?

CARRIE: (*It takes a little more effort for her to invent just now, but she plunges on.*) I just wanted to see if it was this week's issue of *Time* I put under there. It'll get damp. (*She retrieves the magazine from under the bag and looks at its cover.*) Bruce Springsteen? (*looks at the date*) Oh, no, this is November 1978. (*putting the magazine back under the bag, and gathering steam again*) You know, I have this friend who keeps really old copies of *Time* and *Newsweek*. I mean like twenty years old. He keeps them in the bathroom, and then when he can't sleep he gets up and reads all about the Berlin airlift or the Suez crisis. He says it's very relaxing at four-thirty in the morning—because, you see, it's all over now.

NORA: (*really baffled*) I don't get this. You seem more concerned about my defrosting vegetables than you do about your husband.

CARRIE: Oh, dear, is that the way it seems? Not at all. Of course, I do worry about things that drip. But the truth is that right now I'm sort of using it as a delaying tactic because I'm so embarrassed. (*There is a subtle shifting of cogs here, as* CARRIE *seems to make up her mind. She rises and faces away, standing above the chair.*)

NORA: I don't understand. Why are you embarrassed?

CARRIE: (*turning back to* NORA) Because I know all that. Peter told me. Well, not about the wristwatch, but everything else. But that's just half the story. And I can feel it in my bones you don't have a clue about the other half.

NORA: What other half? What are you talking about?

CARRIE: That's what I figured. You don't know. And I don't want to be the one that has to tell you. Though, in all the circumstances, there's no reason why *we* should feel guilty.

NORA: Can I try to pin this down? *Who* is we?

CARRIE: (*deep breath and a step toward* NORA) Me and Oliver.

NORA: You and Oliver what?

CARRIE: The simple answer to that is yes. We are.

NORA: (*getting the general idea, and totally incredulous*) *You* and Oliver?

CARRIE: You're thinking the worst. You're right.

NORA: (*getting to her feet*) Is that so? Well, I think I will take these into the kitchen. (*moves remaining bag of groceries from table, takes it to kitchen*)

CARRIE: You don't ask any questions. Like how did we meet and when did it all happen.

NORA: I have every confidence you are about to tell me. (*returns with a towel, wipes table*)

CARRIE: You're so calm. And I bet you never ate a Ry-Krisp in your life.

NORA: What has that got to do with anything?

CARRIE: A lot. Everything.

NORA: All right. Where did you meet?

CARRIE: In his office. I was a patient. (*sits on the sofa*)

NORA: (*skeptically*) Really? Now, why did I get the definite impression when I phoned Oliver that he had never laid eyes on you before?

CARRIE: (*as though ashamed for* OLIVER) Yes, I heard what he said. It's terrible the way love makes you deceitful. I was a patient, all right. I'll never forget how I suffered in that office, sitting under that weird painting of Saint Sebastian. (*She's done a good enough job of remembering* LEO's *description.*)

NORA: (*forced to buy it, so far*) All right, you *were* a patient—

CARRIE: Of course, it started out on a completely impersonal, professional basis—

NORA: You mean he did not hurl you to the carpet during your first appointment.

CARRIE: (*crossing her legs elaborately and adopting a very worldly posture*) I suppose I deserve the sarcasm. But don't you want to know how it developed?

NORA: (*sitting on edge of the cube*) You mean this thing has a plot?

CARRIE: A plot? You know, that's sort of funny.

NORA: I didn't think so, but then I frequently miss things.

CARRIE: Of course it's not funny. It's a disgrace. (*She has a new thought.*) Oh, I just thought of something terrible!

NORA: Something *else* terrible?

CARRIE: Do you think that's why Peter doesn't wear a wristwatch? So he can pick up girls?

NORA: (*irked, going to table and picking up towel*) I'm hardly a girl, and I don't really think I qualify as a pickup! Peter doesn't wear a watch because he is a very relaxed person. He doesn't want to know every five minutes what time is it, what time is it? Oliver, on the other hand, is the kind of man who always wears his watch—

CARRIE: (*stealing a sudden glance at* OLIVER's *watch, which is still on the arm of the chair where he put it, within reach*) Always?

NORA: Except when he goes to bed. Otherwise, he never takes it off. He—

(CARRIE *has furtively, but not really furtively, palmed* OLIVER's *wristwatch. And* NORA *has broken off her speech because she's noticed the sudden movement. She stares at* CARRIE, *quizzically. Then she crosses to her, stands directly in front of her, and holds out her hand. Caught,* CARRIE *gives up* OLIVER's *wristwatch, a little-girl-guilty expression written all over her face.* NORA *stares at the watch.*)

CARRIE: I'm speechless.

NORA: I'd like to think so. You really are quite a little package, aren't you?

CARRIE: Actually, we have a lot in common. You're the other woman. And *I'm* the other woman. For me, that's progress.

TABLE MANNERS
(from THE NORMAN CONQUESTS)
by Alan Ayckbourn

ACT I, SCENE 1

This opening scene from TABLE MANNERS, which is one of the three plays that comprise THE NORMAN CONQUESTS, takes place in the dining room of a Victorian vicarage-type house outside of London. It is six P.M. on a Saturday night in July. The time is the present. Annie, who lives with and cares for her invalid mother, is waiting for her older brother, Reg, and his wife, Sarah, to arrive for the weekend to take over her nursing chores. Annie is planning to take a holiday weekend at East Grinstead—a suburban town near London that is a very unlikely vacation spot. When Sarah finally arrives, Annie tries to be evasive about her upcoming weekend since she will be spending it with her brother-in-law, Norman, her older sister Ruth's husband. Norman has an eye for the ladies (at least the ones in his family), and he and Annie have already had a lusty go at it during the previous Christmas.

(ANNIE *in baggy sweater, jeans and raffia slippers enters with a flower vase of water. She thumps this down in the middle of the table, picks up the roses which lie beside it and drops them into the vase. She gives the whole lot a final shake and that, as far as she's concerned, concludes her flower arrangement. She is moving to the sideboard, about to lay the table when* SARAH *enters. She wears a light summer coat and dress. She is breathless.)*

SARAH: Hallo! We're here—

ANNIE: Sarah!

SARAH: *(embracing her)* Annie dear . . .

ANNIE: Good journey?

SARAH: Oh yes, yes, not too bad. Reg drove far too fast as usual but we got here—oh, it's lovely to come down. I've been looking forward to this weekend away from it all for weeks. Weekend? It's barely a day. You've no idea how that dreary little house of ours gets me down.

ANNIE: Oh, it's not bad.

SARAH: Try living there sometime. Not a decent shop, not a cinema, not even a hairdresser—except some awful place I can't go into because of the smell. I said to Reg, for goodness' sake you're an estate agent, surely you can get the pick of anywhere and then we finish up in somewhere like this. . . . You're so lucky, Annie, you have no idea. Just to see a tree once in a while and the birds . . . I really miss it. Now then, how are you, let's look. Oh, Annie darling, you look just the same. Your hair . . .

ANNIE: *(self-consciously smoothing her tangle)* I know . . . I haven't brushed it today. I washed it, though, this morning.

SARAH: What's the good of washing it if you don't brush it. It's like a gorse bush.

ANNIE: Well, nobody sees it. The postman, the milkman, couple of cows and Mother.

SARAH: And Tom.

ANNIE: Oh, yes. Tom.

SARAH: You mustn't forget Tom. And how's Mother?

ANNIE: No better, no worse. She hasn't felt like getting up, not for weeks. . . .

SARAH: Well, you should make her. She needs to.

ANNIE: Old Wickham says if she doesn't want to, don't make her.

SARAH: Wickham? Oh yes, I've never really cared for him. His eyes are too close together. Still, I suppose he's all right as a doctor. He must be better than ours. I mean, this business with my back was practically criminal.

ANNIE: Your back?

SARAH: Surely I wrote and told you? I'm sure I did. I was so upset I wrote to everybody.

ANNIE: Oh yes.

SARAH: Annie, I must buy you a new jumper, remind me.

ANNIE: I'm attached to this one.

SARAH: I should think you are.... You were wearing it at Christmas. We'll have to chisel it off you.... Mmm, lovely flowers . . . Now tell me. Where are you going?

ANNIE: When?

SARAH: For your weekend, where are you going?

ANNIE: Well—

SARAH: Oh, come on. Don't be so secretive.

ANNIE: Well . . . I was going to Hastings.

SARAH: Oh, lovely! Hastings is gorgeous. I think I was there with Reg just before we were married. There's a heavenly little pub somewhere. . . .

ANNIE: No, well I couldn't get in at Hastings.

SARAH: Couldn't get it?

ANNIE: No, it was all booked. I forgot it was summer.

SARAH: Oh. Yes. Well, where are you going?

ANNIE: I rather fancied East Grinstead.

SARAH: East Grinstead?

ANNIE: Yes.

SARAH: What an extraordinary idea. What on earth made you choose there?

ANNIE: Well, it sounded—interesting.

SARAH: Yes, I suppose it is. I've never heard of anybody having a holiday in East Grinstead. I suppose they do—but I've never heard of anybody.

ANNIE: Well, I am.

SARAH: Yes. I think I'd have almost preferred Eastbourne but . . . (*displaying her outfit*) Do you like this?

ANNIE: Super.

SARAH: It was like a tent on me when I bought it, but I had it altered. I'm rather pleased. Now, you're to leave everything to me. I'm taking over. Just tell me what pills and potions Mother has and when she has them and then off you go.

ANNIE: I've written it down somewhere. I'll show you. The only difficult things are her drops.

SARAH: Oh well, if they're difficult Reg can cope with them. He's going to do most of the running up and down stairs anyway. I mean, this is a holiday for me too. She's his mother. He can do something for her for a change.

ANNIE: How is he?

SARAH: Reg? (*big sigh*) Oh well, he's still Reg, you know.

I've tried. God knows I've tried but he'll always be basically Reg. You'll know, he's your brother after all. There are times when I think he's sleepwalking. I have to force him to make an effort. Heaven knows how he runs a business. I'd certainly never let him sell a house of mine.

ANNIE: I've left you a cold supper.

SARAH: Oh, you shouldn't have bothered.

ANNIE: Well, I knew you wouldn't want to be . . .

SARAH: You shouldn't have bothered.

ANNIE: I left it all out for you on the—

SARAH: You really shouldn't have bothered.

ANNIE: —kitchen table.

SARAH: Lovely.

ANNIE: I was just laying things in here.

SARAH: Oh, there's no need for that. We'll eat with our fingers. We're on holiday, for heaven's sake.

ANNIE: We do have knives and forks.

SARAH: I'll find them, don't bother. Now please, just get changed and go.

ANNIE: Okay. (*She starts to move to the door.*)

SARAH: Oh. I nearly forgot. How's Tom?

ANNIE: Tom? Oh, fine. I think.

SARAH: Still seeing a lot of him?

ANNIE: Oh, yes. He's generally around. When he's not out curing his sick animals. He's here at the moment, actually. The cat's got something wrong with its paw.

SARAH: It must be fascinating being a vet. It's a pity in a way he's not a proper doctor.

ANNIE: He is a proper doctor. He just prefers animals to people.

SARAH: That came from the heart.

ANNIE: No. He just likes animals. Don't think he's very fond of our cat but he likes most animals.

SARAH: Yes, he's a bit—heavy going, isn't he? I've always found him a trifle ponderous. Perhaps it's shyness.

ANNIE: No, I think he's probably ponderous.

SARAH: He hasn't—er—shown any more interest?

ANNIE: In what?

SARAH: Well, you. At Christmas, we thought he was beginning to sit up and take notice of you just a little. Pricking up his ears.

ANNIE: Like a mongrel with a pedigree bitch.

SARAH: Yes, well . . .

ANNIE: Honestly, stop trying to pair us off. He just comes round when he's bored, that's all.

SARAH: A man doesn't spend as much time as Tom does round here without having a very good reason. Believe you me. You don't have to be psychic to know what that is.

ANNIE: Well, if it's that he's never asked for it and even if he did he wouldn't get it. So I don't know why he bothers.

SARAH: Annie! You're getting dreadfully coarse.

ANNIE: Oh, you're just a prude.

SARAH: No, I'm not a prude. No, I've never been called that. You can't call me a prude. That's not fair, Annie. I mean, I don't care for smutty talk or dirty jokes. I just don't find them funny. Or particularly tasteful. But that isn't being a prude. That's normal decent behaviour which is something quite different.

ANNIE: Yes.

SARAH: I won't have the television set on at all these days.

ANNIE: Anyway, all that happens is that Tom comes round here like he has done for years. I feed him. He sits and broods. Sometimes we talk. That's all.

SARAH: Talk about what?

ANNIE: Oh, super exciting things like does the kitchen ceiling need another coat and distemper and hardpad and foot and mouth and swine vesicular disease. Then I pot Mother and retire to bed—alone—itching.

SARAH: Oh.

ANNIE: And count sick sheep crashing headlong into the gate. Look for all I know he may be passionately in love with me. He may be flashing out all sorts of secret signals which I just haven't noticed. But he's never even put a hand on my knee. (*reflecting*) God forbid.

SARAH: But you're fond of him?

ANNIE: He's—very kind. Yes, I like him a lot. I sometimes miss him when he's not here. I suppose that means something.

SARAH: Yes. You see, I was rather hoping—I know it's wicked of me—I was rather hoping that you were both planning to go off for this weekend together.

ANNIE: Oh. No.

SARAH: You're not, are you?

ANNIE: (*uneasy*) No. Not at all.

SARAH: Are you sure?

ANNIE: Of course I'm sure.

SARAH: You're looking very shifty.

ANNIE: I'm not. Honestly. No. Stop it.

SARAH: Stop what?

ANNIE: Looking at me like that.

SARAH: Like what?

ANNIE: Like that. Stop it.

SARAH: You're a dreadful liar.

ANNIE: I'm not.

SARAH: Listen, if you are, there's no need to keep it a secret from me. I mean, you said I'm a prude but I've just proved I'm not, surely? I mentioned it first. I think it's splendid. I think if you and Tom were to get away from this house, away from Mother and everything—it's the best thing you could do. It's what you both need. (*She kisses her.*) Very sensible.

ANNIE: Yes.

SARAH: Have a lovely time. I only wish it were me. Not with Tom, of course. But I think that's what we all need now and then, don't we? A nice dirty weekend somewhere. Oh, it's so exciting. I am pleased you're doing it. I think the best bit is waking up in the morning in a strange room and finding some exciting looking man beside you and—you've got a double room?

ANNIE: It's a bit more complicated than that.

SARAH: Oh? How do you mean? You haven't got a double room.

ANNIE: No, it's just . . .

SARAH: What? You're not pregnant?

ANNIE: No.

SARAH: Oh, thank God.

ANNIE: No, it's just—oh golly, I didn't mean to tell you.

SARAH: Tell me what?

ANNIE: It's awfully sordid. You're sure you want to hear?

SARAH: Of course, I want to hear.

ANNIE: It'll shock you.

SARAH: My dear, I've been married for eight years. I've had two children. I think I've just about seen everything there is to see. I defy you to shock me. I honestly defy you.

ANNIE: Well. Last Christmas, when you were all here . . .

SARAH: Yes?

ANNIE: You and Reg and Ruth and Norman. And then you and Reg left early. . . .

SARAH: Because Denise didn't want to miss her dancing classes—yes?

ANNIE: And then after that, Ruth was ill. . . .

SARAH: Or so she said.

ANNIE: Well, she was flat on her back with something for a week and that left Norman and me—more or less to cope. Tom was in Scotland on a course.

SARAH: Yes?

ANNIE: Anyway.

SARAH: I am beginning dreadfully not to like the sound of this one little bit.

ANNIE: Anyway. Golly, I'm getting dreadfully hot.

SARAH: Go on. What?

ANNIE: Well, you know Norman, he's . . .

SARAH: Yes, I know Norman very well.

ANNIE: He's not a bit like Tom. I mean, just the opposite to Tom. Norman doesn't bother with secret signals at all. It was just wham, thump and there we both were on the rug.

SARAH: Rug?

ANNIE: Yes.

SARAH: Which rug?

ANNIE: The brown nylon fur one in the lounge . . . (*She starts to giggle.*)

SARAH: (*irritated*) What is it? Why are you laughing?

ANNIE: (*unable to control herself*) Does it matter which rug?

SARAH: I don't think it's funny.

ANNIE: No, nor do I. I'm sorry—it's just I'm so embarrassed— oh, gosh—

SARAH: Annie, pull yourself together.

ANNIE: (*is helpless*) Yes . . .

SARAH: (*thumping the table*) Annie, what happened on the rug?

ANNIE: Everything happened on the rug.

SARAH: Does Ruth know?

ANNIE: No.

SARAH: Or Tom?

ANNIE: No. (*drying her eyes*) Oh dear . . .

SARAH: Well, I blame Norman. That is absolutely typical . . . fur rug! (*This starts* ANNIE *off again.*) It's just the sort of thing— Annie, will you stop making that ridiculous noise . . . typical behaviour. (ANNIE *blows her nose.*) Is that it? Was that the only occasion?

ANNIE: Oh yes. Ruth got better and they both went home.

SARAH: I suppose it could have been worse. That poor woman. I mean, I don't have a lot of time for Ruth, as you know. Personally, I find her snide little remarks, her violent ups and downs just too much to cope with. I know she's your sister, I'm sorry for talking like this. However, I would not wish my worst enemy married to a man like... not even Ruth. Heaven knows why they married. Never understood it. What did she see in him?

ANNIE: Norman says it was uncontrollable animal lust that drew them together.

SARAH: Norman told you that?

ANNIE: Yes. He says it's died out now. They are like two empty husks.

SARAH: Yes. Hardly surprising. Well, believe me, you're well clear of that, dear. You're well clear of that one.

ANNIE: You don't think I should then?

SARAH: What?

ANNIE: Go.

SARAH: Go where?

ANNIE: This weekend.

SARAH: This weekend?

ANNIE: With Norman? To East Grinstead. (*a pause*)

SARAH: You were planning to go with Norman to East Grinstead?

ANNIE: Yes. He couldn't get in anywhere else.

SARAH: You're not serious?

ANNIE: Yes.

SARAH: But how could you even think of it?

ANNIE: He asked me.

SARAH: What has that got to do with it?

ANNIE: Well, I wanted a holiday...

SARAH: Yes but—this wouldn't be just a holiday... I mean, I mean, you just don't go off on holiday with your sister's husband.

ANNIE: It was only a weekend. I needed a holiday.

SARAH: Well, you could have gone on your own.

ANNIE: (*slightly angry*) I didn't want to go on my own. I'm always on my own.

SARAH: But did you realize what you would be getting yourself into?

ANNIE: Well—the way Norman put it—it sounded simple. Just a weekend.

SARAH: Norman will put it any way which suits Norman. Did you think of Ruth? And Tom?

ANNIE: Oh, to hell with Tom. He could have asked me if he'd wanted to but he didn't. If I wait to be asked by Tom, I won't even get on an old folks' outing.

SARAH: Well, what about Ruth?

ANNIE: That's up to Norman. He wrote to me and then he phoned and asked me and I suddenly thought well yes . . . I think actually if I'm being really truthful and, knowing Norman, I didn't think it would ever happen.

SARAH: You were certain enough about it to get Reg and I down. We've had all the trouble of having to take the children to their grandparents so that we wouldn't have to bring them down here because we knew they would disturb Mother. I've had all the trouble of delegating responsibility for the "Bring and Buy Sale" which I'm sure will be a disaster because I'm the only one among them with any sort of organizing ability. And Reg has had to cancel his golf.

ANNIE: I'm sorry. I've been feeling sick all morning. I'm sorry.

SARAH: Yes, well I'm sure we all are.

ANNIE: Well . . . (*She moves to the door.*)

SARAH: Where are you going?

ANNIE: I don't know. I was just—I don't know.

SARAH: I think it's just as well we are here. You quite obviously need a rest. Now, I want you to sit down here and leave everything to me.

ANNIE: No, it's all right I—

SARAH: And let's get this quite clear to start with. You are not going anywhere. Not while I'm in this house.

ANNIE: What about my weekend?

SARAH: You can have your weekend here. Reg and I will cope. That's what we came down for. You can rest. You can certainly forget the idea of going anywhere with Norman. That's final. You're staying here.

ANNIE: Yes, I rather thought I would be.

SARAH: What you need is rest.

THE GREAT NEBULA IN ORION
by Lanford Wilson

Louise and Carrie haven't seen each other since they graduated from Bryn Mawr fourteen years ago. Their lives have led them in very different directions: Louise is a successful fashion designer leading a glamorous New York life; Carrie is a Bostonian housewife and the mother of two children. A chance meeting on the streets of New York brings them together for an afternoon of reminiscences and revelations.

Both women seem to be living the lives they sought. Yet after several glasses of brandy, Carrie confesses her unrequited love for Richard Roth (a former friend of Louise's brother, Sam, whom she knew in college), and she hints that her marriage to David is not all she hoped it would be. Louise shares her own pain over the break-up of her long affair with Phyllis Trahaunt, another Bryn Mawr classmate. Both women alternate between being envious of each other's choices, and commiserating over their mutual loss of innocence.

LOUISE: Have another drink.

CARRIE: Well, I guess. I don't really want to shop. . . . I'm out of the mood. There's nothing I can't really get in Boston.

LOUISE: You're here another day.

CARRIE: (*standing, walking about*) It's really a lovely apartment. You have another room. It's bigger than I— (*opens the door*)

LOUISE: Oh, don't go in there, darling. It's a mess. You know me. (CARRIE *retreats, rather startled, just a little.*) It's just the bedroom.

CARRIE: It's large.

LOUISE: It's such a mess. Here. Cheers.

CARRIE: Yes. (*They sip,* CARRIE *sits back down, looking puzzled.*)

LOUISE: I really am a terrible housekeeper. We're both going

190

to be stone drunk in the middle of the afternoon and create a scandal. Boston Society Girl and famed designer arrested for etc., etc.

CARRIE: I know. Think of the ladies clubs. Well, I suppose Boston has the best fish markets in the country, that's something. There and Maine, and we have a place in Maine. I really—I really hate fish, I—

LOUISE: That's funny.

CARRIE: I can't even walk down half the streets.

LOUISE: Listen, I want to appear sometimes at work in overalls.

CARRIE: What?

LOUISE: I don't know, I think I'm a little fuzzy. What did you call that? The great fuzz in Orion—?

CARRIE: (*away*) Belt. Er, uh, nebula. The great nebula.

LOUISE: I'd like to be there.

CARRIE: Yes, (*pause*) David is very chowder; a chowder person.

LOUISE: (*reviving*) Listen, why don't you write for a change now that I've—that we've re-established some kind of—now—(*laughing*) I don't know what I'm saying.

CARRIE: I know I'm going to be very popular, having—I'll tell them lunch—with my famous alumna.

LOUISE: Tell them to buy something.

CARRIE: Oh, they will; they'll have to.

LOUISE: I want to do a whole line for little girls. Your little girl is so adorable—women overdress their little girls; I'd love that. Call it the—what's her name?

CARRIE: Alice.

LOUISE: The Alice Line.

CARRIE: She'd be very proud. (CARRIE *has on her jacket, she stands now.*)

LOUISE: (*superficially, phony*) It's really been fun, Carrie.

CARRIE: (*the same*) Hasn't it? I'm so glad I— (*stops, biting her lip. Covers her eyes with her hand.* LOUISE *looks at her, painfully.* CARRIE *sits down.* LOUISE *sits down beside her.* CARRIE *is trying very hard not to cry.*)

LOUISE: Carrie. Can I get . . . what?

CARRIE: (*Shaking her head, not looking up. Weakly*) No, nothing. (*now looking at her*) Louise, I saw her picture, Phyllis' picture in your—I'm sorry, I didn't mean—I didn't know . . . I had no idea . . . I'd . . .

LOUISE: (*looking away*) Well, we all have our . . . (*Biting her lip.* CARRIE *begins to cry openly.*) You don't want to go back, do you?

CARRIE: (*breaking down completely*) No. (*sobbing openly, audibly, shaking her head*) No, no, I can't . . . no. (LOUISE *begins to cry now too. They sit at opposite ends of the sofa.* CARRIE *reaches out her hand.* LOUISE *takes it, grasping hard, tightly. The continue crying openly. Not looking at one another.* CARRIE *withdraws her hand, opens her purse, blows her nose.*) Ma-maybe— (*They look at each other now, their faces bathed in tears, both with the same thought, trying to laugh, shaking their heads up and down in agreement.*) Maybe Richard Roth ran off with Phyllis Trahaunt.

LOUISE: (*who has said "Phyllis" with her*) Yes, yes . . . (*wiping her face*) Damn my face.

CARRIE: What are we going to do?

LOUISE: I don't know, Carrie. I don't know. I've not known for six goddamned years.

CARRIE: I know.

LOUISE: Maybe David'll build us a little rocket ship in his workshop, huh? We'll fly off to your . . . (*a motion with her hand, crying again*)

CARRIE: (*crying, trying to laugh*) Nebula.

LOUISE: Do you think he could?

CARRIE: No, No. (*They laugh.*) He's a terrible carpenter. He is.

LOUISE: I suspected as much.

CARRIE: (*blowing her nose again*) Oh, he only spends his time out there because he can't understand why I'm always in such a foul mood. I look like hell—Oh, I don't care. (*She stares off.*)

LOUISE: You could ask his sister where . . .

CARRIE: No, I couldn't. She's married, I don't really know her. I couldn't anyway.

LOUISE: I guess . . .

CARRIE: Where did Phyllis . . . ?

LOUISE: Thin air, darling.

CARRIE: I'd forgotten how lovely . . . .

LOUISE: Oh, don't. Her parents wouldn't answer my "enquiries" —she was very honest with them, so they didn't think much of me. I stay in the apartment because if . . .

CARRIE: (*A long pause. Finally picking up her gloves*) Well.

LOUISE: Oh, don't go.

CARRIE: The thought of that hotel room is a bit—

LOUISE: Stay. We'll fix ourselves up and go out to a film. Have some great fattening dinner—you can have the sofabed; it's miles better than mine. They floodlight the Planetarium at night—it makes a great night light coming through the window.

CARRIE: I don't know if I need that. (*with some humor*)

LOUISE: Take your pick. (CARRIE *smiles.*) Good.

CARRIE: The thought of that hotel . . .

LOUISE: Darling, the thought of anything.

CARRIE: (*Neither moves.*) I had such great ideas of changing the world . . . you remember. I always thought . . .

LOUISE: We're better off than most . . .

CARRIE: They keep telling us.

LOUISE: Umm.

CARRIE: I worked so diligently, and believed so . . .

LOUISE: Yes, didn't we.

CARRIE: (*with a sigh*) Oh, God, Louise . . .

LOUISE: It's all just a great . . . (*They sit, huddled in their separate corners of the sofa.*)

CARRIE: (*pause*) The ironic thing . . .

LOUISE: (*pause*) Of course it's all . . .

CARRIE: Any other woman would be . . .

LOUISE: . . . Yes . . .

CARRIE: (*A long pause. The lights begin to fade, very slowly. They hardly move, staring off, lost in mixed images.*) It's all such a . . .

LOUISE: (*A long pause. With just a touch of humor*) The terribly . . . ironic . . . thing . . . (*A long pause. The lights fade out completely.*)

A DELICATE BALANCE
by Edward Albee

ACT II, SCENE 1

Julia is thirty-six years old and she has returned to her parents' home. Her fourth marriage has just ended and she wants some peace and privacy and comfort to help her through this trying time. When she finds that her parents' close friends, Harry and Edna, have taken up residence in her old room, she is furious. It seems that the night before, Harry and Edna were sitting in their house and—suddenly, inexplicably—they became frightened. So they fled to their friends' home, moved into Julia's room, and locked themselves in.

In the following scene Julia confronts her confused and beleaguered mother, Agnes.

JULIA: (*anger and self-pity; too loud*) Do you think I like it? Do you?

AGNES: (*no pleading*) Julia! Please!

JULIA: DO YOU? Do you think I enjoy it?

AGNES: Julia!

JULIA: Do you think it gives me some kind of . . . martyr's pleasure? Do you?

AGNES: Will you be still?

JULIA: WELL?

AGNES: THERE IS A HOUSE FULL OF PEOPLE!

JULIA: Yes! What *about* that! I come home: my room is full of Harry and Edna. I have no place to put my things. . . .

AGNES: (*placating*) They'll go to Tobias' room, he'll sleep with me. . . .

JULIA: (*muttered*) That'll be different.

AGNES: What did you say, young lady?

JULIA: I SAID, THAT WILL BE NICE.

AGNES: You did *not* say any such thing. You said . . .

JULIA: What are they *doing* here? Don't they have a house any more? Has the market gone bust without my knowing it? I may have been out of touch, but . . .

AGNES: Just . . . let it be.

JULIA: (*between her teeth; controlled hysteria*) Why are they here?

AGNES: (*weary; head back; calm*) They're . . . frightened. Haven't you heard of it?

JULIA: (*incredulous*) They're . . . what?

AGNES: (*keeping her voice down*) They're frightened. Now, will you let it be!

JULIA: (*offended*) What are they frightened of? Harry and *Edna*? Frightened?

AGNES: I don't . . . I don't know yet.

JULIA: Well, haven't you *talked* to them about it? I mean, for God's sake. . . .

AGNES: (*trying to stay calm*) No. I haven't.

JULIA: What have they done: stayed up in their room all day—*my* room—not come down? Locked in?

AGNES: Yes.

JULIA: Yes what?

AGNES: Yes, they have stayed up in their room all day.

JULIA: My room.

AGNES: Your room. Now, let it be.

JULIA: (*almost goes on in the same tone; doesn't; very nice now*) No, I . . .

AGNES: Please?

JULIA: I'm sorry, Mother, sorry for screeching.

AGNES: I am too old—as I remember—to remember what it is like to be a daughter, if my poor parents, in their separate heavens, will forgive me, but I am sure it is simpler than being a mother.

JULIA: (*slight edge*) I said I was sorry.

AGNES: (*all of this more for her own bemusement and amusement than anything else*) I don't recall if I ever asked my poor mother that. I do wish sometimes that I had been born a man.

JULIA: (*shakes her head; very matter-of-fact*) Not so hot.

AGNES: Their concerns are so simple: money and death—making ends meet until they meet the end. (*great self-mockery and exaggeration*) If they *knew* what it was like . . . to be a wife, a mother, a lover, a homemaker, a nurse, a hostess, an agitator, a pacifier, a truth-teller, a deceiver . . .

JULIA: (*saws away at an invisible violin; sings*) Da-da-dee; da-da-da.

AGNES: (*laughs softly*) There is a book out, I believe, a new one by one of the thirty million psychiatrists practicing in this land of ours, a book which opines that the sexes are reversing, or coming to resemble each other too much, at any rate. It is a book to be read and disbelieved, for it disturbs our sense of well-being. If the book is right, and I suspect it is, then I would be no better off as a man . . . would I?

JULIA: (*sober, though tongue-in-cheek agreement; shaking of head*) No. Not at all.

AGNES: (*exaggerated fret*) Oh! There is nowhere to rest the weary head . . . or whatever. (*hand out; loving, though a little grand*) How are you, my darling?

JULIA: (*a little abrupt*) What?
AGNES: (*hand still out; somewhat strained*) How are you, my darling?
JULIA: (*gathering energy*) How is your darling? Well, I was trying to tell you before you shut me up with Harry and Edna hiding upstairs, and . . .
AGNES: ALL RIGHT!

(*pause*)

JULIA: (*strained control*) I will try to tell you, Mother— once again—before you've turned into a man. . . .
AGNES: I shall try to hear you out, but if I feel my voice changing, in the middle of your . . . rant, you will have to forgive my male prerogative, if I become uncomfortable, look at my watch, or jiggle the change in my pocket. . . . (*Sees* JULIA *marching toward the archway as* TOBIAS *enters*) Where do you think you're going?
JULIA: (*head down, muttered*) . . . you go straight to hell . . .

LAUNDRY AND BOURBON
by James McLure

It is a hot and dusty summer afternoon in Maynard, Texas. Hattie Dealing, a "bossy, brassy woman," has escaped the chaos of her children for a few hours and come to gossip and while away the time with her girlhood friend, Elizabeth Caulder. While they fold laundry and sip bourbon and Coke on Elizabeth's front porch, they begin to share some of the problems and discontent that characterize their lives in this small west Texas town. Elizabeth's husband, Roy, has been missing for two days. She keeps looking up the road for a glimpse of Roy's 1959 pink Thunderbird convertible that first captured her heart when she was a teenager. For Elizabeth, this cherished auto has come to symbolize all the passion and dreams of her youth.

HATTIE: Whew it's hot out here. (*pause*) Lordy, how's a body supposed to keep cool?

ELIZABETH: Nothing to do but fix a bourbon and Coke and just sit and sweat.

HATTIE: I can't do that.

ELIZABETH: You can't sweat?

HATTIE: No. Fix a drink in the afternoon in front of the kids.

ELIZABETH: Why not?

HATTIE: Children learn by example.

ELIZABETH: So?

HATTIE: Well, all I need is to come home to a house full of kids sitting around drinking margueritas. You don't know what it's like raising a family.

ELIZABETH: No, I don't.

HATTIE: And lemme tell you, summertime is the worst.

ELIZABETH: What do you do?

HATTIE: I send them outside.

ELIZABETH: In this heat.

HATTIE: I give 'em a salt pill and say, play outside.

ELIZABETH: Don't they collapse from heat prostration?

HATTIE: Anything to slow them down.

ELIZABETH: I wish you'd let me take them sometimes.

HATTIE: Elizabeth, you're not used to kids. The strain would kill you. (*Elizabeth moves D. Leans against porch post looking out over the land. Pause*) Elizabeth, what are you staring out at that road for?

ELIZABETH: No reason. There's nothing to see.

HATTIE: That's the truth. Nothing green to look at. God, it's depressing living on the edge of a desert.

ELIZABETH: But just think millions of years ago all this land was under water.

HATTIE: Well . . . at least it would have been cool.

ELIZABETH: I like this land, but sometimes it gets too hot and burnt for people. It's still too wild and hard for anything to grow. (*pause*) Oh, look, Hattie!

HATTIE: What is it?

ELIZABETH: Look at that cloud.

HATTIE: It's just a cloud.

ELIZABETH: Yeah, but look how it's throwing a shadow across the land. God, doesn't that shadow look peaceful gliding over the land. Doesn't it look cool? It reminds me of a cool dark hand stroking a hot surface. (*pause*) Lately I've felt so hot and hollow inside I've wanted something to come along and touch me like that.

HATTIE: Elizabeth, what's the matter with you?

ELIZABETH: Nothing, Hattie, nothing.

HATTIE: (*pause*) You're doing it again, staring out at that hill. There ain't nothing out there but the highway and the road up to the house. Now, what're you expecting to see?

ELIZABETH: I was hoping to see a 1959 pink Thunderbird convertible come over that hill.

HATTIE: You've got tears in your eyes! Don't you tell me nothing's the matter! What is it? (*pause*)

ELIZABETH: Roy's been gone two days. (*silence*)

HATTIE: Why that son of a bitch! No wonder you've been so weird. Here, you sit yourself down here. I'm gonna fix you a drink and you're gonna tell me all about it.

ELIZABETH: I don't want another drink.

HATTIE: Hush up. Hattie's taking care of you now. The doctor is in. (ELIZABETH *sits.* HATTIE *exits to kitchen, talking.*) I knew there was something wrong the minute I laid eyes on you. First you didn't answer the doorbell, and as soon as I saw you I could tell something was the matter. That son of a bitch. (HATTIE *returns, having mixed drinks in record time.*) Well, what brought it on this time?

ELIZABETH: I don't know. Things haven't been the same since he came back.

HATTIE: From Vietnam?

ELIZABETH: Yeah.

HATTIE: I know. I seen the change. But believe me you've been perfect about it.

ELIZABETH: I haven't been anything. I haven't done anything. He was the one that went off for two years. He was the one got shot up. He's the one that has nightmares.

HATTIE: Nightmares.

ELIZABETH: Yeah, almost every night. (*pause*) Anyway, now he's back and he can't seem to get nothing started. He made me quit the job at the pharmacy. He worked some out at his Dad's place. He's done some rough-necking out in the oil fields. But then always gets in fights and gets himself fired.

HATTIE: Well . . . what's he got to say for himself.

ELIZABETH: He says he's looking for something.

HATTIE: Hmmnnn. What?

ELIZABETH: He doesn't know what. He says everything has changed here in Maynard.

HATTIE: Nothing's changed in Maynard since the Civil War.

ELIZABETH: I want him back the way it used to be.

HATTIE: Elizabeth, he's always been wild and unmanageable.

ELIZABETH: (*flaring*) I don't want to manage him. I don't want to break his spirit. That's why I married him, his spirit. Roy Caulder wasn't going to take no crap from anyone or anything. He and Wayne Wilder were gonna shake up the world.

HATTIE: Need I remind you that Wayne Wilder is currently serving five to ten for car theft?

ELIZABETH: (*quietly*) Roy's different than Wayne.

HATTIE: I wouldn't be too sure.

ELIZABETH: I just wished I knew he was safe. He could be hurt.

HATTIE: Or he could be with another woman.

ELIZABETH: I hope that's all it is.

HATTIE: Elizabeth, how can you say that?

ELIZABETH: Any man worthwhile is gonna look at other women. That's natural. And sometimes they wander a bit.

HATTIE: A bit? That man's done more wandering than Lewis and Clark.

ELIZABETH: You're exaggerating.

HATTIE: Last year? Last year! He took off for five days.

ELIZABETH: (*in spite of herself, smiling*) Yeah. He had himself quite a time.

HATTIE: You mean he told you what he did?

ELIZABETH: Oh, sure.

HATTIE: Well, you never told me.

ELIZABETH: No.

HATTIE: But I'm your best friend. You're supposed to tell me everything.

ELIZABETH: It was different then. We'd had a fight and he left in a huff. Drove off to El Paso. Picked up a girl hitchhiking.

HATTIE: What was her name?

ELIZABETH: Hattie, how should I know? She was a hitchhiker.

HATTIE: A little tramp probably! A little hippie road slut! What's she look like?

ELIZABETH: Blonde.

HATTIE: A little blonde hippie bitch that never washed or nothing I'll bet!

ELIZABETH: Oh yeah, and there was one other thing . . .

HATTIE: What?

ELIZABETH: She had a tattoo.

HATTIE: A *tattoo* on her arm?

ELIZABETH: Not exactly on her arm.

HATTIE: God . . . where?

ELIZABETH: On her behind.

HATTIE: No! On her behind! How disgusting!... What did it say?

ELIZABETH: "Born to be wild."

HATTIE: Oh Lord! Lord!

ELIZABETH: Then Roy went down to El Paso got in a four-day poker game, won a hundred bucks and come on home.

HATTIE: Weren't you mad?

ELIZABETH: Yes.

HATTIE: Didn't you want to shoot him?!

ELIZABETH: Yeah.

HATTIE: I would've.

ELIZABETH: I thought it was what he needed to get something out of his system. For a while it seemed to work.

(*pause*)

HATTIE: Y'know half his trouble is that damn car of his.

ELIZABETH: What do you mean?

HATTIE: He gets behind the wheel of that car and he thinks he's the cock of the walk, the best-looking thing in these parts.

ELIZABETH: (*proudly*) He still is.

HATTIE: (*grudgingly*) Yeah.

ELIZABETH: Even the girls in high school today. I see them in town looking at him the way we did.

HATTIE: I never looked at him that way.

ELIZABETH: Hattie you still do.

HATTIE: I tell you it's that damn car. When he gets in it he thinks he's young and free again. (*pause*) Somebody ought to take that car away from him.

ELIZABETH: (*warming to the memory*) I remember the first day he drove into town in that car.

HATTIE: So do I.

ELIZABETH: He'd worked three years, summers and winters, for the down payment.

HATTIE: Only slightly used.

ELIZABETH: Roy and Wayne drove right through the center of town.

HATTIE: They looked like a couple of sultans.

ELIZABETH: It was a bright pink.

HATTIE: It glistened like sin.

ELIZABETH: I remember I was coming out of the drug store with an ice cream cone.

HATTIE: What flavor?

ELIZABETH: Vanilla. And the sun off the hood was blinding. Couldn't even see the car. Then it passed into one shadow and I saw it. For the first time. It was beautiful, and Roy hardly knew me then but he waved at me, and I dropped my vanilla cone right there on the pavement. And I knew . . . he was the one.

HATTIE: Yeah. All through high school we double dated.

ELIZABETH: Remember drive-ins, Hattie.

HATTIE: I sure do. More like wrestling matches.

ELIZABETH: One couple would get the car one night.

HATTIE: The other the next.

ELIZABETH: We'd drive around and drive around and then go make out.

HATTIE: Wayne and me didn't even drive around.

ELIZABETH: (*rising*) God, I want them back. I wished tonight was ten years ago. And Roy was coming to pick me up in that pink Thunderbird. I wished I could buy back some of the nights of summer I had in that car. When everything was cool and free and driving along the highway away from this stupid town. With the wind coming at you and the stars all the way to the horizon, like diamonds that went all the way to dawn. (*pause*) Then driving off the road somewhere. By a lake maybe. Anywhere. Being off from the town with the boy you loved better than anything ever in your whole life. I remember us making love for the first time. Really slow and gentle. God. He was gentle then. He taught me my body. I'd never really felt with my body before Roy. Suddenly it was like every pore of my skin was being opened like in a rain storm, feeling and holding everything you possibly wanted right there in your arms. What I wouldn't give to have those nights again. Just one night when the back seat of that Thunderbird was sweeter than all the beds in the world. (*slight pause*)

ONCE A CATHOLIC
by Mary O'Malley

Act II, Scene 5

This comedy takes place in the Convent of Our Lady of Fatima, a school for girls near London. All the girls in class 5A are named Mary and all of them are trying to reconcile the dogma they are being taught in school with their own budding needs.

Mary Gallagher is a "sensible, attractive" student. She is going out with Cuthbert, a Catholic 6th former. Mary considers herself quite modern and, in the scene below, she prods her friend and classmate, Mary Mooney, into revealing her own extra-curricular activities with men. Mary Mooney is reticent at first, but gives in to the urge to share her secret.

As the scene opens both girls are in the garden of the Convent. They are supposed to be praying silently.

MARY GALLAGHER: Oh Jesus, I'm bored out of my mind.

(MARY MOONEY *puts her finger to her lips.*)

Don't tell me you're not bored.

(MARY MOONEY *shrugs her shoulders.*)

I'm sure they're trying to drive us mad. It's a well-known fact that too much silence can drive a person insane. It's all right for them. They're already round the bend. Especially Mother Peter. If she hadn't put herself into a convent somebody would have locked her up in a loony bin.

MARY MOONEY: Sssh!

MARY GALLAGHER: It's all right. There's nobody about. Although they've probably put a load of microphones into the bushes. And they're sure to have stationed Reverend Mother down in the basement on a periscope. Why the hell can't they

202

have their idiotic retreats in the holidays. D'you want a Smartie? (*She takes a tube out of her pocket.* MARY MOONEY *shakes her head.*) Oh have one, will you, for Christ's sake. We're not supposed to be fasting, you know. Hold out your hand. (*She pours some Smarties into* MARY MOONEY'S *reluctant hand.*) Are you keeping quiet just to annoy me, by any chance? (MARY MOONEY *shakes her head.*) I suppose you're scared of getting caught.

MARY MOONEY: No I'm not.

MARY GALLAGHER: You are.

MARY MOONEY: I'm not.

MARY GALLAGHER: Well, what are you being so holy for? Come to think of it, though, you always have been a bit that way inclined.

MARY MOONEY: I have not. I'm no more holy than you are.

MARY GALLAGHER: Not much. I doubt if you've ever committed a genuine mortal sin in all your life.

MARY MOONEY: Oh yes I have. I've definitely committed one.

MARY GALLAGHER: Ooooh, one. That's a lot isn't it.

MARY MOONEY: Why, how many have you committed?

MARY GALLAGHER: Millions.

MARY MOONEY: Have you really?

MARY GALLAGHER: Yes. You know that box of Tampax?

MARY MOONEY: Yes.

MARY GALLAGHER: They were mine.

MARY MOONEY: They weren't!

MARY GALLAGHER: They were, you know.

MARY MOONEY: Why didn't you go up and claim them?

MARY GALLAGHER: You must be joking. She didn't suspect me for a minute.

MARY MOONEY: Who got the blame in the end?

MARY GALLAGHER: Maria Zajaczkowski.

MARY MOONEY: That wasn't very fair.

MARY GALLAGHER: She's not bothered. They could just as easily have been hers. She went red when Mother Peter cross-examined her. Did you know she's going out with a really old man?

MARY MOONEY: No.

MARY GALLAGHER: Yes. He must be at least twenty-five. Nearly everybody in our form has got a bloke. It's time you got yourself one, isn't it?

MARY MOONEY: You think I've never been out with a bloke, don't you?

MARY GALLAGHER: Well you haven't, have you?

MARY MOONEY: Oh yes I have, if you want to know.

MARY GALLAGHER: Oh yes? Since when?

MARY MOONEY: Since just after Easter, actually.

MARY GALLAGHER: How come you've kept so quiet about it, then?

MARY MOONEY: If I told you something really confidential would you promise to keep it a secret?

MARY GALLAGHER: Yes, of course.

MARY MOONEY: Would you swear to God never to tell a soul?

MARY GALLAGHER: Yes. You can trust me.

MARY MOONEY: Cross your heart and hope to die.

MARY GALLAGHER: All right.

MARY MOONEY: You know when you were in Fatima?

MARY GALLAGHER: Yes.

MARY MOONEY: Well, I met a bloke in the street and he asked me to go to his house with him, so I did.

MARY GALLAGHER: What, you let a bloke pick you up just like that? And you didn't even know who he was?

MARY MOONEY: No. I mean yes. I did know who he was. That's just the trouble. You know who he is too.

MARY GALLAGHER: Who?

MARY MOONEY: Promise you won't tell anyone in all the world. Especially not Mary McGinty.

MARY GALLAGHER: Why not her?

MARY MOONEY: Well, see, this bloke . . . It was her boyfriend Derek.

MARY GALLAGHER: Cor! No!

MARY MOONEY: Yes.

MARY GALLAGHER: Are you sure you're not making it up? I can't imagine you and him together.

MARY MOONEY: Well we were.

MARY GALLAGHER: Christ. She'd go berserk if she ever knew.

MARY MOONEY: You won't tell her will you? Please.

MARY GALLAGHER: I wouldn't dare. Did he ask to see you again?

MARY MOONEY: I wouldn't want to see him again, not as long as I live. He's horrible.

MARY GALLAGHER: Is he? How come Mary McGinty's so mad about him then?

MARY MOONEY: He was nice at first. But then he turned nasty. Well not exactly nasty but rude. Do all blokes try to do rude things to girls?

MARY GALLAGHER: The majority of them, yes, if they get the chance.

MARY MOONEY: Has Cuthbert ever tried to be impure?

MARY GALLAGHER: He never thinks about anything else.

MARY MOONEY: But he's a Catholic.

MARY GALLAGHER: Yes. Terrible, isn't it.

MARY MOONEY: You've been going out with Cuthbert for a long time, haven't you?

MARY GALLAGHER: What about it?

MARY MOONEY: Is that why you've committed so many mortal sins? Because he makes you?

MARY GALLAGHER: He doesn't make me. What a thing to say. It's the devil who makes you commit sins.

MARY MOONEY: That Derek must be possessed by the devil.

MARY GALLAGHER: Why? What did he do? Oh dear, you haven't lost your priceless virginity, have you?

MARY MOONEY: No. No . . . but . . .

MARY GALLAGHER: What?

MARY MOONEY: I couldn't possibly tell you.

MARY GALLAGHER: I've probably heard it all before.

MARY MOONEY: I couldn't possibly say what he did. But I've got it written down in my diary. (*She takes a book out of her pocket.*) I have to keep it with me all the time in case anyone should ever find it. My Mum'd swing for me if she saw it. You can have a look at it if you like.

MARY GALLAGHER: (*reading the diary*) Cor, fancy letting a bloke do that to you the first time you ever go out with him.

MARY MOONEY: I didn't want him to. But he was a lot stronger than me. He's not like a boy, that Derek. He's a proper big man, you know.

MARY GALLAGHER: They will usually stop if you tell them to.

MARY MOONEY: I did. But he said we all know "no" means "yes". That doesn't make any sense though, does it?

MARY GALLAGHER: It means you liked what he was doing but you didn't want to admit it.

MARY MOONEY: I did not like it.

MARY GALLAGHER: Didn't you? You must be abnormal then.

MARY MOONEY: I'm not.

MARY GALLAGHER: You must be. Everybody else likes it.

MARY MOONEY: Well it wasn't all that bad, I suppose.

MARY GALLAGHER: You want to find a bloke of your own. It's not the done thing to go round borrowing other people's.

MARY MOONEY: Oh, shut your rotten face. And give me back my diary.

MY SISTER EILEEN
by Joseph A. Fields and Jerome Chodorov

ACT 1, SCENE 1

Fresh from Columbus, Ohio, Ruth and Eileen Sherwood are eager to start their new life in New York City. But first they need to find a place to live. Where do an aspiring actress and her writer sister look first? Greenwich Village, of course.

Ruth and Eileen are reluctant to rent the studio basement apartment that Mr. Appopolous shows them. After all, it's tiny, has iron bars on the window and contains a kitchenette and bathroom barely large enough for a full-grown adult. But Mr. Appopolous is very persuasive. He assures them they will get used to the blasting of construction under the sidewalk, promises to return their first month's rent if they are still dissatisfied in thirty days, and takes advantage of the late hour by telling them to "sleep on it." The sisters barely have time to object when he palms their money and skips out the door.

RUTH: You were in such a hell of a hurry to get to bed. (*A* WOMAN, *and white dog, cross from R. to L. back of window.* RUTH *crosses up to window, sees dog stopping at lamppost.*) Oh, get away from there! (*The* WOMAN *and dog go off L.* RUTH *puts hat and purse on mantel.*)

EILEEN: How did I know they were blasting underneath us? (*She opens overnight bag on bed.*)

RUTH: (*crossing to kitchen*) I had an instinctive feeling the moment I saw this place.—But all a man has to do is tell you how beautiful you are, and your ping changes to a purr! (*In a sudden burst of angry energy,* RUTH *pulls curtain back and glares in.*) Model kitchenette! Eileen, promise me you'll never go in there! (EILEEN *rises and looks around helplessly.* RUTH *closes curtains and goes to bathroom, throws door open and looks in with disgust.*) And look at that! Thank God we took a bath before we left Columbus!

EILEEN: (*pathetically*) Oh, Ruth—what are we going to do?

RUTH: (*grimly*) We're going to do thirty days. (*Crossing to R. bed, taking off her jacket.* EILEEN *crosses to L. bed with her jacket, purse and hat.*) We might as well get to bed. (RUTH *hangs jacket in closet, starts to remove blouse and skirt.*)

EILEEN: (*puts jacket, purse and hat on armchair*) Don't you think he'd be willing to give us at least half our money back?

RUTH: And take a loss of twenty-seven fifty, or whatever it is? Do you realize that we've got exactly forty-nine dollars and seventy-one cents to last us until one of us gets a job? (*She steps out of her skirt, hangs it in closet.*)

EILEEN: (*deeply impressed*) And remember what that boy I met on the bus told us? You're not eligible for relief until you've lived here three years. (*She sits on L. bed.*)

RUTH: And while we're on the bright side—we can't get unemployment insurance until one of us gets a job and is fired. (*She starts for bath, notices window, picks up overnight bag and runs to bathroom hurriedly.*) You know this bedroom could be a little more private. (*She goes into bathroom, leaving door half open.*)

EILEEN: (*opening zipper on back of dress*) Ruth, maybe we shouldn't have come to New York just yet—maybe we should have gone to Cleveland first.

RUTH: Yes—I hear they're very short of writers and actors in Cleveland. (EILEEN *rises and steps out of her dress.*)

EILEEN: At least a few people in Ohio *know* us.

RUTH: Wasn't that why we left?

EILEEN: (*puts dress on armchair*) Gee—we've got to make good—if it's only to spite Aunt Carrie.

RUTH: Nuts with Aunt Carrie—we've got to spite practically everybody in Columbus! (EILEEN *nods sadly, and stands for a moment lost in thought.*)

EILEEN: I wonder what Billy Hunnecker thinks now?

RUTH: He's probably at the country club this minute with Annie Wilkinson, drinking himself to death.

EILEEN: (*pulls off bedcover, starts to fold it*) He can have her.

RUTH: Don't you suppose he knows that?

EILEEN: And she can have *him* too—with my compliments.

RUTH: That's the advantage of not leaving any men behind—I don't have to worry about what becomes of them.

EILEEN: Oh, it's different with you—boys never meant anything in your life.

RUTH: Not after they got a load of you, they didn't.

EILEEN: What?

RUTH: Oh, nothing. (*She comes out of bathroom dressed in pajamas. Crosses to her bed*) This Appopolous must be some bingo player—look at all this stuff he won.

(*She pulls cover off bed, very gingerly. Then puts it on floor near armchair L.C.*)

EILEEN: (*pulls blanket to foot of her bed*) You may be right about Billy Hunnecker, but not with that Wilkinson girl. She's not his type. (EILEEN *exits into bathroom.* RUTH *crosses to closet wall and starts to bump her behind against it violently, in rhythm, obviously a nightly ritual to break down the fatty tissues.*)

RUTH: That's an outstanding feature about Columbus. (*bumping on italicized words*) *Nobody* there *is anybody else's type.* (*She stops—tired.*) Oh, the hell with it. Let it spread. (*pulls blanket off R. bed, puts it on armchair*)

EILEEN: (*from bathroom*) Ruth, we'd better send Mother and Dad a wire before they start worrying. And reverse the charges. Dad won't mind.

RUTH: I'll send it on a birthday blank. It's only a quarter. (RUTH *crosses to phone, dials operator, listens a moment, then jiggles hook.*) Hello? (*dials "operator" again*) Hello? (*She hangs up bitterly.*) Disconnected. Imagine Appopolous leaving a hot phone around. (RUTH *crosses to her bed, kneels on it and tucks sheet in at the back.*)

EILEEN: We ought to have it connected in the morning so we can start calling up for jobs. (RUTH *does a "take" on "calling up"—turns around, and opens bed.*)

RUTH: You don't call up for jobs, dear, you go out and look for them. (*She sits on bed R.*) Boy! What Bernard MacFadden would give for these beds! (*takes off stockings*)

EILEEN: Gee, I hope we land something soon so we can start paying Pop back.

RUTH: Don't worry, darling—we will—we've *got* to. It's a cinch Dad can't help us any more.

EILEEN: It doesn't seem fair—Poor Pop works so hard all his life and what's he got to show for it?

RUTH: You'd be amazed at all the things that aren't fair, Eileen. (RUTH *starts to put stockings on floor, then decides to place them under her pillow. Rises, crosses to door and bolts it*) I hope some fresh air gropes its way in here. It's stifling. (*Pauses at light switch and turns out lights.* EILEEN *comes out of bathroom, crosses to bed. The room is bathed in the glow from the street lamp.* RUTH *starts toward her bed when she suddenly realizes that it is as bright as ever in the room.*) Didn't I just put out the light? (*She pushes light button again, looks the room over and then pushes light switch a third time.*)

EILEEN: (*turning to window*) There's a lamppost right in front of the window. Pull down the shade. (*She sits on L. bed.*)

RUTH: (*crossing C., looks at window*) There isn't any shade.

EILEEN: No shade! We're practically sleeping on the street.

RUTH: (*bitterly as she crosses to her bed*) Just wait till I get that Appopolous!

EILEEN: Would it help any to close the window?

RUTH: (*as she lies down*) If we do, we'll suffocate.

EILEEN: (*sitting on edge of her bed*) I'm afraid—you know a dog could chase a cat through there!

RUTH: And probably will. Let's go to sleep. Maybe we can forget. (EILEEN *gets into bed.* RUTH *gets into bed, kicks her feet in the air, pulling sheet out at the bottom of bed. Puts sheet back disgustedly. Then rolls around trying to find a soft spot. Finally quiets down with her arms over her eyes to keep the light out.*)

EILEEN: Good night ...

RUTH: Good night ... (*A moment's silence. Then a* KID *passes from R. to L. outside window, running a stick across iron bars, exultantly simulating a machine gun. Immediately he is back again, going the other direction.* GIRLS *sit up in fright.*)

EILEEN: What was that?

RUTH: It sounded like a machine gun!

EVERYTHING IN THE GARDEN
by Edward Albee

ACT I, SCENE 1

Jenny and Richard need money. Everything is so expensive in their upwardly mobile suburban community: the house, the car, the country club, private school for their 14-year-old son. As a research chemist Richard earns barely enough to keep up with his affluent neighbors. If only they could afford the greenhouse that Jenny wants, or an electric lawnmower for Richard, or nicer clothes—then their happiness would be complete. Jenny wants desperately to get a job, but Richard is too proud to let his wife work. So they skimp and save and bicker about money.

On this particular afternoon their wealthy neighbor, Jack, has stopped by for a martini and some harmless flirting with Jenny. The visit is interrupted by a stranger, Mrs. Toothe enters. She is an Englishwoman who runs a rather unusual business in town: a house of prostitution for suburban housewives who can't make ends meet. She has come to offer Jenny a job.

Just prior to his exit, Jack joked about his attraction to Jenny.

JENNY: You mustn't believe a thing Jack says, Mrs. . . .

MRS. TOOTHE: (*a hand up to silence her*) Oh, really. I can tell a lover from a friend.

JENNY: (*maybe even a little offended*) Oh? How?

MRS. TOOTHE: (*laughs*) Because in this country they're very seldom the same.

JENNY: You're English.

MRS. TOOTHE: Yes. Very. (*small silence*)

JENNY: Would you like some tea . . . or a drink?

MRS. TOOTHE: (*very efficient*) No thank you; this is business. Strictly business.

JENNY: (*pause*) Oh?

210

MRS. TOOTHE: I'm told you need a job?

JENNY: (*somewhat confused*) Who, who told you that?

MRS. TOOTHE: (*airy*) Oh, one of your friends. A woman.

JENNY: (*curious, still puzzled*) Oh? Who?

MRS. TOOTHE: No matter. Am I mistaken?

JENNY: (*a little ill-at-ease*) Well, no . . . that is, I *was* thinking about getting a job. . . .

MRS. TOOTHE: Yes, well, I thought so.

JENNY: Not a . . . a career, you understand, just something . . .

MRS. TOOTHE: . . . part *time*, something to bring a little extra money in.

JENNY: Well, yes; you know how it is: my son's away at school, and I have the spare time. Besides, one can always use money, can't one?

MRS. TOOTHE: (*looking about, noncommittally*) Yes; one can.

JENNY: These days, with taxes, and the private school . . .

MRS. TOOTHE: Oh, yes; yes; quite. What does your husband do?

JENNY: (*uncomfortable, as if being interviewed*) Well, he . . . he's a research chemist, and . . .

MRS. TOOTHE: . . . and that, as so many good things, pays less than it should.

JENNY: (*protecting Richard*) Well, he doesn't do *too* badly; I mean . . .

MRS. TOOTHE: (*the laugh again*) Of course not! But, still; you would like a job.

JENNY: (*Looks to the hallway, guilty—*RICHARD *might come back.*) Well, yes; one . . . one likes to feel useful.

MRS. TOOTHE: (*looking into her handbag*) Yes; useful. (*She takes out a thick bundle of bills, shows them to* JENNY.) Money. (JENNY *just looks at it, her mouth falling open a little.*) For you. (*makes to give it to her*)

JENNY: Yes, but . . . (*laughs a little, astounded*)

MRS. TOOTHE: (*nods her head*) Yes, money. For *you*. A thousand dollars. Here, take it.

JENNY: (*withdrawing a little from it*) Well, no, I . . .

MRS. TOOTHE: Count it if you like. Here; a thousand dollars. (*tries to force it on her*)

JENNY: (*a little panicked*) No!

MRS. TOOTHE: Very well. (*As calm as can be, rises, goes with the money to the fireplace, throws it on the burning logs*)

JENNY: (*reflex, runs to the fireplace, almost puts her hands into the fire, makes a little yell, straightens up, holds on*) Oh—I think you'd better go, Mrs. Toothe.

MRS. TOOTHE: (*enigmatic smile*) Not yet. Let's begin again. (*She takes another bundle of money from her handbag, makes as if to throw it in the fire,* JENNY *holds out her hand,* MRS. TOOTHE *quietly hands her the money, resumes her seat,* JENNY *stays standing.*)

JENNY: (*never taking her eyes off* MRS. TOOTHE) You're quite mad.

MRS. TOOTHE: No. Very rich.

JENNY: (*looks at the money, almost weighs it*) Look, you...you can't just...*give* me money like this. I can't just...take money from you.

MRS. TOOTHE: (*a little laugh*) You have. It's yours. Isn't there something you'd like to buy? For yourself, for...what is his name?...Richard?

JENNY: People can't just give people money. I want to work.

MRS. TOOTHE: Good then. That's an advance of salary. You can work for me.

JENNY: But I haven't *said* I'd take a job at *all*. Richard is *very* much against it, and...

MRS. TOOTHE: (*daring her to refuse*) I was told you needed money.

JENNY: Yes, but Richard wouldn't approve of anything like this, and...

MRS. TOOTHE: Like what? (*indicates the money*) Wouldn't he approve of *that*?

JENNY: (*looks at the money in her hands*) I'm sorry; I didn't mean to be rude, but it's all so vague, isn't it? And...and so unexpected.

MRS. TOOTHE: (*shrugs*) It's a job.

JENNY: (*nervous laughter in her voice*) Well, you'll have to tell me what it *is*. I mean, money isn't everything.

MRS. TOOTHE: No? What isn't money? Here we are; this house is money, that garden, that lovely garden, those clothes you're wearing, it's all *money*, isn't it?

JENNY: The job?

MRS. TOOTHE: What are your husband's hours?

JENNY: He leaves at eight and gets home from town at seven-thirty, but...

MRS. TOOTHE: Very good. *You'll* come in town, four after-

noons a week, from one to five, say. You'll come to my
address—lovely street; psychiatrist's office, doctors...

JENNY: Is this a...uh...a receptionist's job?

MRS. TOOTHE: Receptionist?

JENNY: Making, making appointments, and so on?

MRS. TOOTHE: *I* make appointments. For *you*.

JENNY: *(tiny pause)* For me? Who with?

MRS. TOOTHE: Clients.

JENNY: *(innocent)* What *for*?

MRS. TOOTHE: For a hundred dollars.

JENNY: No, I mean...A hundred dollars?

MRS. TOOTHE: More, sometimes—if they're generous.

JENNY: But these clients...who are they?

MRS. TOOTHE: Some businessmen, some visitors. All
gentlemen; all rich.

JENNY: *(The knowledge is there but not admitted yet.)*
What...exactly...what exactly would I do...for this money?
*(MRS. TOOTHE laughs lightly, JENNY's jaw drops with the
admission, pause. JENNY picks up the bundle of money, holds
it out to MRS. TOOTHE, even, hard.)* Get out of my house. *(Mrs.
Toothe does nothing, JENNY drops the money on the table.)* I'll
call the police.

MRS. TOOTHE: *(as calm as anything, a little superior)*
Whatever for?

JENNY: *(quivering)* You know what for!

MRS. TOOTHE: *(smiles)* I've said nothing.

JENNY: You know what you've suggested!

MRS. TOOTHE: *(shrugs)* That you make money.

JENNY: THAT WAY!

MRS. TOOTHE: You have a friend who does.

JENNY: *Who?*

MRS. TOOTHE: Oh, no; we're very discreet.

JENNY: *(through her teeth)* I don't believe you, not a word!
People around here wouldn't do that sort of *thing*, you don't
realize; you don't know what we're like.

MRS. TOOTHE: *(unconcerned)* Have it your way.

JENNY: One of the tradespeople, maybe; you're thinking of
someone like that.

MRS. TOOTHE: I'm thinking of a friend of yours; a very
nice woman with a lovely house, who keeps it nicely—much
more nicely than this, by the way—a woman who has no more
worries about money, who is very happy. So could you be.

JENNY: You're a filthy woman! IT'S DISGUSTING!!

MRS. TOOTHE: (*very calm*) Nothing is disgusting, unless one is disgusted.

JENNY: YOU'RE EVIL!!

MRS. TOOTHE: Yes, yes . . .

JENNY: I'LL TELL THE POLICE!

MRS. TOOTHE: (*stands up, stretches a little*) Good. Then perhaps they'll arrest me.

JENNY: I hope they put you in prison!

MRS. TOOTHE: Yes, well, they probably will, and then I shall admit everything.

JENNY: Everything?

MRS. TOOTHE: Yes, how you approached me, and we discussed it, but the terms didn't suit you. The *money* wasn't enough.

JENNY: THAT'S NOT TRUE!

MRS. TOOTHE: Perhaps not. I think it would be believed, though. By enough people.

JENNY: GET OUT OF HERE!

MRS. TOOTHE: (*takes a calling card from her handbag*) Here is my card; address; telephone; let me know what you decide.

JENNY: (*change of tone, almost tearful*) Please? Please go?

MRS. TOOTHE: No police then; good. (*sees* JENNY *will not take the card, puts it down next to the bundle of money on the table*) Don't telephone me before ten, though, please. I *do* like my sleep.

JENNY: Please? Go?

MRS. TOOTHE: (*smiles*) I'll see myself out. It's been very nice to meet you. (*looks one final time at the garden*) What a lovely garden. Do you have a greenhouse? (*Smiles, exits, leaving* JENNY *standing in the center of the room.* JENNY *looks after* MRS. TOOTHE *for a long moment, not moving. Then she looks down at the table whereon sit the bundle of money and* MRS. TOOTHE'S *card. She picks up the card, reads it, moving her lips, then, with a grimace, rips the card in half and, as if she were carrying feces, takes it over to a wastebasket and drops it in. She comes back to the table, stares at the money, picks it up, looks at it with detached fascination, doesn't know quite what to do with it, finally, rather firmly, puts it in desk drawer, locks drawer, keeps key, starts toward French doors, looks back at locked drawer, goes, stands at French windows looking out.*)

EVERYBODY LOVES OPAL
by John Patrick

Opal is in danger, but she doesn't know it. As far as she's concerned, she's found three new friends, and given them refuge in her home—a rundown house on the edge of a municipal dump. She doesn't know that they're perfume swindlers on the lam.

After a month in her house, the trio (Gloria, Brad and Solomon) convince Opal to get plenty of insurance and then plot a tragic accident for her that will solve their financial problems.

But Opal seems to be blessed. When the living room ceiling mysteriously caves in, she happens to be in the cellar. When her house suddenly catches fire, her state trooper friend arrives to save the day. Throughout it all the unsuspecting Opal is loving, caring, and generous to her newfound "friends."

The following scene takes place two months after the would-be murderers have moved in. Opal is repairing the collapsed ceiling when Gloria enters. After a sleepless night, Gloria is feeling some twangs of conscience about her part in the murder scheme.

(*We discover* OPAL *hammering the new support under the stairs. She finishes and crosses to the barrel, coming up with various articles of wearing apparel which she appraises critically. As usual, she hums and whistles to herself as she works.*

GLORIA, *in curlers and a bathrobe, comes sauntering down the stairs yawning.* OPAL *hurries to greet her effusively at the bottom of the steps.*)

OPAL: (*crosses to bottom of stairs*) Good mornin', honey! I hope you hadda good sleep. (*tries to put her arm around her*)

GLORIA: (*Crosses to sit table C. Puts purse on table*) Frankly, I slept terrible. (*pushes* OPAL *away*)

215

OPAL: (*crosses to R. of* GLORIA) Well, it don't show. You look fresh as a daisy. (*takes* GLORIA *to sofa*) Sit close to the stove, honey. It's cold as a witch's nose this morning. (*sits her on sofa*) I been worried ragged about you, honey. You ain't slept good for a couple a' weeks now. (*crosses to behind sofa*)

GLORIA: There's a mouse in my room.

OPAL: I'll tell you what I'll do—tonight I'll lock Mister Tanner in with you.

GLORIA: Peachy. That's all I need—a cat prowlin' around. As if a mouse ain't bad enough.

OPAL: You're dead right, honey. You don't wanna wake up hearin' Mister Tanner crunchin' on no mouse. I'll get some traps and cheese. (*pats her head, crosses U.L.*) Now. What can I fix you for breakfast?

GLORIA: Nothin'.

OPAL: Oh, now, honey—you gotta eat somethin'.

GLORIA: *I don't want nothin'!*

OPAL: All right—all right. (*crosses to barrel C.*) You jus' sit an' rest.

GLORIA: (*sullenly*) Where're the boys at?

OPAL: (*stubbornly cheerful*) Oh, they went somewheres early. (*pulls articles out of barrel*) Honey, I been diggin' in one of my barrels an' I think I come up with somethin' nice you'd like. (*holds out a garish shawl*) A real genuine Spanish shawl. Let's see how you look in it. (*Crosses to behind couch. Drapes it over* GLORIA'S *head*) Oh, wait 'til I find you a mirror. (*takes mirror from shelves U. L.*) I'm gonna show you a real Spanish señorita. (*crosses to behind couch, gives* GLORIA *mirror*)

GLORIA: Thanks. (OPAL *to barrel C.*) I know jus' where to wear it. Next time I collect my unemployment insurance. (*takes shawl off*)

OPAL: Now—here's a beaded bag. They're very stylish again. The *ac*-me of beauty. It just goes to prove you shouldn't never throw nothin' away. If you live long enough, everything'll come back into fashion.

GLORIA: (*pushes it aside*) I gotta bag.

OPAL: (*studies* GLORIA *silently for a desperate moment*) Honey— won't you please lemme make you a cup of tea?

GLORIA: (*explodes*) Opal, how many times I gotta ast you? Will you *stop* waitin' on me! Hand an' foot. Day an' night.

OPAL: (*adamant*) No! No—I ain't never gonna stop doin' everything I can for you. Why, you saved my life. (*goes to* *the merry-go-round*) If it hadn't been for this beautiful merry-go-round that stopped me on that rotten ole step, I'd a' been dead on my birthday. (*determinedly*) No, siree! I owe my life to you an' there won't never be enough I can do for you as long as I live. (*crosses back, grabs* GLORIA *and forcibly implants a kiss*)

GLORIA: (*pushes* OPAL *away*) Well, jus' stop givin' me presents. Frankly, I don't want that junk. (*lights cigarette from package in bosom*)

OPAL: (*hurt*) I don't blame you, honey. Judas! It *is* junk. Everything in this whole darn house is junk. The only thing new and sweet and fresh that ever come into it was you. (*crosses to barrel—drops bag in*)

GLORIA: (*with a twinge of conscience*) I'm sorry if I hurt your feelin's.

OPAL: (*fiercely*) You didn't hurt my feelin's. You *couldn't* an' even if you did—you gotta right to. (*crosses to shelves U.L.— gets money*) You know what I want you to have? A bran' new dress. Pink. An' skin tight. You been blessed with a good shape. No use hidin' it in a mu-mu. (*crosses to behind sofa*) Here. (*shoves some bills toward* GLORIA)

GLORIA: What's that for?

OPAL: (*crosses to R. of sofa*) I want you to go in town an' buy yourself a pink dress fresh outta the sewing machine. I don't want nobody else to've tried it on. There's thirty-nine dollars there, honey. (*takes her purse out and counts the coins*) An' here's ninety-eight cents. Things always cost thirty-nine dollars and ninety-eight cents. (*gives to* GLORIA)

GLORIA: (*wearily*) Now, why you doin' that? (*pushes it away*) Take it back.

OPAL: (*fervently*) Gloria—ain't my life worth at least thirty-nine dollars? (*waits for confirmation*) An' ninety-eight cents?

GLORIA: (*suddenly yells*) I never saved your life!

OPAL: (*rises, crosses C.*) I ain't gonna listen to you. (*puts fingers in ears and sings*) Dum-de-dum-dum. Driftwood—

GLORIA: (*yells*) I didn't! (*rises, crosses to L. of* OPAL)

OPAL: (*takes fingers out*) You did, too.

GLORIA: (*crosses to sit L. of table*) All right—all right. I saved your life. (*Jams the money into her own purse. Then truculently*) But I don't like pink. (*relents*) I look naked.

OPAL: (*Crosses to table, sits C.* GLORIA *takes out curlers from hair.*) Any color you want. (*sighs happily*) Oh, honey, how I wish I was you. You got your whole sweet life ahead of you.

(GLORIA *works on her hair.*) You know if I had my life to live over again, there's only two things I'd want that I ain't got. Big bosoms and long eyelashes. (*brushes hair*) There're three things a man can't resist. That's two of 'em. The other's cookin'. (*combs hair*) You got everything. An' I got confidence in you.

GLORIA: I got nothin'. Frankly, I don't even have an opinion any more.

OPAL: Honey—you been awful twitchy lately. You know what I think you need? A husband.

GLORIA: (*groans*) Oh, cripes.

OPAL: (*dogging her*) What about my frien'—that cop you met here. Joe Jankie. (*jabs* GLORIA) Ain't he a handsome devil?

GLORIA: Yeah—for a weddin' present I could give him my finger prints.

OPAL: Well, what about the professor. He ain't married, is he?

GLORIA: (*scoffs*) Brad? Frankly, that man hates the whole female sex.

OPAL: That's all right—so do most women. (*slyly*) I think you could land him if you played your cards right.

GLORIA: Any girl that played cards with him would find herself in a barrel—rooked and raped.

OPAL: Oh, now, Gloria—you don't mean that. Brad's a booky, brainy, educated college professor.

GLORIA: Yeah. He's got six college degrees. An' one lung. Some husband.

OPAL: (*shocked*) What happened to his other lung?

GLORIA: Oh, he got loaded one night and accidentally killed a man with his car. So he went to prison. An' that's where his lung went. No college in the U.S.A. of America wants him now. An' neither do I.

OPAL: Oh, the trouble some people have. And such a nice fella. Real genuine.

GLORIA: Genuine! If he was really so mentally intellectual, he wouldn't use them big words jus' to prove he was so superior.

OPAL: It does seem like usin' a cannon to shoot a rabbit.

GLORIA: Frankly, I wouldn't want him even with two lungs. He's got a dirty mind.

OPAL: (*tolerantly*) He's a man, honey.

GLORIA: Once, when jus' everythin' was goin' wrong, I said I wish't I could dig a hole and climb in an' hide. You know what he said? He said my trouble was I wanted to go back to my *mother's womb*! (*taking mascara out of purse*)

OPAL: That was a mean thing to say.

GLORIA: (*outraged*) Can you imagine! I *hated* my mother. And that's the very las' place I'd wanna go. (*Spits in mascara. Starts doing eyelashes.*)

OPAL: Maybe he jus' had a bad day.

GLORIA: (*fixing eyelashes*) No. He's like that. You ever heard of Jekyll and Hyde?

OPAL: I seen the movie.

GLORIA: Well, wait'll you see his Hyde-side.

OPAL: (*rises, crosses to barrel—puts things in it*) I can't understand how a nice girl like you ain't married.

GLORIA: Well, the fact of the matter is every fella I ever fell for turned out to be dumb, drunk or drafted.

OPAL: (*rolls barrel U.R.*) Well, honey, there's somebody for you somewheres, an' I'm gonna dig him up.

GLORIA: (*nettled again*) Frankly, what's so important about gettin' married?

OPAL: Well, I'll tell you, honey. If you got somebody, everythin's better. Even what's bad is better. An' that's the truth.

GLORIA: (*puts makeup away*) Then why didn't *you* get married?

OPAL: (*crosses to R. of Gloria*) Because I always been ugly as a mud fence. But you—you're as pretty as a peony. (*laughs*)

GLORIA: (*has a moment of remorse*) Well—I'm sorry you was ugly.

OPAL: Oh, it ain't bad. There's one good thing about bein' ugly—you never worry about losin' your looks.

GLORIA: (*laughs in spite of herself*) You know what your trouble is, Opal? You're pig-headed. You jus' won't see bad in anything.

OPAL: Well, *I believe in live-an'-let-live.* Now I made you laugh, lemme make you a cup of tea. (*crosses to C.*)

GLORIA: Okay. If it's gonna make you happy.

OPAL: (*scurries to make tea*) Why, you jus' bein' around makes me happy. You know, I got only one worry. (*hesitates*) That boss of yours and the professor got me scared.

GLORIA: Scared? Whadda you mean?

OPAL: I'm afraid they're gonna move and take you with them.

GLORIA: (*relieved*) Oh.

OPAL: (*crosses to above table with cup and napkin*) I'll tell you somethin'. I don't think I could get use' to livin' alone again. Mister Tanner ain't enough. (*Puts cup down.*) Honey—I want you to know now—if you ever need a home—you got one here as long as you live. I owe you that for my life. (*pats her hand. Adds quickly*) Now, don't say anything! Just sit there an' take it easy while I get some rags an' dust out your room. (*She goes into the kitchen.*) Mister Tanner—Mister Tanner. Where you at? Well, wake up, you bad boy. (OPAL *reappears with dust rags over one arm, carrying the cat under the other. She continues toward the stairs.*) While you're outta your room, I'll jus' lock Mister Tanner in an' let him mouse around your shoes. (*She caresses the cat as she goes up. She stops half-way.*) You know somethin', Gloria? This sweet ole cat and me has been together for fifteen years. We've lasted longer than most marriages. (*She goes out.* GLORIA *notices the tea bag left on the table. She takes it to pin on the tea line, humming and whistling to herself, unaware that she is reflecting* OPAL's *behavior pattern. Her hum changes to a song.*)

GLORIA: (*as she hangs bag up*) "Dum-de-dum-dum. Driftwood. Do-de-do-do. Driftwood."

MY CUP RANNETH OVER
by Robert Patrick

Yucca Concklin is a dizzy, young rock singer who wakes up one morning to find herself famous. Her roommate, Paula, is a struggling and serious writer who has trouble adjusting to Yucca's overnight success.

(*At the desk sits* PAULA TISSOT, *in her middle twenties, attractive and trim, wearing a long bathrobe. She is typing efficiently.*)

PAULA: (*reads from her manuscript*) "One Woman's Manifesto, by Paula Tissot." There. *Cosmopolitan* will print this one. They have to. They printed a dozen just like it last year. (*reads*) "And so we must remember always to join in sisterhood, with respect for one another's talents and abilities, never to follow the loathsome male model of competitiveness..."

(*The phone rings.*) "... maintaining respect not only for one another but for ourselves" (*Phone rings.*) "... especially for our gentleness and kindness, our tenderness with one another." (*Phone rings. Paula screeches.*) Yucca! Yucca! (*She listens. Phone rings.*) Yucca! Yucca! Yuck! (*Phone continues ringing.*)

YUCCA: (*sleepy, offstage*) Whaaaaaat?

PAULA: Get up and take off your sleep mask and put on your robe and stagger in here and answer the phone! (*Off. A long, incoherent mumble.* PAULA, *sharply*) You don't want to get up and take off your sleep mask and put on your robe and stagger in here and answer the *what*?

YUCCA: (*Staggers in in robe, sleep mask on her head. She's funny and awkward.*) I forget why you can't answer the phone.

PAULA: (*making corrections on her manuscript*) Because it's for you.

YUCCA: I forget how you know that.

PAULA: Because my friends know I write in the mornings and they do not call before noon.

YUCCA: Right. I remember now. (*Answers into phone. Italicized dialogue is into phone.*) Hello?

PAULA: (*reading to* YUCCA *with relish*) "We must recognize one another."

YUCCA: *Lola who?*

PAULA: "We must communicate."

YUCCA: *There's no one here named Lola.*

PAULA: "We must revere one another."

YUCCA: *We have a Paula.*

PAULA: "We must encourage one another."

YUCCA: *Paula.*

PAULA: She writes. "We must be without ego."

YUCCA: *She writes.*

PAULA: Brilliantly.

YUCCA: *And me, Yucca, I sing. Pretty well. No Lola.*

PAULA: I'm not in except to the Pulitzer Prize Committee.

YUCCA: (*as Paula returns to work with a pencil*) *Oh, you're Lola? You're an old friend of mine? I remember you? Look, I was up very late last night. I had to go across the street and fill in for somebody.* (*to* PAULA) Hey, I had to go across the street to The Bitter End, I mean The Other End. It used to be The Bitter End.

PAULA: It's not across the street.

YUCCA: It was across the street from where I was. Anyway, I had to go over there last night and fill in for Tod Mitchell, no less. He had a throat.

PAULA: Useful for a singer.

YUCCA: Sore.

PAULA: No, I'm just trying to write.

YUCCA: No, he had a sore throat and I had to fill in for him. And the people actually stayed.

PAULA: Did they like you as well as *Cosmopolitan* is going to like this article which I will finish writing as soon as you stop bothering me?

YUCCA: They loved me. They always love me. I am their spiritual selves delivering a rueful rigadoon from the depths of poverty and obscurity. Also, I'm better than a sore throat. *Oh, were you there? Did you enjoy yourself? Me, I mean.*

PAULA: No, I wasn't there. I was home working. I write.

YUCCA: Not you. Some person called Lola who insists she is an old friend. *You weren't there? How could you like me, then? Huh? You want to read to me? No, don't. My roommate reads to me. I can read, I just don't. She reads. She writes.*

PAULA: (*grimly*) She tries.

YUCCA: *Read it to her.* (*hands phone to* PAULA) It must be some writer-friend of yours. She wants to read something.

PAULA: Oh, really, Yucca! (YUCCA *exits to kitchen.*) Hello? What? The time? Yes, I have the time, it's eleven-thirty and I don't take calls before—The Times? What times? The New York Times? (*yells*) Yucca, you got reviewed in the New York Times! *Wait, read it to me slowly!*

YUCCA: (*Re-enters with banana. She has not understood.*) You got a rejection slip from the *New York Times*? (*pats* PAULA *consolingly*)

PAULA: (*brushing* YUCCA *away*) Wait, start that over.

YUCCA: (*indicating* Cosmo *rejection slips*) You'll have to start a whole new wall.

PAULA: (*with ever-mounting excitement*) Yucca, hush! Hold on, Lily. All right, "Lola!" Yucca, you're in the *Times*!

YUCCA: I never sent anything to the *Times*. They don't print songs.

PAULA: There was a reviewer there last night.

YUCCA: The *Times* reviews folk rock?

PAULA: Listen. (*She repeats what* LOLA *is reading to her.*) *Funky Punk Subs for Tod Mitchell* . . .

YUCCA: Oh, no!

PAULA: *With her tousled hair . . .*

YUCCA: Oh, God, you told me to comb my hair!

PAULA: *In a sweat-stained T-shirt . . .*

YUCCA: You told me to dress better!

PAULA: *A scrawny street punk lumbered onto the stage at The Other End last night . . .*

YUCCA: (*the pits*) Since freshman year you've tried to teach me to walk.

PAULA: Well, it's a hard way to learn, dear, but maybe you'll listen in the future. *Go ahead, Lola.*

YUCCA: (*trying to grab phone*) No, don't.

PAULA: (*expression of shock*) *And what?*

YUCCA: Made a goddamn fool of herself and didn't even get paid!

PAULA: Yucca!

YUCCA: (*strangling herself with phone cord*) Paula, how does a lady kill herself?

PAULA: Yucca, listen. (*hands phone to* YUCCA)

YUCCA: Oh, God. (*listens*) *And proved to be the most exciting and original new pop talent in years.* How many years?

PAULA: Well, what do you know?

YUCCA: (*staring at phone*) I remember her now. Some incredible bore that used to hang around the coffee-houses and knock folk-rock.

PAULA: (*grabs phone, listens*) *She's obviously bled on the streets she sings about so winningly.*

YUCCA: Lola has?

PAULA: You have!

YUCCA: Oh, I have not.

PAULA: *A remarkable lyric style backed by profound musical expertise. The next thing is going to come from this T-shirted essence of the post-Watergate street punk.*

YUCCA: (*grabs phone*) *Lola, does anybody read the* Times? *I've got to wash and hang up my face. I'll call you back.* (*hangs up*) I can't call her back. I don't know her number.

PAULA: Yucca, how fantastic.

YUCCA: (*beginning to realize*) She must have been there to see Tod Mitchell. The *Times* never saw me in their life.

PAULA: Well, they sure 'nuff saw you now. Congratulations, kid.

YUCCA: Congratulations, "punk."

PAULA: (*rising and excited*) This would seem the time to break out a certain bottle of champagne.

YUCCA: (*to phone*) Post-Watergate street punk? I was a street punk early in '68. Champagne? (*pulls sleep mask over her eyes*)

PAULA: (*runs back on with champagne and two glasses*) Champagne it is!

YUCCA: Paula. I'm interrupting your rigid schedule.

PAULA: (*opening and pouring champagne*) One can't hurt. This is an event.

YUCCA: The *Times* can't be of any importance in rock.

PAULA: Darling, enjoy it, have fun.

YUCCA: It's probably some twelfth-string hack. Everybody thinks they're a rock reviewer if they know Helen Reddy from Phoebe Snow.

PAULA: (*very party-mood*) *Is* Helen Reddy from Phoebe Snow?

YUCCA: I have a confession to make. I have no faith in myself. I drank the champagne Tuesday.

PAULA: Well, I had faith in you. I bought some more Wednesday.

YUCCA: (*removes sleep mask*) Oh, you shouldn't have. (*giggles*) Well, as it turns out, you should have.

PAULA: In fact, I bought two—I have faith in me, too. (*offers glass*)

YUCCA: (*takes glass*) Oh, you should. This will happen to you before it does to me.

PAULA: Maybe when Germaine Greer gets a sore throat. But it *has* happened to you, and it's wonderful.

YUCCA: (*hands glass to* PAULA) It's only one review.

PAULA: (*hands glass to* YUCCA) It's only your first.

YUCCA: But that champagne was for my first gold record!

PAULA: We'll just drink a little and keep the rest in a quart jar.

YUCCA: They came for Tod Mitchell.

PAULA: They stayed for you.

YUCCA: They probably thought I was Tod Mitchell.

PAULA: It's those T-shirts. Drink up, darling. Here's to a fantastic fluke. It couldn't happen to a sweeter punk. (PAULA *drinks.* YUCCA *won't.*) Oh, enjoy it, darling. It may never happen again. (*Phone rings.*) Oh, bicentennial bucket of buttered popcorn!

YUCCA: I'll get it, I'll get it. *Hello! Oh, hi, Brad.* (*hands phone to* PAULA) It's your boyfriend from the *Village Voice*.

PAULA: Oh, come on, he's not my boyfriend. *Brad, you brute. You know I never take calls before noon. But you're* *forgiven, this is your lucky day, we're having a little celebration. My little roommate, Yucca? She sings a little? Well she got a sweet little review of all things in the* Times *of all places, and we were just—Oh, certainly.* (*hands phone to* YUCCA) He wants you.

YUCCA: Of all little people. *Hi, Brad. You what? No, no, you want Tod Mitchell. You've had Tod Mitchell? You were? I was? You do?* He wants to interview me over the phone.

PAULA: He is. (*She sits at typewriter.*)

YUCCA: Right. *Oh, sure, I understand. I understand about deadlines. It's all right, really.* This is just a short interview to fill in. He'll do a great big longer one next week.

PAULA: Of course.

YUCCA: *I guess that's all right. Shoot. Huh? Why do I call myself Yucca?* (YUCCA *types answer and hands it to her.*) *Because it's the state flower of New Mexico.* (PAULA *continues typing.* YUCCA *reads from* PAULA's *typewriter.*) *No, I'm from Nebraska but I couldn't very well call myself Goldenrod Concklin, could I? Concklin?* (PAULA *types.* YUCCA *reads.*) *It's your name, stupid. I mean, it's my name. My inspiration?* (*reads as Paula types*) *I've bled on those streets. Where did I get the idea for the T-shirt?* (PAULA *does not type.*) *Uh, I'll tell you next week. No, I've certainly never had a shorter interview. Bye, Brad.* (*hangs up*)

PAULA: (*philosophically*) Bye, Brad.

YUCCA: Imagine the *Village Voice* interviewing me.

PAULA: I think I am.

YUCCA: Maybe they'll make a movie of my life.

PAULA: I think they have.

YUCCA: They liked the same song you like! (*sings*) "Folks Get Up At Nine in California, Because They Know It's Noon in Alabam'."

PAULA: Is that what I like?

YUCCA: (*going to* PAULA's *desk with champagne and glasses*) Sure, you love that one. Oh, Paula, you're always right. It's just like you said a few minutes ago. "This may never happen again." Oh, well, I guess as it turns out you were wrong, but you know what I mean. (*drinks her champagne, pours more*)

PAULA: Well, I'm an unpublished writer, not an unpublished prophet. And speaking of unpublished writing, (*Phone rings.*) —I'm going to kill myself.

YUCCA: Hey, what's wrong? You sound sad.

PAULA: I'm not sad.

YUCCA: But you don't usually look like this until the mailman brings you your rejection slips. Whoops!

PAULA: I think your best move right about now would be to answer the phone.

THE FACULTY LOUNGE
by Michael Schulman

SCENE 5

Linda Garvin teaches English literature in a small New England high school. She spent last night with her ex-husband, Richard—whom she divorced and now wants back. This morning, shortly after she left Richard to go and teach her first class of the new semester, she phoned him and discovered he already had another woman visitor. After an exchange of ugly words, he hung up on her; and he hung up on her again when she phoned him later in the morning.

Linda needs a way to get at Richard, and she quickly devises a scheme when she enters the faculty lounge and finds Rhoda Bootin's mathematics textbook on the floor. During the previous between-period break, Rhoda, the new mathematics teacher, tried to push her way into the faculty room while Norman, another teacher, was holding his foot against the door so that he could continue a very private argument with Linda. Rhoda managed to wedge her book in the door and when she finally broke through, the book dropped to the floor. In her confusion, Rhoda forgot to retrieve it.

Earlier in the day, Rhoda had the misfortune to walk into the faculty room right after Linda's first phone conversation with Richard. Rhoda's timid question, "Am I in the right place?" was answered by Linda with an angry "How am I supposed to know?" From that moment on Rhoda's day has been one of confusion and anxiety. She's been barked at by teachers, locked out of the faculty room, and in a desperate call to her mother, the telephone operator could not understand her deep Texas accent.

(*An hour later.* LINDA *enters, sees* RHODA's *textbook still on the floor and picks it up. She looks at the cover, then quickly looks for something in the book. She hears footsteps, replaces book and rushes to chair to sit.* RHODA *enters. She is still angry and determined to overcome her still considerable confusion and fear. She sees her book on the floor, picks it up and walks to chair and sits. She opens a book and reads. Long silence.*)

LINDA: So. What's new in arithmetic? (*silence*) Have they discovered any new numbers? (*silence*) You know, you might not be able to tell from looking at me, but I used to love math. Just adored equations. They were so neat. Everything accounted for. Immutable laws. And they gave one a sense of power. Shoving x's and y's around, back and forth, up and down. That is, if you knew the rules. Very neat. The area of a circle equals two pi r—forever and ever. (RHODA *looks up, a bit surprised.*) The area of a triangle equals one half its base times its height. The certainty. To know the area of any circle anywhere in the universe. (RHODA *is impressed.*) I'm afraid there's nothing like that in English literature.

RHODA: The circumference.

LINDA: What?

RHODA: Two pi r is the measure of the circumference.

LINDA: Ah, yes, the circumference.

RHODA: Pi r squared is the area of a circle. (*She shows* LINDA *formula chart on the inside cover.*)

LINDA: Of course. How could I have forgotten?

RHODA: Oh, they're easy to forget if you don't use them regularly. But you do seem to understand the love for it. Most people don't know that mathematics is a very passionate subject.

LINDA: That's so true.

RHODA: Do you know that there are equations that make me cry?

LINDA: No!

RHODA: Yes, some are so beautiful they actually bring tears to my eyes. My favorite is the one for the hypotenuse of a right triangle: $a^2 + b^2 = c^2$. Oh, the simplicity of it.

LINDA: Oh, yes. I like that one myself.

RHODA: The Pythagorean Theorem.

LINDA: Those Greeks certainly knew their triangles.

RHODA: And the calculus. Man's *greatest* invention. Nothing quite like it.

LINDA: Nothing.

RHODA: So efficient.

LINDA: So practical.

RHODA: The elegance of it.

LINDA: Like Fred Astaire.

RHODA: Fred Astaire?

LINDA: A poor analogy. Sorry.

RHODA: Well, I certainly am glad we finally got to chat.

LINDA: Rhoda...

RHODA: I would never have thought you had a love for mathematics.

LINDA: Rhoda, would you do something for me?

RHODA: I must admit that I was feeling very... well, alone before... lost...

LINDA: Rhoda...

RHODA: Like a little girl on her first day in school.

LINDA: Rhoda, would you do me a small favor?

RHODA: Oh, yes. Of course.

LINDA: Good. I'd like you to make a phone call for me.

RHODA: A phone call? I'm not very good on the phone. I get kind of nervous, and people up here don't understand what I'm saying.

LINDA: This'll be easy for you.

RHODA: Who do you want me to call?

LINDA: His name is Richard.

RHODA: Richard? That's a man. I don't think...

LINDA: This is right up your alley, Rhoda. You see, what we have here might be called a classic triangle.

RHODA: (*confused*) Oh.

LINDA: I will dial a number for you. When a man answers, say, "Is this Richard Garvin?"

RHODA: His last name is the same as yours. Is he a relative?

LINDA: Sherlock Holmes would be proud of you. Yes, he's my ex-husband.

RHODA: Oh.

LINDA: You'll say, "Is this Richard Garvin?"

RHODA: "Is this Richard Garvin?"

LINDA: And when he says...

RHODA: (*still memorizing the first line*) "Is this Richard Garvin?"

LINDA: Yes, very good. And when he says, "yes," you'll ask him if I'm there.

RHODA: But you're here?

LINDA: Yes, but he doesn't know that, does he?

RHODA: Oh.

LINDA: In this little enterprise we can refer to my where-abouts as "X."

RHODA: Oh.

LINDA: All right, after you ask for me . . .

RHODA: Ring. Ring. "Is this Richard Garvin?" He says, "Yes." Then I ask is . . . oh.

LINDA: What?

RHODA: How shall I ask about you? Should I say, "Is your ex-wife there?"

LINDA: No. Ask if Mrs. Garvin is there.

RHODA: Ring. Ring. "Is this Richard Garvin?" Yes. "Is Mrs. Garvin there?"

LINDA: Katharine Hepburn, watch out. Then . . .

RHODA: Ring. Ring. "Is this Richard . . ."

LINDA: Rhoda. I think you've mastered this part of it.

RHODA: O.K.

LINDA: He'll say, "No. She's not here." And then ask you, "Who's calling?" Then I want you to say, "This is the principal's office at the high school."

RHODA: Oh, I . . .

LINDA: Then you'll tell him that I left the school and told someone I was heading for my ex-husband's house and you're calling for me because I seemed upset.

RHODA: Oh, no. I couldn't say all that.

LINDA: You see, I want him to think I'm on my way over. He knows what I can be like when I'm mad. I want him to panic and throw his new lady friend out. I'm the jealous type.

RHODA: No, I couldn't . . .

LINDA: Why not?

RHODA: Because it's lying.

LINDA: Oh. Because it's lying. Hmm. First day on the job, and filled with scruples. I like that. Well, then perhaps we'll take another approach. No lying. First you ask him, "Is this Richard Garvin?" Then you ask him if I'm there. When he says, "No," you say, "Watch out for her," and hang up.

RHODA: Watch out for her?

LINDA: Yes. I'm *her*. That should do the trick just as well. The sissy! And I assure you, you won't be lying.

RHODA: I don't know.

LINDA: Come on, Rhoda. We women have to stick together.

RHODA: Well, um, um, um . . . all right.

LINDA: Good. Do you have a dime?
RHODA: I think so. (*She finds one and hands it to Linda.*)
LINDA: Good. Ready? (*Rhoda nods.*) Great! I'll dial.

TEACH ME HOW TO CRY
by Patricia Joudry

ACT II, SCENE 3

Melinda and Will are both outcasts in the high school world of prom dates and basketball games. She is self-conscious, inhibited and needing. Will is a "writer type" who has to battle his upwardly mobile parents. Melinda and Will turn to each other for the strength and security to withstand the trials of adolescence.

Their classmate, Polly, is "the personification of success." She is attractive, confident, and a "born leader." But underneath her polished exterior, Polly also feels unwanted and unloved.

The following scene takes place in the corridor of a high school in a small town. It is Parents' Night and all the students are bustling about eager to introduce their parents to their friends. Melinda has just introduced her mother to Polly and stepped into the garden.

After waiting for her parents to arrive, Polly realizes that they are not coming—that they are not concerned enough about her to come to school. Filled with humiliation and anger, she pulls Melinda aside to ask her for a favor.

MELINDA: Of course I like talking to you, Polly. But couldn't we have talked out in the garden?
POLLY: Your mother will be all right, Melinda.
MELINDA: I know she will. But maybe she'll wonder why I left so quickly. Why were you hiding out there?
POLLY: I wasn't hiding.
MELINDA: And I thought you seemed to be crying too.
POLLY: (*laughs*) What a silly little thing you are. But I like you anyway, Melinda. I'm going to have a party soon, a big party, and I'd like you to come.
MELINDA: I'd love to.

POLLY: And then the boys will ask you out—

MELINDA: I don't care about that.

POLLY: Of course not. You've got Will, haven't you? I guess you and Will are terribly in love.

MELINDA: Oh, no, Polly, it isn't anything like that.

POLLY: Isn't it?

MELINDA: Polly, will you come to my house too?

POLLY: I'd adore to. We'll go back and forth. That's what friends are for, isn't it, Melinda, to share things back and forth.

MELINDA: (*eagerly*) Oh, yes!

POLLY: (*A pause . . . she crosses L. Carefully*) Melinda. You know what you said, up on the bandstand? You said you thought I wanted the part of Juliet. . . .

MELINDA: Yes . . .

POLLY: And I said I didn't care about playing Juliet. Well, that was only because I—I wasn't sure if you were my friend or not.

MELINDA: (*slight pause*) Oh.

POLLY: (*comes toward her*) Because the truth of the matter is, I would like to play Juliet, because I happen to have a more or less personal reason. I guess if you'd known I really wanted the part, you wouldn't have accepted it, would you?

MELINDA: (*backs up a step*) Why, I—

POLLY: (*follows her*) Would you, Melinda! Not if I was your friend, and you knew I wanted it. That's what you said—you said that yesterday. You said you were sorry. Well, if you're really sorry—if you dropped out now for some reason—there are lots of reasons you could drop out—the rehearsals have barely started, and I know the whole part off by heart. (*She talks fast and breathlessly.*) It must be a bore for you anyway, having to rehearse every day when Will is waiting for you. To go up to the bandstand. Doesn't he, Melinda? Doesn't he wait for you every day, and you go up there together!

MELINDA: No—not every day—

POLLY: (*intensely*) Yes! Every day! It's every day, and I know, because I've seen you.

MELINDA: (*frightened*) Polly—if you would just—

POLLY: (*Now she smiles.*) But we don't have to argue about it anyway. All I want is for you to drop out of the play, and then we'll never have to mention the bandstand again.

MELINDA: I couldn't. I couldn't do that, Polly. I wouldn't have any reason to drop out of the play.

POLLY: (*her voice hard*) I just told you the reason.

MELINDA: You're only teasing, aren't you, Polly? My mother has made nearly all the costumes. And Mr. Chesley wouldn't understand. How could he? I don't understand. I don't understand at all why you'd—unless—you were crying outside. Why, Polly? Is it because your mother didn't come tonight?

POLLY: (*a tortured cry*) Shut up!

MELINDA: Polly—

POLLY: Shut up, shut up!

MELINDA: Yes, it is. I understand about some things. You picked some violets for your mother.

POLLY: (*Looks front. In wonderment*) She didn't even put them in water . . . just left them lying on the kitchen table till they were dead. That's what they'd like me to be—my parents—dead.

MELINDA: No, they wouldn't.

POLLY: (*swings on her*) What do you know about it? Your mother wouldn't come to the play anyhow. But mine would, and so would my father. They'd bring all their friends, and they'd look at me and see me there. Please, Melinda. Please, please. I'll do anything for you. Please let me by in the play. It's easy for you.

MELINDA: No it isn't.

POLLY: (*pleading piteously*) Please!

MELINDA: I can't—I can't—I want to be your friend, but—

POLLY: (*suddenly in a fury*) My friend! Would you like to know something, Melinda Grant? I've never hated anybody in this whole world as much as I hate you. (*Melinda steps back; Polly follows.*) I'll give you one last chance. You drop out of that play or I'll tell everybody everything about you and Will Henderson!

MELINDA: There isn't anything to tell!

POLLY: There's plenty. There's lots to tell. And I'll start tonight—right away—and you'll be sorry, you'll be sorry—

MELINDA: Stop it! Don't you talk to me anymore! Just don't you ever talk to me again. You said you were my friend. You don't know what it means to have a friend. You must never have had a friend.

POLLY: (*almost hysterically*) You—you—slut!

(*She turns and runs off L.* MELINDA *stands, staring front.*)

SCENES FOR TWO MEN

CHAPTER TWO
by Neil Simon

Act 1, Scene 1

After a four-and-a-half-week tour of Europe George Schneider returns to his lonely New York apartment. Recently widowed, George prowled all the major capitals in an attempt to forgive his beloved wife for having died. His fast-talking, fun-loving brother, Leo, enters and tries to help George put his life in order. This touching, warm play, based on part of Neil Simon's own life, follows George's struggle to form a new relationship while coping with the ghost of his first wife.

Like so many of Neil Simon's plays, the following scene is a wonderful blend of humor and pathos that gives actors the opportunity to perfect their comic technique while playing the reality of human suffering.

LEO: (*coming through the door*) George, you're not going to believe this! I found a place to park right in front of the building. First time in four years... I think I'll buy an apartment here—I don't want to give up that space. (*puts the suitcase down*) Christ Almighty, it's four degrees in here. Whoooo! Whyn't you rent it out for the winter Olympics, pay your expenses. Where do you turn your heat on? (GEORGE *is reading his mail.*) I smell gas. Do you smell gas, George?

GEORGE: (*looks up*) What?

LEO: Gas, for Chrissakes! (*He runs into the kitchen, to the stove.* GEORGE *continues to read his mail.* LEO *comes out.*) It was on. Didn't you check it before you left? Thank God I didn't have a cigar on me. One match, we'd *both* be back in Italy. (*turns on the desk lamp*) Where do you turn the heat on?... *George?*

GEORGE: What?

LEO: Where is the heater?

235

GEORGE: The heater? It's, uh . . .

LEO: Take your time. Accuracy is important.

GEORGE: I'm sorry . . . The thermostat's on the wall as you come in the bedroom.

LEO: (*looks at him*) Are you all right?

GEORGE: No. Am I supposed to be?

LEO: You lost weight, didn't you?

GEORGE: I don't know. A couple of pounds.

LEO: Sure. Who could eat that lousy food food in Paris and Rome?

GEORGE: Do you smell gas?

LEO: What?

GEORGE: I smell gas.

LEO: I think your nose is having jet lag, George. (*He goes into the bedroom.*)

GEORGE: I was going to stay another week in Rome. Then I said, "No, I have to get back. I'm really anxious to be home." (*He looks around.*) I wonder why I thought that.

LEO: (*reentering*) Come on. You walk into Ice Station Zebra with gas leaking in the kitchen and no fresh air in here for four and a half weeks. I mean, this is February and we're standing here breathing January. . . . Why don't you make some popcorn, see what's on TV.

(*He takes the suitcases into the bedroom,* GEORGE *shakes his head.*)

GEORGE: God!

LEO: (*enters*) You've got to see the bathroom. You left the shower dripping with the little window wide open. There are icicles hanging everywhere. It's beautiful. It looks like the john in *Doctor Zhivago* . . . What are you reading?

GEORGE: My mail.

LEO: Anything interesting?

GEORGE: Not unless you like letters of condolence. I thought I answered my last one when I left. . . . Do we have an Aunt Henry?

LEO: (*offstage*) *Aunt* Henry? We have an *Uncle* Henry. In Kingston, New York.

GEORGE: This is signed "Aunt Henry." (*offstage*) Uncle Henry's about sixty-three—maybe he's going through a change of life. (*reading*) "George, sorry to hear about your loss. With deepest sincerity, Aunt Henry."

LEO: (*comes out of the kitchen; holding up the food*) You want to see sour milk? You want to see white bread that's turned into pumpernickel all by itself? You want to see a dish of grapes that have dried into raisins?

GEORGE: (*looking at another letter*) You want to listen to something, Leo?

LEO: (*trying to avoid the past*) George, you just got home. You're tired. Why don't you defrost the bathroom, take a bath?

GEORGE: Just one letter: "Dear Mr. Schneider, My name is Mary Ann Patterson. We've never met, but I did know your late wife, Barbara, casually. I work at Sabrina's, where she used to come to have her hair cut. She was so beautiful and one of the warmest people I've ever met. It seems I always used to tell her my troubles, and she always found some terrific thing to say to cheer me up. I will miss her smiling face and the way she used to come bouncing into the shop like a little girl. I feel lucky to have known her. I just wanted to return a little of her good cheer. God bless you and keep you. Mary Ann Patterson." (*He puts down the letter.* LEO *looks at him, knowing not to intrude on this moment.*) What the hell did I read *that* for?

LEO: It's very nice. It's a sweet letter, George.

GEORGE: Barbara knew a whole world of people I never knew... She knew that Ricco, the mailman, was a birdwatcher in Central Park, and that Vince, the butcher in Gristede's, painted miniature portraits of cats every weekend in his basement on Staten Island.... She talked to people all year long that I said hello to on Christmas.

LEO: (*looks at him*) I think you could have used another month in Europe.

GEORGE: You mean, I was supposed to come home and forget I had a wife for twelve years? It doesn't work that way, Leo. It was, perhaps, the dumbest trip I ever took in my whole life. London was bankrupt, Italy was on strike, France hated me, Spain was still mourning for Franco... Why do Americans go to grief-stricken Europe when they're trying to get over being stricken with grief?

LEO: Beats me. I always thought you could have just as rotten a time here in America.

GEORGE: What am I going to do about this apartment, Leo?

LEO: My advice? Move. Find a new place for yourself.

GEORGE: It was very spooky in London... I kept walking around the streets looking for Barbara—Harrod's, King's

Road, Portobello. . . . Sales clerks would say, "See what you want, sir?" and I'd say, "No, she's not here." I know it's crazy, Leo, but I really thought to myself, It's a joke. She's not dead. She's in London waiting for me. She's just playing out this romantic fantasy: The whole world thinks she's gone, but we meet clandestinely in London, move into a flat, disappear from everyone and live out our lives in secret! . . . She would have thought of something like that, you know.

LEO: But she didn't. *You* did.

GEORGE: In Rome I got sore at her—I mean *really* mad. How dare she do a thing like this to me? I would *never* do a thing like that to her. Never! Like a nut, walking up the Via Veneto one night, cursing my dead wife.

LEO: In Italy, they probably didn't pay attention.

GEORGE: In Italy, they agree with you. (*He shrugs.*) Okay, Leo, my sweet baby brother, I'm back. . . . Chapter Two in the life of George Schneider. Where the hell do I begin?

LEO: I don't know. You want to go to a dance?

GEORGE: You know, you're cute. Does Marilyn think you're cute?

LEO: Yeah. It's not enough. I want *all* the women to think so.

GEORGE: Everything okay at home?

LEO: Couldn't be better.

GEORGE: You sure?

LEO: Never ask a question like that twice. I gotta go. (*He buttons his coat.*) How about poker on Thursday?

GEORGE: I'll let you know.

LEO: Want me to get tickets for the Knicks game Saturday?

GEORGE: We'll talk about it.

LEO: How about dinner on Sunday? Monday? Maybe Tuesday will be my good news day? (*Imitates a trombone playing "The Man I Love." GEORGE doesn't respond.*) Hey! Hey, Georgie . . .

GEORGE: I'm okay, Leo. I promise. Just give me a little time, okay?

LEO: I don't know what to do for you . . . I feel so goddamn helpless.

GEORGE: Well . . . Maybe you can come by tomorrow and show me how to open up tuna fish.

LEO: (*looks at GEORGE*) Now *I'm* mad. I think it stinks, too. I'm not going to forgive her for a long time, George. (LEO *goes over and embraces* GEORGE. *Tears well up in* LEO's *eyes. He pulls away and heads for the door.*) I'm coming back next week and the two of us are getting bombed, you understand? I mean, I want you *disgusting*! Then we'll drive up to Kingston and check out this Aunt Henry. If he's got money, he might be a nice catch for you.

(*He turns and goes quickly.* GEORGE *turns and looks at the apartment, then picks up his attaché case.*)

GEORGE: (*He takes in a deep breath.*) Okay, let's take it one night at a time, folks.

TRUE WEST
by Sam Shepard

SCENE 4

Austin and Lee are brothers, but you'd never know it from appearances. When we first meet Austin he is well-groomed and mild-mannered. He has come to stay at his mother's home in a suburb of Los Angeles while she is on vacation. He has come in order to finish a story-idea for a film. He has an appointment with a film producer and high hopes for a sale.

Lee is a few years older than Austin. He is a drifter and a hustler, taken to robbing houses and training fighting dogs. He is aggressive and unkempt. He spends lots of time alone in the Mojave Desert.

This morning Austin agreed to give Lee the keys to his car if Lee would stay out of the house during his meeting with the producer, Saul Kimmer. But Lee came back early while Austin and Kimmer were working out their deal. Lee hustled Kimmer into agreeing to read a story-idea of his, a "true-to-life Western." As it turns out, though, Lee can't write. So he drafts Austin to write it down for him. As the scene below opens, Austin is at the typewriter and Lee—who has still not returned Austin's car keys—is sitting across from him "drinking beer and whiskey." Austin types for a while, then stops.

LEE: All right, now read it back to me.

AUSTIN: I'm not reading it back to you, Lee. You can read it when we're finished. I can't spend all night on this.

LEE: You got better things to do?

AUSTIN: Let's just go ahead. Now what happens when he leaves Texas?

LEE: Is he ready to leave Texas yet? I didn't know we were that far along. He's not ready to leave Texas.

AUSTIN: He's right at the border.

LEE: (*sitting up*) No, see, this is one a' the crucial parts. Right here. (*taps paper with beer can*) We can't rush through this. He's not right at the border. He's a good fifty miles from the border. A lot can happen in fifty miles.

AUSTIN: It's only an outline. We're not writing an entire script now.

LEE: Well ya' can't leave things out even if it is an outline. It's one a' the most important parts. Ya' can't go leavin' it out.

AUSTIN: Okay, okay. Let's just—get it done.

LEE: All right. Now. He's in the truck and he's got his horse trailer and his horse.

AUSTIN: We've already established that.

LEE: And he sees this other guy comin' up behind him in another truck. And that truck is pullin' a gooseneck.

AUSTIN: What's a gooseneck?

LEE: Cattle trailer. You know the kind with a gooseneck, goes right down in the bed a' the pick-up.

AUSTIN: Oh. All right. (*types*)

LEE: It's important.

AUSTIN: Okay. I got it.

LEE: All these details are important.

(AUSTIN *types as they talk.*)

AUSTIN: I've got it.

LEE: And this other guy's got his horse all saddled up in the back a' the gooseneck.

AUSTIN: Right.

LEE: So both these guys have got their horses right along with 'em, see.

AUSTIN: I understand.

LEE: Then this first guy suddenly realizes two things.

AUSTIN: The guy in front?

LEE: Right. The guy in front realizes two things almost at the same time. Simultaneous.

AUSTIN: What were the two things?

LEE: Number one, he realizes that the guy behind him is the husband of the woman he's been—

(LEE *makes gesture of screwing by pumping his arm.*)

AUSTIN: (*sees* LEE'S *gesture*) Oh. Yeah.

LEE: And number two, he realizes he's in the middle of Tornado Country.

AUSTIN: What's "Tornado Country"?

LEE: Panhandle.

AUSTIN: Panhandle?

LEE: Sweetwater. Around in that area. Nothin'. Nowhere. And number three—

AUSTIN: I thought there was only two.

LEE: There's three. There's a third unforeseen realization.

AUSTIN: And what's that?

LEE: That he's runnin' outta' gas.

AUSTIN: (*stops typing*) Come on, Lee.

(AUSTIN *gets up, moves to kitchen, gets a glass of water.*)

LEE: Whadya mean, "come on"? That's what it is. Write it down! He's runnin' outta gas.

AUSTIN: It's too—

LEE: What? It's too what? It's too real! That's what ya' mean isn't it? It's too much like real life!

AUSTIN: It's not like real life! It's not enough like real life. Things don't happen like that.

LEE: What! Men don't fuck other men's women?

AUSTIN: Yes. But they don't end up chasing each other across the Panhandle. Through "Tornado Country."

LEE: They do in this movie!

AUSTIN: And they don't have horses conveniently along with them when they run out of gas! And they don't run out of gas either!

LEE: These guys run outta gas! This is my story and one a' these guys runs outta gas!

AUSTIN: It's just a dumb excuse to get them into a chase scene. It's contrived.

LEE: It is a chase scene! It's already a chase scene. They been chasin' each other fer days.

AUSTIN: So now they're supposed to abandon their trucks, climb on their horses and chase each other into the mountains?

LEE: (*standing suddenly*) There aren't any mountains in the Panhandle! It's flat!

(LEE *turns violently toward windows in alcove and throws beer can at them.*)

LEE: Goddamn these crickets! (*yells at crickets*) Shut up out there! (*pause, turns back toward table*) This place is like a fuckin' rest home here. How're you supposed to think!

AUSTIN: You wanna' take a break?

LEE: No, I don't wanna' take a break! I wanna' get this done! This is my last chance to get this done.

AUSTIN: (*moves back into alcove*) All right. Take it easy.

LEE: I'm gonna' be leavin' this area. I don't have time to mess around here.

AUSTIN: Where are you going?

LEE: Never mind where I'm goin'! That's got nothin' to do with you. I just gotta' get this done. I'm not like you. Hangin' around being a parasite offa' other fools. I gotta' do this thing and get out.

(*pause*)

AUSTIN: A parasite? Me?

LEE: Yeah, you!

AUSTIN: After you break into people's houses and take their televisions?

LEE: They don't need their televisions! I'm doin' them a service.

AUSTIN: Give me back my keys, Lee.

LEE: Not until you write this thing! You're gonna' write this outline thing for me or that car's gonna' wind up in Arizona with a different paint job.

AUSTIN: You think you can force me to write this? I was doing you a favor.

LEE: Git off yer high horse will ya'! Favor! Big favor. Handin' down favors from the mountain top.

AUSTIN: Let's just write it, okay? Let's sit down and not get upset and see if we can just get through this.

(AUSTIN *sits at typewriter. Long pause*)

LEE: Yer not gonna' even show it to him, are ya'?

AUSTIN: What?

LEE: This outline. You got no intention of showin' it to him. Yer just doin' this 'cause yer afraid a' me.

AUSTIN: You can show it to him yourself.

LEE: I will, boy! I'm gonna' read it to him on the golf course.

AUSTIN: And I'm not afraid of you either.
LEE: Then how come yer doin' it?
AUSTIN: (*pause*) So I can get my keys back.
(*Pause as* LEE *takes keys out of his pocket slowly and throws them on table, long pause.* AUSTIN *stares at keys.*)

MASS APPEAL
by Bill C. Davis

Act I

Father Tim Farley is the priest at St. Francis' Church. His life is comfortable, his parishioners are comfortable, and his sermons carefully avoid saying anything to disturb his or their comfort. Without fully realizing it, he has become part politician and part entertainer. Enter seminarian Mark Dolson. Mark *believes*. And when he takes action or gives sermons based on his convictions, he disturbs everyone—the community, the church hierarchy, and Father Farley.

But Father Farley cannot dismiss Mark as easily as the others can. Some shard of recollection of his own youthful idealism gnaws at his conscience. He wants to protect Mark and teach him to avoid offending those who will sit in judgment on whether or not he becomes a priest. He has arranged for Mark to become the Deacon at St. Francis so he can help him become a priest.

Now Mark is in trouble again—this time with Monsignor Burke, the rector of the seminary. Mark defended two seminarians who were accused of having homosexual relations, and in the process called the Monsignor a "homophobic autocrat." In his first sermon he condemned the parishioners for being "shackled" by their material possessions—their mink hats and cashmere coats and blue hair. He also drew shocked silence on the line "the purpose of the Church is to become obsolete."

As the scene begins Father Farley has just gotten off the phone with the steaming Father Burke. Burke wants to see Mark right away.

TIM: Mark—come in here.

MARK: (*from offstage*) I'm helping Margaret with the dishes.

TIM: Never mind about the dishes. Come in here now. It's important.

MARK: (*as he enters*) I just have a few more pots...

TIM: Monsignor Burke wants to see you as soon as I'm through with you.

MARK: He's upset about the sermon.

TIM: He says it's not about the sermon.

MARK: It's not?

TIM: Monsignor Burke has appointments with several seminarians and now—you.

MARK: Why?

TIM: Some dress funny—others hang out together too much—

MARK: What did I do?

TIM: It seems you were too vehement in your defense of Frank Kearney and Alfred Virasi.

MARK: He's nuts.

TIM: That's just the kind of intelligent approach he's hoping you'll resort to.

MARK: Do I have to put up with this? Can't I see the bishop?

TIM: The bishop is so paranoid about this Frank and Alfred business, he wishes all the altar boys were girls, so he'll let Burke do what he wants.

MARK: What do you think he's going to ask me?

TIM: It's hard to say. These interviews change according to the person he's inter... Let's do it.

MARK: What?

TIM: The interview. I'll play Monsignor Burke and you play you.

MARK: I shouldn't have to go through this—at all.

TIM: Mark—relax. You don't have anything to be afraid of— do you? Come on—just go out and come in like you're coming for the interview.

MARK: I don't want to play a psycho game.

TIM: Mark—you have to go through this with as much grace and tact as you can. You can't afford a repeat of your last encounter with him.

MARK: (*pause*) All right. (MARK *goes off and reenters as if coming in for his interview with* MONSIGNOR BURKE.)

TIM: (*as* BURKE) Good day, Dolson.

MARK: (*laughing at the apparent accuracy of the impersonation*) Hello, Monsignor Burke.

TIM: (*as* BURKE) You're late.

MARK: I am? Well—sorry—I've been fasting all week and meditating every night so time and space are . . .

TIM: That's very interesting, Dolson. Have you considered a career in a contemplative order?

MARK: Funny you should say that. Father Farley suggested that very thing to me just today.

TIM: (*as* BURKE) Well—he manages to have a few good ideas every so often. (*as himself*) Leave me out of this. (*as* BURKE) Now—I'd like to ask you a few questions. My first question has to do with Frank Kearney and Alfred Virasi.

MARK: He wouldn't get into that right away.

TIM: (*as himself*) Yes, he would. He's a busy man.

MARK: If he's so busy, he can skip my interview.

TIM: (*as himself*) All right—have it your way. (*as* BURKE) How's your family?

MARK: Fine—thank you.

TIM: (*as* BURKE) There's one thing I've always been curious about, Dolson, in regards to your family life. Why did you leave home at sixteen?

MARK: I wanted to be on my own.

TIM: But so young. Was there something at home pushing you out?

MARK: I don't think I was aware of it at the time, but there was a silence in my house that . . . crushed me. There were choruses going on inside of me, and at dinner we all chewed and clanked—and there were times I thought the fork would melt right in my hand.

TIM: So you left?

MARK: Yes.

TIM: And they let you go?

MARK: I think they were relieved.

TIM: Where did you go?

MARK: (*pause*) What were you asking about Frank and Alfred?

TIM: (*as* BURKE) Well . . . I have been wondering why you reacted so strongly to the . . . suggestion they take a year off from their studies.

MARK: It was not a suggestion—it was a demand. They did not take a year off—you kicked them out.

TIM: All right—if you want to be direct. (*as* BURKE) Do you think priests should be allowed to sleep together?

MARK: They weren't priests—they weren't even deacons. A vow of celibacy was far off for them.

TIM: (*as* BURKE) Do you think such practices are easily dispensed with?

MARK: Is your question something along the lines of, "How you gonna keep 'em down on the farm after they've seen Paree?"

TIM: (*as* BURKE) Stop your verbal acrobatics and give a response to whatever you interpret my question to be.

MARK: Yes—I think Frank and Alfred would have stayed down on the farm after they had seen "Paree."

TIM: (*as* BURKE) How do you know?

MARK: I said I "think." I did not say I know.

TIM: (*as* BURKE) Let me ask my next question in your native tongue. Have *you* ever seen "Paree"? (*silence*) And if you have seen "Paree," were they "Parisiettes" or "Parisians"?

MARK: (*long pause*) Both.

TIM: (*as himself*) Really?

MARK: That's it—no more. You were shocked.

TIM: I was playing Monsignor Burke. Both?

MARK: Yes—women and men—two sexes. Monsignor—before I came to the seminary, I enrolled myself in a three-year orgy that laid waste to every fiber of my character. Does that sound apologetic enough? How about this? Monsignor Burke—please understand—I explored the world by indulging my sexual ambivalence. I searched with my body and I discovered that I could never reconcile my inner emotional world that way. Others have—but my unique, personal and human condition called for another way. So I invite celibacy. I will be happy to stay down on the farm because it's there I will be calm enough to help others and the only real joy in this world is helping other people. I feel determined and perfectly prepared to become a priest. What would he say to that?

TIM: (*as* BURKE) Both?

MARK: Will you stop?

TIM: I'm sorry—it's just that I've never seen you in this light before.

MARK: What light?

TIM: Red light.

MARK: And you've *never* been in "red light"?

TIM: By the time my father left and my mother died, I was so confused I didn't want to be near man, woman or piano leg. Celibacy came naturally to me. (*pause*) Mark—if Monsignor Burke asks you, say, "Yes—I have made love with 'Parisiettes.'"

MARK: That's a half-truth.

TIM: Don't start throwing principles around now, Mark. This is too serious for principles. In the larger scheme of things, he's not that important.

MARK: But the truth is. I won't become a priest on a lie.

TIM: Better that than not at all.

MARK: I can't believe you're saying this. I won't listen.

TIM: All right—don't listen to me. Go in there and do your martyr number. Just leave a forwarding address behind.

MARK: He can't get rid of me.

TIM: He can. Mark—once you're a priest you can fight him all you want. You'll end up hearing confessions in the cornfields of Iowa if you do, but at least give yourself a chance. Make sure you do become a priest. Try it my way. Be diplomatic. Avoid answering questions directly. You can steer the questions. Phrase your answers certain ways. . . .

MARK: You mean lie.

TIM: Even Christ said to his apostles, "Be as innocent as doves and as cunning as serpents." Christ said that.

MARK: Does cunning mean lying?

TIM: If you can afford not to be a priest—tell the truth. If you want to be a priest—lie. (*silence*) Mark—I want you to be a priest. I asked for you.

MARK: You asked for me? You said . . .

TIM: I know. I told you Monsignor Burke made me do this—but he didn't. I asked him to let me help you.

MARK: Why?

TIM: Because you're a lunatic. And the Church needs lunatics— and you are one of those priceless lunatics that come along every so often and makes the Church alive. The only problem with lunatics is that they don't know how to survive. I do. (*Pause. Holds out his keys*) Here—take my car. (MARK *takes the keys and exits.*)

SAY GOODNIGHT, GRACIE
by Ralph Pape

Jerry is an out-of-work actor who lives in a shabby East Village apartment with his girlfriend, Ginny. His school chum, Steve, who tends to see the world as a situation comedy, is frantically trying to make his mark as a television writer. When Steve is not out looking for work, he likes to hang out in Jerry's apartment.

In the opening scene of the play, Jerry returns home after another unsuccessful audition. He is in a crisis over what to do with his life and in no mood for pranks. But Steve is full of them.

(*Upstage left, a door opens and closes.* JERRY *enters. He has a traveling bag over his shoulder. He is carrying an 8x10 glossy of himself. There are a few moments of indecisive action. At last, he sits on the couch, stares at his picture and tears it up.*)

JERRY: What next?
STEVE: (*He has been hiding behind the sofa. Quietly, he appears. He is wearing a gorilla mask and a brown derby.* JERRY *has not seen him.*) Excuse me, do you know that time it is?
JERRY: Holy shit!
STEVE: Wait. Before you say anything, I've got something wonderful to tell you! (*He removes mask as he speaks.*)
JERRY: WHAT ARE YOU DOING IN MY APARTMENT?! You trying to give me a heart attack or something?!
STEVE: Oh, it's OK, Ginny let me in. She went to pick up her dress at the cleaners. How'd the audition go?
JERRY: What are you doing in my apartment, Steve?!
STEVE: You weren't right for the part, were you?
JERRY: Never mind! (JERRY *moves to kitchen area.*)
STEVE: Jerry, it doesn't *matter*! Wait till you hear what—

JERRY: Not now! Please.

STEVE: Oh boy! Just wait till you hear what I've got to tell you! Come on: ask me what it is. I haven't told *anybody* yet—Ginny'll be right back, Bobby'll be here, we'll be leaving for the reunion—Come on!

JERRY: (*turning around; holding an empty pot by the handle*) Where's the Chunky Turkey soup?

STEVE: Soup? Soup? Who cares about soup?

JERRY: Where's the Chunky Turkey soup?

STEVE: I ate it! It was delicious! I thank you from the bottom of my heart!

JERRY: You ate the Chunky Turkey soup?

STEVE: Yes! I was all alone, I was excited and hungry and I wanted to celebrate and here was this little can crying out: Take me, open me, eat me, I'm yours!

JERRY: In *my* cabinet, Steve, in *my* kitchen, in *my* apartment, there are the following items—

STEVE: And do you know *why* I was so excited???

JERRY: —3 cans of Chunky Beef soup, 3 cans of Chunky Vegetable soup, 3 cans of Chunky Split Pea and Ham soup, and 7 family-size cans of Franco-American Spaghettios. Are you listening?

STEVE: What are you doing? (*almost immediately*) Rehearsing a monologue! (*He watches and listens to Jerry.*)

JERRY: Early this morning, as I was about to leave *my* apartment, I paused for a moment in *my* kitchen and looked in *my* cabinet, and I made certain that hidden away behind all those other items, there was still one remaining can of Chunky Turkey soup. Why did I do this?

STEVE: (*checking imaginary watch*) 10...9...8...

JERRY: I did this because Chunky Turkey soup, as you know, for some mysterious reason, has become almost impossible to locate in this part of the city, and because I like it very much. In fact, I love it! Why do I love it? I don't know. I can't honestly tell you why I love Chunky Turkey soup. All I know is—

STEVE: Hey, thanks so much for coming. We would have preferred hearing something from Shakespeare, but this gives us a damn fine idea of your talents, and believe me, if a part *should* turn up—

JERRY: All I know is: I love it! It is dependable. It is there. It is the last thing I can be certain of in a world filled with uncertainty; and in any case I don't believe that an emotion such as love has to be explained. Do you agree?

STEVE: Are you all right?

JERRY: *Do* you agree?

STEVE: My God, it was only a can of soup!

JERRY: It was only a can of soup. Was that what you said?

STEVE: Yes.

JERRY: Guess what word you left out?

STEVE: I have no idea.

JERRY: Guess.

STEVE: I don't know!

JERRY: Take a guess!

STEVE: But I don't know!

JERRY: What's the word?!

STEVE: (*as Groucho*) Hmmm. It wouldn't be "swordfish," would it?

JERRY: My! The word is "my." My, my, my, my, my! It was only my fucking can of soup!

STEVE: You are really angry.

JERRY: Oh, yeah? How can you tell? Seriously. As an actor, it's important that I be able to recognize such things. Come on. How can you be sure I'm angry?

STEVE: All right. Put down the pot.

JERRY: You want me to put down the pot? OK. I'll put *down* the pot, Steve. Oh, I'll put down the pot! Are you sure you *really* want to see me put down the pot??

STEVE: Oh, stop it. You sound just like Jackie Gleason!!

JERRY: DON'T YOU EVER TELL ME I SOUND LIKE JACKIE GLEASON!!

STEVE: I'm sorry. That was the wrong thing to say.

JERRY: Don't you *ever* say that again!

STEVE: I'm sorry.

JERRY: Now I've got a headache.

STEVE: It's my fault.

JERRY: I know it's your fault.

STEVE: I said—

JERRY: Don't say another word!

STEVE: But— (*Jerry sits down on couch.*)

JERRY: Don't say another word! (*closes his eyes*) I've got to relax. Dear God, I've got to relax. Don't say another word. Just let me relax. . . .

STEVE: May I make an observation? Do you know why you have so much trouble at auditions? It's because you're tense.

It's very hard to feel at ease in the presence of someone who's unnaturally tense. Do you know what your body says to the average person? It says: Tension. Do you realize what the—

JERRY: Why don't you ever listen to me?

STEVE: Because I'm your friend. What's the matter? Did your boss give you more static about taking off to go to auditions?

JERRY: Can't you see I've got a lot on my mind? And it's more than just an audition or a job that's bothering me?

STEVE: Of course I can see that. I'm not insensitive. Will you just let me tell you what I've been trying to tell you?

JERRY: Would you like a beer?

STEVE: Sure. Fine. (JERRY *gets the beer, hands one to* STEVE.) Thanks. OK. Are you ready for this? You know that girl with the red hair who comes in the book store where I work? Miriam? Well, she knows I'm a writer, and she said she didn't know why she never thought of it before, but this morning she tells me if I ever come up with an outline for a situation comedy pilot, she has got contacts with Norman Lear and can get him to read it! Do you believe this?! Norman Lear?! Producer of *All in the Family; Mary Hartman, Mary Hartman;* right? OK. *Now.* By a strange coincidence, what do you suppose I have been working on in secret for the past two months? A completely original TV series in which—now, hold on to your seat!—I have modelled the central character on you. I even gave him your name! His name is Jerry! One day it just comes to me: a situation comedy about a group of people who are members of the very *first* TV generation, born and raised during the dawn of the Atomic Age, whose lives have gone nowhere, whose dreams have been shattered, who see themselves as hopeless failures, or, at best, historical curiosities, and who do not have the slightest idea what to do about it! I mean: I firmly believe the time is ripe for something like this: it cannot miss! Do you see what I'm getting at? You'll never have to work in an office again. When the show is picked up, guess who I'm going to recommend for the part? There will be no way they can turn you down! Well? What do you think? (*pause*)

JERRY: Steve, I hate to tell you this.

STEVE: Tell me what?'

JERRY: You're fantasizing again.

STEVE: No, no, no! I'm not fantasizing again. You're wrong! What I'm writing now is the cumulative result of everything that has happened to me in the last ten years: this is it! I know it! OK, OK, so maybe it sounds a little pretentious, but I'm convinced that I have finally achieved some form of maturity as an artist.

JERRY: (*holding up gorilla mask*) Maturity, Steve?

STEVE: Don't you appreciate what I'm trying to do for you? I was trying to cheer you up. I thought it would make you laugh!

JERRY: It was a great success, Steve. Thank you.

STEVE: (*taking mask quickly*) Hey, don't tell me you don't remember this? I found it in a box in my closet last week. You used to have one, too. Don't you remember in grammar school we used to watch the *Ernie Kovacs Show* over at Bobby's house, and there was this routine called The Nairobi Trio with these guys in gorilla suits, so the three of us went out and bought these masks and we used to get all dressed up every—

JERRY: Steve, we're almost 30 years old!

STEVE: So what!

JERRY: You know why I feel sorry for you?

STEVE: You know I do. (*pause*) It's been 15 years since Ambrose died, but to me he was always more than just a parakeet. . . .

JERRY: Because you're silly! Let's face it, *you are a silly man*. There's no other word for it. I, on the other hand, am a stupid man. But you know what? I would *rather* be a stupid man than a silly man, because a stupid man at least *tries,* a stupid man *cares,* a stupid man, in his own *stupid* way, has integrity! Not like a silly man! How can a silly man *care* about anything, or *have* integrity, or—or—

STEVE: Don't stop now. This is much better than the speech about the soup.

JERRY: Goddammit, Steve! Does it amuse you to watch my mind turning into a piece of Swiss cheese? Well, does it?

DA
by Hugh Leonard

ACT ONE

Charlie loved his father, Da—and hated him. He learned so much from him yet was so often confused by him. Da made him laugh and, sometimes, he made him cry. Now Charlie is in his early forties and Da has died. He returns to Ireland to the house of his childhood to settle Da's affairs.

Charlie is a successful playwright now living in London. He is a grown man with a child of his own—yet he is obsessed with the memory of his father. Something was left unresolved. What kind of man was Da—really? Da's ghost haunts Charlie. He won't be gotten rid of. They resume old battles and relive events from the past. Sometimes Charlie sees himself as "Young Charlie," and sometimes he remains himself, conversing with Da in the past or present.

In the scene below Charlie is himself. He and Da, and Blackie, their dog, are going for a walk.

(CHARLIE *and* DA *go into the hall.* DA *dips his fingers into a holy-water font and flicks the water at* CHARLIE.)

DA: (*opening the front door; to the dog, stumbling*) Blast you, don't trip me up . . . hoosh owa that! (*They stop on the doorstep,* DA *looking at the sky. During this scene,* CHARLIE *does not attempt to imitate a child. He is an adult re-enacting a memory. Trust is evident in his attitude towards* DA.)

DA: (*continued*) That's a fine mackerel sky. Sure isn't it the best bloody country in the world!

CHARLIE: Da, say it.

DA: Say what?

CHARLIE: What you always say. Ah, you know . . . what the country mug in the army said. Say it.

253

DA: (*feigning innocence*) What did he say?

CHARLIE: Ah, do . . .

DA: Yis, well, he joins up. And he sits down to his dinner the first night, and says he . . .

CHARLIE: Yeah, yeah!

DA: Says he: "Yes, sir; no, sir; sir, if you please. Is it up the duck's arse that I shove the green peas?" (CHARLIE *laughs delightedly. They walk hand in hand up and around the stage, both singing "Waxie Dargle." Lights go down on the kitchen. They stop at an upper level.* DA *reaches back to help* CHARLIE *up.*)

DA: (*continued*) Come on, now . . . big step.

CHARLIE: I can't, da.

DA: Yes, you can.

CHARLIE: I'll fall.

DA: You won't fall. Catch a hold of me hand. That's the lad . . . and there you go! Looka that, looka them mountains. There's a view, if you were rich enough you couldn't buy it. Do you know what I'm going to tell you? . . . There's them that says that view is better nor the Bay of Naples.

CHARLIE: Where's Naples, da?

DA: Ah, it's in Italy.

CHARLIE: What's Italy like, da?

DA: (*pause, then gravely*) Sticky, son . . . sticky.

CHARLIE: Da . . .

DA: What?

CHARLIE: Will I go to Italy when I grow up?

DA: (*comforting*) Not a fear of it . . . we wouldn't let you.

CHARLIE: (*looking out and down*) There's a ship. Is that it, da? . . . is that our ship coming in?

DA: Where? No . . . no, son, that ones going out.

CHARLIE: Will ours come in tomorrow, da?

DA: Begod now it might.

CHARLIE: We'll be on the pig's back then, da, won't we? When we're rich.

DA: We won't be far off it.

CHARLIE: And what'll we do?

DA: Do?

CHARLIE: When we win the Sweep.

DA: (*the standard answer*) We won't do a shaggin' hand's turn.

CHARLIE: (*awe and delight*) Gawny!

DA: (*deadpan*) Sure the girl drew out me ticket the last time, and bad cess to her, didn't she drop it.

CHARLIE: (*dismay*) She didn't?

DA: She did.

CHARLIE: The bloomin' bitch.

DA: The what? Where did you hear that expression?

CHARLIE: I dunno, da.

DA: Don't ever again let me hear you saying the like of that. That's a corner-boy expression.

CHARLIE: Sorry, da.

DA: Women is different from you and me: y'ought to grow up to have respect for them. No, never call a woman a name like that, son, not even if she was a right oul' whoor. (*pause*) Do you know where we are now?

CHARLIE: Dalkey Hill, da.

DA: Not at all. In my day this was called Higgins' Hill, and oul' Higgins used to chase us off it and him up on a white horse. He never set foot in church, chapel or meeting, and sign's on it when he died no one would have him, and (*pointing off*) that's where he's buried, under that stump of what's left of a cross after it was struck by lightnin'. Sure they say he sold his soul to the Oul' Fella himself.

CHARLIE: What oul' fella?

DA: (*pointing down*) Your man. Isn't the mark of his hoof on the wall below on Ardbrugh Road where he tripped running down to the mailboat to go back to England?

CHARLIE: Da, let's go home.

DA: What ails you?

CHARLIE: I'm afraid of old Higgins.

DA: Are you coddlin' me?

CHARLIE: And it's getting dark. I want to go home.

DA: Sure ghosts won't mind you if you don't mind them.

CHARLIE: Da . . .

DA: Wait now till I light me pipe and then we'll go.

CHARLIE: Da, you know the thing I'm worst afraid of?

DA: What's that?

CHARLIE: Well, you know me mother? . . . not Ma: me real one.

DA: What about her?

CHARLIE: Me Aunt Bridgie says when it gets dark she comes and looks in at me through the window.

DA: Looks in at you?

CHARLIE: And she says she's tall and with a white face and a black coat, and she comes out from Dublin on the tram, and she wants me back.

DA: Is that a fact?

CHARLIE: And me Aunt Bridgie says it wasn't true what you told me when I was small, about me mother being on Lambay Island where she wasn't able to get hold of me, and living on pollack and Horny Cobblers.

DA: Not true? Did I ever tell you a word of a lie?

CHARLIE: I don't believe she's on Lambay Island.

DA: No. No, she's not there. That wasn't a lie, son: it was . . . a makey-up. Because you were too young, do you follow me . . . you wouldn't have understood.

CHARLIE: (*apprehensive*) Understood what? Why, where is she? (DA *looks impassively out to sea.*)

CHARLIE: (*continued*) Da, tell us.

DA: (*seeming to change the subject*) Do you see that flashing light?

CHARLIE: That's the Kish lightship.

DA: Well, that's where she is.

CHARLIE: (*stunned*) On the Kish?

DA: God help her.

CHARLIE: What's she doing on the Kish?

DA: She . . . cooks.

CHARLIE: For the lightshipmen?

DA: Yis.

CHARLIE: What does she cook?

DA: Ah, pollack, son, and Horny Cobblers.

(CHARLIE *gives him a suspicious look, then peers out to sea.*)

CHARLIE: Gawny.

DA: So now you know.

CHARLIE: Da . . . what if she got off the Kish? What if she's at home now before us and looking through the window?

DA: Well, if she is, I'll tell you what we'll do. I'll come up behind her and I'll give her the biggest boot up in the arse a woman ever got.

CHARLIE: (*pleased*) Will you, da?

DA: I will. And bejasus it'll be nothing compared to the boot I'll give your Aunt Bridgie. (*rising, brushing his trousers-seat*) Now where the hell is that whelp of a dog?

CHARLIE: Da, I love you.

DA: (*staring at him in puzzlement*) Certainly you do. Why

wouldn't you? (*moving away*) Blackie, come here to me!
(DA's *reply has the effect of causing* CHARLIE *to revert to his
present-day self.*)

CHARLIE: (*fuming*) Why wouldn't I? I'll tell you why bloody
wouldn't I. Because you were an old thick, a zombie, a
mastodon. My God . . . my mother living on a lightship, trim-
ming the wick and filleting Horn Cobblers. What a blazing,
ever-fertile imagination you had—Cobblers aren't even edible!

DA: (*whistles*) Blackie!

CHARLIE: And pollacks!

DA: You're right, son, bolloxed that's what he is.

CHARLIE: The black dog was the only intelligent member of
the family. He died a few years later. He was poisoned, and
no one will convince me it wasn't suicide. God knows how
Ma ever came to marry you.

GEOGRAPHY OF A HORSE DREAMER
by Sam Shepard

ACT ONE

In an old sleazy hotel room Cody lies spread-eagle on his back
on a bed with his arms and legs handcuffed to each bedpost. He
is a dreamer of winning horses and he is being held captive by an
organization headed by a man called Fingers. But Cody's astounding
powers are leaving him and he hasn't dreamt a winner in six
months.

Beaujo and Santee, two small-time hoods, guard Cody. Santee
is fed up with waiting for a lucky dream and he's tired of Cody's
demands for more freedom. Santee decides to contact Fingers
and ask him to help them out of their "slump" by moving them
to another city or giving them another "dreamer."

In the scene below Santee has just left Beaujo and Cody in the
hotel room. Although he's anxious for Cody to start dreaming
winners again, Beaujo is also sympathetic to his captive and tries
his best to make him comfortable.

BEAUJO: What the hell are you tryin' to pull? You know better than to get Santee pissed off like that. We're all in this together ya' know.

CODY: Yeah. Sorry.

BEAUJO: I mean it's mostly up to you ya' know. I mean the dreaming end of it. You're actually the big shot in the situation. You can call all the shots. All you gotta do is dream right.

CODY: It ain't so easy Beaujo. I'm dried up. I need a break.

BEAUJO: Yeah, I can see that and I'm doin' everything I can to make that happen. But in the meantime you gotta play it cool. When Santee's nerves are on edge you gotta go slow.

CODY: If I could just talk to Fingers myself maybe I could convince him. I can't talk to Santee. He hates my guts. He don't understand my position. It's very delicate work, dreaming a winner. You can't just close your eyes and bingo!, it's there in front of you. It takes certain special conditions. A certain internal environment.

BEAUJO: Well how did it happen before? It used to be a snap for you.

CODY: I don't know. It was accidental. It just sort of came to me outta' the blue. You know how that is. At first it's all instinct. Now it's work.

BEAUJO: Yeah, but you can't explain that kinda' stuff to mugs like Santee and Fingers. They don't buy it. All they understand is results. The process don't interest them.

(BEAUJO *lights a cigarette and walks around.*)

CODY: If I could just listen to my record again. That's all. Just a couple of tracks off my record.

BEAUJO: No show. It drives Santee crazy. Besides, like he says, that's part of what got you goin' downhill.

CODY: He's nuts. In the beginning I came up with six fifteen to one shots in a row. Six of 'em. And all of 'em came from the music. It's a source of inspiration, Beaujo.

BEAUJO: It's just impossible right now. We gotta go slow. Maybe later we can sneak the music back into it.

CODY: Then tell me where we are at least. What country is this?

BEAUJO: Can't do it Cody. It's strictly against the rules.

CODY: It's stupid! It's really stupid! I'm dreaming American horses and we're probably in Morocco somewhere. It don't make sense. I gotta know where we are so's I can adjust. I've lost track of everything. I need some landmarks.

BEAUJO: Fingers says the dreams are a gift from God. It don't matter what country you dream in.

CODY: Fuck Fingers! I'm the dreamer. I oughta' know.

BEAUJO: I could describe the general area to you maybe. The neighborhood around the hotel.

CODY: That'd help. Anything would help.

BEAUJO: It's a city. We're in a certain area of a city. The workers wear handkerchiefs around their heads. Their main concern is getting laid. They use rough language and swagger their manhood around.

CODY: That could be anywhere.

BEAUJO: It's a gambling town. Racing all year round. It's the poor people who lose. Dozens of big bookmakers for every block. A few sheisters work a system. All of 'em work with high stakes. The government has hooks directly into the bookmakers. There's protection on every level except for the bums. The police are paid off by high syndicates. For the rich it's a sport. For the poor it's a disease.

CODY: That doesn't help. It don't put me in touch with anything. I need firm ground to stand on.

BEAUJO: That's all I can give you.

CODY: What kind of cars do they drive?

BEAUJO: No more. I overstepped my bounds already.

CODY: What do the cops look like?

BEAUJO: That's it Cody. No more.

CODY: If I could just take a walk. You think you can talk Santee into letting me have a short walk?

BEAUJO: We'll see.

CODY: Oh man, I wish I was dead.

BEAUJO: It'll pass.

CODY: I got a feeling I'll never see daylight again.

BEAUJO: Now come on. Don't go gettin' morbid about it. This is just a slump we're in. Fingers'll pull us out of it.

CODY: Fingers is in the same boat as us. We're like his mirror. We never see him but we're always in touch. When he's winning we're in the Beverly Wilshire. When he's losing we're in a dump like this.

BEAUJO: He's got other dreamers. As soon as things pick up he'll move us.

CODY: Why is he keepin' me on! I wanna go back to Wyoming and raise sheep. That's all I wanna do. I got no more tips. I'm from the Great Plains not the city. He's poisoned my dreams with these cities.

BEAUJO: You want a sleeper?

CODY: Yeah. Gimme four of 'em. The blue ones.

BEAUJO: Oh no. Last time you had four you didn't come around for three days. We thought we lost ya'.

CODY: Gimme three then.

BEAUJO: Two's enough. Put you in a nice light sleep. Who knows, you might even dream a winner.

CODY: Just gimme the pills!

(BEAUJO *hands* CODY *two sleeping pills and a glass of water.* CODY *gobbles them down.*)

BEAUJO: You know your problem Cody? You don't accept the situation. There's no way out. Even if you could escape you're too weak to get very far. Even if you got very far we'd know where to find you. You gotta give into it boy.

CODY: Yeah. Maybe you're right.

BEAUJO: You gotta use some smarts. If you just relaxed into it and accepted it then everything would come to you. We might even let you have a little more freedom. No blindfolds. Walks in the park. All that stuff would come to you.

CODY: Yeah. I keep thinking this is temporary. How long's it been going on anyway?

BEAUJO: No time hints. Just forget about the other possibilities. This is all you got.

CODY: I can't remember how it started.

BEAUJO: You had a dream.

CODY: Yeah. I had that big dream.

BEAUJO: Then you got publicized.

CODY: Yeah. *Life* magazine. Then my folks started cashin' in. My brothers.

BEAUJO: Then half the state of Wyoming. You were the hottest thing in the West. Then we nabbed you.

CODY: I was kidnapped.

BEAUJO: Well, not exactly.

CODY: I was wined and dined. Where was that? (*Through this* CODY *is getting drowsy until he finally falls asleep.*)

BEAUJO: Hollywood Park. Aqueduct. Yonkers.

CODY: What happened?

BEAUJO: We had to keep you secret. Too many scabbies cashin' in.

CODY: I used to wake up and not know where I was. As long as I can remember.

BEAUJO: It'll be all right now. It'll all come back to you. (*melodramatically*) You'll find that special area. A huge blue space. In the distance you'll see 'em approaching the quarter-mile pole. The thunder of hooves. Whips flying. The club-house turn. You'll get a sense of it again. It'll all come back just like it used to. You'll see. You got magic Cody. You'll see.

(CODY *falls into a deep sleep.* BEAUJO *gets up and walks around. He comes to a stop and looks around the room.*)

BEAUJO: (*to himself*) Huh, for a second there I thought I was lost.

G. R. POINT
by David Berry

ACT I, SCENE 4

Micah Bradstreet is a long way from the genteel New England surroundings of his childhood, and the safe Amherst campus of his college days. His mother said that the army would be good for him, as it was for all the generations of Bradstreet men. So now Micah is in Tay Loi, Vietnam, stationed at G. R. Point, the *Graves Registration* area, where the bodies of Vietnam combat victims are processed before burial.

When Micah first enters this gruesome and grotesque world of bodies and body parts, he asserts, "I intend to remain civilized." But one doesn't remain civilized long in a world where slaughter and rape are too common to be noticed, and where drugs are the only escape from fear and hatred. Micah quickly sees that this war only makes men *less* than they were, and writes the "truth" home to his mother.

In the scene that follows, Micah has returned to the barracks after his first battle. He was on guard duty during a Viet Cong attack. He fought heroically. He killed a great many Vietnamese and saved many of his comrades' lives. He is dirty from the fight, and he carries a charred sandal of one of the enemy. His comrades have left him alone with his one friend in the company, Zan. Zan has been through battles, although he didn't take part in the one last night.

ZAN: You need sleep?

MICAH: I'm wide awake.

ZAN: Shoulders said you got a pile of gooks.

MICAH: I did.

ZAN: It isn't easy the first time.

MICAH: What isn't?

ZAN: Zapping gooks.

MICAH: Oh, really?

ZAN: Yeah, really. Tell me about it, Micah.

MICAH: Firefights are fucken beautiful.

ZAN: Where've you been?

MICAH: Taking a walk.

ZAN: Sightseeing?

MICAH: You bastard!

ZAN: Everybody wants to look at least once.

MICAH: Yeah.

ZAN: I hear the bunker next to you got blown away.

MICAH: Like the Fourth of July.

ZAN: Shoulders said you saved the dudes between you and him.

MICAH: You win some . . . lose some . . .

ZAN: There sure was beaucoup shit flyin' last night. . . .

MICAH: Bullets don't move like in my dreams . . . they don't bounce off flesh. . . .

ZAN: Take off your flak jacket, man.

MICAH: (*doing as told*) I stink, Zan. I smell really bad.

ZAN: Not like the carcasses in G. R.

MICAH: (*dangling the sandal*) I got a Ho Chi Minh.

ZAN: Looks like it caught some fire.

MICAH: I think I'm . . . gonna be sick.

ZAN: Be it, man. (MICAH *goes to a waste barrel, dry heaves.* ZAN *follows and touches his shoulder.*)

MICAH: Don't touch me!

ZAN: Okay . . . easy . . . easy. I got sick, too. Half my guts came up.

MICAH: I want a shower . . . gotta get off the fucken dirt.

ZAN: Nobody's expectin' you to be clean.

MICAH: I think I burned out my sixteen. . . .

ZAN: Don't do it to your mind, Micah.

MICAH: I want a shower.

ZAN: Forget it. You got nothin' to do.

MICAH: I want to wash up.

ZAN: Talk to me, brother.

MICAH: There must be . . . two hundred of them out there. . . .

ZAN: Somebody'll get promoted.

MICAH: I saw a foot dangling in the wire. . . . no more steps for that one. I have things to do. . . . gotta clean up.

ZAN: Stay right where you are.

MICAH: I don't want to!

ZAN: You better. Plug in!

MICAH: What the fuck do you want?!

ZAN: I don't know. But . . . don't bury the shit.

MICAH: Barker was one of the guys zapped next to me. Know how I know?

ZAN: Tell me.

MICAH: I-found-his-dog-tag-on-his-boot-by-my-bunker-this-morning. Know what else I found?

ZAN: Tell me.

MICAH: I . . . I . . . found his foot in the boot! I couldn't look for the rest.

ZAN: That's somebody else's job. C'mon, sit down before you fall down.

MICAH: There's a head on the road by the laundry, just a head, maybe a little piece of shoulder. The eyes're open, staring at the dust. People are taking pictures. . . . I saw the Deacon taking pictures . . .

ZAN: C'mon, Micah, sit down—now! (*takes off* MICAH's *helmet*)

MICAH: (*icily in control*) Zan . . . they're all fucken liars . . . smart fucken liars . . . fucking whoring lies right down to me. Fucken imposters! They didn't tell me . . . they . . . *liked* . . . the blood. I LIKED THE BLOOD!! *That's* a man, huh? That's a *man*.

(*pause*)

Out there, man . . . raggedy gook bodies with stiff blooming cocks seeping semen, Zan . . . bloody rigormortising cocks fucking the obscene air. . . .

(*pause*)

"Dear Mother, I want to tell you about corpse cocks." MOTHER!! Don't touch me, Zan! "Dear Mother—"

ZAN: Cut the crap, Micah!

MICAH: They're out there now picking up the bodies *I* made!

ZAN: That's right—

MICAH: This morning, almost dawn, this morning just before the end, I got three of 'em with my fougas, three of 'em, fucken scared kids, I got 'em with my crazy-gas, deep fried 'em with my napalm barrel, they were fucking *hiding* behind the barrel! They almost made it to the end, but I pushed the button AND I MELTED THEM!!! I did that. I burned those gook kids, didn't I?!

ZAN: Uh-huh, you did. But we all did, Micah. Everybody pushes the same-same button.

MICAH: Zan . . . I . . .

ZAN: Yes, Micah?

MICAH: (*rising*) Man, I fucken *begged* Charlie to come for me! Come for me, you motherfuckers, I'm gonna tear your throats! Get near me, you bastards, and I'm gonna eat you, gonna cut open your fucken stomachs 'n wrap your steaming guts around my neck 'n rip your veins wide open and drink your warm blood 'n pound your fucken heads on the bunker beams 'til there's nothing fucken left of you for G. R. to shovel into the truck and take to the dump and push into a hole and pour diesel on and burn, you motherfuckers, BURN!!!

ZAN: Easy, man, easy.

MICAH: I had . . . I had . . . I want to get clean! I stink!

ZAN: You smell alive.

MICAH: Zan! The bunker was hit next to me and I couldn't hear anything anymore and the colors rushed into me and out of me and I slammed home clips and sprayed beaucoup shit and no more fear anymore and no more wanting to piss and I couldn't hear anything anymore except in my head, no more outside, just inside, all the noise inside me, in my head, everything was alive and breathing in the dark—I'm so fucken dirty—I've never been alive like that . . . I was alive . . . I have to wash . . . so alive . . . and I . . .

(HE *suddenly grabs* ZAN, *then lurches away.*)

. . . I had . . . I killed all those people and . . . I had . . . I . . . I . . .

ZAN: (*shaken*) *What*, Micah? What?

MICAH: I CAME!!! (*pause*) In the middle of that . . . I came. Like some animal . . . (ZAN *begins to hold him.* MICAH *resists but* ZAN *doesn't let go.*) . . . filthy . . . DON'T TOUCH ME . . .

don't. Please...don't...please...don't...touch...me... please...

ZAN: Stop it, Micah! Stop it! It isn't dirty, for for Christ sake. So what...so you came. You were alive. Maybe your cock voted for the truth.

MICAH: I didn't want to kill anybody.... I didn't...

ZAN: I know, Home, I know. We're all the same. It's like they're somebody else, 'til you kill one. Then you know.

(*pause*)

Let me help you, Micah. Let it out...let it in...let me in.

MICAH: (*begins to sob*) Leave me alone...please...I can't ...think...I'm tired...I'm...

(HE *trails off into sobbing.*)

ZAN: Don't listen to me anymore. It's okay, Micah, it's okay. Yeah...cry...cry. We got each other, man, all of us here. We're an oasis. That's the miracle in this fucken desert.

LOOSE ENDS
by Michael Weller

SCENE 2

Paul is a Peace Corps dropout when he meets Susan on a beach in Bali. She is bumming around the world with a girlfriend trying to "find herself" and decide what she wants to do with her life. They are attracted to each other, but Paul is leaving for Philadelphia in the morning to start a teaching job.

When Paul returns to the States he manages to track Susan down and they resume their relationship. In the scene below they are visiting Paul's friend, Doug, in New Hampshire. The two men are repairing Doug's trailer home and catching up on their lives. Paul is trying to tell his friend how he first met Susan, but Doug just can't stop talking about his sex life.

DOUG: Listen, man, I've been there, you don't have to tell me about horny. Shit, when I found out ole Maraya was pregnant with baby Jake I got a hard on—wouldn't go down for six months. Everything got me off and I mean everything. Even ole Doofus the dog. Even looking at flowers.

PAUL: Well, what I was . . .

DOUG: Man, there was this one time it was raining and I was walking home from the swimming hole and I just started thinking wow, this rain reminds me of Maraya's big ole tummy. Don't ask me why. And before I knew what I was doing there I was standing in the rain, standing, man, holding my pecker in my hand, pumping away just like I was in the shower or something, I don't know. This dude came driving right by, I didn't give a shit, nothing was gonna stop me. He gets about fifty yards down the road and hits the brakes, tires screeching all over the place when he realizes he's just seen a sex maniac whacking off in the rain. I'm telling you, man, when the feeling hits you like that, fuck holding back, right.

PAUL: Yeah, but the thing is . . .

DOUG: I don't know. Maybe I'm just getting weird living up here. I'm not saying I'd ever go back to the city, ungh-uh, you can have that shit, but still . . . (PAUL *hands him piece of 2x4.*) What's this one for? Oh, yeah . . . Damn, I interrupted you again, I *am* getting weird, I'm telling you. Cisco came up here a couple weeks ago, stayed for two days, I couldn't stop talking. Nobody up here talks. How do I seem?

PAUL: What do you mean?

DOUG: Since the last time you saw me. Do I seem any weirder?

PAUL: No.

DOUG: You do.

PAUL: What do you mean?

DOUG: I don't know. So you're walking on this beach in Bali and you see this chick, right?

PAUL: Well, you know. we started talking and it felt really good. I mean after two years in Africa it felt really good to be talking to someone again. . . .

DOUG: So you whipped out the big boy and shagged her on the beach.

PAUL: Douglas, you have a mind like a sewer, you know that.

DOUG: You didn't fuck her? You mean I been listening to all this shit for nothing?

PAUL: You haven't been listening, you've been talking the whole time.

DOUG: O.K., you got five minutes to get to the fuck or I'm quitting for lunch.

PAUL: You want to hear this or not?

DOUG: Shit, man, she really got to you, huh?

PAUL: I guess you could say that.

DOUG: And I did. So it's real serious, huh?

PAUL: Well, you know, for now. What do you want me to say?

DOUG: You don't know if it's serious?

PAUL: We'll see.

DOUG: O.K., you go to bed at night sometimes and you lie there together but you don't feel like you *have* to fuck before you go to sleep, right.

PAUL: What are you talking about?

DOUG: Just answer me, does that ever happen?

PAUL: Sure, sometimes.

DOUG: Then it's serious. So you fucked her on the beach. Hey, O.K., I'm sorry, what happened?

PAUL: I've been trying to tell you.

DOUG: Well I been waiting for it to get interesting. I can't help it if you don't know how to tell a story.

PAUL: O.K., look, the school closed. . . .

DOUG: What school . . .

PAUL: Doug!

DOUG: What school? You didn't say anything about a school.

PAUL: Philadelphia. Where you wrote me that time?

DOUG: Oh, yeah. How come it closed?

PAUL: Oh, you know, it was one of those experimental places, develop the inner person, that kind of shit. Anyway, the parents must've got wise or something 'cause the school ran out of money halfway through the year and they had to close down. So there's me out of a job, nothing to do, so I got a bus up to Boston to check out a few possibilities and she was on the bus.

DOUG: You're shitting?

PAUL: I swear. I couldn't believe it.

DOUG: You didn't even know she was back in America? That's really far out. I mean that's definitely in the land of spooky events.

PAUL: Well, actually, I left out the part where I called her family in Denver and found out she was living in Boston.

DOUG: Why you little devil.

PAUL: I mean I wasn't sure I was going to try to look her up or anything. In fact I had a little thing going in Philadelphia and I wasn't even sure I wanted to leave.

DOUG: Listen.

PAUL: What?

DOUG: She's real cute. I like her. Really. And I want to get back to the part where you fucked on the beach. And I want a sandwich. You want a sandwich?

PAUL: You're never gonna get this house built.

DOUG: Fuck the house, man, I'm hungry.

LONE STAR
by James McLure

Things just aren't the way they used to be, even in Maynard, Texas. As far as Roy is concerned, everyone is "either married, moved to Oklahoma or shot their foot off." All Roy has left from the good old days is his 1959 pink Thunderbird convertible. When he first drove down Main Street in that car, he was the most envied kid in town; girls fell for him on the spot and guys spoke to him with respect. Yes, things used to be good for Roy.

Then Roy went off to Vietnam and came back a changed man. He still had his car, and his loving wife, Elizabeth, and the respect of most of the men in Maynard; but these things no longer gave him the same pleasure they used to.

It's one A.M. on a summer morning behind Angel's Bar. Roy and his younger brother, Ray, are drinking their usual Lone Star beer while Roy engages in his usual activity: reminiscing about his past sexual triumphs in the back seat of his famous pink automobile.

(Note: James McLure's *Laundry and Bourbon* is the companion play to *Lone Star*. Actors will find it helpful to read the scene on p. 196 in which Elizabeth, Roy's wife, reminisces about her early married days.)

ROY: Yes. (*pause*) You know, I been thinkin' about that car lately, Ray.

RAY: Me, too.

ROY: Do you realize that I've had more tail in that car than anybody else in this whole town?

RAY: Well, sure. You wouldn't let no one else drive it but you.

ROY: I had myself the pleasures of my life in that back seat.

RAY: You used to let me smell the seats after you come home from a date. You used to say, "that's the smell of a woman." I appreciated it.

ROY: It was nothin'. That car's gonna be a museum piece in time. I'd like to pass on to my children and their children, somehow, a piece of that car.

RAY: You can give them each a piece, Roy. (*pause*) Roy, I got somethin' to tell you.

ROY: All right.

RAY: It's bad.

ROY: All right.

RAY: It's terrible.

ROY: Uh-huh.

RAY: It's like an open wound. (*pause*) When you were in Vit Nam.

ROY: Yes.

RAY: Me and Elizabeth.

ROY: You and Elizabeth what?

RAY: Me and Elizabeth . . .

ROY: Yes . . .

RAY: Well, me and Elizabeth . . .

ROY: I've heard this part, Ray. (*pause*) Stop playin' with that tractor gasket. (*Pause. Slowly*) Ray—

RAY: Made love.

ROY: You and Elizabeth.

RAY: Elizabeth and me.

ROY: It's the same thing.

RAY: Yes.

ROY: While I was in Vit Nam?

RAY: Yes. (*Pause.* ROY *looks at* RAY. RAY *looks at ground.*)

ROY: Damn. Shit damn. (*pause*) What have you got to say for yourself.

RAY: I'm sorry.

ROY: Is that all?

RAY: I'm real sorry.

ROY: (*standing, pacing*) Well, shit. I just can't believe it.

RAY: Roy—

ROY: Shut your mouth. (*pause*) My own little brother. I can't believe it! I taught you your life! I taught you how to swim, how to drive a car, how to pass a football, I taught you how to jack off! The most important things in life, I gave to you. And this is my reward?

RAY: What can I say?

ROY: Not a damn thing. I can't believe this is happening to me! My own goddamn little brother and my own goddamn wife! You know that's against the Ten Commandments, don't you? You've just broken one of God's biggest laws, that's all! You have coveted your own brother's wife.

RAY: What does coveted mean?

ROY: IT MEANS FUCK, YA DAMN FOOL! You have fucked your own brother's wife! You know what that's called?

RAY: No what?

ROY: Sodomy.

RAY: (*with terror*) No!

ROY: That's right, Ray. Sodomy. Boy, I'd hate to be in your shoes. It says it right there in the Bible: "Thou had better not commit adultery, nor fuck thy brother's wife, nor covet thou his sheep, nor covet thou his ox. . . ."

RAY: I wouldn't fuck my brother's ox.

ROY: (*groaning*) NO . . .

RAY: I wouldn't even fuck my own ox.

ROY: That not what it means!

RAY: You said "covet" meant fuck.

ROY: Sometimes it does, sometimes it doesn't. See what I mean, Ray? See what I'm drivin' at?

RAY: No.

ROY: I'm talkin' about the Bible, Boy! I'm talkin' about the goddamn Garden of Eden!

RAY: You are?

ROY: Of course. In the Garden of Eden, God made Adam. And he made animals. And He looked down and he saw that it was good. Then He looked down and saw Adam was alone and he saw that that was perverted.

RAY: Why was it?

ROY: Because Adam was alone. He had nothing to occupy his mind. He was walking around perverting the Garden of Eden.

RAY: What was he doing?

ROY: Figure it out, Ray. The guy was alone and he was horny.

RAY: Oh. Then what?

ROY: Then God made Eve, and the bitch screwed the goose and they all got kicked out on their ass. Get my point?

RAY: No.

ROY: God punished them. They broke some of his major laws just like you and he punished them. (*pause*) When did you and Elizabeth fornicate on me?

RAY: Uh... about two years ago...

ROY: When two years ago?

RAY: Winter... no the air conditioner was on the first time—

ROY: The first time! Was there more than once?

RAY: Huh?

ROY: More than once? How many times? Did you do it a lot?

RAY: No, not a lot.

ROY: You better tell me the truth. How many times?

RAY: I'm not good at countin'. (*a horrible silence*)

ROY: Where?

RAY: In your bed.

ROY: My weddin' bed! Is that all?

RAY: Once on the floor.

ROY: The floor!

RAY: Once in the bathroom.

ROY: What!

RAY: Once on the kitchen table.

ROY: The kitchen table. I'll never eat off it again. You goddamn degenerate. I swear. This is the most perverted thing that ever happened to me. My whole house defiled. Guess I'll just have to pitch a tent in the back yard.

RAY: Once in the back yard. (RAY *still seated.* ROY *stalks around with contained rage.*)

ROY: I wonder what I'm going to do with you, Ray?

RAY: I don't know.

ROY: I think what I ought to do... (ROY *picks up a two by four near the shed.*)... is take this here two by four upside your skull.

RAY: Don't do that, Roy.

ROY: Why the hell not?

RAY: It might kill me.

ROY: You ought to be killed.

RAY: Don't say that to me. I'm your little brother.

ROY: I oughta smash your skull in.

RAY: War has made you bloodthirsty, Roy.

ROY: That's what it's supposed to do you damn fool!

RAY: But if you killed me . . .

ROY: What?

RAY: I'll die.

ROY: So?

RAY: If I die . . . I won't know what to do. (ROY *throws away lumber.* RAY *braces for the blow he feels sure is coming.* ROY *walks to* RAY *slowly. Stands over him.* ROY *snatches* RAY'S *cap and beats* RAY *furiously with it. His anger subsiding,* ROY *walks over to the side of the bar, leans against it, roaming like an animal in pain.*)

ROY: The thing is . . . nothing has been the same since I come back. Things I see . . . people I see . . . . it's like they never was. The thing is . . . I can't seem to get nothin' started no more . . . 'cause . . . 'cause . . . see, me and Elizabeth, we had it good once. And I never thought she would do me like . . . I mean I know I'm a hard man to live with . . . but . . . she's a wonderful woman . . . a wonderful woman . . . see, the thing is . . . goddamnit all to hell. (ROY *comes back to where* RAY *is sitting. Gives him his hat*)

RAY: Are you gonna hit me now, Roy?

ROY: No.

RAY: Please. It'll make you feel better.

ROY: No.

RAY: Wish you would. You'll feel better. I promise.

ROY: No.

RAY: All right. (ROY *walks in front of where* RAY *is sitting. Without breaking stride he suddenly turns and belts* RAY *in the mouth.* RAY *flies off the car seat he is sitting on.* ROY *goes back U. to side of bar.*) You said you weren't going to hit me.

ROY: Changed my mind.

RAY: Do you feel any better?

ROY: No. (*pause*) You see, me and Elizabeth we were real close once. It's like, she trusted me . . . she knew I had my faults when she married me . . . but deep down we always loved each other. And I'll always love her, no matter what.

RAY: That's good, Roy.

ROY: No matter what comes between us, I'll always love her. (*quietly*) See. We were together. And we'll always be together. (ROY *crosses to bench, sits.*) But now I got this hurt that I'm carrying around with me.

RAY: I understand.

ROY: No you don't. How could you understand? Ain't nobody can understand my hurt. It's deep down. No one understands. Who could possibly understand my hurt?

RAY: (*pause*) Hank Williams.

SCAPINO!
by Frank Dunlop and Jim Dale

PART TWO

Scapino wants revenge. His master, Geronte, found out that Leandro (Geronte's son) was about to marry a gypsy girl. When confronting Leandro, Geronte claimed he got this news from Scapino. Not so. Scapino, angered at being falsely accused of being Geronte's henchman, decides to teach him a lesson. He fabricates an elaborate lie. He tells Geronte that Leandro has been kidnapped by Turks and they are demanding a 500,000 lire ransom. The worried father gives Scapino the money and orders him to save his son.

In another twist of the plot, Geronte has a scheme to marry off his daughter to Ottavio, his friend's son. But Ottavio has married someone else. Scapino concocts yet another lie to frighten Geronte: that Ottavio's wife's brother is after him to prevent Geronte from ruining his marriage.

Loosely based on a French farce and set in Naples, *SCAPINO!* is a madcap comedy that combines a *commedia del'arte* style with modern humor.

The scene opens with Geronte meeting Scapino in front of a dockside café. Geronte is anxious for news of his son.

GERONTE: Well, Scapino, how are you getting on with saving my son?

SCAPINO: Your son, your son, is now perfectly safe. But it's you who now run the risk. You're in the greatest danger, sir. What I wouldn't do to see you locked up safely back home.

GERONTE: Why?

SCAPINO: Why, at this very moment, sir, they're searching everywhere to murder you.

GERONTE: Me?

SCAPINO: Yes.

GERONTE: Who?

SCAPINO: The brother of the girl Ottavio married. He thinks that your plan to put your daughter in the marriage bed reserved for his sister will succeed. Thinking this, he's determined to wreak vengeance on you and make you pay with your life for the slight on his family's honor. At this moment all his friends, bullies like himself, they are questioning every person in this town. I myself saw a squad of soldiers, all friends of his, beating up and questioning people, and laying siege to every way back to your house so that you can't get home or take a step to right or left without falling into their hands.

GERONTE: My dear Scapino, what shall I do?

SCAPINO: Well, I don't know, sir, do I? It's a funny situation. I'm so frightened for you I'm trembling from hand to mouth. (*He pretends to go and look up every alley, then claps his hands.*) Sir, I have it. I have a way to rescue you. But first you must get into that sack.

GERONTE: Oh, noooo.

SCAPINO: Ah! Oh, my God, look over there!

GERONTE: (*jumping into sack, in fear*) Who is it?

SCAPINO: Good, good, now you there, all you have to do is get to the bottom of that sack. Don't make a sound. Don't make a move. I can then lift you up, you see, as if you were a bundle. Put you on my back, carry you through your enemies back to your house where we can then barricade ourselves in and then phone for the police.

GERONTE: (*getting down in sack*) A brilliant idea.

SCAPINO: (*helping him*) None better, sir. That's it. In you go, sir, all the way to the bottom, sir, and do not make a sound whatever happens.

GERONTE: Just leave it to me. I'll not even breathe.

SCAPINO: Good, good, all the way to the bottom, sir. That's it. (GERONTE *is now in sack. However, his umbrella is sticking out.* SCAPINO *pushes it in, sticking* GERONTE *who yells.*) . . . Just in time, sir, just in time. Here's a real villainous-looking one. . . . Now do not make a sound whatever happens. . . . He's a . . . he's just sailing up in a boat. (*takes sausage, runs into boat and picks up broom, fixes hat as a pirate, jumps out of boat using broom as a crutch, starts walking to the sack* *with parrot [imaginary] on shoulder, and takes on assumed voice.*)

SCAPINO: (*as Long John Silver*) Ah ha! Sixteen men on a dead man's chest. Yo ho ho and a bottle of gin. Avast there, ye landlubbers—can any man Jack of you tell me, Long John Silver, where I can find that pirate, Geronte? ("Pretty Polly.") Shut up, you. You over there, you with the sack, it's Jim lad, isn't it? You tell me where I can find this Geronte, Jim, and I'll give ye a gold balloon—I'll give ye a gold doubloon.

SCAPINO: (*as himself*) Sir, sir, are you searching for my very good friend, Signor Geronte?

SCAPINO: (*as Long John Silver*) Ay, that I am, lad, so that I can keel, haul him, hang him from the highest yardarm, peck him to death with my parrot. ("Pretty Polly.") Shut up, you, or I'll stuff you.

SCAPINO: Sir, I do not know where Signor Geronte is.

SCAPINO: (*as Long John Silver*) Jim, lad, you don't happen to be a shipmate of his, do ye?

SCAPINO: Yes, sir, yes, sir. "I do ye." A very devoted shipmate.

SCAPINO: (*as Long John Silver*) Right then, Jim—then you take this to him from me—("Pretty Polly.")—and her, too. (*attacks the sack, shouting, etc., as if he were being beaten*) Ar, you let that be a lesson to you, Jim. Tell this Geronte that when I find him he'll be my little bit of treasure, and you know what a pirate does with a little bit of treasure? ("He buries it.") He buries it. Right. So now I'm off. Up sail, up anchor. Up, up and away in my beautiful doubloon . . . up into the sky . . . (SCAPINO *lies down and begins screaming.*)

SCAPINO: Sir, ooh, damn the bully, may they take his guts for garters.

GERONTE: (*thrusting his head out of the sack*) Oh, Scapino, I can't bear it any longer.

SCAPINO: Sir, my back is broken.

GERONTE: How's that? It was my back that he beat.

SCAPINO: Oh, no, no, it wasn't. That was my back he was having a go at.

GERONTE: What do you mean? I felt every single stroke and I can feel every one of 'em still.

SCAPINO: No, that was only the end of his . . . er, yardarm that was reaching you.

GERONTE: You should have moved off a bit then, and none of it would have reached me.

SCAPINO: Aagh! (*making* GERONTE *go back into the sack again*) Don't look now, sir, get back in as quick as you can. Just spotted another one. (*repeat same umbrella business*) Just in time, just in time. It's a real vicious Eastern type. Not a sound! Not a move, sir! (*long "spiel" in stage Japanese à la Karate*.) Pardon? *If you think I'm going to repeat all that, you're a stupid idiot. Moment please, there is something moving in the saki. I think I am going to give gigantic Karate chop suey to saki.* No, sir, please don't. Sir, that will be over my dead body. *If necessary.* Please don't, sir. I've already been beaten up once this morning already. *Then this is not your lucky day! Con foo...Ow!...Ah so, etc.* (*short "spiel" and he hits sack again, screaming in mock Karate*) *You, let that be a lesson to you, soony Jim....Teach you not to be so insolent. Now I go, Chow...Mein.* Oooh, may they take his guts for garters. (*falls on floor*)

GERONTE: (*popping his head out of the sack*) Oh, I'm beaten to death.

SCAPINO: Oh, I'm killed.

GERONTE: Why the devil must they keep hitting the sack?

SCAPINO: I don't know, sir. I mean...the ushers just let them down the aisle. Sir, don't look 'round. I've just spotted another, sir. Get in as quick as you can. That's it, all the way to the bottom, and do not make a sound, whatever happens. (*He goes to do umbrella business again but this time* GERONTE *pulls it in first.*) Just in time, sir, just in time. It's a whole squad of English soldiers. (*asks audience to get ready to march*)

SCAPINO: (*as Squad*) I say, sergeant...Yes, sir!...I say, sergeant, have you seen that chappie Geronte anywhere? Hey what, what, what, what. *No, sir! He's not over here.* Sir, I say, there's his servant laddie over there with a sack. Let's investigate. (*to audience*) *Company by the left. Quick.* (*Audience starts feet, making marching sounds.*) *Wait for it...* (*hits someone on head who has started sound*) *By the left, march, left, right, left, right, left...* (*to audience*) *Keep up in the back there. Left...right...left...right, left. Brass bands ...forward.* (*puts sausage to lips, imitates brass band marching and playing theme from "The Bridge on the River Kwai."*) Then, I say there, chappie, can you tell us where we can find Signor Geronte; hey, what, what, what, what, tally-ho what.

SCAPINO: Sir, look, I swear I do not know where he is.

You're the third lot of people that have looked for him today.

SCAPINO: (*as Squad*) Now look, chappie, either you tell us where he is or we shall attack your sack. (*Sack falls over;* GERONTE *has fainted.*)

SCAPINO: Sir, sir, for the last time, sir, I do do not know where he is.

SCAPINO: (*as Squad*) Right, then. Sergeant, bring up the cavalry. Right! Cavalry—Forward. (*imitates cavalry; stomping and neighing of horses*) I say, sergeant! Yes, sir? Keep those damn horses quiet. (*then orders*) Horses—Quiet! Now for the last time, are you going to tell us where we can find Signor Geronte?

SCAPINO: Sir, look, for the last time, I swear I don't know.

SCAPINO: (*as Squad*) Right then, sergeant, prepare to charge. GERONTE *pokes head out of sack and sees* SCAPINO *acting as Squad.*) Yes, sir! Artillery, brass band, platoon, my lords, ladies and gentlemen, prepare to charge. . . . Charge! (*Just as he is going to turn around and beat the sack, he sees* GERONTE, *who has come out of the sack. They stare at each other, then* SCAPINO *runs off, out the upstage exit.* GERONTE *can't catch him because the sack is around his legs.*)

GERONTE: The traitor. The villain. The scoundrel. (*He kicks sack and strains his leg and back.*) I'll make you pay for this.

GALILEO
by Bertolt Brecht
(English version by Charles Laughton)

SCENE 7

In 1609, in the city of Padua, Galileo stunned the scientific world and the Vatican court with the news that the earth and, therefore, mankind, was not the center of the universe. He claimed that the earth moved around the sun, and the moon and Jupiter reflected the sun's light. This heretical announcement earned Galileo the wrath of the Church and the ostracism of his fellow scientists who were afraid to challenge the powerful theologians. Persecuted by the Inquisition, he was branded a heretic and excommunicated.

In the following scene a Monk comes to see Galileo. The Little Monk has read Galileo's revolutionary treatise and spent "four sleepless nights" trying to reconcile Galileo's findings with the Church's doctrine. The Little Monk has decided that even if his findings are true, Galileo should abandon his work in favor of a higher good.

GALILEO: Let's hear it. That robe you're wearing gives you the right to say whatever you want to say. Let's hear it.

LITTLE MONK: I have studied physics, Mr. Galilei.

GALILEO: That might help us if it enabled you to admit that two and two are four.

LITTLE MONK: Mr. Galilei, I have spent four sleepless nights trying to reconcile the decree that I have read with the moons of Jupiter that I have seen. This morning I decided to come to see you after I had said mass.

GALILEO: To tell me that Jupiter has no moons?

LITTLE MONK: No, I found out that I think the decree a wise decree. It has shocked me into realizing that free research has its dangers. I have had to decide to give up astronomy. However, I felt the impulse to confide in you some of the motives which have impelled even a passionate physicist to abandon his work.

GALILEO: Your motives are familiar to me.

LITTLE MONK: You mean, of course, the special powers invested in certain commissions of the Holy Office? But there is something else. I would like to talk to you about my family. I do not come from the great city. My parents are peasants in the Campagna, who know about the cultivation of the olive tree, and not much about anything else. Too often these days when I am trying to concentrate on tracking down the moons of Jupiter, I see my parents. I see them sitting by the fire with my sister, eating their curded cheese. I see the beams of the ceiling above them, which the smoke of centuries has blackened, and I can see the veins stand out on their toil-worn hands, and the little spoons in their hands. They scrape a living, and underlying their poverty there is a sort of order. There are routines. The routine of scrubbing the floor, the routine of the seasons in the olive orchard, the routine of paying taxes. The troubles that come to them are recurrent troubles. My father did not get his poor bent back all at once, but little by little, year by year, in the olive orchard; just as year after year, with unfailing regularity, childbirth has made my mother more and more sexless. They draw the strength they need to sweat with their loaded baskets up the stony paths, to bear children, even to eat, from the sight of the trees greening each year anew, from the reproachful face of the soil, which is never satisfied, and from the little church and Bible texts they hear there on Sunday. They have been told that God relies upon them and that the pageant of the world has been written around them that they may be tested in the important or unimportant parts handed out to them. How could they take it, were I to tell them that they are on a lump of stone ceaselessly spinning in empty space, circling around a second-rate star? What, then, would be the use of their patience, their acceptance of misery? What comfort, then, the Holy Scriptures, which have mercifully explained their crucifixion? The Holy Scriptures would then be proved full of mistakes. No, I see them begin to look frightened. I see them slowly put their spoons down on the table. They would feel cheated. "There is no eye watching over us, after all," they would say. "We have to start out on our own, at our time of life. Nobody has planned a part for us beyond this wretched one on a worthless star. There is no meaning in our misery. Hunger is just not having eaten. It is no test of strength. Effort is just stooping and carrying. It is not a virtue." Can you understand that I read into the decree of the Holy Office a noble, motherly pity and a great goodness of the soul?

GALILEO: (*embarrassed*) Hm, well at least you have found out that it is not a question of the satellites of Jupiter, but of the peasants of the Campagna! And don't try to break me down by the halo of beauty that radiates from old age. How does a pearl develop in an oyster? A jagged grain of sand makes its way into the oyster's shell and makes its life unbearable. The oyster exudes slime to cover the grain of sand and the slime eventually hardens into a pearl. The oyster nearly dies in the process. To hell with the pearl, give me the healthy oyster! And virtues are not exclusive to misery. If your parents were prosperous and happy, they might develop the virtues of happiness and prosperity. Today the virtues of exhaustion are caused by the exhausted land. For that, my new water pumps could work more wonders than their ridiculous super-human efforts. Be fruitful and multiply: for war will cut down the population, and our fields are barren! (*a pause*) Shall I lie to your people?

LITTLE MONK: We must be silent from the highest of motives: the inward peace of less fortunate souls.

GALILEO: My dear man, as a bonus for not meddling with your parents' peace, the authorities are tendering me, on a silver platter, persecution-free, my share of the fat sweated from your parents, who, as you know, were made in God's image. Should I condone this decree, my motives might not be disinterested: easy life, no persecution and so on.

LITTLE MONK: Mr. Galilei, I am a priest.

GALILEO: You are also a physicist. How can new machinery be evolved to domesticate the river water if we physicists are forbidden to study, discuss, and pool our findings about the greatest machinery of all, the machinery of the heavenly bodies? Can I reconcile my findings on the paths of falling bodies with the current belief in the tracks of witches on broomsticks? (*a pause*) I am sorry—I shouldn't have said that.

LITTLE MONK: You don't think that the truth, if it is the truth, would make its way without us?

GALILEO: No! No! No! As much of the truth gets through as we push through. You talk about the Campagna peasants as if they were the moss on their huts. Naturally, if they don't get a move on and learn to think for themselves, the most efficient of irrigation systems cannot help them. I can see their divine patience, but where is their divine fury?

LITTLE MONK: (*helpless*) They are old!

(GALILEO *stands for a moment, beaten; he cannot meet the* LITTLE MONK'S *eyes. He takes a manuscript from the table and throws it violently on the ground.*)

LITTLE MONK: What is that?

GALILEO: Here is writ what draws the ocean when it ebbs and flows. Let it lie there. Thou shalt not read. (*The* LITTLE MONK *has picked up the manuscript.*) Already! An apple of the tree of knowledge, he can't wait, he wolfs it down. He will rot in hell for all eternity. Look at him, where are his manners? Sometimes I think I would let them imprison me in a place a thousand feet beneath the earth, where no light could reach me, if in exchange I could find out what stuff that is: "Light." The bad thing is that, when I find something, I have to boast about it like a lover or a drunkard or a traitor. That is a hopeless vice and leads to the abyss. I wonder how long I shall be content to discuss it with my dog!

LITTLE MONK: (*immersed in the manuscript*) I don't understand this sentence.

GALILEO: I'll explain it to you, I'll explain it to you.

MR. ROBERTS
by Thomas Heggen and Joshua Logan

Act I, Scene 2

Everyone aboard the U.S. Navy Cargo Ship AK 601 hates the Captain. It is 1945. The war in Europe has just been won. The big final battles with Japan are beginning. The AK 601 plies the non-combat areas of the Pacific.

Lieutenant J.G. Roberts is the ship's cargo officer. He cares about the seamen on board and fights for them against the Captain. It is only because of the men's commitment to Mr. Roberts that Cargo Ship AK 601 has earned one of the best records in the fleet.

But Mr. Roberts wants desperately to be reassigned to a combat zone. He feels that others are fighting his battles, taking the risks, proving their mettle—while he safely loads and delivers cargo. All his requests for transfer have been blocked by the Captain who knows that his own advancement depends on keeping Mr. Roberts on the job as his cargo officer. Hoping to embarrass the Captain into letting him go, Roberts' latest transfer-request letter describes his conflicts with the Captain and the overall disharmony on board.

Ensign Pulver shares Mr. Roberts' stateroom. *He* also hates the Captain, and has devised various schemes to annoy him. But he has never found the courage to carry any out. As Roberts describes him, Pulver is "a hell of a likable guy . . . but also the most hapless, lazy, disorganized, and, in general, the most lecherous person" he has ever known.

The following scene takes place in Roberts' and Pulver's stateroom. A newly arrived nurse has promised Pulver a date on

the condition that he brings some Scotch. Roberts and Doc have
come to his rescue. They have filled a large vinegar bottle with a
concoction of alcohol, Coca-Cola, iodine, and Kreml—and to
their surprise, "By God, it does taste a little like Scotch."

The scene begins with Pulver thanking his buddies. As the
scene progresses, Roberts learns that Pulver has intercepted his
latest transfer-request letter out of fear that this man he admires
so much will be killed if he gets reassigned to a combat zone.

(Doc is on stage during this scene, but has no lines. For
scene-study purposes, the scene may be thought of as just
between Roberts and Pulver. Roberts' comments to Doc about
Pulver will also make sense if they are altered slightly and
spoken directly to Pulver.)

PULVER: (*singing softly*) Won't know the difference... won't
know the difference. (DOC *starts to drink from Coca-Cola
bottle as* PULVER *comes over and snatches it from his hand.*)
Thanks, Doc. (*Puts cap on the bottle and hides it under the
mattress. Turns and faces the others*) Thanks, Doug. Jeez, you
guys are wonderful to me.

ROBERTS: (*putting bottles back in medicine chest*) Don't
mention it, Frank. I think you almost deserve it.

PULVER: You do—really? Or are you just giving me the old
needle again? What do you really think of me, Doug—honestly?

ROBERTS: (*turning slowly to face* PULVER) Frank, I like you.
No one can get around the fact that you're a hell of a likable
guy.

PULVER: (*beaming*) Yeah—yeah...

ROBERTS: But...

PULVER: But what?

ROBERTS: But I also think you are the most hapless...
lazy... disorganized... and, in general, the most lecherous
person I've ever known in my life.

PULVER: I am not.

ROBERTS: Not what?

PULVER: I'm not disorganized—for one thing.

ROBERTS: Have you ever in your life finished anything you
started out to do? You sleep sixteen hours a day. You pretend
you want me to improve your mind and you've never even
finished a book I've given you to read!

PULVER: I finished *God's Little Acre*, Doug boy!

ROBERTS: I didn't give you that! (*to* DOC) He's been reading

God's Little Acre for over a year! (*takes dog-eared book from* PULVER'S *bunk*) He's underlined every erotic passage, and added exclamation points—and after a certain pornographic climax, he's inserted the words "well-written." (*to* PULVER) You're the Laundry and Morale Officer and I doubt if you've ever seen the laundry.

PULVER: I was down there only last week.

ROBERTS: And you're scared of the Captain.

PULVER: I'm not scared of the Captain.

ROBERTS: Then why do you hide in the passageway every time you see him coming? I doubt if he ever knows you're on board. You're scared of him.

PULVER: I am not. I'm scared of myself—I'm scared of what I might do to him.

ROBERTS: (*laughing*) What you might do to him! Doc, he lies in his sack all day long and bores me silly with great moronic plots against the Captain and he's never carried out one.

PULVER: I haven't, huh.

ROBERTS: No, Frank, you haven't. What happened to your idea of plugging up the line of the Captain's sanitary system? "I'll make it overflow," you said. "I'll make a backwash that'll lift him off the throne and knock him clean across the room."

PULVER: I'm workin' on that. I thought about it for half an hour—yesterday.

ROBERTS: Half an hour! There's only one thing you've thought about for half an hour in your life! And what about those marbles that you were going to put in the Captain's overhead—so they'd roll around at night and keep him awake?

PULVER: Now you've gone too far. Now you've asked for it. (*Goes to bunk and produces small tin box from under mattress. Crosses to* ROBERTS *and shakes it in his face. Opens it*) What does that look like? Five marbles! I'm collecting marbles all the time. I've got one right here in my pocket! (*Takes marble from pocket, holds it close to* ROBERTS' *nose, then drops it in box. Closes box*) Six marbles! (*puts box back under mattress, turns defiantly to* ROBERTS) I'm looking for marbles all day long!

ROBERTS: Frank, you asked me what I thought of you. Well, I'll tell you! The day you finish one thing you've started out to do, the day you actually put those marbles in the Captain's overhead, and then have the guts to knock on his door and say,

''Captain, I put those marbles there,'' that's the day I'll have some respect for you—that's the day I'll look up to you as a man. Okay?

PULVER: (*belligerently*) Okay!

(ROBERTS *goes to the radio and turns it up. While he is listening,* DOC *and* PULVER *exchange worried looks.*)

RADIO VOICE: . . . intersecting thirty miles north of Hanover. At the same time, General George S. Patton's Third Army continues to roll unchecked into Southern Germany. The abrupt German collapse brought forth the remark from a high London official that the end of the war in Europe is only weeks away—maybe days . . .

(ROBERTS *turns off radio.*)

ROBERTS: Where the hell's Dolan with *that* letter! (*starts toward the door*) I'm going to find him.

PULVER: Hey, Doug, wait! Listen! (ROBERTS *pauses at the door.*) I wouldn't send in that letter if I were you!

ROBERTS: What do you mean—*that* letter!

PULVER: (*hastily*) I mean any of those letters you been writin'. What are you so nervous about anyway?

ROBERTS: Nervous!

PULVER: I mean about getting off this ship. Hell, this ain't such a bad life. Look, Doug—we're a threesome, aren't we—you and Doc and me? Share and share alike. Now look, I'm not going to keep those nurses all to myself. Soon as I get my little nursie organized today, I'm going to start working on her twin sister—for you.

ROBERTS: All right, Frank.

PULVER: And then I'm going to scare up something for you too, Doc. And in the meantime you've got a lot of work to do, Doug boy—improvin' my mind and watching my grammar. And speaking of grammar, you better watch your grammar. You're going to get in trouble, saying things like ''disharmony aboard this ship!'' (ROBERTS *looks at* PULVER *quickly.* PULVER *catches himself.*) I mean just in case you ever said anything like ''disharmony aboard this ship'' . . . or . . . uh . . . ''harmony aboard this ship'' or . . .

ROBERTS: Where's that letter?

PULVER: I don't know, Doug boy . . . (*As* ROBERTS *steps toward him, he quickly produces the letter from the blanket.*) Here it is, Doug.

ROBERTS: (*snatching the letter*) What's the big idea!

(ROBERTS *goes to desk, reading and preparing to sign the letter.* PULVER *follows him.*)

PULVER: I just wanted to talk to you before you signed it. You can't send it in that way—it's too strong! Don't sign that letter, Doug, please don't! They'll transfer you and you'll get your ass shot off.

LUTHER
by John Osborne

ACT I, SCENE 2

Martin Luther is a tormented man. A year after his initiation into the Augustinian Order of Eremites, he is about to celebrate his first Mass. But he is not sure he is worthy. "Baited and surrounded by dreams" of carnal sin, Martin strives for a purity of soul and mind that is beyond attainment. He becomes frantic if he misinterprets a line of scripture or feels a twinge of resentment at doing an unpleasant chore in the monastery. He fasts and indulges in mortifications in order to cleanse his soul and erase every hint of doubt. But in his heart, Martin cannot truly believe that God will forgive his sins.

Just before the Mass is to begin, Martin kneels by his bed to pray. Brother Weinand, a member of the Order, enters.

BRO. WEINAND: Brother Martin! Brother Martin!
MARTIN: Yes.
BRO. WEINAND: Your father's here.
MARTIN: My father?
BRO. WEINAND: He asked to see you, but I told him it'd be better to wait until afterwards.
MARTIN: Where is he?
BRO. WEINAND: He's having breakfast with the Prior.
MARTIN: Is he alone?

BRO. WEINAND: No, he's got a couple of dozen friends at least, I should say.

MARTIN: Is my mother with him?

BRO. WEINAND: No.

MARTIN: What did he have to come for? I should have told him not to come.

BRO. WEINAND: It'd be a strange father who didn't want to be present when his son celebrated his first Mass.

MARTIN: I never thought he'd come. Why didn't he tell me?

BRO. WEINAND: Well, he's here now, anyway. He's also given twenty guilden to the chapter as a present, so he can't be too displeased with you.

MARTIN: Twenty guilden.

BRO. WEINAND: Well, are you all prepared?

MARTIN: That's three times what it cost him to send me to the University for a year.

BRO. WEINAND: You don't look it. Why, you're running all over with sweat again. Are you sick? Are you?

MARTIN: No.

BRO. WEINAND: Here, let me wipe your face. You haven't much time. You're sure you're not sick?

MARTIN: My bowels won't move, that's all. But that's nothing out of the way.

BRO. WEINAND: Have you shaved?

MARTIN: Yes. Before I went to confession. Why, do you think I should shave again?

BRO. WEINAND: No. I don't. A few overlooked little bristles couldn't make much difference, any more than a few imaginary sins. There, that's better.

MARTIN: What do you mean?

BRO. WEINAND: You were sweating like a pig in a butcher's shop. You know what they say, don't you? Wherever you find a melancholy person, there you'll find a bath running for the devil.

MARTIN: No, no, what did you mean about leaving a few imaginary sins?

BRO. WEINAND: I mean there are plenty of priests with dirty ears administering the sacraments, but this isn't the time to talk about that. Come on, Martin, you've got nothing to be afraid of.

MARTIN: How do you know?

BRO. WEINAND: You always talk as if lightning were just about to strike behind you.

MARTIN: Tell me what you meant.

BRO. WEINAND: I only meant the whole convent knows you're always making up sins you've never committed. That's right—well, isn't it? No sensible confessor will have anything to do with you.

MARTIN: What's the use of all this talk of penitence if I can't feel it.

BRO. WEINAND: Father Nathan told me he had to punish you only the day before yesterday because you were in some ridiculous state of hysteria, all over some verse in Proverbs or something.

MARTIN: "Know thou the state of thy flocks."

BRO. WEINAND: And all over the interpretation of one word apparently. When will you ever learn? You must know what you're doing. Some of the brothers laugh quite openly at you, you and your over-stimulated conscience. Which is wrong of them, I know, but you must be able to see why.

MARTIN: It's the single words that trouble me.

BRO. WEINAND: The moment you've confessed and turned to the altar, you're beckoning for a priest again. Why, every time you break wind they say you rush to a confessor.

MARTIN: Do they say that?

BRO. WEINAND: It's their favourite joke.

MARTIN: They say that, do they?

BRO. WEINAND: Martin! You're protected from many of the world's evils in here. You're expected to master them, not be obsessed by them. God bids us hope in His everlasting mercy. Try to remember that.

MARTIN: And you .tell me this! What have I gained from coming into this sacred Order? Aren't I still the same? I'm still envious, I'm still impatient, I'm still passionate?

BRO. WEINAND: How can you ask a question like that?

MARTIN: I do ask it. I'm asking you! What have I gained?

BRO. WEINAND: In any of this, all we can ever learn is how to die.

MARTIN: That's no answer.

BRO. WEINAND: It's the only one I can think of at this moment. Come on.

MARTIN: All you teach me in this sacred place is how to doubt—

BRO. WEINAND: Give you a little praise, and you're pleased for a while, but let a little trial of sin and death come into your day and you crumble, don't you?

MARTIN: But that's all you've taught me, that's really all you've taught me, and all the while I'm living in the Devil's worm-bag.

BRO. WEINAND: It hurts me to watch you like this, sucking up cares like a leech.

MARTIN: You *will* be there beside me, won't you?

BRO. WEINAND: Of course, and, if anything at all goes wrong, or if you forget anything, we'll see to it. You'll be all right. But nothing will—you won't make any mistakes.

MARTIN: But what if I do, just one mistake. Just a word, one word—one sin.

BRO. WEINAND: Martin, kneel down.

MARTIN: Forgive me, Brother Weinand, but the truth is this—

BRO. WEINAND: Kneel.

(MARTIN *kneels.*)

MARTIN: It's this, just this. All I can feel, all I can feel is God's hatred.

BRO. WEINAND: Repeat the Apostles' Creed.

MARTIN: He's like a glutton, the way he gorges me, he's a glutton. He gorges me, and then spits me out in lumps.

BRO. WEINAND: After me. "I believe in God the Father Almighty, maker of Heaven and Earth. . . ."

MARTIN: I'm a trough, I tell you, and he's swilling about in me. All the time.

BRO. WEINAND: "And in Jesus Christ, His only Son Our Lord . . ."

MARTIN: "And in Jesus Christ, His only Son Our Lord . . ."

BRO. WEINAND: "Who was conceived by the Holy Ghost, born of the Virgin Mary, suffered under Pontius Pilate . . ."

MARTIN: (*almost unintelligibly*) "Was crucified, dead and buried; He descended into Hell; the third day He rose from the dead, He ascended into Heaven, and sitteth on the right hand of God the Father Almighty; from thence He shall come to judge the quick and the dead, And every sunrise sings a song for death."

BRO. WEINAND: "I believe—"

MARTIN: "I believe—"

BRO. WEINAND: Go on.

MARTIN: "I believe in the Holy Ghost; the holy Catholic Church; the Communion of Saints; the forgiveness of sins;"

BRO. WEINAND: Again!

MARTIN: "The forgiveness of sins."

BRO. WEINAND: What was that again?

MARTIN: "I believe in the forgiveness of sins."

BRO. WEINAND: Do you? Then remember this: St. Bernard says that when we say in the Apostles' Creed "I believe in the forgiveness of sins" each one must believe that *his* sins are forgiven. Well?—

MARTIN: I wish my bowels would open. I'm blocked up like an old crypt.

BRO. WEINAND: Try to remember, Martin?

MARTIN: Yes, I'll try.

BRO. WEINAND: Good. Now, you must get yourself ready. Come on, we'd better help you.

(*Some* BROTHERS *appear from out of the bagpipe with the vestments, etc. and help* MARTIN *put them on.*)

MARTIN: How much did you say my father gave to the chapter?

BRO. WEINAND: Twenty guilden.

MARTIN: That's a lot of money to my father. He's a miner, you know.

BRO. WEINAND: Yes, he told me.

MARTIN: As tough as you can think of. Where's he sitting?

BRO. WEINAND: Near the front, I should think. Are you nearly ready?

(*The Convent bell rings. A procession leads out from the bagpipe.*)

MARTIN: Thank you, Brother Weinand.

BRO. WEINAND: For what? Today would be an ordeal for any kind of man. In a short while, you will be handling, for the first time, the body and blood of Christ. God bless you, my son.

(*He makes the sign of the cross, and the other* BROTHERS *leave.*)

MARTIN: Somewhere, in the body of a child, Satan foresaw in me what I'm suffering now. That's why he prepares open pits for me, and all kinds of tricks to bring me down, so that I keep wondering if I'm the only man living who's baited, and surrounded by dreams, and afraid to move.

BRO. WEINAND: (*really angry by now*) You're a fool. You're really a fool. God isn't angry with you. It's you who are angry with Him.

(*He goes out. The* BROTHERS *wait for* MARTIN, *who kneels.*)

MARTIN: Oh, Mary, dear Mary, all I see of Christ is a flame and raging on a rainbow. Pray to your Son, and ask Him to still His anger, for I can't raise my eyes to look at Him. Am I the only one to see all this, and suffer?

TEAHOUSE OF THE AUGUST MOON
by John Patrick

ACT III, SCENE 2

Yesterday, the natives of Tobiki, a small village in Okinawa, were happy. Yesterday, thanks to Captain Fisby, the American officer of occupation in Tobiki, the first teahouse the village ever had was opened by the village's first geisha girl, Lotus Blossom. Yesterday, also thanks to Captain Fisby, the villagers were making lots of money selling homemade sweet-potato "brandy" to various officers' clubs of the American occupation forces. And yesterday, because the villagers were happy, Captain Fisby, whose assignment it was to turn Tobiki into a democratic and productive community, was also happy.

But today Colonel Purdy arrived. Colonel Purdy, an officer who does things by the book, wants to know why Fisby has not filed any bimonthly progress reports during his two months at Tobiki, and also why Fisby has not delivered even one lecture to the villagers on democratic theory. He is even more concerned with what happened to the truckload of wood he sent Fisby to build a schoolhouse, and is extremely curious about how the villagers got so prosperous all of a sudden. The answers to all these questions make Purdy very unhappy, to say the least. He orders the brandy still and the teahouse destroyed—and soon, no one in Tobiki is happy anymore.

Before all is saved in the final scene, Fisby and his villagers get a hefty dose of anguish from the narrow-minded Colonel, while we, the audience, are treated to a great deal of laughter as we watch all their respective squirmings. As the scene opens, Purdy has already begun his interrogation, and has just dismissed Captain McLean, one of Fisby's accomplices.

PURDY: (*turns back to* FISBY) Now! Is the schoolhouse finished?

FISBY: (*sighs*) No, sir.

PURDY: *Why* isn't it finished?

FISBY: It isn't finished, sir, because it isn't started.

PURDY: I have a splitting headache, Fisby. I ask you not to provoke me needlessly. Now, where is the schoolhouse?

FISBY: I never built it.

PURDY: Don't stand there and tell me you never built it. I sent the lumber down two months ago.

FISBY: (*impressed*) Is it *that* long, sir?

PURDY: What did you do with the lumber I sent?

FISBY: Well, I built a teahouse.

PURDY: (*stares at him*) I don't suppose you have any aspirin here?

FISBY: No, sir, I haven't.

PURDY: Now, sit down. Fisby. I want to be fair. (FISBY *sits down.*) I'm a patient man. When I run into something that defies reason, I like to find the reason. (*explodes*) What in the name of Occupation do you mean by saying you built a *teahouse* instead of a *schoolhouse*!

FISBY: It's a little hard to explain, sir. Everybody in the village wanted one . . . and Lotus Blossom needed it for her work.

PURDY: And just what is your relationship with this woman?

FISBY: Well, she was a present. So to speak. She's a geisha girl—after a fashion.

PURDY: You built this teahouse—this place for her to ply her trade—with lumber belonging to the Army of Occupation of the United States Government?

FISBY: Well, it just seemed like lumber at the time.

PURDY: Fisby, are you operating a house of prostitution here on Government rice?

FISBY: No, sir! Geishas aren't what you think.

PURDY: Don't tell me what to think. Army Intelligence warned me I'd find something mighty peculiar going on in Tobiki.

FISBY: What's Army Intelligence got to do with it, sir?

PURDY: You're not very cunning, Fisby. With all the Occupation money on the island finding its way to this village, did you think it wouldn't come to the attention of Intelligence?

FISBY: Oh.

PURDY: Why did you do it, Fisby, why!

FISBY: Well, Lotus Blossom had to have a place to teach the Ladies' League how to become geishas and—

PURDY: Fisby! You mean to say you've turned all the decent women of this village into professional . . . (*He slumps into the chair.*) How could you sink to such depths, man!

FISBY: I was only giving in to what the majority wanted, sir.

PURDY: I don't doubt that statement—not at all. It is a sad thing that it took a war to convince me that most of the human race is a degenerate. Thank God I come from a country where the air is clean, where the wind is fresh, where—

FISBY: (*interrupts*) For heaven's sake, sir, would you please listen to me instead of yourself! There is not a thing goes on in that teahouse that your mother couldn't watch.

PURDY: (*leaps to his feet and points a warning finger*) You be careful how you use my mother's name, Fisby.

FISBY: Well, *my* mother then. I swear there's nothing immoral about our teahouse.

PURDY: Then answer me this. What is bringing all that Occupation money to this particular village? There is only one thing that attracts that kind of money.

FISBY: Well, evidently there are two things.

PURDY: And if it isn't honor that you sell here, what is it?

FISBY: (*sighs unhappily*) We . . . make things.

PURDY: What?

FISBY: Mats . . . and hats . . . and cricket cages.

PURDY: One hundred and fifty thousand yen finds its way to this village every month. You can't convince me that the American soldier is spending that much on "cricket cages."

FISBY: Well, naturally . . . not all of it (*The telephone rings.* FISBY *looks at it apprehensively.*)

PURDY: Answer it.

FISBY: (*pauses*) It's nothing important, sir.

PURDY: It might be for me. Answer it.

FISBY: (*airily*) Oh, it rings all day, sir. Pay no attention.

PURDY: Then I'll *answer* it! (*He picks up the telephone.* FISBY *covers his face.*) Hello? *What* do you want? Who is this? Well, Commander Myers, I think you have the wrong connection. This is not a brewery. Yes...Yes...yes! (*He turns to look at* FISBY.) Oh...I see. I see. I see. (*He hangs up. He turns to* FISBY, *who smiles weakly.*)

FISBY: It was the only thing we could make that anyone wanted to buy, sir.

PURDY: Brandy! (*sadly*) I don't know which is worse. Putting your country in the white slave trade or the wholesale liquor business. Congress will have to decide.

FISBY: We've the most prosperous village on the island, sir.

PURDY: This ends my Army career. I promised Mrs. Purdy I'd come out a general. You've broken a fine woman's heart, Fisby.

FISBY: You said to make the village self-supporting, sir.

PURDY: I didn't tell you to encourage lewdness and drunkenness. You've sullied the reputation of your nation and all the tears—

FISBY: All right, sir, shall I kill myself?

PURDY: Oh, don't minimize this. You don't know the enemy's genius for propaganda.

FISBY: Does anyone have to know, sir? We're doing all right.

PURDY: (*explodes*) Yes, they have to know! I requested an investigation myself. I've notified the Inspector General. Now I'll have to radio the whole story to Washington.

FISBY: Oh.

PURDY: (*calmer*) Well, what have you done with all this money you've made so dishonestly?

FISBY: Banked it in Seattle.

PURDY: Oh, that's despicable—making a personal fortune off the labor of these ignorant people.

FISBY: I haven't touched a cent for myself, sir. It's been deposited in the name of the Tobiki Cooperative. The whole village are equal partners. Share and share alike.

PURDY: (*leaps up*) That's *Communism*!

FISBY: Is it?

PURDY: (*sinks down again*) I'll be lucky to get out of this war a private. (*He is a beaten man.*) Well, there is only one thing for me to do.

FISBY: What is that, sir?

PURDY: First, you are to consider yourself under technical arrest. You will proceed to H.Q. at once to await court-martial.

FISBY: Yes, sir.

PURDY: (*steps to the door*) Gregovich! (*He turns back to*

FISBY.) I must go on to Awasi this afternoon on an inspection tour. But before I leave, I intend to wipe this stain from our country's honor.

THE ANDERSONVILLE TRIAL
by Saul Levitt

ACT I, SCENE 2

In August 1865 in Washington, D.C., Captain Henry Wirz of the Confederate Army was tried by a United States military court for the murder of Union soldiers when he was the superintendent of the Andersonville Prison Camp in Georgia. The indictment accused him of responsibility for the deaths of over fourteen thousand prisoners by failing to provide adequate shelter, food, or medical treatment, of ordering guards to shoot on sight prisoners that crossed a "deadline," of using bloodhounds that killed over fifty escaped prisoners, and of killing thirteen men by his own hand.

James Davidson—nineteen years old and from Vermont—was one of the prisoners that survived. He has told the court that he and a fellow prisoner had escaped, but were "treed" by the bloodhounds. He said that Wirz soon rode up, yelling, "Get those Yankee bastards." After he and his companion climbed down from the tree, he saw "those dogs tear my companion." He also described another occasion when he saw Wirz and two guards bring back to the stockade another escaped prisoner who had been captured by the dogs: "...his legs was torn and his...neck bloody...[He] made as if to get up and then lay back. Didn't move after that."

As the scene below begins, the defense counsel, Otis H. Baker, starts to cross-examine Davidson.

(The stage direction "To Wallace" in the scene indicates that Davidson speaks this line to the President of the Court, General Lew Wallace.)

BAKER: (*His manner is gentle in conscious contrast to*

CHIPMAN'S.) Mr. Davidson, we will not detain you long, sir. In that first instance you have described—when you made your escape attempt—you say Captain Wirz cursed, urging on those dogs, that were tearing your companion.

DAVIDSON: Yes, sir.

BAKER: Tell me, Mr. Davidson, at any time in your career as a soldier—did you ever yell—"Get those rebel bastards"?

DAVIDSON: I guess so.

BAKER: And what was it that Captain Wirz yelled?—

DAVIDSON: Get—those—Yankee—but that was different.

BAKER: How different?

DAVIDSON: He meant for those dogs to tear that man, and I saw them do that.

BAKER: You were close enough to see that—

DAVIDSON: Yes—

BAKER: Well—*how* close, would you say?

DAVIDSON: Ten, fifteen feet away maybe. No more'n from here to there.

BAKER: And how was it, Mr. Davidson, those dogs did not tear you? (DAVIDSON *stares at* BAKER *in shocked puzzled silence.*) How do you account for that? (DAVIDSON *shakes his head inarticulately.*) Can you think of any reason, Mr. Davidson? (*more silence*)

DAVIDSON: I wouldn't know why, sir.

BAKER: Now, since you admit those ferocious dogs didn't attack you, shall I understand you were completely unhurt when you were brought back to the camp?

DAVIDSON: (*slowly*) No, sir.

BAKER: You were bruised some, as a result of rushing pell mell through the swamps, weren't you?

DAVIDSON: Yes.

BAKER: Bloodied a bit, too?

DAVIDSON: Some. From all that running and stumbling against rocks—

BAKER: Yes. And from bramble bushes and whipping branches and dead cypress limbs, some of them as pointed as knives?

DAVIDSON: Yes, sir.

BAKER: It would bruise and bloody any man, trying to beat a pursuit through a Georgia swamp, wouldn't it?

DAVIDSON: I guess so.

BAKER: So in that second instance you spoke of, when you saw a man brought back to the stockade—couldn't those marks on him that you say were caused by the dogs—couldn't they have been caused by his rushing headlong through the swamps, as yours were?

DAVIDSON: That man was torn by dogs—

BAKER: Well, now you didn't *see* him being torn by dogs, did you, Mr. Davidson?

DAVIDSON: It was commonly known that the dogs—

BAKER: Many things are commonly known, sir. (*Rises. Crosses to R. of witness*) Could you identify the bruises on this man as being indisputably caused by dogs?

DAVIDSON: (*feebly stubborn*) He was bit by the dogs and he died—

BAKER: (*Shrugging. Crosses above table R.*) Possibly. How long did you remain at that spot after this man—you don't happen to know his name, do you?

DAVIDSON: No, sir.

BAKER: How long did you remain there after that man fell down?

DAVIDSON: Three—five minutes.

BAKER: And did you have occasion to look that way later?

DAVIDSON: Some time later—yes.

BAKER: And was he still lying there?

DAVIDSON: No, sir—taken off to the dead house—

BAKER: Or to the sick ward? (*waiting*) Mr. Davidson, you can't say this man died as a result of being mutilated by dogs and you can't identify this man, is that correct?

DAVIDSON: (*to* WALLACE) Sir, please. I got to go back home.

BAKER: And Captain Wirz riding around that man . . . without a word—that sounds mighty unfeeling. You wouldn't know whether he notified the guard at the gate to have that man moved, would you?

DAVIDSON: I got to go home.

BAKER: Thank you, Mr. Davidson. That will be all. (*sits R.*)

SCENES FOR THREE CHARACTERS
(AND A NARRATOR)

THE LIFE AND ADVENTURES OF NICHOLAS NICKLEBY
by Charles Dickens,
(Adapted for the stage by David Edgar)

PART II, ACT III, SCENE 3

One of the greatest theatre events in modern times, *Nicholas Nickleby* is a saga of Victorian England. Adapted from Charles Dickens' novel, the play follows the escapades of Nicholas, his sister Kate, their mother, and a host of unusual characters through a series of humorous and moving events. In the process, the virtuous Nicholas battles injustice, poverty, and corruption and, in the end, emerges a champion of man's essential goodness.

The play begins with the Nickleby family arriving penniless in London after the death of Nicholas' father. Nicholas has come to seek his fortune in the bustling city. But times are hard and he is forced to take a position at Dotheboys Hall, a dilapidated boys school in Yorkshire run by a tyrannical headmaster. There he befriends Smike, a crippled orphan with no recollection of his life before the misery of Dotheboys Hall. Nicholas and Smike escape from the school and, after a brief stay with a travelling theatrical company, they return to London. Smike is welcomed by the Nickleby family and becomes a member of the household. For the first time in his life he knows kindness and friendship.

Despite the loving care bestowed upon him by the Nicklebys, Smike's health deteriorates. When it becomes clear that he is dying, Nicholas and Kate take him to the country home of their youth to spend his last days amid the happy memories of their childhood.

During the course of their stay, Nicholas and Kate both decide that they will not marry their respective sweethearts. Pride has led them to a mutual decision. Kate's beau, Frank, is very rich and she is poor. Nicholas' love, Madeline, has recently inherited a fortune. Neither want to appear avaricious, and they resign themselves to a life together as brother and sister.

As the end draws near for Smike he begins to relive earlier happy times with Nicholas. While they were with the theatrical group both men performed in *Romeo and Juliet,* Nicholas as Romeo, and Smike as the apothecary. Smike was unable to remember his lines and Nicholas drilled his friend night and day. Now, as he is dying, Smike recalls the poetry that Nicholas so lovingly helped him learn. Near death and half-delirious, Smike mutters his opening line, "Who calls so loud?"

NARRATOR: Dividing the distance into two days' journey, in order that their charge might sustain the less exhaustion and fatigue from travelling so far, Nicholas and Kate found themselves at the end of the second day back in the village where they had grown up together.

NICHOLAS: Look, there's our garden, Smike. That's where we used to play, and run, and hide.

SMIKE: You used to hide?

NICHOLAS: Yes, Smike, you know, the game.

KATE: And Nicholas would climb that tree: that big one, over there, to look at young birds in their nests—and he'd shout down, look Kate, how high I've climbed.

NICHOLAS: And you'd be frightened, and you'd tell me to come down.

KATE: And you, you wouldn't come down. But climb even higher, waving all the time.

SMIKE: You climbed up there.

NICHOLAS: And that's the house, Smike, where we used to live, that was Kate's room, behind that tiny window.

KATE: I remember still, the way the sun would stream in, every morning.

SMIKE: Every morning? Winter too?

KATE: I think . . . I can't remember.

NICHOLAS: I suspect that it was always summer here. (SMIKE *has been looking at "the tree."*)

SMIKE: Is it the same. As when. Is it the same. (KATE *and* NICHOLAS *look at each other.*)

NICHOLAS: Things look a little different, Smike. The tree looks smaller. And the garden has become a little overgrown. But still—it is the same. (SMIKE *goes towards the tree.*)

SMIKE: You climbed up there. (KATE, NICHOLAS *and* SMIKE *move round the stage.*)

NARRATOR: And from the house they walked on to the churchyard, where their father lay, and where Kate and her brother used to run and loiter in the days before they knew what death was, let alone its meaning.

NICHOLAS: Once, Smike, Kate was lost, and we searched for an hour, and we couldn't find her, and at last we found her here, beneath that weeping willow, fast asleep. And so our father, who was very fond of her, picked up her sleeping body in his arms, and said that when he died he wanted to be buried here, where his dear, little child had lain her head. Do you remember, Kate?

KATE: I've heard it told so often, I don't know.

SMIKE: You lay down here?

KATE: (*smiling*) Yes. So they say. (KATE *wanders a little away.* SMIKE *takes* NICHOLAS' *hand.*)

SMIKE: Please promise me.

NICHOLAS: What promise? If I can, you know I will.

SMIKE: Please, if I can, may I be buried near—as near as possible—to underneath that tree?

NICHOLAS: Of course. Yes, yes, you will. (KATE *turns back from her wander. She puts out her arms and spins round.*)

NARRATORS: And in a fortnight, Smike became too ill to move about. And he would lie upon an old couch, near the open doors that led into a little orchard. (*Two actors set a couch upstage.*) And Nicholas and Kate would sit with him and talk for hours and hours together. Till the sun went down, and Smike would fall asleep.

(SMIKE *on the couch. It's sunset.* KATE *and* NICHOLAS *leave* SMIKE *and walk downstage. During the scene, it grows darker, and we can no longer see* SMIKE *through the dusk.*)

KATE: Nicholas.

NICHOLAS: Yes, what?

KATE: What is it?

NICHOLAS: I was thinking about those we left behind.

KATE: One person, in particular? (*Pause.* NICHOLAS *turns to* KATE.).

NICHOLAS: It is, I suppose . . . I love her, Kate.

KATE: I know. Your feelings are as obvious to me, as mine must be to you. (*pause*)

NICHOLAS: Oh, Kate. Oh, both of us. Has he—

KATE: He has proposed.

NICHOLAS: What did you say?

KATE: I said—that it was very painful for me, very difficult. But, still, I had to tell him, no.

NICHOLAS: And why?

KATE: Because—you know why.

NICHOLAS: Tell me, Kate.

KATE: Because—of all the kindness of the brothers, to you, and to all of us. Because—Frank's rich, and we are poor, and it would look as if, we'd taken gross advantage of...

NICHOLAS: There's my brave Kate. (*pause*) You've no idea, how much your strength in making your, this sacrifice, will help me making mine.

KATE: But Nicholas, it's not the same.

NICHOLAS: It is the same. For Madeline is bound to our two benefactors with ties just as strong—and she too has a fortune. (*pause*)

KATE: So—we shall stay together.

NICHOLAS: Yes. And when we're staid old folks, we will look back, on these times, and wonder that these things could move us so. And, even, who knows, we might thank the trials which bound us to each other, and which turned our lives into a current of such peace and calm. (*pause*) We'll always be the same.

KATE: Oh, Nicholas. I cannot tell you how, how happy I am, that I've acted as you would have had me.

NICHOLAS: And you don't, at all, regret...

KATE: I don't regret. At least. Perhaps...No, no. I don't regret. (*slight pause*) And, yes, I hope and pray we'll never change. (SMIKE *stands there.*)

SMIKE: Who calls? Who calls so loud? (NICHOLAS *and* KATE *look at* SMIKE, *but* NICHOLAS *stops her with a touch.* SMIKE, *insistent.*) Who calls so loud? (NICHOLAS *a step towards* SMIKE.)

NICHOLAS: Come hither, man. I see that thou art poor. Hold, there is forty ducats. Let me have—

SMIKE: Such mortal drugs I have, but Mantua's law is—is—

NICHOLAS: Oh, Smike—

SMIKE: Is death to any he that utters them. (*prompting*) Art thou so bare—?

NICHOLAS:
Art thou so bare and full of wretchedness,
And fearest to die? Famine is in thy cheeks,
Need and oppression starveth in thy eyes.
Contempt and—

SMIKE: No. No, I don't fear to die. My will consents. (NICHOLAS *turns to embrace* SMIKE, *who throws his arms round* NICHOLAS' *neck to stop himself collapsing*.) You know, I think, that if I could rise up again, completely well, I wouldn't want to, now.

(SMIKE *looking over* NICHOLAS' *shoulder at* KATE.) For nothing—can be ill, if she be well.

NICHOLAS: Then she is well, and nothing can be ill. (*pause*) Her body sleeps in Capel's monument. (*pause*) But her immortal part with angels lives. (NICHOLAS *lifts* SMIKE *up into his arms*.)

SMIKE: Is it. E'en so. I see a garden. Trees and happy children's faces. And her body sleeps. Light on the faces. Living with the angels. Dreamt my lady came and found me dead. Such happy dreams. (*He pulls himself up to whisper in* NICHOLAS' *ear. Then, out loud, to* KATE:) I'm going home. Who calls. Who calls so loud? (SMIKE *is still.* NICHOLAS *realises he is dead. He turns to* KATE. *He is crying.*)

NICHOLAS: He said—I think you know. (*Pause.* KATE *can say nothing.*) And then he said he was in Eden.

MONOLOGUES FOR WOMEN

A LOVELY SUNDAY FOR CREVE COEUR
by Tennessee Williams

SCENE 5

The place is St. Louis, 1935. Dorothea, a "marginally youthful but attractive" school teacher, dreams of marriage to the principal of her school. Hopelessly romantic, she is convinced this is possible. She doesn't know that he is engaged to another, and her roommate, Bodey, tries to shield her from the shattering news.

Despite her charmingly fragile and attractive qualities, Dorothea has never been successful with men. In the following monologue she reminisces about an early beau.

DOROTHEA: (*taking a large swallow of sherry*) Best years of my youth thrown away, wasted on poor Hathaway James. (*She removes his picture from the vanity table and with closed eyes thrusts it out of sight.*) Shouldn't say wasted but so unwisely devoted. Not even sure it was love. Unconsummated love, is it really love? More likely just a reverence for his talent—precocious achievements...musical prodigy. Scholarship to Juilliard, performed a concerto with the Nashville Symphony at fifteen. (*She sips more sherry.*) But those dreadful embarrassing evenings on Aunt Belle's front porch in Memphis! He'd say: "Turn out the light, it's attracting insects." I'd switch it out. He'd grab me so tight it would take my breath away, and invariably I'd feel plunging, plunging against me that—that—frantic part of him...then he'd release me at once and collapse on the porch swing, breathing hoarsely. With the corner gas lamp shining through the wisteria vines, it was impossible not to notice the wet stain spreading on his light flannel trousers....Miss Gluck, MOP IN!!

(*Miss Gluck, who has timidly opened the bathroom door and begun to emerge, with the mop, into the bedroom, hastily retreats from sight.*)

Such afflictions—visited on the gifted . . . Finally worked up the courage to discuss the—Hathaway's—problem with the family doctor, delicately but clearly as I could. "Honey, this Hathaway fellow's afflicted with something clinically known as—chronic case of—premature ejaculation—must have a large laundry bill. . . ." "Is it curable, Doctor?"—"Maybe with great patience, honey, but remember you're only young once, don't gamble on it, relinquish him to his interest in music, let him go."

AGNES OF GOD
by John Pielmeier

ACT I, SCENE 10

Dr. Martha Livingstone is assigned by the court to determine the mental stability of Sister Agnes, a young nun whose infant was found dead in her room. Mother Miriam, head of the convent, is opposed to "psychiatric probing" and fears the doctor will destroy her belief in Agnes' "unconscious innocence."

In the following monologue Mother Miriam shares an event from her childhood with the doctor.

(See also the scene between Agnes and Dr. Livingstone on page 145.)

MOTHER MIRIAM: When I was a child I used to speak with my guardian angel. Oh, I don't ask you to believe that I heard loud, miraculous voices, but just as some children have invisible playmates, I had angelic conversations. Like Agnes' mother, you might say, but I was a lot younger then, and I am not Agnes' mother. Anyway, when I was six I stopped listening and my angel stopped speaking. But just as a sailor remembers the sea, I remembered that voice. I grew, fell in love, married and was widowed, joined the convent, and shortly after I was chosen Mother Superior, I looked at myself one day and saw nothing but a survivor of an unhappy marriage, a mother of two angry daughters, and a nun who was certain of nothing. Not even of Heaven, Doctor Livingstone. Not even of God. And then one evening while walking in a field beside the convent wall, I heard a voice and looking up I saw one of our new postulants standing in her window, singing. It was Agnes, and she was beautiful; and all of my doubts about God and myself vanished in that one moment. I recognized the voice.

(*silence*)

Don't take it away from me again, Doctor Livingstone. Those years after six were very bleak.

THE WEST SIDE WALTZ
by Ernest Thompson

ACT I, SCENE 2

Robin Bird answered a notice on a bookstore bulletin board requesting a companion. It read, "Wanted. Someone to live in. Free room and board, light housekeeping, companionship, arrangements to be negotiated." She finds her way to the West Side (New York City) apartment of Margaret Mary Elderdice and announces, "I'm here about the job."

Margaret Mary is a fiesty lady who intends to hold on to her independent way of life despite advancing age and failing health. She will hire someone to do what she can no longer do for herself.

After she quiets her neighbor, Cara, who is upset that her own offer to move in with Margaret Mary has been refused, Margaret Mary asks Robin to sit down beside her ("so I can hear you"), and inquires, "Why would you be interested in this sort of situation?"

Robin, who has changed her name from Roseanne Mazzarella, tries to avoid answering, but finally she begins.

(For audition and scene study purposes, Margaret Mary's and Cara's lines in the middle of the story may be omitted.)

ROBIN: Um. Well, you know. I'm an actress. (*She looks quickly for a response. All she gets is a look at the ceiling from* CARA.) Although nobody else really knows that. I intend to be an actress, that's my dream. Um. I'm from Brooklyn, which you might be able to tell, although most recently I've been living in Connecticut, which is probably why I seem a little crazy. I've had a lot of jobs, I was married for seven years—I hope that doesn't screw up my, you know, eligibility. I'm not married now, I'm unmarried. But I've had some experience in housekeeping, though I've never won any prizes for it. (*She looks about.*) This place is huge. So, anyway, somewhere along the way my husband became gay and um . . .

MARGARET MARY: Became what?

CARA: Homo.

MARGARET MARY: Oh, oh, gay. Go on, this is good.

ROBIN: Well, anyway, when Peter Pan flew away, I counted the rooms in our house for a couple of months—there's only four rooms—and then I said, "What are you doing, dummy?" And I decided to do something incredible with my life, and I came into the city and was an incredible waitress for three months, until that made me crazy, and then my cousin, who I've known all my life, crapped out on me, and said I had to move out of her apartment 'cause I was threatening her libido, so I've been staying in this rooming house for women, which is like the ultimate answer to the all-time question: "How low can you go?" Then I was in the Rainbow Bookstore looking for something interesting to read, but they didn't have anything, and then I saw your little card, and I'm sorry I took it down. Can I use your bathroom? I figured I'd at least get to use the bathroom.

NUTS
by Tom Topor

Act III

Claudia Faith Draper is being held in New York City's
Bellevue Hospital while awaiting trial on manslaughter charges.
But first the State asked that she receive a psychiatric evaluation
to determine whether she has the capacity to stand trial on the
indictment. Two psychiatrists declare her to be a paranoid
schizophrenic, incapable of standing trial. In a countermove,
Claudia and her lawyer file a motion to challenge, and she
presents evidence to the court that she isn't "nuts."

During the fierce cross-examination, Claudia valiantly holds
her own. She describes with poignant clarity the reasons why a
"nice, bright middle-class girl" like herself might become a
high-priced call girl.

Just prior to the monologue below, the prosecuting attorney
has asked Claudia if she loves her mother.

CLAUDIA: (*pause*) When I was a little girl, I used to say to
her, I love you to the moon and down again and around the
world and back again; and she used to say to me, I love you to
the sun and down again and around the stars and back again.
Do you remember, Mama? And I used to think, wow, I love
Mama, and Mama loves me, and what can go wrong? (*pause*)
What went wrong, Mama? I love you and you love me, and
what went wrong? You see, I know she loves me, and I know
I love her, and—so what? So what? She's over there, and I'm
over here, and she hates me because of things I've done to
her, and I hate her because of the things she's done to me. You
stand up there asking, do you love your daughter, and they say
"yes," and you think you've asked something real, and they
think they've said something real. You think that because you
toss the word love around like a frisbee we're all going to get

311

warm and runny. No. Something happens with some people: they love you so much they stop noticing you're there because they're so busy loving you. They love you so much their love is a gun, and they keep firing it straight into your head. They love you so much you go right into a hospital. Yes, I know she loves me. Mama, I know you love me. And I know the one thing you learn when you grow up is that love is not enough. It's too much and not enough.

DEATH COMES TO US ALL, MARY AGNES
by Christopher Durang

SCENE 5

Christopher Durang's black comedy takes place in the decaying mansion of the Jansen-Hubbell family. The wealthy Mr. Jansen-Hubbell is dying and has called his family together for the reading of his will. When his daughter, Vivien, arrives, she is surprised to find her ex-husband, Herbert, present. While they all wait for the elder Jansen-Hubbell to pass into the next world Vivien reminisces about the first time she saw Herbert.

VIVIEN: (*tearing at the eyes*) Oh, Herbert, we had good times, didn't we? Scurrying about the continent, knowing dukes and earls. Do you remember how you met me? You were just 17 and you went to your first brothel. I was just 14 and it was my first brothel too. My first night. And I remember the Madame, Madame Leore, said to me, she said, Vera—she got my name wrong even then—Vera, you'll turn many a trick in your day, but you'll never turn one like your first one. And so my heart was aglow and you came up to me and in your adolescent voice you said to me, "How much?" And I thought to myself that that was the most romantic thing I had ever heard. And so you and I retired to that little room with the cobwebs and the dank smell of urine and we sat on the bed. Is this your first? I asked, and when you said no I didn't believe you. And is this your first? you asked me, and when I said yes, you didn't believe me. And one of us was lying, and to this day I don't know which one it was, but I don't care because the night air was so fragrant and love was so new, and we were so young. So very, very young. And then you began very methodically to take off my clothes, which were soaked in perspiration from my busy day and from so many other bodies. And then I bit off your buttons, one by one, and your eyes grew larger at every pop. And then I took off your pants. I was very young, you understand, and I had never seen a man, not even a statue of one because they didn't have museums in those days and I wouldn't have gone even if they had. And so then your slender form got on top of my slender form and then—pump! Pump! PUMP! You pumped away, and I gave in to my first experience of love—OH! Oh! Ohhhhh-Ohhhhhh. OHHHHHHHHHHHHH. Uh. Uh. And then when it was all over, I got off of you, and I looked into your blue eyes—your eyes were blue then—and I said in the pale, frightened voice of a school girl, "Herbert, it is you I love." (*pause*) Do you remember, Herbert? Herbert? (*kindly*) Children, I think your father's fallen asleep. (*She lets go of* HERBERT, *and he falls to the ground.*) Oh. Has he had a stroke? Do you think it's a stroke? (*enter* MARTIN)

STOPS ALONG THE WAY
by Jeffrey Sweet

SCENE 1

Stops Along the Way is a bittersweet exploration of a romance gone bad. After five weeks together Larry and Donna are breaking up. A woman in her forties, Donna was infatuated by this young teacher, and left her husband to live with him. But the relationship didn't work out, and Larry is driving her back to Baltimore and her former life.

The following monologue takes place in a diner near a

highway. The couple have stopped for a quick bite during their journey. Their conversation is strained as they attempt to cope with the awkwardness of parting.

(For auditioning and scene-study purposes Larry's lines may be omitted.)

DONNA: Actually, I think we both deserve to be congratulated— you and me. Really, hooray for us. In my considered and impartial opinion, we're being very adult. Handling it very well. You remember in physics, when they told about the atom, about splitting the atom?

LARRY: What about it?

DONNA: When they split an atom, all this energy gets released. When they separate the electrons from the protons—or maybe it's the wontons. Anyway, there's this explosion of energy, and that's the basic principle behind the atom bomb, right? Well, I think it's the same with people. I mean, you take two people who've had a very tight, close thing, and you split them—for whatever reason, whether it's their idea or not—but you do with them like they're an atom, and there's all this energy that's released. And if it's the wrong kind of energy, you can have a Hiroshima on your hands. Hey, *that's* a metaphor, isn't it?

LARRY: That qualifies.

DONNA: But what I'm saying is it can be good energy too, sometimes. In certain cases. Like in our case. Which surprises hell out of me, to tell you the truth. I'm in a good mood. I really am. Of course, I would have been even happier if it had worked out. Jeez, has it only been five weeks? Wow. Spooky. (*a beat*) Wouldn't it be terrific if you could insure emotions? Say you'd go to Prudential, and they'd sell you insurance against getting hurt or feeling guilty or something. Probably the premiums would be incredibly high, though. And can you imagine the claims adjusters, what they'd have to go through? Though right now I do wish I were covered. (LARRY *looks uneasy.*) No, I'm O.K. Actually, to tell you the truth, I think that this is going to turn out to be a very positive thing. Not that I'm glad it didn't work out. But even taking that into consideration, I can truthfully say I think it was a good thing. The whole experience. Taken as a whole. (*a beat*) It's sure as hell going to mean a change in things between Elliot and me. For the better, I think. O.K., the first few days I'm back, it's going to be a little awkward. But I predict, with a little time, he'll accept what happened. I mean, I don't expect him to come right out and admit it, but I bet you he'll come to see it was a good thing in the long run. He'll forgive. (*a beat*) No, fuck forgive! I don't want him to forgive. Or if he insists on forgiving me, well, two can play that game. I'll just forgive him right back. Believe me, there's a lot I could forgive. I don't have to tell you.

A SEA OF WHITE HORSES
by Peter Dee

ACT I

When his wife died two years ago, Ed Shaw left his children and isolated himself in a shack by the sea. But now they have descended on him and shattered the peace he found.

Ed's daughter, Janice, is a young woman whose "rawest need is her father's love." When she finds him living like a hermit by the sea, her already unstable mental state gives way and she tries to take her life. Her brother, Stephen, who has followed her to their father's retreat, finds her and she is swiftly taken to the hospital.

A week later Janice is back. She has recovered physically, but is now sinking again into a helplessly lost state of confusion. She desperately needs her father, but doesn't know what to ask him for or if he is capable of giving it to her.

In the monologue below, Stephen has just asked his sister why she tried to kill herself.

JANICE: I thought you'd never ask. I don't know yet. I'm still trying to figure it out when I can. I had the equipment to do it for a long time. Stored in my hotel drawer. Two little bottles hidden under one of mama's dresses. How's that for a touch. Didn't know I took one of her dresses did you. You all thought I just walked out clean. I had a little poem in my head that sometime I'd wear that dress and drink my little bottles.

But you never do your planned poems—at least not the conscious ones. I took them from a photographer's studio. He saw me looking them over and he said be careful they're poison and I dropped them in my pocket like a couple of Hershey bars. He said I had an "interesting" face. Me and Marilyn Monroe, you know—we're "interesting." He laid me and then took some pictures and then he laid me again. Know what my interesting face was, Stephen; boredom. I kept waiting for him to wake me up. See I don't know how I suddenly got this stray dog attraction for people. Maybe he talked to some of his friends. Because at different times not too far apart people would come into the store—the A & P boutique you know—and I'd go off with them because I had nothing else to do. I did some pretty wild things, Stephen. I never told you when you dropped by because I was ashamed. But I don't ever remember wanting to kill myself. I think I wanted to die but I didn't want to kill myself. It wasn't the sex that did me in or all the crazy shit I took, all that showed me was that somehow I'd gone to sleep forever. Then I got the postcard. From Dad. And I picked up my little bottles and came down here like in a dream. Those bottles were my life, having death near me kept me alive. Knowing I had the controls kept me strong, understand? Anyway, I stood up on that dune, looking at what he'd come to. There was no one around. Just that simple little shack. And sky and the sound of ocean and the smell of it and birds and the sea. And I was suddenly the leper come to rot it all. And I guess still in my dream I went like a rat under his shack and opened my bottles and drank. Just like Juliet.

THE FACULTY LOUNGE
by Michael Schulman

SCENE 4

Rhoda Bootin is in trouble. She has come all the way from Texas to New England for her first job as a high school mathematics teacher, and she is having a very bad first day. The other teachers have mistaken her for a student, have shouted at her, and have locked her out of the faculty lounge while they were arguing among themselves. Tired of roaming the halls between classes, she finally musters the courage to burst in, just as the other teachers vacate the room. Alone now, Rhoda "lurches her way" to the pay phone and dials.

RHODA: Operator. Operator. I want to place a collect call to Mrs. Laura Jean Bootin, and please hurry. Where? She's in Texas, of course—and hurry, 'cause I'm in big trouble. The number? Ah...the number. Sure I know the number. It's my mother's house. I live there *too*. At least I did live there up until yesterday. But now I live here—and that's the reason for the trouble. I should never have left home, operator. I thought it was time for me to go out on my own, but...Oh, yes, the number. Her number is...hold on, it'll come to me. Sure. Good idea. Call information. The city? Ah...I knew it yesterday. I was born there...ah...Amarillo. Yeah. No, no, not Armadillo—*Amarillo*. Never mind. I remember the number. It's area code eight-oh-six, then six-eight-four, four-eight-three-one. Yep, four-eight-three-one. One. I said ONE! Sorry. It's just that my nerves feel like they're sizzling like pork fat in a hot skillet....I said like pork fat in a...forget it. Just dial the number, please. It's from her daughter: Rhoda Sue Honey Mae Bootin. I'm holding. Hello, Mama. Mama, oh, Mama. It's so good to hear your voice again. It's been such a long time. Yes, I know I left only yesterday, Mama, but it seems like it's been such a long time. Mama, I don't think they like me here. No, the other teachers don't like me. I don't know why. These Northerners here—they have no hospitality. And some of them can't even understand English. I don't know if I can last out the rest of the day. Well, I know I signed a contract, but...No, I wouldn't want Daddy to think his little girl was a quitter. Course, not, but...But my feet hurt and I'm not happy here. Well, sure I remember the story of the littlest cowgirl. Sure I do. It was my favorite story. You know that. No, Mama, she wasn't a quitter. I know—she caught all the rustlers, and stopped a herd of stampeding cattle, and delivered the payroll to the snow-trapped railroad men, and doused out the raging prairie fire— all by herself—and still had the time and strength to cook her twelve orphaned brothers their full-course suppers. Oh, Mama,

I'll try again. I won't quit. Thank you, Mama. Don't tell
Daddy, O.K.? O.K. I love you. Bye.

IT'S BEEN WONDERFUL
by John Patrick

ACT III, SCENE 1

Gussie Goddard is a "no-longer-youthful" but still beautiful
Hollywood star who is hoping to land the lead in the film version
of her friend, Paula's, successful novel. She has come to Paula's
weekend party intent on charming the producer and director into
giving her this chance at a career comeback.

In the following monologue she is talking to Paula's younger
brother, Hank, who has come into her bedroom hoping to sleep
with the famous star. In a reminiscent mood, she recalls her early
days in Hollywood and her first husband.

GUSSIE: He was an agent. I was young—alone—scared to
death—broke—and hungry. I used to go to cocktail lounges
and pretend I was waiting for someone so I could eat the
peanuts. I've given some star performances in those joints. I
still can't eat peanuts without feeling depressed. But I survived.
Dear god—there was so much I wanted. I think the most
wonderful moment in my life was realizing I was able to buy
something without asking what it cost. Then there was the
wonder of being able to buy everything. (*Rises and paces,
absorbed in her nostalgic soliloquy.*) And most wonderful of
all—not needing anything to buy. But the things I want now
aren't things I *needed* on the way up. One of the troubles with
being on top is—you've spent so much learning how to get
there that you haven't learned anything about how to live there
once you've made it. You think you're going to be the same
person. But you change. And you don't know where it began.
You take a ballet dancer—if she wants to get to the top, she's
got to use certain muscles other people don't use. Then one
night she looks down at her feet and sees they've become

ugly. So she cries a little. But she knows—if you want something, you pay something. So she goes on dancing. But it isn't so much to pay when you know that so many people *like* you. Because that's all success is—making millions of people like you. That's the best part. But it scares you. Because I can't stand not being liked. And the thing I haven't learned is—how am I going to take it when they stop. I'm afraid of what it'll do to me. You see, they put my mother in a mental institution when I was three. Until I was fifteen I lived with an aunt—a real fruitcake. She looked like Bertrand Russell in drag. But she was a dedicated woman. Dedicated to playing bingo. We had fifteen statues she won of Venus de Milo with a clock in her belly. She'd put me to bed with a bag of potato chips and off she'd go on her bingo binge. Oh, I tell you—I was raised like you throw a pair of dice. I remember when I was six, my aunt gave me a dime for my birthday. I went out and bought jelly beans. I wanted to give a birthday party. You know who I invited? God. I wanted somebody who loved me. I waited. And waited. I'll tell you something. I'm still waiting. Anyhow, as soon as I started making money, I took my mother out of that pig pen and put her in a private sanitarium. She's still alive. If you call it that. I go to see her when I can. A lot of good it does. She doesn't know me. She's gotten fat. Her skin bulges out over her ankles like something loose and swollen. Or dead. But I bring her candy. She likes that cheap hard candy on a stick she can suck like the kids do. At least it's something to please her. I feel so sorry for her. And when I leave, she just stands there with her legs apart and her chin quivering—and—and urinates on the floor.

(*She covers her eyes for a moment.*)

For *weeks* after I've seen her, I can't sleep. I keep thinking— she was young once—and probably pretty—and maybe looked a lot like I do now. I'm so afraid it will happen to me. (*She is silent for a moment. Then she turns to* HANK. *There is no response. He lies with his head back, asleep.*) Oh, dear God—do I have to die to sleep in peace? (*She sits down beside* HANK *and brushes the hair back from his forehead.*) Wake up, sleepy head. (HANK *sits up and blinks sleepily.*)

LOVE IS A TIME OF DAY
by John Patrick

Act II, Scene 2

Skipper Allen is convinced that April MacGregor wants him to move in with her. She does not. In fact, she is quite adamant that she is not in love with her fellow college student and has no intention of sleeping with him. Fortunately for Skip, his bad back suddenly acts up while he is visiting her, and April has no recourse but to permit the amorous Skip to stay in her apartment.

Weeks go by but April continues to fend off Skip's advances. Starved for some affection, Skip brings home a female window dummy from the department store where he works and puts her in his bed. April sees the dummy and thinks it is a real woman. Suddenly, she is very jealous. She gets Skip out of the apartment on the pretext that her dog desperately needs to be walked, and she asks Skip's new "girlfriend" to leave.

(The diapers April refers to are part of an assignment for her Parenthood course in babycare.)

MAC: (*sweetly*) Excuse me. Could I speak to you? (*She waits.*) Look—I don't know who you are and you don't have to say anything if you don't want to but I wish you'd listen to me. I'm not judging you. If you want to get drunk and go to bed with a total stranger—that's your business. Personally, I think it should mean something. At least to the girl. Unless she's being paid. If you're expecting to be paid anything, I think I owe it to you as woman to woman to warn you. He hasn't anything in his pockets but peanuts. I really think, for your own sake, you ought to go. (*waits*) Look—this is my apartment, too, and I can't concentrate on my baby's diapers with this sort of thing going on. My mother gave me that sofa. And she wouldn't approve of using it for—for hanky-panky. Besides, I have to use the bathroom once in a while so I'm

320

asking you to leave. Are you going to leave? (*waits*) *Will* you leave? Please. Miss—don't make me do anything I'll be ashamed of. (*She starts to cry and crosses to desk.*) It's awful to discover you're in love and jealous. It's awful. Awful. I just hate myself. (*Now she begins to get mad. She storms back to end of sofa.*) Now I've been perfectly objective and dispassionate but if you insist on being wanton and sluttish, I'll have to descend to your level. I want you out of this apartment right away. I'll turn my back so I'll never know who you are, but if you haven't grabbed your things and left by the time I count to ten, I'll drag you out of that bed and pull every hair out of your head *one by one*. I mean it! This is zero hour. Off that launching pad! All right—this is your countdown. (*She crosses D. to table, and with her back to the sofa begins to count.*) Ten—nine—eight—seven . . . (SKIP *returns. He comes down and stands between the sofa and* MAC, *listening.*) six—five—four—three—two—(*hesitates*) One! (*waits*) One minus—two minus—

WAITING FOR THE PARADE
by John Murrell

SCENE 14

The setting is Canada during World War II. The men have gone off to war. The play is about the women left behind. Earlier today Catherine received a telegram that her husband, Billy, is missing in action in France. Her friends have come to console her. To relieve her anguish, she gets drunk and sings bawdy songs and talks about her life.

Catherine tells how hard it is sometimes to remember what Billy really looks like and how yesterday she nearly said yes to an attractive man at work who has been asking her out. She goes on to talk about Billy and her marriage.

(To use the scene as a monologue, omit Margaret's line.)

CATHERINE: When Billy and I were first married—we fought all the time. About everything. My clothes. His clothes. My friends. His friends. Whether or not to have children. How many to have. Girls or boys. We fought about baseball teams, which I didn't know anything about. We fought about religion and politics, which neither of us knew anything about. We fought about whether or not it was healthy for us to fight so much. (*pause*) One day—we'd only been married a few months—Billy borrowed some rope and came home from work early. I was having a nap. When I woke up, I was bound—hand and foot! I couldn't move an inch! And Billy was standing there—grinning like a halfwit. ''From now on,'' he said, ''no more fighting. We're going to make love instead. Whenever we feel a fight coming on, we're going to make love instead. And if you don't agree, I'm going to strangle you and dump your remains in the river!''

(*She laughs.*)

MARGARET: I don't see anything very amusing about that.

(*pause*)

CATHERINE: When I think about those times, I can almost see Billy again. At least, I can see his eyes. I can see his hands. And his teeth. He has perfect teeth. Not like mine. That's something else we fought about. (*pause*) But the rest of the picture—is in shadow. (*pause*) Listen. If they want to make the Hollywood blockbuster of all time—one of those stories of tragic romance—sure to have every woman in the theatre reaching for her hanky—they should tell the story of a woman—whose husband goes away—but he goes away, one piece at a time. First an arm vanishes. Then a leg. Then his eyes. His hands. His teeth. Finally she can't remember what he looked like—at all. (*pause*) That's what hurts. (*pause*) That's what's—peculiar. (*pause*) Losing him—a little at a time.

MONOLOGUES FOR MEN

SLY FOX
by Larry Gelbart

ACT I, SCENE 2

Abner Truckle is enraged. When Foxwell Sly's servant, Able, maliciously describes Mrs. Truckle as "the toast of the Coast," and adds that, "Market Street's never fuller than when she sashays down to church," Abner all but explodes with fury. He hurries home to his pious and devoted wife and sets down new rules of conduct for her designed to keep her hidden from any admiring eyes.

TRUCKLE: Air? (*During the following, he slams the window shut, closes the shutters, and secures the crossbar.*) I've forbidden you a thousand times to hang out the window! Showing your body! You think men can't tell that's a body? They know that's a body! How many stopped to talk to you, eh, Jezebel? What obscene gestures were made? Who were they? I'll hang' em by their clockweights! (*He begins using fireplace tools as wedges to secure the window.*) Oh, I'd like to know one day without shame, know before I die that I'd bought and paid for the respect of others. My God, two eyes are too few to watch over one wife! A man's got to be rich! They steal poor men's brides. If I had money, *real* money; if Sly would only breathe his last foul breath! I'll have the windows walled up, buy me a house with a garden on the inside where you can breathe your head off with no lechers peeking up your nostrils! (*He goes to the stage left archway and gets a broom, which he also wedges into the shutters.*) That'll be the day! I'll hire servants to spy on you. They'll have to be eunuchs—for at least ten years before!

KEY EXCHANGE
by Kevin Wade

Scene 5

Michael, Lisa and Philip bicycle together every Sunday in Central Park. Michael has just married a girl he loves very much. Unfortunately, she is a dancer who spends most of her time rehearsing with her composer. Philip, who is unsure if he will ever be ready for married life himself, asks his friend how things are going.

(For auditioning and scene study purposes Philip's lines may be omitted.)

MICHAEL: (*pause*) If you really want to know, married life sucks. My wife left me.

PHILIP: What happened?

MICHAEL: The composer. The guy she's been working with. He tells her he can't help himself. And she can't help herself. So they're out there somewhere helping themselves.

PHILIP: Shit. I'm sorry.

MICHAEL: I can't believe it. We're in bed. I'm trying to get something started, and she up and turns on the light and starts to cry and says we've got to talk. "There's this man, Michael. You've met him. Eric. The musician. I don't know how this happened. I have, we have feelings for each other. I've been trying to rationalize them away, pressure from the wedding, the intimacy of working together, but I can't. I'm with you now, but I'm thinking about him, and that's not fair to either of us. I can't sneak around on you. I have to figure out what I'm doing. I can't just live in this limbo." Then we're in the bathroom, and she's putting all her makeup and shit into a bag, and she's telling me that it's nothing I've done, this Eric guy is totally different, they connect on a whole other level. I still can't believe it. She starts to pack up

326

her diaphragm and jelly, and I say can't you hold off on the fucking until you know a little better just what the fuck you are doing? And she says physical attraction is part of what's between them, and it's her body. We fight. She's really crying hard now, and she goes back into the bedroom. (*pause*) I see the tube of diaphragm jelly lying next to the sink. I'm nuts, you know, I'm really crazy. I empty the tube of jelly into the toilet, take my tube of muscle liniment, hold them nozzle to nozzle, and fill up the jelly tube with Tiger Balm.

PHILIP: That Chinese stuff?

MICHAEL: Super Ben-Gay. Tiger Balm.

PHILIP: You're kidding me.

MICHAEL: I was crazy. I've never seen myself like that.

PHILIP: Jesus.

MICHAEL: I figure I'd give them something to remember me by.

PHILIP: Jesus Christ.

MICHAEL: If they're so fucking hot for each other, let them feel like a couple of fucking firecrackers.

INDIANS
by Arthur Kopit

SCENE 2

It is the late 1800's and three senators have come to an Indian Reservation to hear the grievances of Chief Sitting Bull and to investigate conditions. The Chief had requested the "Great Father" (the President of the United States) to come himself, but he is prepared to swallow his pride and accept the senators as representatives.

Sitting Bull has chosen John Grass to speak first at the hearing. Grass is an Indian who attended "the white man's school" and "understood something of their ways." He delivers an eloquent and moving speech that summarizes the Indians' dilemma and pleads for justice for his people.

JOHN GRASS: *Brothers!* I am going to talk about what the Great Father told us a long time ago. He told us to give up hunting and start farming. So we did as he said, and our people grew hungry. For the land was suited to grazing, not farming, and even if we'd been farmers, nothing could have grown. So the Great Father said he would send us food and clothing, but nothing came of it. So we asked him for the money he had promised us when we sold him the Black Hills, thinking, with this money we could *buy* food and clothing. But nothing came of it. So we grew ill and sad. . . . So to help us from this sadness, he sent Bishop Marty, to teach us to be Christians. But when we told him we did not wish to be Christians but wished to be like our fathers, and dance the sundance, and fight bravely against the Shawnee and the Crow! And pray to the Great Spirits who made the four winds, and the earth, and made man from the dust of this earth, Bishop Marty hit us! . . . So we said to the Great Father that we thought we would like to go *back* to hunting, because to live, we needed food. But we found that while we had been learning to farm, the buffalo had gone away. And the plains were filled now only with their bones. . . . Before we give you any more of our land, or move from here where the people we loved are growing white in their coffins, we want you to tell the Great Father to give us, who still live, what he promised he would! *No more than that.*

LONE STAR
by James McLure

Roy loves to reminisce about his adolescent adventures as the owner of the only 1959 pink Thunderbird convertible in Maynard, Texas.

It is one A.M. on a summer morning behind Angel's Bar. Roy is telling his younger brother, Ray, about his first sexual encounter in the back seat of his beloved car.

(See also the scene between Roy and Ray on page 268.)

ROY: In the spring of nineteen hundred and sixty-one I took Edith Ellen Hyde out in that car a mine. Took her parkin' out to Thompson's road. That was the night I looked up her dress. Up until then I had no idea what life was all about. (*pause*) We kissed and kissed till we got half way good at it. Then she took off her shirt. (*pause*) That was the first nipple I'd had in my mouth since Mom's. But nipples are like bicycles: once you learn you never forget how. Finally we got the windows all steamed up, and I couldn't wait. Got the car to smell like the smell of a woman and I just had to see it. Edith Ellen didn't want me to see it. Said it was bad enough me touchin' it without wantin' to look at it. She even tried to scare me. Said it looked God awful. But she couldn't talk me out of it. I was a man with a mission. So I scooted over and scrunched down under the steerin' column like this and she lifted up her skirt and I lit a match like that. And I looked at the damn thing. (*pause*) And y'know, y'wonder what the first explorer felt. The first explorer that climbed over that hill and saw—stretched out before him, in all its God glory—the grand canyon. Well that's what I felt like when Edith Ellen Hyde lifted her skirt and said, "here it is," I looked, and it was AWE-INSPIRING. I felt like Adam. I felt like the man who discovered the Grand Canyon.

STILL LIFE
by Emily Mann

SCENE 7

Mark is an ex-Marine who served in Vietnam. In this "documentary" play by Emily Mann, Mark, his wife, Cheryl, and his mistress, Nadine, describe how their relationships have been affected by the nightmare of Vietnam and its aftermath.

In the monologue below, Mark confesses that he murdered children during the war.

MARK: I killed them with a pistol in front of a lot of people. I demanded something from the parents and then systematically destroyed them. And that's . . . that's the heaviest part of what I'm carrying around. You know about it now, a few other people know about it, my wife knows about it, Nadine knows about it, and nobody else knows about it. For the rest of my life . . . I have a son. . . . He's going to die for what I've done. This is what I'm carrying around; that's what this logic is about with my children. A friend hit a booby-trap. And these people knew about it. I knew they knew. I knew that they were working with the VC infra-structure. I demanded that they tell me. They wouldn't say anything. I just wanted them to confess before I killed them. And they wouldn't. So I killed their children and then I killed them. I was angry. I was angry with all the power I had. I couldn't beat them. They beat me. (*crying*) I lost friends in my unit. . . . I did wrong. People in the unit watched me kill them. Some of them tried to stop me. I don't know. I can't . . . oh, God . . . a certain amount of stink went all the way back to the rear. I almost got into a certain amount of trouble. It was all rationalized, that there was a logic behind it. But they knew. And everybody who knew had a part in it. There was enough evidence, but it wasn't a very good image to put out in terms of . . . the Marines overseas, so nothing happened. I have a child . . . a child who passed through the age that the little child was. My son . . . my son wouldn't know the difference between a VC and a Marine. The children were so little. I suppose I could find a rationalization. All that a person can do is try and find words to try and excuse me, but I know it's the same damn thing as lining Jews up. It's no different than what the Nazis did. It's the same thing. I know that I'm not alone. I know that other people did it, too. More people went through more hell than I did . . . but they didn't do this. I don't know . . . I don't know . . . if it's a terrible flaw of *mine*, then I guess deep down I'm just everything that's bad. I guess there is a rationale that says anyone who wants to live that bad and gets in that situation . . . (*long pause*) but I should have done better. I mean, I really strove to be good. I had a whole set of values. I had 'em and I didn't. I don't know. I want to come to the point where I tell myself that I've punished myself enough. In spite of it all, I don't want to punish myself anymore. I knew I would want to censor myself for you. I didn't want you to say: what kind of a nut, what kind of a bad person is he? And yet, it's all right.

I'm not gonna lie. My wife tries to censor me . . . from people, from certain things. I can't watch war shows. I can't drive. Certain things I can't deal with. She has to deal with the situation, us sitting around, a car backfires, and I hit the deck. She knows about the graveyards, and R.J. and the woman. She lives with all this still hanging out. I'm shellshocked.

ROMANTIC COMEDY
by Bernard Slade

ACT II, SCENE 2

When Phoebe discovers that her long-time writing collaborator, Jason, is having an affair with Kate Mallory, the leading lady of their new play, she breaks up the partnership. After all, Jason is married to Allison and Phoebe is very fond of their two children. She is also secretly in love with him.

Just before Phoebe walks out on their 10-year partnership, Jason decides to tell her who he "really" is.

(See also the scene between Jason and Phoebe on page 36.)

JASON: My real name isn't Jason Carmichael. It's Joey Mahovalich. I didn't graduate from Yale—I never even finished high school. I grew up, a fat little kid with a bad nose and a worse accent on 12th Street in the South Side of Detroit. Did you ever notice I have no relatives? My father wasn't a lawyer—he worked for the Gas Company. I never knew him—he ran off with a woman who lived upstairs when I was four years old. My mother took a job in the cafeteria at the G.M. plant so I lived pretty much on the streets. She died when I was thirteen and I was put in a series of foster homes. I was arrested three times before I was fifteen for stealing—mostly food from vending machines. (*He looks at her.*) Do you know who I really am?

PHOEBE: Oliver Twist? (*He doesn't smile. She makes a gesture of "forget that."*)

JASON: I'm a totally manufactured man. I didn't like my life, hated what I was—so I became someone else. You know why I married Allison? I couldn't get over the fact that a girl with her background would want someone like *me*. But she did. My God, now I had the "right" wife. So there I was—the successful, urbane playwright—the host of the most glittering dinner parties in town. Fooled a lot of people; but *I* never believed it. Inside the Saville Row suits there was always the ugly, fat little kid waiting to be found out. So much for the past. Lately, I've been feeling more—unattractive than usual. Things between Allison and I haven't been— Look, I'll be forty-six next month. Middle age. Pick your cliché. (*She remains silent, her face impassive. Finally*) And none of that is the real reason this happened. I was angry at you—because of Leo. I suppose—in some way—I wanted to lash back. (*She is too astounded to say anything. A pause*) All right. I was terrified of losing you. So you see before you an insecure, middle-aged man who just this afternoon made a complete ass of himself and couldn't regret it more.

THE FACULTY LOUNGE
by Michael Schulman

SCENE 2

This is the first day of school. When Norman Barnes went to his car this morning to drive to his job as Chairman of the high school English Department, he discovered that his trunk had been broken into. Among the items missing were some home movies that, to say the least, could be very embarrassing if shown to the wrong people. He rushes to the faculty lounge to make a phone call. After a brief encounter with the new mathematics teacher he is left alone and dials.

NORMAN: Roger. Roger. The movies were stolen. What am I going to do? They stole them from my car—right out of the trunk. I don't know what do do first, take poison or slit my wrists. I'd jump out the window, but the goddamned building has only two floors. Roger, I'm desperate. Help me! . . . It's NORMAN, YOU ASS-HOLE. Who do you think it is? Well, yes, Roger, I do tend to lose my sense of humor when I'm thinking of killing myself. God, don't you understand how serious this is? This is a small town. My whole life is . . . How the hell do I know who stole them? One of our postgraduates, no doubt—and definitely one who failed in industrial arts from the mess he made of the back of my car. (*With repugnance*) Industrial arts—a training ground for second-story men, if you ask me. What difference does it make why I left them in the trunk? I was tired last night when I left your party—as I am always tired when I leave your parties. I thought they'd be safe there. Don't you tell me to calm down. By the time this day is over the whole town will know that *crusading* Mayor Bertram and his head speech writer, yours truly, who also happens to be the *respected* chairman of the high school English Department, are homosexual lovers. Or will they prefer fags or faggots or queers or . . . It's not serious? I can't believe you. You idiot. We're REPUBLICANS! It's the end of our careers. And it's all your fault. You and your goddamned cameras and lights and darkroom, and sick imagination. (*Mimicking* ROGER *lisping*) Oh, please let me film you. I majored in cinema in college. Oh, please, please. (*own voice*) I should have shoved the camera, the lights and the microphone into each of your always well-lubricated orifices. No, I didn't call Bertram. What could I say to him? And anyway, he wouldn't be in his office now. He's at the Kiwanis breakfast. Oh, God, he's making a speech about returning to traditional family values. God, and I wrote it for him. He'll be so humiliated. Roger, you must do something. Save us. I don't know what. You're rich. You must have friends in low places: the Mafia, the C.I.A. Come on. This is America. There's got to be somebody who keeps tabs on who steals what from whom. We'll offer them anything—all your money, your house, your entire Ethel Merman record collection. Everything. No, I didn't call the police. That's all I'd need is for the police to catch them and decide to look at one of the films. How do you know the police wouldn't do that? Wouldn't *you* look if you found a reel of developed film? (*As if he is talking to an imbecile*) Yes, and the police have also been known to be curious about things. Of course we'll know if they found them. If next week Bertram announces that police salaries have been raised to a hundred thousand dollars a year, you'll know they found them. What else is missing? I don't know. I haven't even thought about what else I had in the trunk. My tennis racket. They took my THREE HUNDRED DOLLAR Ille Nastase tennis racket. BASTARDS! And I had an old clock in the trunk I kept forgetting to take to the repair shop. That's all. Some books too, I think. Yes, it is possible that they just threw the films away, but then we have to worry about who will find them, don't we? Yes, that's possible too. Anything's possible, Roger. The moon may crash into the earth this afternoon and then no one at all will care about technicolor movies of Bertram and me dancing naked to "I Can't Get No Satisfaction." But, Roger, I just want you to know that if we go under, I'm taking you with us. Yes, I know, dear. Your family came over on the second boat after the Mayflower. But I'm afraid, Roger, that that just doesn't arouse any sympathy in me right now. What can we do? We can run like hell, that's what we can do. Oh, I have it. You'll take your camera and the three of us will go on the road together. Yes, Bertram and I can become the Mickey and Judy of gay sleaze. That's a good idea, Roger. You go to church and pray for us. But Roger . . . *Roger.* Remember, when you're in church praying to God, do me a favor—don't mention any names. (*He hangs up.*) Idiot!

FATHERS AND SONS
by Thomas Babe

ACT 1, SCENE 4

In 1876 Wild Bill Hickok is an old, partially blind gunslinger, but he still holds court at the "Number Ten" saloon in Deadwood, Dakota Territory. He is still respected and feared by his old cronies, although now and then someone hints that Wild Bill actually shot his victims in the back. Still, the legend lives on.

When Jack McCall, a hot-tempered youth, rides into town claiming he is his illegitimate son and threatening to kill him, Wild Bill gathers his faithful group around him and prepares to do battle. But his long-time friend, California Joe, can't help him out this time.

JOE: I hate to do this to you, Bill. I know we made our plans already and I value our long association. We both got to be pretty famous men in our times. But, as a matter of highly regrettable fact, I'm dying, of consumption, it seems, or somethin like it which does not yet have a name to it, and for which there's no known remedy. I've been in possession of this information six months now, but it ain't felt bad enough yet to complain about till now, and now it's pretty bad, the pain's there all the time, it don't quit, and it's been longer than life itself, it's been a lifetime the last week already. (*drinks to quiet a coughing spell*) Which I haven't said nothin of to you, because I don't want to trouble you none, us bein *confreres* of long standing, but also because I'm finding this peculiarity in me, especially when the fever's way up, that I'm startin to hate you and everybody who's young and comely, them women, the boys, Carl, Charlie, specially you, Bill, because you'll all goddamn survive my miserable end, coughing like a fool and bloody and all, and I'd get to hate your pity a great deal and get to despise generally all of you, for your life. If I could, I'd take you down to death with me, and a couple others, that's true, and it's a dangerous thought because I just might kill you, Bill, some night when the delirium ain't beneficial and dreamy and I think of bein a child again, but some night when it gets me killin crazy. So I gotta fold—nothin personal. I'm goin up someplace there in the hills, and live alone till I die. I just can't stand the sight of your goddamn lovely face.

TEACH ME HOW TO CRY
by Patricia Joudry

Act III, Scene 2

The scene is a deserted bandstand. Will and Melinda often meet here to be together. In the month they have known each other, these two lonely teenagers have given each other strength and security.

But now Will is leaving. Yesterday, he was expelled from school for fighting with a classmate who insinuated that Melinda was a tramp. This morning, Will's father decided that it would be best for the family to move. Heartbroken about leaving the first person he has ever loved, Will tells Melinda how much she means to him and promises they will meet again.

In the following monologue he tries to give her courage by relating an incident from his childhood.

(See also the scene between Melinda and Polly on page 230.)

WILL: Nothing is so very terrible. (*Cornet begins to play. He goes over to her, speaks honestly and forcefully.*) There was a house once down by a lake near where we used to live. The house was all boarded up and deserted, and the kids all said it was haunted and were afraid of it. I was too. More afraid than any of them. And then my mother and dad decided we'd live in that house, and I nearly ran away. I was going to, but I didn't. I decided to be brave, but I didn't know how I could do it I felt so sick. But I went inside that house and I looked at it, every bit of it, up close. It was just an ordinary old house and there I was being afraid of nothing at all.

(MELINDA *begins to cry, looking at him. The weeping becomes a tearing sobbing, and she puts her head down and continues to sob for a long time. She sinks down onto the steps.* WILL *stands quietly, watching her. Once he starts to reach out his hand to her, but takes it back. When the crying has subsided a little*)

WILL: Some people say men don't like it when girls cry, but they're the kind of people that don't like girls to laugh either. Or anybody. I think if you can do one, then it's easier to do the other, and both of them make you feel good. Will you write to me too, Melinda, every day? You don't have to stop crying. Just nod.

A PRAYER FOR MY DAUGHTER
by Thomas Babe

ACT I

Sergeant Kelly and his assistant, Jack, bring in two men suspected of killing an old woman. During the course of the interrogation, Kelly's daughter, Margie, calls him. Her problems with her husband have come to a head and now, in a distraught state, she is threatening to kill herself. Like her mother, Margie is emotionally fragile and she is accustomed to playing the little girl to her indulgent father. Since she has left her apartment, Kelly puts a trace on the phone call and sends a squad car to get her. But he has a premonition that she may succeed in ending her life.

In the monologue below, Kelly describes his feelings for his daughter. As the stage directions indicate, Jimmy, one of the suspects, giggles occasionally.

KELLY: Jesus, what a bunch of hyperventilated creeps. I don't know. (KELLY *drinks again;* JIMMY *stifles his giggles.*) What it is there is that Margie's the only person in the world I'm on a sure foot with. I don't want anything from her, except I'm her father and she's my daughter and that will never get removed. It goes back to the times she was little and all the stuff along the way, and the smiles, and she'd shout at me and get pissed off sometimes . . . but that there is permanent; even when she sticks it to me, it's permanent. It's more like a thing I read about Alfred Einstein, who invented the big bomb, who said when he was a kid he read a lot of dead scientists and authors and said he didn't feel alone, he didn't think he ever would feel alone, because those dead guys were his unloseable friends. That's how I think of her, my daughter, my unloseable friend. And I don't want a goddamn thing from her but she knows it, she's unloseable, and she prospers. That's the limit of it.

INDEX

Agnes of God, 145, 308

Albee, Edward, 48, 193, 210

Album, 166

American Clock, The, 95

Anderson, Maxwell, 104

Andersonville Trial, The, 294

Anne of the Thousand Days, 104

Awake and Sing!, 108

Ayckbourn, Alan, 68, 181

Babe, Thomas, 334, 337

Barefoot in the Park, 3

Bedroom Farce, 68

Berry, David, 261

Betrayal, 59

Brecht, Bertoldt, 277

California Suite, 18

Caligula, 111

Camus, Albert, 111

Chapter II, 235

Chodorov, Jerome, 206

Clark, Brian, 45

Collector, The, 75

Come Back, Little Sheba, 134

Coupla White Chicks Sitting Around Talking, A, 172

Crimes of the Heart, 148

Da, 253

Dale, Jim, 273

Davis, Bill, 243

Death Comes to Us All, Mary Agnes, 312

Dee, Peter, 315

Delicate Balance, A, 193

Dresser, The, 41

Duet for One, 80

Dunlop, Frank, 273

Durang, Christopher, 312

Edgar, David, 299

Everybody Loves Opal, 215

Everything In the Garden, 210

Faculty Lounge, The, 226, 316, 332

Fathers and Sons, 334

Fields, Joseph, 206

Galileo, 277

Gelbart, Larry, 325

Geography of a Horse Dreamer, 257

Gigi, 128

Gingerbread Lady, The, 152

Giraudoux, Jean, 131

G.R. Point, 261

Great Nebula in Orion, The, 190

Harwood, Ronald, 41

Heggen, Thomas, 281

Henley, Beth, 148
Heuer, John, 138
Hopscotch, 89
Horovitz, Israel, 89

Indians, 327
Inge, William, 134
Innocent Thoughts, Harmless Intentions, 138
It's Been Wonderful, 318

Jimmy Shine, 119
Joudry, Patricia, 230, 335

Kempinski, Tom, 80
Kerr, Jean, 176
Key Exchange, 25, 326
Kopit, Arthur, 327

Lapine, James, 72
Laundry and Bourbon, 196
Leonard, Hugh, 253
Levitt, Saul, 294
Life and Adventures of Nicholas Nickleby, The, 299
Logan, Joshua, 281
Lone Star, 268, 328
Loos, Anita, 128
Loose Ends, 265
Love is a Time of Day, 320
Lovely Sunday for Creve Coeur, A, 307
Lunch Hour, 176
Luther, 285

Mann, Emily, 329
Mass Appeal, 243
Mastrosimone, William, 55
McClure, James, 196, 268, 328
McIntyre, Dennis, 98
Miller, Arthur, 95
Modigliani, 98

Mr. Roberts, 281
Murrell, John, 321
My Cup Ranneth Over, 220
My Sister Eileen, 206

Nicholas Nickleby, The Life and Adventures of, 299
Noonan, John Ford, 172
Nuts, 311

Odets, Clifford, 108, 114
O'Malley, Mary, 202
Once a Catholic, 202
Ondine, 131
On Golden Pond, 161
Osborne, John, 285

Pape, Ralph, 248
Parker, David, 75
Patrick, John, 215, 290, 318, 320
Patrick, Robert, 220
Pielmeier, John, 145, 308
Pinter, Harold, 59
Prayer for My Daughter, A, 337
Prisoner of Second Avenue, The, 29

Rimmer, David, 166
Romantic Comedy, 36, 331
Runner Stumbles, The, 124

Say Goodnight, Gracie, 248
Scapino!, 273
Schisgal, Murray, 119
Schulman, Michael, 226, 316, 332
Sea of White Horses, A, 315
Shepard, Sam, 239, 257
Simon, Neil, 3, 18, 29, 152, 235

Slade, Bernard, 36, 331
Sly Fox, 325
Still Life, 329
Stitt, Milan, 124
Stops Along the Way, 313
Sweet, Jeffrey, 313

Table Manners, 181
Table Settings, 72
Tally's Folly, 12
Teach Me How to Cry, 230, 335
Teahouse of the August Moon, 290
Thompson, Ernest, 161, 309
Topor, Tom, 311
True West, 239

Uncommon Women and Others, 159

Vieux Carré, 63

Wade, Kevin, 25, 326
Waiting for Lefty, 114
Waiting for the Parade, 321
Wasserstein, Wendy, 159
Weller, Michael, 265
West Side Waltz, The, 309
Williams, Tennessee, 63, 307
Wilson, Lanford, 12, 190
Who's Afraid of Virginia Woolf?, 48
Whose Life is it Anyway?, 45
Woolgatherer, The, 55

ABOUT THE EDITORS

Having taught acting at the Lee Strasberg Theatre Institute and at The Actors Studio, MICHAEL SCHULMAN now teaches at his own workshop in New York City. He has also written and directed a number of plays for Off and Off-Off Broadway theatre. He is director of The British-American Acting Academy, a school with branches in New York and London, dedicated to the synthesis of the best of British and American acting techniques. In addition to his theatrical career, he is a clinical and research psychologist who has held assistant professorships at Fordham and Rutgers universities. His Ph.D. is from the City University of New York.

EVA MEKLER is both a playwright and actress who has performed on and off Broadway. Trained in psychology, with a master's degree from New York University, she divides her time between her work as a clinician and acting.

DISCOVER
THE DRAMA OF LIFE
IN THE LIFE OF DRAMA

SPECIAL
MONEY SAVING
OFFER

Now you can have an up-to-date listing of Bantam's hundreds of titles plus take advantage of our unique and exciting bonus book offer. A special offer which gives you the opportunity to purchase a Bantam book for only 50¢. Here's how!

By ordering any five books at the regular price per order, you can also choose any other single book listed (up to a $4.95 value) for just 50¢. Some restrictions do apply, but for further details why not send for Bantam's listing of titles today!

Just send us your name and address plus 50¢ to defray the postage and handling costs.

We Deliver!
And So Do These Bestsellers.

DON'T MISS
THESE CURRENT
Bantam Bestsellers

☐	23983	**CIRCLES** Doris Mortman	$3.50
☐	24184	**THE WARLORD** Malcolm Bosse	$3.95
☐	22848	**FLOWER OF THE PACIFIC** Lana McGraw Boldt	$3.95
☐	23422	**NOMADS** Chelsea Q. Yarbro	$2.95
☐	23922	**GIRI** Marc Olden	$3.50
☐	23920	**VOICE OF THE HEART** Barbara Taylor Bradford	$4.50
☐	23638	**THE OTHER SIDE** Diana Henstell	$3.50
☐	23845	**THE DELTA STAR** Joseph Wambaugh	$3.95
☐	23709	**THE OMEGA DECEPTION** Charles Robertson	$3.50
☐	23577	**THE SEEDING** David Shobin	$2.95
☐	20476	**THE UNBORN** David Shobin	$2.95
☐	23198	**BLACK CHRISTMAS** Thomas Altman	$2.95
☐	22687	**TRUE BRIDE** Thomas Altman	$2.95
☐	24010	**KISS DADDY GOODBYE** Thomas Altman	$3.50
☐	23637	**THE THIRD WORLD WAR: THE UNTOLD STORY** Gen. Sir John Hackett	$3.95
☐	24561	**THE VALLEY OF HORSES** Jean M. Auel	$4.50
☐	23897	**CLAN OF THE CAVE BEAR** Jean M. Auel	$4.50
☐	23224	**A SEPARATE PEACE** John Knowles	$2.50
☐	20822	**THE GLITTER DOME** Joseph Wambaugh	$3.95

<u>Prices and availability subject to change without notice.</u>

Buy them at your local bookstore or use this handy coupon for ordering: